Routledge Revivals

The Diary of Dudley Ryder 1715–1716

Originally published in 1939, *The Diary of Dudley Ryder 1715–1716*, comprises an early diary and a few related notes by Sir Dudley Ryder when he was a student at the Middle Temple. The diary is a fascinating record of the character and life of a moderately well-to-do student of Nonconformist leanings. Its chief interest lies in the wealth of intimate detail concerning the writer, his family and friends, but it has too, considerable importance as a social and historical document. The reading and tastes of a serious young man of the early eighteenth century, his opinions on the chief social, religious and political topics of the time. It gives an interesting, at times exciting, account of the daily life of London during the rebellion; it contains eye-witness accounts of trials, executions, riots, battles; it gives fresh details and stories about many public men; it throws new light on the attitude of Nonconformity and the Church towards each other.

The Diary of Dudley Ryder
1715–1716

Edited by
William Matthews

First published in 1939
by Methuen & Co. Ltd

This edition first published in 2025 by Routledge
4 Park Square, Milton Park, Abingdon, Oxon, OX14 4RN

and by Routledge
605 Third Avenue, New York, NY 10017

Routledge is an imprint of the Taylor & Francis Group, an informa business

© 1939 William Matthews

All rights reserved. No part of this book may be reprinted or reproduced or utilised in any form or by any electronic, mechanical, or other means, now known or hereafter invented, including photocopying and recording, or in any information storage or retrieval system, without permission in writing from the publishers.

Publisher's Note
The publisher has gone to great lengths to ensure the quality of this reprint but points out that some imperfections in the original copies may be apparent.

Disclaimer
The publisher has made every effort to trace copyright holders and welcomes correspondence from those they have been unable to contact.

A Library of Congress record exists under LCCN: 40000654

ISBN: 978-1-032-89842-1 (hbk)
ISBN: 978-1-003-54490-6 (ebk)
ISBN: 978-1-032-89848-3 (pbk)

Book DOI 10.4324/9781003544906

SIR DUDLEY RYDER AS ATTORNEY-GENERAL, C. 1754
From the engraving by J. Faber after the painting by James Crank

THE DIARY
OF DUDLEY RYDER
1715–1716

Transcribed from shorthand and Edited by
WILLIAM MATTHEWS
Author of
Cockney, Past and Present

METHUEN & CO. LTD. LONDON
36 Essex Street, Strand, W.C.2

First published in 1939

PRINTED IN GREAT BRITAIN

TO
THE GRACIOUS MEMORY OF
JOHN HAY LOBBAN

EDITOR'S PREFACE

AMONG the many valuable manuscripts belonging to the Earl of Harrowby is a large boxful of papers written in shorthand. They consist of diaries and law notes written by Sir Dudley Ryder from 1715 until 1756, and of diaries, Parliamentary notes and estate notes written by his son Nathaniel, first Baron Harrowby.

By far the greater part of Sir Dudley's shorthand is made up of notes of trials. The diaries fall into two sections, the larger being a series of journals kept from 1746 until his death in 1756, during the period when he was Attorney-General and Chief Justice. The other section comprises an early diary and a few related notes kept in 1715 and 1716, when he was a student at the Middle Temple.

The present book is a selection from my transcription of the early diary. The manuscript is a bundle of twenty-nine sections containing 918 octavo pages. The diary ends in the middle of a sentence at the end of a section; the rest of it is missing. The shorthand is minute, much smaller even than Pepys's, but it is extremely neat and clear. The system is unknown to me by name, although it is similar to Jeremiah Rich's in which so many diaries of the eighteenth and late seventeenth centuries were written: most of them have yet to be transcribed, but they include John Wesley's, Sir Peter King's and Dr. Doddridge's.

The complete transcription[1] amounts to about 350,000 words although the diary relates to only eighteen months: many daily entries are well over 2,000 words long. The diary is a fascinating record of the character and life of a moderately well-to-do student of Nonconformist leanings. Its chief interest

[1] A copy of the complete transcription has been given to the Library of Birkbeck College (University of London).

naturally lies in the wealth of intimate detail concerning the writer, his family and friends; there are few franker diaries. But it has, too, considerable importance as a social and historical document. The reading and tastes of a serious young man of the early eighteenth century, his opinions on the chief social, religious and political topics of the time, his amusements (far more frivolous than one would expect) are fully represented here. It gives an interesting, at times exciting, account of the daily life of London during the rebellion; it contains eye-witness accounts of trials, executions, riots, battles; it gives fresh details and stories about many public men; it throws new light on the attitude of Nonconformity and the Church towards each other.

The selection now published is somewhat less than half of the whole. The greater part of the omissions consists of summaries of books, sermons, and conversations, notes of visits to friends and relations which reveal little except where he went, and brief notes on his law reading and visits to Westminster Hall. I have also pruned many repetitions (particularly of his opinions and his feelings for Mrs. Marshall and Mrs. Loyd). I have omitted some reports of speeches in Parliament and at trials, where they do not differ from authoritative accounts, and I have omitted or abbreviated many of his reflections on religion and conduct. The limits made necessary by a single volume have compelled me to excise many passages I should have liked to retain, but I believe that the selection contains almost everything of considerable interest in what Ryder did, saw, heard and thought, and everything that reveals his life and character—except the full extent of his religious feelings, his tendency to moralize, and his reading of law-books. I have by no means left these unrepresented, but proportionate representation would have necessitated many extra pages.

Like Pepys, Dudley Ryder occasionally wrote isolated words in longhand, and some of them are abbreviated or in archaic spelling. I have not felt justified in following the lead of Pepys's editors by giving an antique spelling to the transcription from shorthand, and so have thought it better to regularize the whole. I have not interfered, however, with the variant grammatical forms; and, except for the few words in square brackets, I have not filled in the occasional omissions of pronouns, etc. The shorthand does not provide punctuation marks; so the punctuation, which has been kept to a minimum, and the paragraphing are mine, too.

It is a great pleasure to acknowledge here the kindness of the Earl of Harrowby and Viscount Sandon in allowing me to publish the diary and to examine other manuscripts at Sandon Hall. I am also deeply indebted to the Librarian of Hackney Municipal Library, who gave me the run of the invaluable Tyson collection of Hackney books and manuscripts, and also lent me the notes of his lectures on old Hackney; to the Rev. F. N. Robathan, M.A., Rector of St. John-at-Hackney, who allowed me to examine the records of his church; to the Librarian of the Middle Temple, who kindly answered several inquiries; to my friend Mr. A. J. Carlton of Geneva, who, having transcribed part of one of Nathaniel's diaries, suggested me as a possible transcriber of the rest; to Professor J. Sutherland, who made many helpful criticisms; and to my good friend Dr. M. C. Hildyard, who checked the final proof. To the late John Hay Lobban, I owe a deep obligation for generous advice and expert help during all the stages of the book; his death in February last robbed English literature of one of its most gracious figures and me of one of my dearest friends.

WILLIAM MATTHEWS

UNIVERSITY OF WISCONSIN
March, 1939

CONTENTS

EDITOR'S PREFACE	vii
INTRODUCTION	1
THE DIARY, JUNE 6, 1715—DECEMBER 30, 1715	29
THE DIARY, JANUARY 1, 1716—DECEMBER 7, 1716	161
INDEX	375

ILLUSTRATIONS

Facing page

SIR DUDLEY RYDER AS ATTORNEY-GENERAL, *c.* 1754
Frontispiece

PART OF JOHN SELLER'S MAP OF MIDDLESEX, INCLUDING HACKNEY AND DISTRICT, 1710	32
A PAGE OF DUDLEY RYDER'S DIARY	64
INCIDENTS OF THE 1715 REBELLION	102
FROST FAIR ON THE RIVER THAMES, 1715–16	162
MARE STREET, HACKNEY, 1731	208

(*Reproduced from a print in the Hackney Municipal Library, by courtesy of the Librarian*)

INTRODUCTION

IF, as he sometimes thought, men preserve in the next world the character that they have in this, Dudley Ryder's feelings upon the publication of this diary must be very mixed. Few diaries are so self-revealing as his. Most diarists pose even to themselves. Here is the complete picture of a man, not only what he did, saw and thought, but all his contradictions, his meanness and virtue, his impudence and diffidence, his vanity and modesty, his harshness and generosity. Those two creatures who are united in every man, he who speaks and acts and he who mocks and applauds, march side by side behind the screen of his shorthand. The one's attempts to impress his friends and acquaintances, his assumed moods of wisdom and knowledgeableness, his efforts to appear a man of the world among the ladies, his love-longings flirtatious or desperately sincere, all prompt the critical *alter ego* to the mocking comment, 'What a fool am I!' Dudley Ryder, ever anxious to present himself to the world as a model product of eighteenth-century culture, calm, wise, witty and respectable, would have shuddered to think that this record of his mental and emotional fluctuations, the petty things he did, thought and felt, was to be presented for the entertainment of the world from which he had so sedulously tried to conceal them. But would this man, who half in pity and half in amusement, recorded his inability to refrain from admiring himself as he passed by the mirrors of the New Exchange, and who was anxious that people should notice the love-lorn melancholy of which he was so ashamed, would he still wish to keep these things hidden in the obscurity of his shorthand notes? I think not. Dudley Ryder, who desired marriage and children because they preserved the life of him who begot them, would relish the more personal immortality of a published diary. It is ironic that the diary which was undertaken as a means of knowing and controlling himself, and so of hiding himself from all but himself, should make us more familiar with him than were any of his contemporaries or descendants. It is not less ironic that the fame to which he aspired should come not from the political and legal successes on which he counted, but, I believe and hope, from the old neglected diary of his youth, whose merit is that it raises an echo in other hearts.

Dudley Ryder created no great stir in the world. He had numerous acquaintances but few friends : throughout his life he regretted his inability to inspire warm friendships. He attained to the highest rank in his chosen profession of the law. His abilities and character were such that he might have made an equal success in the Church, to which, according to Hughes's poem, *The Causidicade*, he had once aspired :

> The Cloak and the Band, it is very well known,
> I've, like R-d-r, declined for the sake of this gown.

He was welcome at court and acquainted with most of the eminent politicians, courtiers and dignitaries of the time. But such was his external character that they were seldom prompted to comment upon him. He became wealthy, was knighted, became one of the landed gentry, and was nearly ennobled. But he has stimulated the curiosity of no man. Even Campbell, who had to give an account of him in his *Chief Justices of England*, never came to regard him as more than one of the unavoidable inconveniences in his history. Campbell is hardly to be blamed (except for his rash and inaccurate generalizations), for even in his personal letters Dudley Ryder wore a mask. That epistolary style which he had carefully cultivated, modelling himself upon Addison and the letters of Voiture, had given him an unrivalled facility in saying nothing at inordinate length, but the picture it gives of the writer is characterless. The unaffected colloquialism of the diary gives a very different impression.

Two stars shone at his birth, Trade and Dissent, the Castor and Pollux of the late seventeenth century. To the first he owed his solid ambition and his belief that reputation and happiness depended upon property ; to the second, his introspection and moral honesty. It would be unjust, however, to suggest that his wagon was hitched to these alone. Not the least merit of his diary is that it illustrates almost every cliché in the criticism of early eighteenth-century life and letters—the triumph of the middle class, the age of conversation, the age of sensibility, urbanity,

A TRADITION OF NONCONFORMITY 3

culture. In one respect, however, he does not fulfil expectations. The Nonconformist renunciation of worldly pleasures was not for him. He could not have enjoyed flirtation, fine clothes, poetry and theatres with greater zest had he been brought up in the Church of England. Thinking of him one thinks of the Spectator Club, Pamela Andrews and the Man of Feeling but not of Law's *Serious Call*.

His grandfather, Dudley Ryder, was one of the martyrs of Nonconformity, ejected from his living at Bedworth in Warwickshire in 1662 following upon the Act of Uniformity. The tradition of Nonconformity was maintained by the Rev. Dudley's eldest daughter, Sarah, who married another dissenting preacher, Robert Billio, the son of the ejected minister of Wickham Bishops in Essex. When Dr. William Bates, the first minister of the Presbyterian meeting in Mare Street, Hackney, died in 1699 and the congregation, despite numerous entreaties, were unable to secure the services of the famous Matthew Henry, Robert Billio applied for that coveted ministry in the prosperous parish where Adoniram Byfield and Philip Nye had formerly preached, and was appointed. So he came from St. Ives in Huntingdonshire to the meeting opposite the present St. Thomas's Square, where he officiated until he was carried off by smallpox in 1710.[1] He was survived by his wife, the genial tattling Aunt Billio of the diary, and two sons, Robert and Joseph, both of whom had been educated for the Nonconformist ministry in Scotland and Holland. Robert, when the diary opens, was a married man and an expectant father—it was gratifying to his dainty cousin Dudley, who had quizzed Robert's wife on the subject, that when the child arrived it proved to be more agreeable and cleanly than children of that age generally are. Robert, who was looking out for a settled appointment—he hoped, vainly as it proved, to get the ministry at the new meeting in Hackney and also the vacancy at St. Bartholomew Close caused by Mr. Freke's death—was hampered by his unsympathetic manner in preaching and his refusal to adopt what he thought to be the ridiculous style of the Nonconformists in prayer. Cousin Jo was a livelier soul, fond of talking nonsense to the ladies. Not that Jo was a zany; when he liked he could hold his own with cousin Dudley

---

[1] His name is inscribed on the communion plate which is preserved at Hackney Municipal Library.

in a discussion on astronomy or centrifugal and centripetal forces.

The Rev. Dudley's sons took to trade. The eldest, Dudley, was a draper in Nuneaton. His critical nephew thought him a rather dull dog, a man who could talk sense only about his own affairs. Of his numerous children, the most talented was John, a promising student at Queen's, Cambridge. He had a few pleasing Cambridge anecdotes and he could keep his end up in a learned discussion with cousin Dudley and cousin Nathaniel Marshall on Mr. Locke or the Church Fathers. But too much of his company was tiresome; a book and the house of office was one of Dudley's refuges after a day or so of his company. John, like his cousin, broke the tradition of Nonconformity and, in the style of the worldly clerics of the eighteenth century, did very well for himself. After serving as vicar of Nuneaton from 1721 until 1742, he became successively Bishop of Killaloe, Bishop of Down and Connor, and Archbishop of Tuam and Bishop of Ardagh. For this ecclesiastical advancement he owed not a little to his cousin.

Richard, the Rev. Dudley's fourth son, was also in trade. He was partner with Mr. West and Mr. Bailey in a prosperous linendraper's at the sign of the Plough and Harrow in Cheapside, at the corner of Ironmonger Lane, the shop to which the diarist came so often to get money, to choose a suit length, or merely to look at the pretty young customers. Richard had joined his brother-in-law Robert Billio in that Arcadia beyond Moorfields, Hackney, the rural retreat of so many well-to-do City merchants with Nonconformist leanings. 'The greatest ambition of the London shopkeeper', says *The Idler* (No. 75), 'is to retire to Stratford or to Hackney.' He had married Elizabeth Marshall [1] and had three sons. Richard, the eldest, was in a prosperous way of business as a draper in Bishopsgate Street, thinking of applying for the office of King's Draper. He had made a good match in Anne Lomax, who had brought into the marriage settlement the manor of Westbrook Hay and other property in Hertfordshire. If she had brought an uncertain temper, too, and the company of a valetudinarian mother, Richard with his gift for abstractedness was not the kind to suffer badly, although Dudley pitied him at times. The youngest son, William, was a sore trial. Although

[1] *The Complete Peerage* says she was his second wife.

he was coming towards the end of his apprenticeship in his father's business, he still had an unhappy knack of getting into scrapes. At the shop they had learned by experience to keep a sharp eye on the till. His fine clothes made all the family (except the strangely purblind father) wonder where he got the money for them. Was it by borrowing at a high rate of interest, as Dudley thought, or by turning highwayman as Aunt Billio melodramatically supposed ?—prompted possibly by the history of Joseph Saunders, the Hackney apothecary, who just escaped hanging for this offence and whose son John was not so lucky.[1] Or William would narrowly miss having a child fathered on him by one of the whores from the Hundreds of Drury. Or he would be overheard entertaining cousin Bibby Ryder and Mrs. Loyd just on this side downright bawdy or arranging assignations. It was perhaps hardly fitting of Dudley to cast the first stone; in some of these faults he was no less guilty than his brother. But it was a relief to everyone when William decided it was time to settle down into married respectability, although finding a suitable bride proved more difficult than that sanguine young man imagined. Before he married Mrs. Burton of Hackney in 1717 several possibilities and their dowries had to be examined discreetly and the stormy courtship with Mrs. Walker had to be passed through.

Dudley, the diarist, was the second son, his father's Benjamin. In some ways he was as much a cause of worry as his brother; his fits of melancholy, his muscular pains, his susceptibility to feminine beauty—it was only for novices, his father once told him, to fall in love with a pretty face—all distressed his parents. But he was a son to boast of, a man of talent who could out-argue even the senior members of the Hackney congregation. Dudley often found his father's pride in his accomplishments embarrassing.

When he began to write his diary, taking a hint from his friend Mr. Whatley, he was 24. He had been at a Nonconformist academy in Hackney, one of those excellent schools forced upon the dissenters by the persecution of the Church and the State. Defoe's praise of these schools as represented by the neighbouring academy at Stoke Newington kept by Mr. Morton is confirmed by the accomplishments which Dudley Ryder had acquired in Hackney. It was probably here that he learned to speak French

[1] Newcome MSS., Hackney Municipal Library.

and acquired the beginnings of that knowledge of Latin which enabled him later to carry on a conversation in that tongue with cousin Jo about their love for Sally Marshall. And he may well have learned shorthand there, too, for it was an art popular among the Nonconformists and taught in many of their schools. The importance of this accomplishment cannot be overrated. Even without considering the cover it gave to the secret thoughts he committed to his diary—and it is incredible that he would have ventured to pen them without such cover—the speed and facility of shorthand enabled him to capture his moods and to escape from the intolerable stiltedness of his ordinary prose style into a natural colloquialism. It is no accident that the greatest diaries of the seventeenth and eighteenth centuries, Pepys's and Wesley's, were both written in shorthand. I doubt whether Pepys's diary would have been either so intimate or so well written as it is, had it not been written in shorthand; he, too, was a tedious writer in the ordinary way. Certainly, if Dudley Ryder had taken the infinite pains in writing his diary that he took in writing to Aunt Stevenson and Edward Leeds, it would have been infinite pain to read.

Debarred from Oxford and Cambridge because of his Nonconformity, Dudley was sent to Edinburgh. He took no great pride in his Scottish education. He had that dislike of the Scottish nation which became almost a mania among Englishmen later in the eighteenth century. He looked upon the English Universities with jealous suspicion, professing to believe the stories about their corruptness and neglect of learning, and maintaining that Whigs would soon be forced to send their sons to Leyden, so low was learning fallen in this country. It was a little inconsistent in him to send his only son Nathaniel to Eton and Cambridge. Perhaps the good job that Queen's had made of cousin John, the archbishop, had changed his opinion by that time. Even so, Natty went up with strict warnings about the society not to keep, the King's College men especially. But if Dudley did not derive from Edinburgh the pleasure he might have done, he made one acquaintance at least, who must have prompted many an hour's conversation later, Alexander Cuming. At the time when Ryder was beginning to make a name in the legal profession, Cuming was induced by a dream of his wife's—in 1715 Ryder thought her a sensible woman enough—to visit the Cherokee Mountains, where in 1730 he was proclaimed lawgiver, commander, leader and chief of the Cherokee Nation. Whether Ryder was present when Cuming returned with his seven Cherokee braves I do not know, for his later diaries do not begin until some years after this historic event. But he must have heard about that solemn agreement of Peace and Friendship with the Cherokee Nation which Cuming, in the name of the British Nation, signed at his room in Spring Garden, and the scheme for settling three million Jewish families in the Cherokee Mountains, and also about the unfortunate rumours of jobbery which soon followed.

Leyden, to which he afterwards went, following the custom of Scottish law students, to study Roman civil law, proved congenial. Uncle Robert Billio had taken refuge there during the reign of James II, and there were many Hackney acquaintances there. Holland and the state of the University were good conversational subjects; it was quite impressive in coach or club to touch upon the learned Perizonius and his successor Burmann, or to descant on the charms of 'my old mistress, the beautiful Elzevira', now married and living at The Hague. It was then, too, that he had visited Paris, although his recollections of the place were now becoming so confused that a guide book might prove useful. Probably he acquired there that discriminating taste in prints which enabled him to form his enviable collection and to gain, on that memorable occasion when he climbed to the dome of St. Paul's to see Mr. Thornhill at work on the new paintings (as so few had done despite Mr. Thornhill's first pretensions that the crowd had to be kept away), the reputation of being a virtuoso. Not that Dudley was deceived himself; he was careful not to say too much lest he should correct Mr. Thornhill's flattering opinion.

When the diary opens, he had been a student at the Middle Temple for nearly two years.[1] The reputation of law students was not high at the time. Ned Ward [2] hits it off pretty accurately in his character-sketch of a young student of the Temple:

> The *Law* was his Profession, but Poetry his Study. *Love* was the sphere he mov'd in, and *Fornication* the Center of all his Happiness. His *Books* were of no other use but to Adorn his Study; and he never thought of Pleading at any

---

[1] He was granted special admission on 22 June 1713.
[2] *The Rise and Fall of Madam Coming-Sir*, 1717.

other *Bar* but a *Vintners*. The Morning he spent in *Dressing*, the Afternoon in *Courtship*, and the most part of the Night in *Debauchery*.

Although Dudley was not free from all these defects, this picture does not hit him off. He did give some of his time to the study of the Law. Except on those days, far too numerous perhaps for a zealous student, when he was entertaining or being entertained at breakfast, writing a letter to Aunt Stevenson or Mr. Leeds, or doing nothing in particular at Hackney except play the viol, he devoted his mornings to reading Coke upon Littleton, Perkins or the *Practical Register*, or he went to Westminster Hall, by boat from the Temple as often as not, to study the method of presenting a case and of arguing so as to impress the jury. Not that he was ever greatly impressed himself; in his more confident moments he thought he could present as good a case himself, or sum-up at least as clearly and succinctly as the judges he heard. Sometimes of an afternoon he would go to his civil law club at John's Coffee House, but this part of the day was nearly always engaged in more pleasing activities, some of those which are set out in Ned Ward's sketch.

Dudley was sadly perplexed what to think of his future as a lawyer. Sometimes when he set about Coke, often as early as seven in the morning, things would go swimmingly. He would grasp the argument of even a long case, and feel that with luck he might make a considerable figure in the law. At other times, he would be utterly despondent. He was too easily distracted, flustered by responsibility, his memory was not good, he was a poor speaker, repeating himself or prone to get stutteringly excited, he had no originality and could only develop other people's ideas. Harsh self-critic that he was, he exaggerated his own defects. If at times this self-confessed mighty critic is repellently ungenerous to his friends and relations, it may be pleaded in extenuation that he was at least as ungenerous to himself. His friends and relations had a better opinion of him. But he had not yet acquired any great love for the law. He may have been posing when he wrote to Mr. Potter in Holland expressing a distaste for Westminster Hall, Coke and Littleton as substitutes for Leyden, Plato and Cicero. But the entries in his diary relating to his legal studies would have been more copious than they are had he been greatly interested in them. Nor would a keen student have passed over his first Inn exercise to a

A MAN OF MANY ACCOMPLISHMENTS

friend as he did, with the excuse that it was so out of the way that it was not worth doing. True he liked to argue at the club, but that was because he shone more brightly in such company than elsewhere. The best hope for legal advancement, he felt, lay in forming useful acquaintances. The introduction to Chief Justice Peter King, which Mr. Freke the parson offered to arrange, seemed promising, although Dudley, diffident as ever, was ashamed of his father's bluntness in hinting at the probable benefit. Mr. Freke died before fulfilling his promise, but the introduction came in time, and very useful it proved.

There were too many distractions for Dudley Ryder, pathetically eager like so many shy people to shine in all companies, to settle down to one course of life. He had many accomplishments. He could read Greek and Latin, French and Italian; he played the bass-viol and the flute, not so well as he could have wished but well enough at times to please even himself; he could dance country dances well and was passably good at those French measures, the minuet and the rigadoon. He collected prints. He had a catholic and genuine love of fine literature and philosophy. Not many young men could boast, although Dudley did not brag of it, of having read in the course of two years, Homer and Horace in the original and in translation, Virgil, Cicero, Quintilian, Sallust, Buchanan, Strada's *Prolusions*, Spenser, Shakespeare, Waller, Milton, Butler, Rowe, Swift, Pope, Addison, Steele, Tickell, Young, Wotton, Tom Brown, Locke, Berkeley, Dr. Clarke, Sharrock, Rushworth, Tillotson, Hoadley, Grotius, Perizonius, Pufendorf, Molière, Le Sage, Regnard, Boileau, Voiture, Fontenelle, Madame Dacier, Fénelon, and others, to say nothing of numerous books and pamphlets on history, travel, antiquities, languages, conversation, economics and theology, and a wide selection of the current journals. Nor was this undigested reading. He read many books two or three times, and he was a sound and independent critic. By taste and training he was fitted for the society of scholars and men of letters. But his shyness would not permit him to get beyond the fringe of the society at the Grecian and Button's. He knew Sam Humphries,[1] Hughes,[2] Harris,[3] and other young fry, but he admired the celebrities from afar. He had an instinctive fear of wits; even Mr.

[1] Handel's librettist. [2] John Hughes, the dramatist.
[3] John Harris, the editor of *The Patriot*.

Isles, the talented raconteur of his club at John's, always put him into a strange fit of bashfulness that took long to wear off. The criticism of his *alter ego* caused him to belittle his own accomplishments and to envy those of other men; instead of consolidating his reputation as a man of taste and reason he had been led to vain thoughts of success as wit, rake, dancing master. And his susceptibility to female charm drew him into company that rarely failed to humiliate him. The ladies never appreciated sense or good judgement; they delighted only in rattling and romping. His own attempts in that way were heavy-footed and unconvincing; his fancy wilted under his own criticism. He suffered bitterly in appreciating the success of cousin Jo or young Sam Powell. What a fool he was, he sometimes reflected, to hanker after female applause when he might enhance his reputation among his own sex as a man of knowledge and judgement.

In London his clubs at John's and Sue's claimed most of his time. Here among his intimates he was respected and most happy. Indeed, they were a company who might have attracted any man of discrimination. Some of them demand the affectionate artistry of Lamb for suitable description. Who else could convey the fine enthusiasm of Mr. Potter, whose speculations extended far beyond his trade of apothecary into the Berkeleian realm of abstraction? What other pen could adequately describe Mr. Street, that amiable young eccentric? Sometimes he would be found hobnobbing with porters, sometimes giving elaborate instructions to a waiter for the preparation of his dinner—a single smelt, sometimes sitting, spectacles on nose and confronted by a grinning skull, poring over grimy treatises on witchcraft. Or he might be missed for several days because he had followed a pretty face all the way to its home, for the simple pleasure of seeing it in church the following Sunday. Impulsive, lovable Street, who laughed with the people who laughed at him.[1] And many others. Witnoom, who was a little too full of his own opinions and began to stutter as the talk grew heated. Jackson, whose talent lay in raillery and ridicule. Heathcote, who knew a lot about Parliamentary affairs but preferred to talk about hunting and hawking. Isles, the raconteur of the party, who gave life to his stories by the most entertaining

[1] Ryder gave an account of him in another manuscript.

minute details. Bowes and Leeds, both men of Ryder's own stamp. Smith, the young parson, who pursued the Higher Thought, leading the conversation towards Immortality and Mr. Berkeley, but who was too insistent in his criticism of conversational style, often embarrassing Dudley by nudging him every time he thought anything ill said. And Whatley, in some ways the most congenial of them all. He had talent and knowledge. His first essay in philosophy had won the applause of no less a person than Mr. Addison, and he enjoyed the friendship of Chief Justice King. Out of the fullness of his knowledge he was apt to run into what might appear pedantry, quoting Latin and Greek freely, and he was so subject to the spleen that he could keep to no settled study but fell into an even deeper gloom than his friend Dudley. But on his best days he was an ideal companion, a talented conversationalist, equally adept in fanciful triviality and cosmic profundity. These and a dozen more, West, Skinner, Warren, Porter, Atkins, Samson, Abney, Forster, made up the company of his friends. They were a talented set on the whole. None of them set the Thames on fire, but most of them achieved success in their chosen way of life.

The subjects they talked about in coffee houses and taverns? Much the same as young men of this type have always discussed, politics, philosophy, literature, religion and bawdry. The news and possibilities of the rebellion, Charles XII's heroic defence at Stralsund, the victories of Prince Eugene, the advisability of executing the condemned lords, the Triennial, Schism and Occasional Conformity Bills, Berkeley's notions on abstract ideas, Clarke's doctrine of the Trinity, Cicero, Horace and Addison, immortality and evil, stories learned and lewd. ' Next to the Pleasure arising from a good Conscience and the standing in Favour with God and Man ', said an anonymous author a few years later,[1] ' are those of Conversation.' These young men enthusiastically subscribed to this article of faith. Such a spate of talk, day after day! It would often start at John's soon after lunch, and, surviving numerous removes to Tom's, Sue's and various taverns, conclude perhaps at midnight. The more raffish young men of the Temple were perhaps engaged in those debaucheries for which they were notorious : these were more decorous, preferring the higher thought to the lower living. But they,

[1] *Gentleman's Magazine*, 1731, p. 198.

too, had their moments. Heated by wine and conversation beyond the love of the spirit, Dudley would sometimes, on his way home, fall from grace. Next to the Pleasures of Conversation, he then found, are the Displeasures of a Bad Conscience.

Dudley Ryder was not such an inveterate sightseer as Samuel Pepys, but he found the pageantry of London another powerful distraction from study. So many varied things were happening in that exciting time. Even Nature seemed affected by the general turbulence; she matched the bonfires of Smithfield with comets and strange apparitions in the sky, and when the tide of rebellion was stopped at Preston she froze the Thames at Westminster. Dudley satisfied his curiosity to the full. Now he would be at the ceremonies and dances of the City Companies, now at the Drawing Room, catching a sight of the Royal Family and, loyal Whig that he was, melting at the charms of the little princesses who were beginning to speak English so prettily, or watching the Court dance minuets and country dances. At other times he would stroll by the booths that had been constructed on the frozen Thames from Temple Stairs to London Bridge, or inspect the great camp that had been set up in Hyde Park. He would take his pleasure with the gentry and the mob at Southwark Fair or Spring Gardens, go by boat to Greenwich to see the great new ship the *Royal George* or to India House to examine the magnificent new orrery to be presented to the Emperor of China. Plays did not draw him much. More often than not he would stay for only one Act—and the whores in the passages always embarrassed him. Other shows there were in abundance, Lord Mayors' pageants, the riotous processions of Whigs and 'Jacks' in which effigies of the Pope, King William, Marlborough, the Pretender and Scaramouche were carried to the burning at Smithfield, the riots and scrimmages which ensued, the arrival of the prisoners from Preston, the trial of the rebel lords, the execution of Kenmure and Derwentwater, hangings, pilloryings. For all these things he had an eager curiosity. At times he displayed an unwonted confidence in his determination to see the show. His impudence was as superb as it is unexpected when he resolved to see the trial of Lord Wintoun by slipping into the Lord Chancellor's procession as one of the Lords' eldest sons—as it turned out he had to line up, under the very noses of the Yeomen of the Guard, with the Lord High

SHYNESS AND IMPUDENCE

Steward's gentlemen. The realization that 'if a person has but courage and could put on a good impudent face, he may always find out means of getting to any of these public sights' must have served him in good stead later. Almost as remarkable was his determination when, after several rebuffs, he succeeded in gate-crashing into the State Ball at St. James's. If it sometimes appears strange that Dudley Ryder should have been so successful in the Law's hurly-burly, it must be remembered that when it was needed he was capable of the shy man's reckless impudence.

If the attractions of London left little time for his legal studies, the social and family claims of Hackney were hardly less insistent. He was there every week-end and often during the week he would leave the Temple for his father's house near the Church of St. John. Sometimes he would go by coach—that stage-coach of Edmund Taylor's, I suppose, which was robbed three years later 'coming from London at night between Mr. Ward's House & Mr. Emmett's in the Lane'.[1] If it were fine he preferred to walk, lunching first with brother and sister Ryder at the shop in Bishopsgate and chatting with some of the numerous relations who were nearly always to be found at brother's table, and then through Moorfields, where he would usually pick up some little book or pamphlet to serve for entertainment the rest of the way over the fields to Hackney.

> Mrs. Pen carried us to two Gardens at Hackn'y (which I every day grow more and more in love with), Mr. Drake's one, where the garden is good, and house and the prospect admirable; the other my Lord Brooke's, where the gardens are much better, but the house not so good, nor the prospect good at all. But the gardens are excellent; and here I first saw oranges grow, some green, some half, some quarter, and some full ripe, on the same tree, and one fruit of the same tree do come a year or two after the other. I pulled off a little one by stealth (the man being mighty curious of them) and eat it, and it was just as other small green oranges are, as big as half the end of my little finger. Here were also great variety of other exotique plants and several labarinths, and a pretty aviary. Having done there with very great pleasure we went away back again, and called at the Taverne in Hackny by the church and there drank and eate, and so in the coole of the evening home.

Thus wrote Samuel Pepys on 25 June 1666. Fifty years later the village had attracted many wealthy citizens, and had become a straggling town of some two thousand inhabitants. Along Mare Street from Bethnal Green to the brook by the Church of

[1] Newcome MSS.

St. John-at-Hackney, along Church Street (the continuation of Mare Street towards Clapton), and along Well Street, Dalston Lane and the other roads which led to the neighbouring hamlets, Homerton, Shacklewell, Clapton, the country seats of the middle-class had been springing up with increasing rapidity. The pillars and stucco of their Palladian architecture survived even into the late nineteenth century. Little now remains of the elegant prosperity of this old suburb, but when Mr. Richard Ryder came to Hackney he could warm himself in the glory of such neighbours as Sir Gilbert Heathcote, the richest commoner in Great Britain (and the stingiest, Strype thought), Sir John Cass, the philanthropist (Newcome the vicar seemed to share the general dislike of him in Hackney), John Gould, the wealthy director of the East India Company and the Bank of England, William Dawsonne, a director of the East India Company. At least three fairly recent Lord Mayors had been resident here, Viner, Pilkington and Heathcote. Most of his neighbours, however, were like himself, reasonably prosperous merchants or professional men, Samuel Powell the grocer, Allard Denn the brewer, John Bickley the upholder, Joshua Iremonger the brewer, Edward Anthony the lawyer, Mr. Marsh the solicitor, Daniel Dolins, Mr. Swaine and many more.

The town had no more beauty and little more of antiquarian interest than the average suburban retreat. By the church where the Ryders lived was the most attractive part. Over the brook, where the tram station and the cottages of Bohemia Place now stand, was the Black and White House built in Queen Elizabeth's reign and later supposed to have been the residence of the Elector Palatine and Elizabeth, James I's daughter. In the middle of the seventeenth century it had been the home of the Vyner family, but in 1720 and probably at the time of the diary it was one of the boarding-schools for which Hackney was famous. It was here, probably, that Dudley, forgetting for the moment his compunctions about brother William's love-brokerings, helped young Mr. Hudson to an acquaintance with the young ladies over the garden wall. Next door, by Church Field where Mr. Ryder built a new house in 1716, was the vicarage newly erected by the old Tower, and behind the vicarage was the Church of St. John-at-Hackney.

The church had been rebuilt too often to have any great

attraction for the lover of antiquity, but it was interesting in other ways, as Mr. Pepys discovered—

> So after dinner . . . took coach and to Hackney church, where very full, and found much difficulty to get pews, I offering the sexton money, and he could not help me. So my wife and Mercer ventured into a pew, and I into another. A knight and his lady very civil to me when they come, and the like to my wife in hers, being Sir G. Viner and his lady—rich in jewells, but most in beauty—almost the finest woman that ever I saw. That which we went chiefly to see was the young ladies of the schools, whereof there is great store, very pretty ; and also the organ, which is handsome, and tunes the psalm, and plays with the people ; which is mighty pretty, and makes me mighty earnest to have a pair at our church, I having almost a mind to give them a pair, if they would settle a maintenance on them for it. I am mightily taken with them. April 21, 1667.

The organ was now in charge of Hugh Reading, a true representative of St. Cecilia : having failed to secure an increase on his salary of £20, he had soon after to be rebuked for making his voluntaries too long and playing tunes that were unbecomingly airy and jigging.[1] The vicar was Peter Newcome, M.A., who was appointed by Francis Tyssen in 1703 and continued to hold the vicarage until his death in 1738. Newcome, whose gift of shrewd irony is applied in his journal to the detriment of many of his solid parishioners, was suspect among the Nonconformists, but being a practical man he had tempered his Toryism since the accession of George I. His son Henry was headmaster of a school in the parish which achieved such fame that he was spoken of as a possible headmaster for Winchester. The church lecturer is now better known than any other person in Hackney at that time, but William Strype did not seem to interest his congregation. Dudley Ryder knew him merely as an old man with an unpleasing style in preaching, and seemed to know nothing of his biographies or antiquarian works. The vestrymen and lay officials of the church were nearly all acquaintances of Mr. Ryder ; in 1714 he and his friends Thomas Powell and Joseph Brooksbank were overseers.

Facing the church on the other side of Church Street was a boarding-school for young ladies (probably that ruled over by Mrs. Wallis) where Dudley honoured the ladies of Hackney with his presence at a dance—the company of so many young ladies of the school threatened to be unpleasing—and where Sam

[1] St. John-at-Hackney Vestry Minutes.

Humphries, Handel's librettist-to-be, displayed an undue anxiety to die for the love of a lady by challenging the captain who had engrossed the attention of his inamorata. The Mermaid Tavern, famous in the history of Hackney, also faced the church. Here Pepys drank and ate after his visit to Lord Brooke's gardens, and here the churchwardens of Hackney continued to drink and eat (mostly to drink, judging by the substantial charges for wine in their accounts) when auditing their accounts or settling such thorny problems as what to do about Mr. Tyssen's leaky waterplug which was spoiling the highway by Mr. Merreal's wall. The Mermaid had fine gardens, and it was on its bowling greens that Dudley saw the gentlemen of the parish trotting after their woods, crouching over them and coaxing them. Beyond the tavern towards Clapton was Dalston Lane, where several of Mr. Ryder's friends had their homes, Mr. Merreal and Mr. Emmett, and where the lord of the manor Francis Tyssen lived, that Francis Tyssen whose funeral ceremonials in 1717 were so splendid and costly that scandalized comment was heard far beyond Hackney.

In Mare Street, on the City side of the church, were several buildings of interest to us. Among the group of buildings at the corner of Well Street were the curious old building later called King John's Palace (it actually seems to have been the former residence of the Prior of the Order of St. John of Jerusalem) and the old house called Shore Place because, Strype writes, 'they say, *Jane Shore* had an Habitation here. And in this House, to preserve this Tradition, now or late, was her Picture.' Here, it seems, lived Aunt Billio and the Sykes family. Opposite the present St. Thomas's Square was the dissenters' meeting-house, first preached in by Dr. Bates and subsequently by uncle Robert Billio and the celebrated Matthew Henry. Dudley, although he was impressed by Matthew Henry's commentaries on the New Testament, was not so impressed that he could forget the dullness of his sermons. Since Henry's death in 1714 the meeting had been a storm centre among the Hackney Nonconformists. When John Barker, the young preacher from Crosby Square, was elected to fill the vacancy instead of the elder Mr. Mayo, forcible possession of the meeting had to be kept for some weeks. This 'division among our Dividers' was still strong in 1715 and Dudley's father was engaged in negotiating with St. Thomas's

Hospital for a site for a new meeting. When they secured one, the gravel ground near the old bowling green just along Mare Street, Dudley's friend George Smith became the parson, although father had hoped to secure the appointment of cousin Robert Billio.

Opposite Mr. Barker's meeting was the old Nag's House. As Mr. Defoe of the adjoining parish of Stoke Newington so truly stated—

> Wherever God erects a house of prayer,
> The Devil always builds a chapel there.
> And 'twill be found upon examination,
> The latter hath the larger congregation.

Such it was, this London *sur le champs*, a place where the prosperous shopkeeper and the citizen knight might retire to enjoy the healthy climate and to live like Sir Roger de Coverley. Surrounded by fields and farms—thirty years ago sheep still grazed at Temple Mills—it was in the eighteenth century a bourgeois paradise, a place from which the retired merchant need hardly stir to gather in his dividends.

Here Dudley passed a good deal of his time. But his was far from a retired life. The Ryders always had visitors or were out visiting. Dudley might complain that the people of Hackney lacked elegance and that the ladies were too much given to scandal, but at least their houses were open. To the Ryder home came all their many relations, fathers, mothers, uncles, cousins, and many of the neighbours. Coming from London, Dudley never knew when he might be expected to entertain a crowd of ladies or relations from the country. Father, with his fitful generosity, often invited people to stay, even people he hardly knew. Business acquaintances, Nonconformist associates, parsons from town and country, all seemed to smell dinner at the Ryders' from afar. To Dudley this gregariousness was often disturbing. To be forced to keep the company of young Mr. Henry or cousin John, to maintain table-conversation with parsons who could talk of little but religion, to hazard the company of a crowd of chattering women—this was a social round repellent to a man who doubted his urbanity and shone only in a selected company. The conduct of the house was not what it should be, moreover. Mother's peevishness and inability to make things run smoothly, father's alternations of petulance and kindliness, sister's shrewishness, William's lapses from respectability, all served to maintain his apprehension. When grandmother was staying with them, the case was even worse; he never knew when that formidable old widow would turn upon him for his attempts to keep a fine appearance. What right had he, the son of a tradesman, to go as fine as her first husband the counsellor? When the little man's own conscience had been pricked by the elegance of his new silver-hilted sword, his scarlet riding cloak, or his new wigs from Colebuck, it was hard to suffer the rebukes of the old lady. It was a happy day when she moved over to Kentish Town with her son John, the vicar there, and his wife, those dogged Tories, whose refusal to admit the truth of Whig arguments rarely failed to put their loyal nephew into an ill humour.

But life at Hackney had its compensations. His viol and flute and the company of a friend to play duets or sonatas, the garden, skating in the Marsh, riding to Edmonton or Enfield, bowls, dances, were all pleasant enough distractions. And though Dudley was a mighty critic both of the manner and matter of most preachers, the sermons at the meetings and church were often agreeable stimulants to thought and argument—and the ladies of the congregation were entertaining reliefs from dull ones, Mrs. Hammond in the next pew, Mrs. Alworthy with the strange roving eye. There were young ladies for whom he had a *tendre*, Mrs. Lee (though he was concerned to hear that she thought he had serious intentions), Mrs. Loyd at Aunt Bickley's, a goodlooking young woman with several beaux to her string, but like himself a mighty critic. How much he was attracted by her own qualities and how much by the familiarities which she allowed brother William and others, Dudley could never quite determine.

In this life of infinite leisure, other diversions were not lacking. There were the visits to the spas, to Hampstead and Islington Wells, and to Epsom, the short holidays at brother's estate at Westbrook Hay, the visit to the Bath. This last was an outstanding event in his life. For a long time the family had been very worried about him; his frequent languidness and the pains in his arm made them think that he was going into a consumption like young Mr. Crisp. Numerous remedies had been tried, cupping, blue flannel (Aunt Marshall had found that efficacious in her own case), a private remedy in which mustard-seed played a large part, the nostrum of Mr. Fowles the quack, all without effect. At length he was prevailed upon to join sister at the Bath. They did not know that his expectations were turned less upon a cure than upon the society of the lady whose charms had swept him away on the first occasion he saw her, going to Bath in the same coach as sister Ryder. Alas, he was doomed to his usual disappointment in love, this time intensified to despair. What chance had he, a student with no certain prospects, short and unprepossessing despite his fine clothes, so lacking in self-assurance that all his intended gallant speeches and lively banter died on his lips as he came into her presence? What chance had he to secure the regard of Sally Marshall, the greatest beauty in Bath, the toast of beaux and officers? None but the brave . . . She, who loved to be entertained with wit and banter (though she was no great wit herself) was easier prey for the unfettered rattling and familiarity of young Sam Powell, an Oxford student of no great sense or respectability, not yet 19. Dudley dissolved in love and jealousy. What heart can fail to be moved by that tragicomic scene in Mr. Blathwayt's garden, when, tortured by Sally's complaisant acceptance of Sam Powell's familiarities and her callous disdain of his own proffered salutes, he was constrained to quit the company for the adjoining wilderness, there to find relief in unmanly tears. Who but Henry Mackenzie could fitly express the sensibility of this Man of Feeling? Little wonder if he returned from the Bath lower in health and spirits than when he went.

The rest of the diary is dominated by his infatuation and despair. It makes a fascinating study, the ineffectual ardour of the draper's ambitious son for the regard of the tailor's aspiring daughter. At times one is apt to be as impatient as Ryder himself; it is unbecoming to languish for what cannot be attained. At times one sympathizes with his bitter-sweet affection for Cupid's painful dart. Nor is the study unrelieved by comedy, Dudley lisping in numbers (with a hint or two from *The Rape of the Lock*) to gratify the Fair with the flattery of the poetic Muse, Dudley consoling himself with cousin Jo, equally stricken by Sally's fateful charm, by railing Timon-like on the failings of women, Dudley attempting to fly from love's sickness on the fumes of hot punch.

When the diary breaks off in the middle of a sentence—what

wretch destroyed the rest of it?—he is still love's slave. He might in a more confident mood write to Sam Powell:

> The soft ideas of love have almost entirely given place to those of the law, and in the room of those bewitching charms with which Sally M—— has so often pleased and distracted my heart, the generous passion for justice, equity and glory inflames my breast.[1]

But some months later he could still write to cousin Jo:

> As I passed through the fields the sun seemed to be hanging over Sally's house, from whence it shot its beams joined with hers, for they brought her strongly before my eyes.[2]

How long his hopes and fears continued, or what became of Sally, I cannot say. That self-possessed and calculating young lady made a match, I imagine, that enabled her to maintain the state she thought fitting—unless, indeed, his relations were right in thinking her too masculine to be really a beautiful woman. Dudley remained unsettled for many years. It was not until 1734, when he was 43, that he entered into that state whose felicities he had craved for so long. That the pangs for Mrs. Marshall were driven out by pangs for Mrs. —— and Mrs. —— we cannot doubt. The sensibility of the man who, even when a highly respectable Attorney-General, confessed himself an admirer of female beauty, could be bruised by the gentlest hand. But when he at last married Anne Newnham of Streatham, he found a bride who repaid the years of waiting. His letters to her, written when the demands of the law or her visits to the Bath separated them, show that his hopes had not been misplaced:

> I look upon matrimony, as it really is, not only as a society for life, in wch our persons & fortunes in general are concern^d, but as a partnership wherein our very passions & affections, our hopes & fears, our inclinations & aversions, all our good & ill Qualitys are brought into one Common Stock.[3]

and—

> I receive your letters as ye most welcome presents y^t can come to me. To find them so full of Love gives me Raptures y^t even ye hurry of Business can't drive out of my soul.[4]

---

[1] Letter in shorthand dated 1 December 1716.
[2] Letter in shorthand dated 14 July 1717.   [3] Letter undated.
[4] Letter dated 12 October 1734.

Lord Chief Justice Campbell mistook the solicitous affection for uxoriousness. He did not know the real Dudley Ryder. He had learnt in suffering.

He had met Anne Newnham at a concert in March 1728/9 in the company of Mr. Worven of Hackney. 'It gave me no little satisfaction', he wrote, 'to see you accompanied by two ladies in whom not only beauty, but good nature and good sense were visible.' Six months later he wrote[1] in answer to her letter 'insisting upon my refusing any application or offers made in relation to her' and agreed to obey her directions in the most religious manner—'I have learnt to have too great a respect for you not to prefer your satisfaction to my own.' One is inclined to see in the five years' delay before their marriage a repetition of earlier misfortunes. That the result was ultimately happier may have been due to the lessons of experience; at least, he learned from the example of Sally Marshall that his own versifyings were not the happiest ambassadors of love. Anne received copies of verses by the author of *The Fair Quaker*.

But perhaps the delay was due to his insistence upon the necessity of a sound financial basis for marriage. His peculiar amalgam of excessive sense and excessive sensibility would have interested Jane Austen. Anne Newnham was to bring him a highly satisfactory dowry, but when he first met her he had still to make his way as a lawyer. He had been called to the bar at the Middle Temple on 8 May 1719, after six years as a student, and had transferred to Lincoln's Inn in 1725.[2] Material is lacking for an account of his progress in the next few years. Campbell suggests that he made a success at the bar, helped largely by the friendship of Lord Chancellor King, who like himself was the son of a tradesman, brought up among dissenters, and a former student at Leyden. Soon Ryder added to these resemblances by forsaking Nonconformity for the Church of England.

His success, Campbell suggests, came when King introduced him to Sir Robert Walpole, who decided to employ him. He entered Parliament as member for St. Germains in 1733 and in 1734 for Tiverton, a seat which the Ryders continued to hold for

[1] Letter dated 26 September 1729.
[2] July 26, 1725—these dates are taken from the Lincoln's Inn Admission Register. The dates given in Campbell and Foss differ.

a century. Upon the promotion of Talbot to the Chancellorship and of Yorke to the office of Chief Justice, he was appointed Solicitor-General in November 1733. Four years later, when Willes was made Chief Justice of Common Pleas, he succeeded to the Attorney-Generalship, a post he retained for over seventeen years. In 1738 it was announced that he would succeed Sir Joshua Jekyll as Master of the Rolls, although he had actually refused the post as the remuneration was insufficient. In 1740 he was knighted.

As first law officer he proved a useful assistant to Walpole. He made no brilliant figure; there is no record or tradition of any great speech, gesture or intrigue associated with him. Even in the few great events in which he took a leading part the limelight of history has played upon the other actors. He seems never to have bullied and browbeaten in the style of other lawyers and politicians, he does not appear to have abused his office to line his pockets as others did. In an age when, according to his great leader, every man had his price, he seems to have held his office by hard work and competence. His virtues were those everyday ideals of his dissenting forbears, which draw neither great praise nor great blame. Knowing him as we do from his early diary—and that his character had not changed greatly is evident from his later diaries—we may wonder how he achieved the eminence that he did. Luck and the assistance of King played their part, but Walpole, a shrewd judge, must have perceived valuable qualities in him. What they were is fairly clear, I think. His own modest estimate that he reasoned well upon the ideas of other people, although he could claim few original ideas, the respect of the more solid of his young friends, and the copiousness of his surviving law notes as advocate and judge, all suggest that in legal affairs he joined painstaking thoroughness with convincing reasoning, qualities admirable in an advocate and Parliamentary debater. He may even have risen to eloquence at times. 'If I were to be so unhappy', the Duchess of Marlborough once wrote to him,[1] ' as to have any more Causes, I had rather have you for my advocate than St. Paul.' Even Horace Walpole described one of his speeches as ' glorious '.[2] And the diffidence that might have held him back was, as we have already seen, redeemed on necessary occasions by a remarkable boldness.

[1] Letter dated 3 August 1742.   [2] Letter to Mann, 22 January 1742.

A SELF-PORTRAIT

His own estimate of his character in later years is as just as any that could be made by another:

> My present character in the world as to my ability is, I believe, that I am a good lawyer and [of] some parts. As to the heart, that I am thoroughly honest and of great humanity and candour. I am sometimes tempted to attack the enemies of the administration in a severe manner, but I check myself in that design. I am more fitted to act the part of candour, mildness, sincerity and good nature and reasoning. My own disposition leads me to this. . . . It will better likewise secure me against enemies and fall in more with my talents, which are not formed for bustle and controversy, management and design. It is indeed as much the reverse as can well be. I should therefore keep out of all scrapes, all enmities. Nor am I much fitted for friendship, and therefore in such disputes should want zealous friends and have none or few but such as are so for their own ends or from public considerations and from my public character [1]

His first important duty had been to conduct through the Commons the bill of pains and penalties against the city of Edinburgh following upon the murder of Captain John Porteous. Despite his arguments and the speech reported (or invented for him) by Dr. Johnson, the feeling of the Commons was so strong that the only penalty inflicted was a fine for the benefit of the widow.[2] When he dreamed [3] in 1715 that he was actively engaged against the rebels, much of his later work was presaged. In 1744, when Prince Charles Edward was about to lead the Jacobite rebellion, he moved the suspension of the Habeas Corpus Act, and in the same year he supported Hardwicke's bill making forfeit the property of rebels' children and attainting the Pretender's sons of high treason should they ever land in England. Ryder's defence of this highly unpopular bill was his greatest Parliamentary speech, one of enormous length but well marshalled and extremely learned. He quoted, among others, Grotius, Pufendorf and Cicero (favourite authors of his student days) and surveyed historically the treason laws of England and of Jews, Athenians, Romans, Saxons and Normans. The bill was passed. His speeches on other bills reveal considerable ability but the same prolixity. Walpole briefly commented upon his last speech in Parliament, in support of Hardwicke's bill to prevent clandestine marriages, that he 'did amply gossip' over the bill.

[1] Later Diary, 22 August 1741.
[2] *Parliamentary History*, x, pp. 274–5.
[3] cf. Diary, p. 46.

THE DIARY OF DUDLEY RYDER

With one notable exception the cases in which he was engaged as Attorney-General have little general interest. That exception was the impeachment of Simon, Lord Lovat, in 1746 for his part in the Jacobite rebellion. Sir Dudley bore the chief responsibility for the conduct of the trial, as one of the managers for the Commons. Throughout the long proceedings his manner was irreproachable, he was fair and he did not bully, and he showed himself an excellent lawyer. But those whose loyalties and passions were deeply stirred by the trial (and in New Zealand at least some people are still passionate about it) found such qualities disappointing to their desire for drama. The glory of the trial fell upon his inferior officer, Murray, the Solicitor-General, whose eloquence, rivalling that of the elder Pitt, had already made him in fact the leader in Parliamentary affairs. Ryder, Walpole admitted, was a much better lawyer than Murray, but his conduct of the trial was 'cold and tedious'.[1] As with Sally Marshall, so with Horace Walpole.

The nearest he came to fame was in almost the last case he conducted as Attorney-General. In 1753 he had to prosecute William Owens for a libel against the House of Commons for its committing the Hon. Alexander Murray to Newgate because he had refused to fall on his knees before them. This heroic defiance endeared Murray to all good Englishmen and Tories. Ryder was not as tactful as he might have been; he maintained that the Commons were the good people of England and the rest the mob. The jury claimed the privilege of all free Englishmen of thinking for themselves; despite the prosecution's clear proof of libellous publication and the direction of Chief Justice Lee, they brought in a verdict of 'Not Guilty'. The decision was greeted with the usual gusto of the time; there were bonfires all over London. Ryder, afraid to face the mob, hid in the Lord Mayor's closet. A few hours later when he ventured to seek the sanctuary of his house in Chancery Lane, he found a great bonfire in Fleet Street, and before he was allowed to pass he was forced to give money to the mob to drink the health of the jury. Fortunately, they did not recognize him. As his coach passed by they threw him, for his amusement, a copy of the song freshly composed by an Irish porter—

[1] Letter to Mann 20 March 1747.

BARON RYDER OF HARROWBY

> Sir Doodley, Sir Doodley, do not use us so rudely;
> You look pale, as if we had *kilt* ye:
> Sir Doodley, Sir Doodley, we shamefully should lye,
> Were we to say the defendant is GUILTY, &c.

Shortly afterwards, Sir William Lee died of an apoplectic fit, and in 1754 Sir Dudley took his place as Chief Justice in the Court of King's Bench, and was made a Privy Councillor. The hope of his student days, that he might make a considerable figure in the law, had been completely justified. He was not a great Chief Justice, he made no decisions of great importance, and he disappointed the expectation that he would reform common law procedure. But he nearly achieved his own ambition and vindicated the law's dignity by being raised to the peerage. Hardwicke, the Lord Chancellor, was still averse to having a rival law-lord in the House of Peers, but the legal profession urged Ryder's ennoblement as essential to the public welfare and the respect due to the law. Ryder himself pressed its importance upon all his influential friends, especially the Duke of Newcastle. After two years' agitation, Hardwicke's resistance was broken. On 17 May 1756, Sir Dudley recorded in his diary that he had inquired whether he might assume the title of 'Grantham' and whether he would take precedence of Villiers and Horace Walpole. Three days later he wrote: '20 May: I ordered Mr. Child to make me a Baron's robe by Tuesday next' and wondered whether he should still call the judges in his court 'brothers'. On 24 May, the King signed a warrant to the Attorney-General to make out a patent of peerage to Sir Dudley under the style of Lord Ryder, Baron Ryder of Harrowby in the county of Lincoln.

That evening, Sir Dudley died quite unexpectedly of apoplexy. He is buried at Grantham, where there is a marble monument to him in the parish church.

W. M.

1715

PREFACE

Mr. Whatley told me the other day of a method he had taken for some time of keeping a diary. And I now intend to begin the same method and mark down every day whatever occurs to me in the day worth observing. I intend particularly to observe my own temper and state of mind as to my fitness and disposition for study or the easiness or satisfaction it finds within itself and the particular cause of that or of the contrary uneasiness that often disturbs my mind. I will also take notice especially of what I read every day. This will be a means of helping my memory in what I read. I intend also to observe my own acts as to their goodness or badness. I think there will be many advantages from this way of setting down whatever occurs to me. I shall be able then to review any parts of my life, have the pleasure of it if it be well spent, if otherwise know how to mend it. It will help me to know myself better and give a better judgement of my own ability and what I am best qualified for. I shall know what best suits my own temper, what is most likely to make me easy and contented and what the contrary. I shall know how the better to spend my time for the future. It will help me to recollect what I have read.

Monday, June 6. Rose between 6 and 7 in the morning. Employed till breakfast in reading Locke upon the lowering interest. My thoughts pretty much taken up with my journey I was to take in the afternoon especially upon the account of the dancing. Did little from breakfast to dinner but play upon my viol.

At 3 o'clock went with Skinner and Swain to Hampstead.[1] Both of them good humoured and very civil and obliging.

---

[1] Matthew Skinner (b. 1689) of Welton, Northants, entered Lincoln's Inn 1709; Chief Justice of Chester, 1734. His cousin was probably Thomas Swaine, son of Bennett Swaine of Hackney, whose sister married into the Skinner family.

Swain is a man of very little conversation. Skinner very pleasant, tells abundance of stories and does it pretty well. Apt to make a jest of his cousin Swain and seems to despise him mightily. In my journey was thrown down by a hog but without any hurt. Came to the Wells, drank a pint of wine together and went into the dancing-room. Tolerable diversion, much company but little genteel. Most that danced were either dancing masters or their prentices, I suppose because a holy day. Walked upon the walks. Looked at the gamesters. The place very full. Met Mrs. Lee with her father and sister. Returned home about 10 o'clock and soon went to bed. At Hackney.

Tuesday, June 7. Rose at 8. Read Boileau's reflections upon Longinus,[1] wherein he particularly exposes Perrault for his unjust treatment of Homer, Virgil and all the best authors of antiquity. They are admirably well made and worth a second reading. Played upon my viol. Aunt Billio[2] and cousin's wife and daughter dined with us. Cousin Billio treats her daughter harshly and severely.

Mr. Cumming[3] came to see me. Told me of the very strict examination he passed through in Edinburgh in order to be admitted as advocate. I am much concerned about the studying the law. I don't seem to gain that knowledge and insight into it that might be expected from my time at it. Went to bed at 12.

Wednesday, June 8. Rose at 7 though called at 6. Dined at my brother's. Bought 5 yards of cloth to make a suit of clothes at 18s. per yard. Met with Cousin Watkins. Saw his house and shop he is fitting up. Will cost him a great deal of money to finish it. I wish it may turn to account. Bespoke a wig of Colebuck.

Read in Madame Dacier's discourse upon the corruption of the taste wherein she defends Homer against the censures and

---

[1] In the 1694 edition of his works.

[2] *Aunt Billio* was Sarah, sister of the diarist's father. She married the Rev. Robert Billio (1645–1710), who was minister at the Presbyterian meeting in Mare Street, Hackney, from 1699 to 1710. Her sons, both of whom appear frequently in the diary, were Robert (m. to Mrs. Jeffries) and Joseph. Both of them were Nonconformist parsons.

[3] Sir Alexander Cuming (d. 1775), called to Scottish Bar 1714. Became Chief of the Cherokee Indians in 1730 [cf. *D.N.B.*].

criticism of Mr. de la Motte.¹   She does not manage this adversary with that spirit and wit that Boileau did the same against Mr. Perrault but however sufficiently exposes her adversary.

After 7 o'clock brother called me to go to park with sister. Saw great deal of company at least there but little good. Never was walking there before with a lady. A little perplexed how to behave with respect to the giving her the right or left hand when we turned back. At first changed sides with her to keep her of my right hand but at last observing that ceremony not much regarded by others, I kept my own side in going backwards or forwards.

Thursday, June 9. Mr. Samson ² breakfasted with me. We talked French together some time. He told me of the method of bringing a case to trial and of the process from the taking out of the original writ to the trial of the issue. Has an esteem for me I believe.

Went to dancing. My master told me I don't dance firmly and strongly enough. It tires me very much to dance.

Read Sir Richard Steele's dedication of his account of the state of the Roman Catholic religion to the Pope. A generous disinterested charitable spirit runs through the whole. Extremely pleased to see the book writ with so much wit, raillery and art. Immediately after read over some of my last letters. Extremely pleased with them. It is the most agreeable state of mind a man can be in to be pleased with his own performances.

Friday, June 10. Rode out in the evening with brother, Gregg and West.³ Run my sister's horse against one that Gregg rode upon. Won a treat of him. It made him mighty dull and out of

---

¹ *Causes de la Corruption du Gout*, 1714, by Madame Dacier, wife of the Secretary of the Academy. Antoine de la Motte, who knew no Greek, had used her translation in making his French version of the *Iliad*, 1699. This quarrel formed the second stage in the Battle of the Books, which raged for some thirty years in France. The first controversialists were chiefly Perrault, La Bruyère and Boileau. The battle was taken up in England by Temple, Swift, Wotton and Bentley, among others.

² Attorney of Bartley's Buildings.

³ Possibly Richard West (d. 1726); admitted to Inner Temple 1708, M.P. for Bodmin 1722–6. His play *Hecuba* was performed at Drury Lane on 2 February 1726.

humour all the time after. Came to town again and heard the agreeable news that the House of Parliament was upon the impeachment of Oxford and Bolingbroke. And several of the House of Commons impatient to hear whom they will impeach besides of high treason.[1]

Saturday, June 11. Went after dinner to John's Coffee House.[2] Met with Mr. Witnoom [3] and Jackson and Smith [4] and two or three more. Discoursed about the impeachments. Jackson the same as usual sees everything in a ridiculous light, laughs at everything he says. Smith, also still like himself, corrected Mr. Witnoom for a small error in his words. Smith has a very ill custom of observing upon everything that is said and jogging me with his feet or hands to make me take notice of any that he thinks is ill said in the company. It puts me in pain for fear the company should observe it and think that I am in conspiracy with him to make remarks upon them. Returned to brother's. He and I went to hire horses to go to Epsom on Monday. Met with Mrs. Lee there. She was extremely good humoured, mighty obliging to me, loves my company, I believe. Told me she had vindicated me in the company of ladies at Hampstead from the charge of being full of the vapours. Found a secret pleasure in hearing I was talked of. It's indeed a pleasant thing to hear one's own name mentioned, and this makes it that it is a much more taking and agreeable way of address to call a man by his name when you speak to him than by his common appellation of ' Sir ', and sometimes to mention his name in the third person when you are addressing yourself to himself as ' How does Mr. Such an one do ' when you are speaking to the man himself whose health you inquire after.

Came to Hackney with Mr. Tickell's new translation of the first book of Homer's *Iliad* in my hand. Read part of it. Seems to be done well in the general. Should be glad to see Mr. Pope's.

[1] The report of the committee appointed on 22 March 1715, to examine the conduct of the late ministers, was issued on 9 June. It resulted in resolutions for the impeachment of Bolingbroke, Harley, Ormonde, and Strafford.
[2] In Bow Lane near the Exchange.
[3] A Cornelius Wittenoom, vinegar merchant, died on 5 November 1756 (Musgrave).
[4] George Smith, M.A. (d. 1746), first minister of the Old Gravel Pit meeting in Mare Street, Hackney.

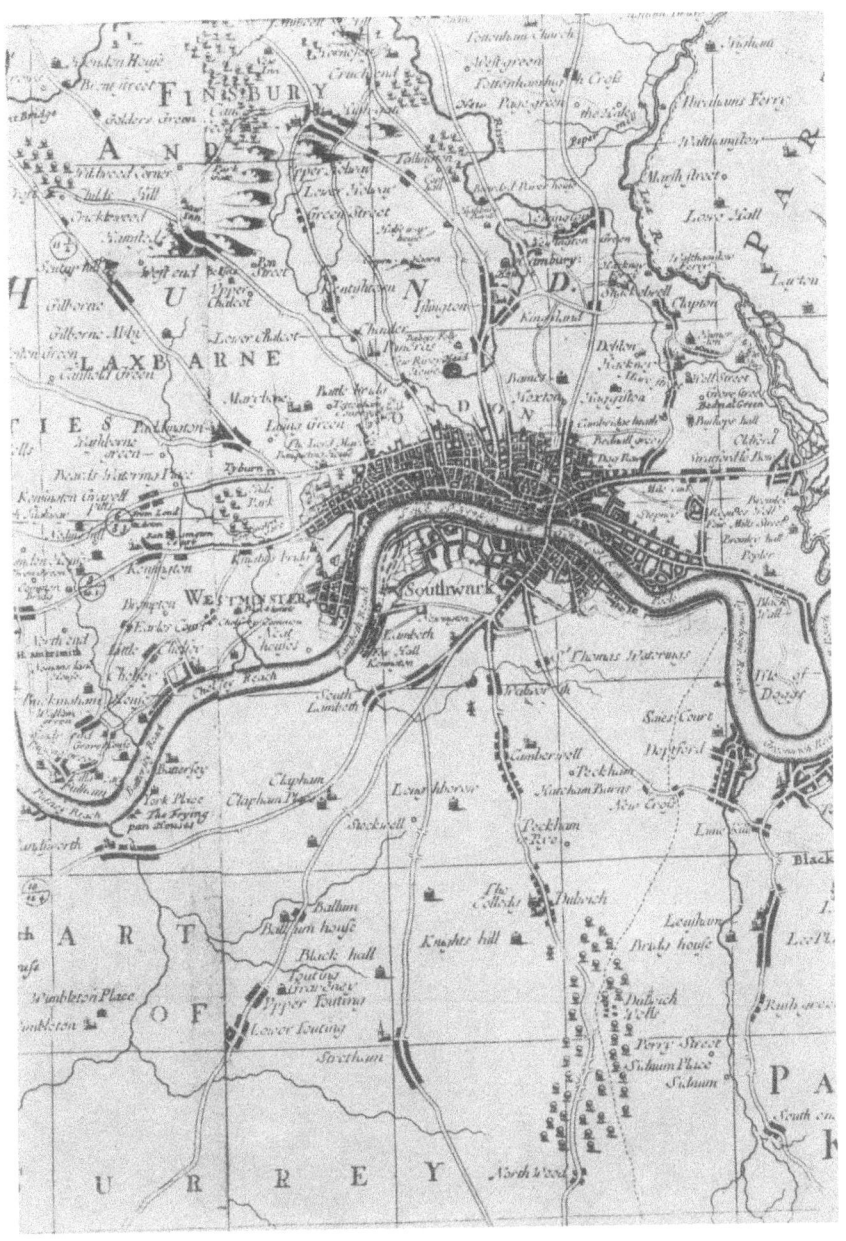

PART OF JOHN SELLER'S MAP OF MIDDLESEX, 1710

Emulation will I hope be a spur to their geniuses that something extraordinary may be produced.¹ Went to bed at 11.

Sunday, June 12. Walked in the garden a little before breakfast. Went to prayers in the family. Went to church, heard Mr. Barker. Was mightily pleased with the passage that was read before sermon in the 1 Isaiah where God is angry with his people for their disobedience and very emphatically expresses his anger to them : ' Bring me no more vain oblations, your new moons and your feasts are all abominations to me &c.' I thought it extremely sublime. Went to London in the afternoon with Cousin Joseph Billio. We talked together about the great advantage of a proper pronunciation and of that natural way of delivering a discourse which is scarce ever to be met with when men talk in the pulpit in the same tone of voice as they do in common conversation. Heard Mr. Trapp ² the poet. He is a man of a very mean aspect and behaves very strangely in the pulpit, full of uncouth gestures and postures. His sermon was not very extraordinary, not what one would have expected from a good poet.

Monday, June 13. Was extremely sick in the night and vomited. The cause of it was some meat pie I eat for supper which always makes me sick in the night. Slept very little all night.

Rose at four to get ready to go to Epsom. Went to brother's and got out with them about half an hour after 6. Came to Epsom between 9 and 10, set our horses up at an inn, eat some breakfast, and brother and sister went to my Lady Harrison's while I looked about the town and went to the bowling green and the long room. The gentlemen here divert themselves in the morning very much at bowls. There was a great many gentlemen there. Some of them employed themselves all day long at the dice table. One would be apt to think that they valued

---

¹ Pope's translation was published later in the same year. The merits of the rival translations were hotly debated. Addison's opinion, which led to a bitter quarrel with Pope, was that they were both well done, but that Tickell's had more of Homer in it.

² Joseph Trapp (1679–1747), first professor of Poetry at Oxford and author of *Abra-Mule.* One of the nine Oxford poets impaled in the distich ' Bubb, Stubb, Grubb, Crabb, Trapp, Young, Carey, Tickell, Evans.' He was a noisy supporter of Sacheverell.

money very little to see how soon a heap of guineas were thrown away. When I looked upon them in this light, as persons that valued a guinea no more than a halfpenny, I was apt to desire to engage with them not doubting but I should win because they valued the money so little. In the afternoon they have music that plays in the bowling green for the common diversion of all the company that is there or in the house. There were no ladies there that appeared while we were there, that is till near 7 o'clock.

I was invited to my Lady Harrison's and accordingly dined there. My lady herself is a woman of a great deal of polite breeding and endeavours to keep up the dignity of her ladyship by an appearing reservedness and something of a distance. As to the four young ladies her daughters, the two eldest seem to be persons of a very good sense and genteel and good humoured, but not beautiful at all. Mrs. Celia the second is to me the most agreeable. She has a great deal of sweetness and civility in her conversation that is mighty taking. The two youngest, though women grown, seem to have a great awe of their mother upon them and therefore say but little and don't seem to be so genteel as the others. The son who is an only one is a man of, I believe, a good temper and pretty tolerable conversation but nothing as I can discover extraordinary in him. Mrs. Celia rode with us four miles towards home and is extremely civil and obliging. When she left us we rode very hard home, it being light, that we rode 8 miles in an hour's time.

We were as we came near London under apprehension of being robbed by a man who was followed by a servant that carried a red cloak. What made us suspect was his turning into the road upon us, going to the hedge and looking through it, then speaking to his man and affecting to talk with us, but he did not think fit to attack us and we came safe home.

Tuesday, June 14. Went to Mr. Warren's where we talked together about an hour and then went together to Mr. Whatley's [1] where we were entertained for a considerable while with his usual philosophy. I forgot that I had called in at my return from the city at Paul's, where I was well pleased with the anthem I heard

---

[1] Robert Whatley, fifth son of Thomas Whatley, late of Mells, Somerset, was entered at the Inner Temple 11 November 1710. He later wrote a number of pamphlets, some addressed to Sir Peter King.

there. It was the 104th Psalm. Hughes had the chief part in it. I think to those that have a taste for music this kind of church music might be improved to very good purpose to raise the mind into a higher pitch of devotion and spiritualize it. It is a very unhappy thing though that they make so ill a use of singing in the cathedral by using it even in their prayers and recitations of the Psalms that are no better at all than the Italian recitativo's.

Wednesday, June 15. Dined at brother's. Met there with Cousin Billio [1] and his wife. She is very big, it makes her look a little dull and heavy. Sat with her alone half an hour. We found it very difficult to find discourse for so long a time. We seemed both uneasy.

Went to our club. Mr. Samson told us of a very odd sort of a custom in the West of England. Cudgelling it seems is a mighty diversion among them and it's handed down from father to son. The father teaches his sons to cudgel by playing with them himself and never allows them to spare him, but when they have once broke his head he then thinks them fit to shift for themselves and go into the world. There was a father cudgelling with his son and the young man was afraid to strike his father who continually pressed him to it. ' Sirrah,' says he, ' why don't you strike me ? ' But the boy refused until the father at length gave him a smart blow that raised his spirits and the young rogue had courage enough to break his father's head. ' That is well done,' says the father. ' Now you are fit to go into the world.' It seems they beat one another most furiously, and the father will set his children to cudgel and stand by and encourage them to thrash one another.

Supped at my brother's where we had the treat that we won of Gregg at racing. Mr. West came sooner than Gregg and told us of the strange and unaccountable love that Gregg seemed to have for Tristram and that he was afraid he would marry her. At length Gregg himself came, and we went to supper. And after that we sat down to punch where we stayed till 1 o'clock. Came home and went presently to bed.

Thursday, June 16. Rose at 8. Did nothing but mend my clothes till breakfast, when Mr. Samson came and after him

[1] Rev. Robert Billio, elder son of Aunt (Sarah) Billio. Later Vicar of Lutterworth and Swepstone, Leicestershire.

Mr. Smith. Samson went away first and left Smith and I together. It is very difficult for us two to find discourse to entertain ourselves with when we are alone. Mr. Warren or Whatley are more proper for my conversation. They generally say something that leads me to say something too and continue the discourse. And the reason is because they have got the art or rather habit of introducing subjects of extensive view, matters of speculation that leave room for diverse people's thoughts, whereas when the conversation turns only upon little matters of fact that occur, it's immediately put an end to by the end of the story. The conversation thus finishes sooner and must have more renewals than when it turns upon a point of law or philosophy or observations upon mankind &c. in which everything that is said raises new thoughts in the company and gives occasion to say more. This kind of conversation is also more particularly adapted to me because I cannot retain matters of fact enough in my memory to tell stories and maintain a conversation upon that foot.

Went to brother's. My father just come from the Hay. He was in mighty good humour. Went with him and Mrs. Lee and sister to Skinners' Hall where we were entertained upon the occasion of the choice of a master and wardens. There got acquainted with Colonel Day's son. He is a man of a good pleasant conversation. I believe of no great learning or solid sense but something of a wit. He sings well enough to entertain the company with some humoursome songs. My Lord Peterborough [1] who was brought up in the school that belongs to the company honoured them with his presence. The ladies dined first by themselves and then the men. The entertainment was very magnificent, music playing all the while at dinner. After dinner they chose the master and wardens. They have a ceremony of bringing the caps of these with the sound of the instruments into the hall and giving them into the hands of the last master, who presents it to the company that is at his table, that is the court of assistants, who all of them try each of them at several times one upon their heads till they come to the persons appointed to be master and wardens who then keep them upon their heads and at every time a cap is fixed the trumpet and music sounds.

[1] Charles Mordaunt, 3rd Earl of Peterborough (1658-1735). The *D.N.B.* states he was educated at Eton.

After this we went about 6 o'clock to dancing and ladies were got into the room of cedar where those men that would dance came and took the ladies out. There were but few that danced French dances at first while my Lord Peterborough was present. Afterwards I ventured to dance a minuet with Mrs. Lee and so we continued dancing minuets or country dances till 12 o'clock when I waited upon her home. And returned to my own lodgings in the same coach. And went presently to bed.

Friday, June 17. Rose at 7. Wrote down yesterday's diary. Employed till breakfast in mending my shelf and trying on my new clothes. Found myself ill. Was afraid it would prove a fever. Was preparing to go to Hackney that I might be ill there. Began at past 10 to read Dacier's discourse upon the corruption of the taste. Upon reading upon the controversy between her and Mr. de la Motte the rule that Mr. Whatley gave me some time ago upon my contradicting him in some of his notions came into my head. It was this, that one should never read or hear any new thing with a kind of a resolution to contradict it before we hear it. But yet this is too common a practice especially in conversation. A man no sooner advances a new thing but somebody or other in the company without observing whether it be just or no is seeking about for an answer against it, as they do in the schools.

Went to Button's.[1] Read the *Grumbler*.[2] He is very tolerable now. He in one of his papers gives a long account of the controversy between Dacier and M. de la Motte. Went to the auction. Bought two or three French books. Came back and went to Tom's[3] and the Gill house but did not stay at either of them.

Saturday, June 18. Rose at 8. Wrote yesterday's diary. Went to Hackney in the hackney coach with two women, one of them a very pretty agreeable face, seemed to be a servant maid. We had very little conversation. Went up to my grandmother's. She gave us some cherries and told us some old stories.

[1] Near Will's in Russell Street, Covent Garden.
[2] By Squire Gizzard (George Duckett and Sir Thomas Burnet). One of many imitations of *The Tatler*, it was first published in February 1715.
[3] A favourite coffee-house of Ryder's set in Devereux Court. It was frequented by men of letters and was later a favourite resort of Garrick's.

Went to the bowling green.¹ Saw Mr. Reed and old Mr. Thomson there.² Thomson seems to be a good sensible man and talks well. He told us that when he was a youth he had given £5 to learn the art of wrestling, and that there was as much art and variety of things to be learnt in that as in fencing. Our discourse continued upon the subject of fighting, boxing, wrestling, and fencing.

Came into my closet. Read some of the *Tatlers*. His characters of human life are extremely fine and judicious, his method of raillery very delicate and exact. Intend to read them often to improve my style and accustom myself to his way of thinking and telling a story and manner of observing upon the world and mankind.

Sunday, June 19. Concerned to see my mother so peevish and fretful, continually saying some ill-natured thing or other to my father or the maid. I will endeavour if possible not to have a fretful uneasy wife. How easy it is to observe the faults my mother is guilty of in contradicting another, though I am too apt to be guilty of the same kind of peevishness myself. I have too much of her temper, but I am resolved to endeavour to quell at its first rise every secret resentment and uneasiness that comes upon me. I know how to do it already pretty well with respect to others by preventing its being discovered to others but this is not enough.

Went with my father to Newington Green though I was very unwilling upon the account of the heat. It was extremely hot and troublesome. Heard Mr. Tonge³ preach a funeral sermon. I don't much admire his preaching or praying. Father went to prayers. After that walked into the garden together and went to supper. It is the misfortune of our meals that the sweetness of them is very much taken away by my mother's peevish uneasy temper. She grows angry and cross upon every little occasion and sometimes makes the most innocent things a handle for saying

---

[1] In the extensive gardens of the Mermaid tavern which stood nearby, opposite the parish church of St. John-at-Hackney.
[2] Possibly Samuel Reade who died at Hackney in 1733, worth £80,000. A Joseph Thomson was overseer at Hackney in 1708.
[3] William Tonge (1662–1727), the eminent Presbyterian minister. He was appointed minister at Salter's Hall in 1702.

harsh things. I have been myself to-day but in an ill humour and discontented, mighty apt to take offence. The heat of the weather makes me very dull and heavy and lazy, unfit and disinclined to do anything. I have now an ill cold upon me that makes me cough much. Went to bed about 11.

Monday, June 20. Rose at 6. Very uneasy, extremely dull and feverish. Grew by degrees better. Read 5 Matthew; it contains the complete account of the christian morality. Went to London on foot at 7 o'clock. Came home with the report from the committee of secrecy.[1] It is full of the discovery of the treachery, perfidy, and treasons of the ministry in their management of the peace. My cough that had almost left me in the day is now come upon me again. Went to bed at one o'clock.

Tuesday, June 21. Coughed very violently the great part of the night. Sweated very much. Rose at between 10 and 11. Not well. Found myself hot and feverish. Determined to go to Hackney lest I should fall sick. Eat a pretty good dinner of boiled beef. Found myself much better after it. Went to John's coffee-house. Met Mr. Smith, Witnoom and Mr. Isles. A certain awe and damp came upon my spirits when I saw Mr. Isles there. Afraid to speak before him. He is a man very agreeable for common ordinary conversation, tells a story well and with a great deal of humour, but a man of no great depth or solid judgement. Went out and met young De Foe.[2] Had a little talk about the behaviour of the late ministry. He did not say much to justify them.

Went to Gill House. Talked there in strange company about the peace, the cessation of arms. I thought I spoke very well. Read three or four *Guardians*. Went to bed between 10 and 11.

Wednesday, June 22. Mr. Whatley came to see me. He affects to be singular in his opinions. Thinks himself very much taken notice of and observed by the world. He told me Mr.

[1] cf. note, p. 32.
[2] From later entries it appears probable that this is Benjamin Defoe who was entered at the Inner Temple on 29 August 1712 as the son and heir apparent of Daniel Defoe of Stoke Newington. Among Ryder's shorthand letters is one in the pastoral style to young Mr. De Foe.

Witnoom told him that I was in love. We talked some time upon that subject, whereupon he told me that he had conquered that passion in a very violent degree. But by his discourse about it he does not seem much to understand that passion. Went to the auction. Bought two or three Italian and French books.

Went to Mr. Witnoom's club by the Change with him and Mr. Jackson and one Mr. Potter whom I never saw before. Mr. Witnoom still maintained his opinion that the Whigs were going on too violently in impeaching the Duke of Ormonde of high treason because it would but the more incense the people against the King. We were all but Mr. Serjeant of the opposite mind, that nothing but putting the law in strict execution would quell the rage and fury of the tories.

Returned home about 11 o'clock. I find I am mighty apt to be surprised and put into a confusion and disorder upon any sudden accident that requires an immediate action. One instance of my want of presence of mind I had when I was at Skinner's Hall. Sir Samuel Clark [1] came to me and desired me to dance, that it would be an entertainment to my Lord Peterborough who had honoured the company with his presence. I was so confounded with the suddenness and strangeness of what he said that though I had no awe of him before upon me I called him 'My Lord' several times while I was excusing myself from dancing. Went to bed between 11 and 12.

Thursday, June 23. Went to dancing master whom I paid for my quarter and told him I should learn no longer. He is as I believe a tory but knows nothing at all of the public affairs or the present state of affairs and indeed does not trouble himself much about them. When I talked to him of the crimes of the last ministry he seemed to be satisfied that they were rogues but is not one that concerns himself much about these matters.

Went on horseback to Uncle Marshall's at Kentish Town.[2] All the family at home but cousin. Soon got upon public affairs and a little warm dispute followed. They seemed to be a very

---

[1] Created baronet in 1698 : married Mary Thompson of Newington Green.

[2] John Marshall (Mrs. Ryder's brother) was vicar at Kentish Town. His son Nathaniel was curate there in 1715. Nathaniel later became one of the King's chaplains and was Canon of Windsor in 1722. He published several works, including *The Genuine Works of St. Cyprian, with his Life, written by his Deacon Pontius; all done into English.* . . . London, 1717.

hardened family and incapable of conviction or appearing to be convicted. They gave the most strange, absurd, improbable turns to any matters of fact that look ill towards the tories that it is shocking to hear them. They have got also a method of denying whatever is not strict legal demonstration. Thus whatever is said in the report to the disadvantage of the late ministry is only the misrepresentation of their enemies and a setting the things in the worst light. When I talked of the insults and riots that had been committed by the high church mobs throughout England they said they were well assured that many of the mobs were hired by some Whig lords. The breaking the windows in London upon public nights was laid entirely upon the glaziers whose interest it was it should be so and the tories suffered equally by it with the whigs. The dissenters themselves as they say pulled down Dr. Burgess's meeting-house [1] in the time of Sacheverell. By such methods as these they elude the force of whatever is said against them. And they generally have some little story or other to tell upon every such occasion which they will set against a multitude of others that show the contrary. No matter whether the story be true or no as long as you cannot disprove it. When they talked with me in this manner, upon reflection I find I did not talk against with that modesty and submission to them as became me and spoke in too harsh terms that looked a little too ungenteel. As when I said, by the same method that they took they might prove whatever they would or make black white and white black, and the like.

Met my father at the stable-keeper's. Told my father what they said at Uncle Marshall's. He misrepresented my stories at Hackney to my mother and Aunt Lomax. He is not cautious enough in what he says. I find I must be cautious how I tell him anything that is dangerous to be told again. He has not memory good enough to retain all the circumstances of a story and tell it again as it ought to be told.

Friday, June 24. Rose at 8. Did nothing all the morning being obliged to keep my sister company, except playing upon the viol and began to read Cicero's *De Officiis*.

[1] On 1 March 1710 the Sacheverell mob gutted the meeting-house of Dr. Daniel Burgess in New Court, Carey Street, and made a bonfire of the pulpit and fittings.

In the afternoon between 3 and 4 was preparing to go to London when cousin Marshall and his son and daughter came in. It was a good while before we came to talk of politics but at last the report came into play. I find by his discourse the two great things that will be said by the Tories with respect to the report will be to vindicate the ministry from treason which not being so very plainly or evidently proved upon them by the report will give them an opportunity of turning off the discourse concerning their villainy and knavery by talking that there is nothing contained in it sufficient to charge them with high treason. And then as to the affair of high crimes and misdemeanours, since they cannot deny but that there has been some underhand dealings in it they will confess that the ministry did not keep to the strict rules of moral honesty but that this is but in common to them with all politicians in the management of treaties and the like, so that now all their treachery, knavery, and cheating the nation and destroying its trade is to be accounted nothing else but politics.

Saturday, June 25. Rose at 7. Went soon after to Westminster with Mr. Warren, Mr. Samson and Mr. Price[1] in a boat. Found Mr. Witnoom, Street, Atkins,[2] Goodall at the tavern where I was very agreeably entertained. Mr. Jackson and Smith came in afterwards. We never want mirth when Mr. Jackson and Street are there, for Mr. Street is the fittest person in the world to show Jackson in his proper light and in all his colours to the best advantage. For Jackson's character lies in seeing the ridiculous side of things and making merry with whatever occurs. Mr. Street is a man of perfect good humour, takes nothing ill, but is apt to make use of odd sort of expressions, commits some errors or says something out of the way. This presently sets Jackson to work and everything that Street says furnishes matter for him to burlesque upon and laugh at. This was one thing Street said—that pleased me very well because it was extremely natural. Upon occasion of an attempt being made to lift up a sword with two fingers by the point of it, 'I believe', says he, 'I

[1] This may be Robert Price, son and heir of John Price of Edmonton, Middlesex, who was entered at the Middle Temple on 25 October 1705, and called on 19 May 1710.
[2] Possibly John Tracy Atkins of the Middle Temple: appointed Cursitor Baron of Exchequer 1755.

can do more in this way than any one in the company. See', says he, 'how apt we are to be vain. I remember when I was a boy I used to think it a very great thing if I could but spit further than another or piss &c.'

Sunday, June 26. Rose between 7 and 8. Did nothing in the morning but dress myself and breakfasted till I went to church. Heard Mr. Barker.[1] He has a pretty good style. Don't much wonder if he is liked. He has now and then some good turns and thoughts. His great defect is want of judgement to give a clear account of his subject and also to choose what to say and what to leave out, for he generally says a great deal upon every head, turns a thought every way and gives the same thought over and over in different expressions.

After church went to Cousin Billio with a design to go to London. Aunt Billio and Cousin Joseph were there also. There happened a sort of a quarrel between these two, wherein he did not show that regard to his mother that he ought to have done. He would not in the least yield to his mother, but stood firm to what he had said though by what I could judge he was in the wrong. I am vexed with myself to find I had an ill-natured pleasure rise in me upon seeing this dispute.

Returned home. Did little till prayers. Then read Mr. Henry's [2] sermon upon ending the day with God from these words : 'I will lay me down in peace and sleep, for thou, Lord, makest me to dwell in safety.' I think I never was more pleased with a sermon than this. And it gives me a greater idea of Mr. Henry than ever I had.

Monday, June 27. Went to father's shop and desired some money of him. Found him in a very good humour, told him

[1] John Barker (1682 ?–1762) succeeded Matthew Henry as minister of the Mare Street meeting about Christmas 1714. The choice between the rival candidates, as Newcome, the Hackney rector, ironically noted, ' Caused some division among our dividers'. Barker did not become settled until ' after guard and forcible possession had been kept for him of the meeting for some weeks'. Barker became an eminent preacher, being appointed to the Salter's Hall lectureship in 1741.

[2] Matthew Henry, the eminent dissenter, was minister at Mare Street from May 1712 until his death in June 1714. His *Expositions on the Bible*, 1710, were famous throughout the eighteenth century.

what a good husband he was and how little company I kept for fear of spending money. He is very willing to let me have money. If I could but use an agreeable forwardness with him of telling my circumstances to him I should never have him grumble when he gives me money. Nothing is more agreeable to me and more affecting to me than when I see my father give me money with willingness and readiness. He gave me £12.

Tuesday, June 28. Went from dinner to the Six Clerks' office to inquire about Aunt Allen's [1] suit with Lord Huntington. Her attorney's clerk did not seem very well pleased that another should come to inquire about him when his master used to send a constant account of it to Mrs. Allen. Saw there another clerk to an attorney who I used to dance with at Fernley's. It is useful to take the opportunity of conversing with these sort of men. A seat in their office is worth a considerable sum of money if the possessor of it has a good business and helps it over to the buyer of it. A seat is worth £1,000. The bare seat without any business annexed to it is worth £600.

Went to Moorfields and bought two or three little books and so went on to Hackney and read in the way a little pamphlet that I had bought about a shorter method of teaching of Greek and Latin than usual, which he proposes by making them the first languages that they learn, which by conversing with them only in that language will be as easy to them as English.

Wednesday, June 29. Rose at 6. Took some purging water upon the account of a tumour that was rising upon my hand and which has been very sore all day. At different intervals read Farquhar's Miscellany of letters and poetry.[2] He writes his letters in a good humorous style enough, shows him to be a man of a sprightly ready fancy and wit. Is apt now and then to come in with a witticism a little too refined and not natural. However, they are very diverting. Have been mighty uneasy almost all

---

[1] Ryder's grandmother had remarried old Mr. Stevenson of Gresley, Derbyshire: Aunt Allen and Aunt Stevenson were related through this marriage.

[2] George Farquhar's *Love and Business*: in a collection of occasionary verse and epistolary prose, 1702. The letters are mainly concerned with his love affairs.

day, in a restless posture, not knowing what to do to keep myself in employment, and because I lived so in the morning in doing nothing in the afternoon. When sister and aunt and father were gone to London I did not know how to fix to any one thing, but read sometimes the *Tatlers*, turning to one thing and to another, sometimes sitting in a drowsy careless posture wishing for company though when I had it wanted to be alone. I am too apt to fall into this state of mind when I have no one fixed business to mind as I have when I have my law books about me.

Thursday, June 30. Rose at 7. Took purging waters again. The tumour in my hand grows more and more. Walked about the parlour and prayed to God that he would turn the current of my affections towards himself. This as soon as I had done praying put me upon reflecting upon myself. And I could not but conclude that the most prevailing passion or view that I had was a love of esteem. There is indeed another thing that goes hand in hand with that and this is the prospect and hope of an agreeable woman for my wife. To these two I think all my other ends may be reduced.

Friday, July 1. Rose between 7 and 8. Began to read Mr. Locke's treatise against Filmer's patriarchal scheme, by which he accounts for monarchy and absolute power.
Came to London to my brother's. Saw Mrs. Lee there. Stayed there till 10 at night with her. We were good company to one another. I think I kept up a humorous strain pretty well all the while. We had a great deal of female conversation, the great part of it turned upon scandal and stories of other people, especially their own sex. But not a word of anything to the commendation of any one of the sex. However, what they said seemed to come very naturally from them rather from the humour of conversation than with any ill malicious design, though perhaps all the while there may be a secret vanity which they don't perceive themselves that makes them delight in such stories and nourishes them. Came home and went to bed at 11.

Saturday, July 2. Sent for my periwig maker for my wig, paid him £5 for it. Went to Cousin Watkins's new shop, saw him there working hard in making up medicines. He had got a surgeon's bill for a lady, as I guess for a venereal distemper by the use of mercury, which he was making up into an ointment with nothing else but pomatum beat together. It takes up I perceive a great deal of time to make the mercury mix with the pomatum. He is still the man he was, full of a good opinion of himself. Is upon the affair of matrimony, after disappointment in two attempts before. Talks that he has good hopes, I am afraid upon as little foundation as his former were.

Came to Hackney in the stage coach with a merchant and a gentlewoman that lives in Yarmouth. Her husband deals in corn beyond sea. She is come up to town to show her daughter the city, who was in the coach with her. I perceive she is an only daughter and the parents are rich. The mother seemed to be a woman of good sense but talks very broad English.

Came home and read some dialogues in French between the diable boiteux and the diable borgne.[1] The design of this I perceive is a satire upon the manner and characters of the persons that make a figure at Paris. There are abundance of different characters exposed in it and I think pretty well. At least I think it is very useful to be acquainted with books that treat of characters. Nothing fits a man more for conversation. This is indeed what the *Tatlers* and *Spectators* are most of all remarkable for, that you see the different manners of men set in a very clear and distinguishing light.

Sunday, July 3. Dreamt a very disturbing dream about the Pretender that he was come and had got possession of the throne, that I was myself a very active man against him. This dream made such an impression on me that it is not yet wore off.[2] Went to meeting in the afternoon, heard cousin Billio. He has a very ill manner and method in prayers. I am always in pain for him when I hear him pray. Is mighty apt to say things over again and sometimes make blunders in prayer. I wonder he does not take more pains with himself on that score. I don't admire his manner of preaching neither. He has something puerile both in his delivery and his discourse. He affects in his manner of delivery a familiar easy way without any tone but he does it but

---

[1] *Le Diable Boiteux*, 1707, by A. R. Le Sage.

[2] This dream is very interesting in view of Ryder's part in prosecuting the rebels of the '45.

awkwardly. Besides, he has one constant tone at the ending of a period.

Father uneasy to hear the bellows blow because it consumes the coals too fast. I find I am too apt to be sensible of little things myself and to fret upon little occasions. As to-day my head has run almost all day long about the new wig I have bought. Been uneasy because I think it not so good as the last and yet gave as much money for it.

Monday, July 4. Rose at 7. Read to the end of Mr. Locke's treatise of government against Filmer.[1] Played upon the viol. Ended the morning with reading over again the letters of Farquhar. He has for the generality a true epistolary manner and style. He writes with that freedom and ease that you would think he was talking with you. And at the same time shows he is a man full of wit and good humour of a very pleasant gay turn of thought, full of humour and good sense too. In short by all his letters it appears very plain that he was a man of a very agreeable conversation that made pleasure his chief business and had a very quick and polite relish of it. Could say the most shocking things with a good grace and make them easily passed over by the humorous turn he gave them.

Went in the afternoon to Aunt Billio. Cousin Billio was brought to bed of a boy last night. Cousin Joseph Billio came in and then came Cousin Robert. We had a great deal of conversation together, the chief part of it turned upon matrimony and the pleasures and delights of that state.

One thing was told me (which I never heard before) for a certain truth, that the Elector of Hanover a little before the Queen's death had by the means of Bothmer[2] kept a correspondence with the dissenters more especially in Ireland and also in many counties in England, that there was a combination made among them for the maintenance of the Hanoverian succession. And particularly that a dissenting minister in the country was employed in it. That Bothmer had made a calculation of the

---

[1] The first of Locke's *Two Treatises of Government*, 1690, attacks Sir Robert Filmer's views as expressed in *Patriarcha, or the Natural Power of Kings Asserted*, 1680.

[2] Hans Caspar von Bothmer, the Hanoverian envoy at the court of Queen Anne in 1710 and 1714.

number and riches of the dissenters and sent them to Hanover and that great quantities of arms were bought up by the dissenters to be ready upon occasion. Mr. Billio of Maldon [1] came from the country while I was at Shore house.[2] He says it is spread all about the country that there is nothing in the report from the committee of secrecy and that they will make nothing of the impeachments, that the tories there are not ashamed to deny the most plain and evident matters of fact that make anything against them.

Wednesday, July 6. As I was going to dinner met Mr. Crisp. Went with him to the coffee-house where he met with several of his friends. After some time they were going to dinner. He would have had me going with them but I excused it. Was a little confounded upon this occasion. I find I still want that presence of mind that is necessary to go through such an affair as this is.

From thence to Mr. Whatley's who had a friend with him. He still continues to brag of his philosophy. Very unconstant as to his settling in the world. Went to supper and to home, where my father had left word to meet him at the tavern. Went there and met Uncle Ryder,[3] father, Mr. Gregg and Mr. Mears. Mr. Gregg proposed to me to take part of chambers with a friend of his an attorney in business. I believe it may be of use to me in the study of the law by seeing the practical part. Mr. Gregg I believe has a kindness for me and will do me service when I come to be in the way of business.

Thursday, July 7. Went out to dinner. The rain kept me where I dined till 3 o'clock. As I was coming home met with Uncle Ryder. Went with him to the coffee-house. Stayed half an hour with him. Very little conversation with him. He is not communicative at all nor free of talking even about what he does understand. Gave my letter in at the coffee-house, a little concerned for fear it should be lost. I am indeed too apt to be concerned about the letters I write. The reason is because I take

---

[1] Joseph Billio, aunt B.'s brother-in-law. He was Nonconformist minister at Maldon in Essex.

[2] In Well Street. Strype mentions a tradition that Jane Shore lived there.

[3] Dudley Ryder, the Nuneaton haberdasher, elder brother of the diarist's father.

so much pains about them, indeed I take too much pains in them. It is not so much because I want something to say but the manner of saying it costs me most time and I am apt to turn it every way before I let it go.[1]

Friday, July 8. Rose about 8. Read Coke all the morning, comprehended what I read very well. Pretty well pleased with the law. Hope I shall be able to make something of it.

Went to playhouse. The whores are always in the passage to it and continually lay hold of me. I have not yet got over the surprise it puts me into when they speak to me, though I think of it beforehand. Did not stay there. Went to Button's, did not stay there neither. Came to Tom's. Supped upon milk and toast there.

Saturday, July 9. Cousin Hardin[g] came to my lodgings. Gave him an old suit of clothes and a pair of shoes. Bought the pair of shoes this morning. Very idle, did not know how to employ my time. Stayed in the shop for near an hour with sister looking about us upon the people that passed by. Were going with brother and sister by water to Chelsea but were afraid of the rain and so came home again at length. Went with brother and sister to Stocks Market.[2] I treated them at one of the fruit shops: it cost me 2s. Came to Hackney. Found father there and in a very good humour, very kind and full of tender expressions of his love to me. He is indeed a very fond father to me and loves me very well. My mother also expressed herself very kindly to me. But what makes me uneasy is to see that my father and mother sometimes cannot agree in any[thing] else but in loving me. Mother is mighty apt to be touchy and see everything my father says in the worst light and take in the worst sense; continually little differences arise in which my mother seems to be chiefly and generally in fault by a cross peevish way of talking. Not but that these differences pass over in a moment and they are the next moment as loving together as ever. From this example I will endeavour to check every hot rising of my passions if ever I

[1] His letters at this time are remarkable for their emptiness, however, as well as their painstaking lightheartedness. Like many people of his day (even John Wesley), he succumbed to the fashion for pastoral fancies.

[2] A fruit market on the site of the present Mansion House.

should be married, especially keep the furthest possible from little offences, anything that may give uneasiness to my wife, pass by every little failing.

Sunday, July 10. Rose about 8. Did nothing material this morning. Spent it till church time in dressing and breakfasting. This is too commonly the way in which I spend Sunday morning; I think a very ill one. I am resolved to rise earlier for the future and make better use of that time.

Went to London with Cousin Joseph Billio in the afternoon. Cousin Billio and I are pretty well fitted for conversation together because we can fall into subjects that are speculative and philosophical and are not confined to matters of fact to entertain one another.

Went to Pinner's Hall and heard Mr. Hunt.[1] He has got a very genteel congregation, a great many substantial hearers, men of fashion. He has the most of the familiar way of any that I know. Tells his hearers in a plain familiar style and manner his sentiments. He is not a man of a very fluent way of speaking and therefore will never be a very popular man, but is very much liked by men of judgement that prefer good sense before a good style.

Went from thence to brother's. Drank tea there. From thence went to Salter's Hall where Bradbury[2] was haranguing to very crowded congregation. The people were standing without the doors to hear him. Could not get in. Heard him talk a little. He has a good commanding voice.

Went to Hackney.

Read some of Mr. Henry's exposition upon the New Testament. His expositions are much better than his sermons used to be.

Monday, July 11. Rose at 6. Drank two bottles of purging waters. A very fine morning. Walked in the long walk. Thought of the being of God.

Spent my morning in nothing else material. Went to dinner to Cousin Billio's. Saw her abed, after her lying in, and her son. Went from thence to Shore House, where there were at Mr.

---

[1] Jeremiah Hunt, D.D. (1678–1744), became pastor of the independent congregation at Pinner's Hall, Old Broad Street, in 1705.

[2] Thomas Bradbury (1677–1759), congregational minister at Salter's Hall. His vehement political sermons made him the stormy petrel of Nonconformity.

Sikes's my sister and Mrs. Ironmonger,[1] Mrs. Betty Sikes,[2] and Cousin Joseph Billio. I happened to be but in an ill humour for ladies' conversation, though never very fit for it. I sat all the while silent and dumb while my Cousin Billio entertained himself and us with them. His chief talent by which he maintains the conversation with the ladies is by being perfectly free and familiar with them, and saying whatever comes next into his thoughts without considering either the goodness of the thought itself or the tendency it has to disoblige or affront. By this means he comes to be as I guess very much liked by them in conversation, though he oftentimes says those things that would be taken very ill from another hand, but by being himself unconcerned at it and saying it in a familiar way it passes off well enough. The ladies value such a man for his present conversation that they may pass the time away agreeably, but I am apt to think they regulate their esteem of a man rather by the value that is put upon a man by his own sex though he does not make so gay and pleasant a figure in their company. I find I am mighty apt to look silly and a little uneasy when I am in the company of ladies. And this bashfulness comes upon me upon very little occasions, even the change of a room of a house shall alter my state of mind in this respect. I can behave myself and talk with a great deal of forwardness sometimes in the very same company in one place that in another place puts me into a deal of confusion and disorder how to behave and talk.

Went to brother's. Father had got a man there with him who was so over complaisant, made such low bows to me and did it in such a manner that I really took him to be half drunk. He looked like a man that is very good-natured when he is fuddled but it seems it is only his manner and was perfectly sober. Went home, stayed a little while, and went to the tailor's about making a pair of breeches out of old silk stockings. Read the comedy of Regnier called *Attendez moi sous l'Orme*.[3] It is a good humoursome plot and the dialogue pleasant enough. The honest

---

[1] Mary and Elizabeth, the daughters of the late Joshua Ironmonger, brewer, of Hackney.

[2] Elizabeth, daughter of the late John Sikes of Well Street, Hackney.

[3] *Attendez-moi sous l'orme* by Jean-François Regnard (1647-1709), produced in 1694. ' Qui ne plaît pas à Regnard,' said Voltaire, 'n'est pas digne d'admirer Molière.'

innocent simplicity of a country girl is very well represented and the vanity and conceit of an affected gay officer well exposed. Went to bed at past 12.

Tuesday, July 12. Went to brother's to dinner. There was Cousin Robert Billio. At 3 o'clock went to John's where met with Mr. Jackson and Witnoom and two or three more friends. At length by chance a gentleman whom none of us knew, hearing us discourse about religion, joined to our company and at last was free in talking. He is a man well versed in the manufactures of England. He would have our holidays, all but necessary ones, entirely cut off and thinks that every holiday costs England £100,000 by the loss of so much labour. Another observation he made upon our manufactures is that they are capable of very great improvement and he thinks it would tend very much to it if in our manufactures that consist in several parts, as most of them do, and require different sorts of work to bring them to an end, every distinct part be put into different hands and one person be not used upon different parts of it.

We talked also about our foreign trade. He said it was a very difficult matter to know the balance of trade in general and which nation has the advantage on its side, because as to our exportation the entries in the Custom House are seldom according to what is really exported, for the merchants, out of policy that their markets may not be overstocked, generally enter much more at the Custom House than they really export (since they pay no duties) that those that come in there, seeing so much goods sent to such a market, may think it too much stocked to make it worth while to send more to the same.

He also talked of the improvement that might be made of the land itself by the manner of manuring. He says he knows a method by which ten times less seed than usual may be sown upon the ground and a better crop produced.

Wednesday, July 13. I went to John's where met with Mr. Milley, a gentleman that comes among our society there, and with him and Mr. Heathcote [1] went to our club. Mr. Witnoom and

---

[1] Probably John Heathcote of Hackney, son of Sir Gilbert Heathcote, ex-Lord Mayor of London. He married Elizabeth Holworthy in 1720 and was M.P. for Bodmin in 1733.

Street and Jackson, and one Mr. Blackbourn came afterwards who is high steward for the county of Essex and others. We had good company and not at a loss for discourse. The affair of the impeachments was talked over.

Mr. Blackbourn is a talkative man, says a great deal, tells stories and is merry and good-humoured and what may be called a good companion. I said but little myself as I generally do in this public company, but when I ventured to tell one story I found I committed an error in the playing of my hands and setting it out with my hands. I perceived it by Mr. Jackson's behaviour. Came home with Mr. Milley who lives in Wine Office Court. I invited him to come to see me, as he did me to see him and look upon the library which he has. He seems to be a man of a good solid judgement that can distinguish well between things that differ. He does not talk much but has good sense. I believe his acquaintance may be useful. Came home between 11 and 12. Went to bed at 12.

Thursday, July 14. Went to Hackney to dinner, where Cousin Wilkinson and Marshalls from the country.[1] They stayed with us till 7 o'clock and then coaches were sent for and sister and Aunt Lomax were to go in one. One coach was hired before the others that were sent for came, and when they came my father had some little dispute with them about their fare and they two went away. Upon this my sister, who it seems was mightily set upon going to-night, took it so very ill that the coaches were gone without her that she cried and was extremely uneasy. I never saw so much of my sister's temper before in my life. She said my father did it on purpose to cross her mind, to keep her here against her will, and it was her temper she said never to be forced to do a thing and therefore she was resolved to walk it to London rather than not go. There was not the least ground to think my father had any such design in the letting the coaches go nor did he at all desire or press her to stay, but still nothing could persuade her but my father did it on purpose to force her against her will to stay at Hackney to-night. I never saw a child that cried for a plaything more obstinate and stubborn and regardless of reason than she was upon this occasion. I find she behaves herself much after the same manner towards her husband, continually teasing

[1] At Wisbech.

him and construing everything that is done to be done on purpose to cross her. I pity him. Such a temper is the worst thing can be in a wife. I am resolved therefore to be very careful as to the temper of the woman I choose to be my wife. It is of the greatest consequence to my peace and happiness to have her of a meek, humble and modest one. There is no wife in London can be better treated than she is both by her husband and his relations; they are fond of her, take all opportunities of discovering their particular pleasure and satisfaction in her; and her husband denies her nothing. She does, says and acts as she pleases and has what she pleases, and yet in this fit of passion she was complaining how she had always been a fool in being imposed upon continually, that everybody made her do what they pleased, and the like. At this rate it is impossible to make such a temper easy or pleased. However, she got a coach at last and went to London. Father was very much vexed to see my sister so childish and so unreasonably angry. But said but little.

Friday, July 15. Rose at 7. Intended to have drank purging waters, but they were not good. Played upon the bass viol. Aunt Billio came to dine with us. She has one good quality, that either when she entertains others or is entertained at others' houses she has always a pleasant look, appears well pleased and cheerful without any fretfulness or uneasiness.

After dinner we were talking about my grandmother's unaccountable behaviour towards my mother and all of us. Her reservedness and strangeness. She has nothing of that freedom with us that is becoming. If I do but come into her chamber she looks upon me with that shyness and distance, puts herself into that formal posture of reservedness one would think a stranger had surprised her in her room. This temper, with her continual finding fault, her appearing never obliged, her rash censuring upon every little occasion and impregnable obstinacy in whatever she once asserts, though never so false or absurd, makes it a very uneasy thing to live in the house with her. My Aunt Billio attributes this temper of hers to that mean, poor-spirited, confined, narrow way of living she was engaged in all the time of her marriage with Stevenson, and I am apt to think there is a great deal in that. She was such a slave, had so little money at command then that she does not now know how to use the plentiful fortune that is entirely at her own disposal. She has also a little pride mixed with her other qualities, and I perceive values her mightily upon being the husband[1] of Mr. Marshall. Hence it is she is so much offended at my dress and looks upon it with a great deal of indignation that the son of a tradesman should go as fine as her husband the counsellor.

Went to London. Received a letter from Aunt Stevenson. Went to the Park alone. Met Mr. Jobson there. After a little walking there we met two ladies his cousins, who walked with us. He begged leave of the ladies just to go into the Drawing-Room and promised to return to them in half an hour. So I had the sole care of the ladies. We walked several turns. One of them entertained herself mightily with the dress and manner of those of her sex that walked there, continually criticizing upon the shape, face or dress of those that passed by. She is a lady of a good deal of wit and spirit and a mighty air of familiarity. We were grown as familiar in a few minutes, though I never saw her before, as if we had been long acquainted and she made her remarks to me upon everybody that passed. It was not very difficult to keep up the conversation with a lady of this humour, and so we went on very merrily. The other was something of the same temper but not so brisk and lively. They both seem to be very good-humoured. We began at last to be thinking what had become of Mr. Jobson, but he did not come. We waited till they were tired of walking and I assisted them both with my arms. We stayed there till all the company, excepting very few, were gone, till about 10 o'clock, and then we took a coach and came home together. I set them down at Basinghall Street near the end of the street. They were obliging, thanked me for my trouble and asked me to come in, but because it was so late hoped I would come another time and drink a dish of tea with them. So came home. Went to bed at past 12.

Saturday, July 16. At breakfast the maid came to me and told me her mistress thought she did not please because I had not given her when I paid her as I used to do the other maids. I was a little surprised at this, but I told her there was nothing of that in it and I

[1] A slip for 'wife'. The first husband of Mrs. Frances Stevenson, the diarist's maternal grandmother, was William Marshall of Lincoln's Inn, second son of John Marshall of Wisbech.

should make it up to her. Would not give her anything lest it should look as if was compelled to give.

Went to Mr. Smith; found him at home. Stayed with him almost an hour. Little discourse that was material. He walked with me as far as London Fields. Talked in the way of Mr. Berkeley's notion concerning abstract ideas,[1] that there are really no such things. I don't yet rightly conceive his notion and how he distinguishes general ideas, which he allows, from abstract ones. I intend to borrow his book of Mr. Smith some time or other. Supped: played upon the flute. Went to bed about 11.

Sunday, July 17. Rose at 8. Went into my closet, read the 5 and 6 of Matthew. Mightily pleased with the perfect morality of our Saviour. I cannot too often read that sermon upon the mount. Went in the afternoon to Bethnal Green, heard Mr. Chapman. He has a very ill manner of speaking and a most dismal face to look at when he is praying or preaching. His sense is good and he made a good sermon. Talked with my father in the way there about brother and sister. He is very much displeased with her for her ill-treatment of him last Thursday about the coaches.

Talked with him about Uncle Lomax's will by which he gave his estate to brother and his heirs if he married his daughter, so that according to that my sister has not so much as her life in it if he dies before her.[2] So that what kind of a jointure she has I don't know nor as I can perceive my father neither.

Went to Aunt Billio's, where met Uncle Dudley and Cousin Joseph Billio besides my aunt. Talked about Cousin Katherine and her being so deeply in love. Uncle is very angry with her though she has strove so much against it in obedience to him. She is now very ill and in danger of dying by reason of it and he has now given my father leave to write her word that he leaves it to her to do what she will. But he is so averse to the marriage

---

[1] George Berkeley, later Bishop of Cloyne, published in 1710 his *Principles of Human Knowledge*, in which he maintained, contrary to existing theories of externality, that visual consciousness is merely a system of arbitrary signs which symbolize for us certain actual or possible tactual experience.

[2] The diarist's elder brother Richard had married Anne Lomax, daughter of Thomas Lomax of Westbrook Hay, Hertford.

that he said he had rather follow her to her grave. If she marries he says he must marry too.

Monday, July 18. Rose at 7. The front of the house was begun to be pulled down.

Walked to London. Saw a pinner and things that belonged to a woman lying in my room that made me suspect that somebody had lain in my room when I was absent. Asked the maid whether there was. She told me no. Said no more of it.

Mr. Mills [1] came and stayed with me till 5. Our conversation turned pretty much upon books, he being a man that studies polite learning as well as law and keeps up his respect for the classics. Mr. Mills does not seem to be a man well skilled in criticism by his great admiration of Rapin.[2]

When he was gone took a boat and went to Lambeth Wells.[3] Paid threepence for entrance. There was a good deal of company but all made up of rakes and whores. There seemed to be scarce a sober man or woman there. Met young Mr. Dry[4] there, who it seems is a constant customer to the place. I never was among more wretched sad company in my life. The men were almost all either such as have nothing else to do but to spend their time this way, as officers of the Guards or young fellows that are glad of every opportunity to gratify their pleasure, as attorneys' clerks and the like, and as for the women they seemed to be all whores and of the meanest sort, not one dressed like a gentlewoman. Yet the men that were there that seemed to be men of fashion were as familiar with them as if they were their equals. A strange nauseous familiarity appeared there. Mr. Dry I perceive has got the true taste of the rake, can talk with all the whores and jest with them without any concern. There were country dances but such very mean company that I was ashamed to be seen in the room, much more to have danced with them. And yet this is constant rendezvous of abundance of your polite officers.

[1] A chancery lawyer; possibly Edward Milles of the Inner Temple.
[2] René Rapin (1621-1687), the Jesuit theologian and classical critic.
[3] These Wells were in Three Coney Walk (later Lambeth Walk). In 1755 the dancing licence was refused on grounds of nuisance and the Great Room was thereafter used for Methodist meetings.
[4] This is probably Benjamin Dry of Ticehurst, Sussex, who was entered at Lincoln's Inn on 6 May 1712. Ryder knew two Mr. Dry's. The elder was Filacer (an officer of the Courts at Westminster) of Cambridge.

Tuesday, July 19. Went about 3 o'clock to Change. Met none of my friends there except Mr. Street upon Change. Walked with him a little while there and talked about our shortsightedness. Proposed a method of finding out whether the glasses we use make us more shortsighted. Went thence to Mr. Cynelum my viol master. From thence went to playhouse. Saw part of the first Act in the sidebox and came away.

Came to Tom's Coffee-house where met Mr. Whatley. Talking of the law he told me he thought I had but little proficiency in it and knew little of it, that my head was not turned that way. It struck me very sensibly that he told me that. He takes me, I believe, to be one that am too gay and minds a genteel manner of behaviour and the company of the ladies too much to make any great matter of the law. Though this character is true enough that I affect a polite way, yet he mistakes me very much when he thinks that I don't apply myself to the law.

Read the beginning of Steele's *Englishman*.[1] It seems to be a very good antidote against that lukewarmness and coolness that appears in some people in the cause of their country that are afraid of being thought hot and party men and therefore can appear indifferent and careless in matters of the greatest concern. Went to bed at past 11.

Wednesday, July 20. Went to brother's again and with him to Cousin Wilkinson where were my mother, Aunt Lomax, sister. Saw them make their earthenware: it is indeed an art very ingenious. Went to our club behind the Change. Mr. Porter who is an apothecary was talking of the cold bath and the service it had done him by making him of a more strong, firm constitution than before. He says it is extremely good against the headache, strengthens and enlivens the body, is good against the vapours and impotency and that the pain is little. I have almost determined to go in them myself. Went to bed at between 12 and 1.

Thursday, July 21. Went to Westminster by water. The Parliament was just broke up as I came. Went into Waghorn's Coffee-house. Heard some Parliament men talking there. It is

[1] A journal which Steele published immediately after the failure of *The Guardian* in October 1713. It failed but was revived in 1715.

very encouraging to hear them speak of the designed invasion of the Pretender as of a thing that can do no harm. Went to Banqueting House into the chapel where the ceiling is painted by Rubens. He did it in Flanders and when he came over here as ambassador he brought it as a present to our court. Went home and read part of the *Légataire*, a comedy of Regnard. I remember I saw it acted at Paris. The chief character of this man's plays seems to be to me this, that they have something of humour and diverting but without any judgement in the maintaining the characters. Went to supper between 8 and 9 and then came home. Played upon the flute and went to bed.

The King came yesterday to the House of Lords and passed several bills, among the rest that against riots,[1] and made a speech to them wherein he told them he had certain intelligence that the Pretender was preparing to invade us and desired the assistance of the Commons. The Commons immediately resolved to assist him with their lives and fortunes and desired to know what provision of arms, men and shipping will be necessary. To-day the Commons read twice a bill for suspending the Habeas Corpus Act that the King may have power to take up suspected persons and retain them in custody.

Friday, July 22. Visited Mr. Burroughs.[2] Had a good deal of discourse with him about making sermons and the manner of preaching. Afterwards he played upon the viol and I played also. He has much more the command of the viol than I have, plays with more freedom and ease.

From thence to John's where met with Mr. Jackson, Witnoom and Mr. Porter. After some talk in the coffee-house us four went to the tavern where our first discourse was about Mr. Berkeley's notions concerning matter. Mr. Witnoom is under apprehension of the ill consequences of the present temper of the people and is mightily confirmed in his opinion that the King had acted a prudent and politic [part] to have kept in with the Tories by admitting them into a share of government. We all on the contrary maintained that that would have ruined us and they

[1] 'An Act for preventing tumults' by which an assembly of twelve or more persons was obliged to disperse upon proclamation by a single magistrate.
[2] Jeremiah Burroughs, assistant to Dr. Samuel Wright at the Presbyterian meeting in Carter Lane, Doctors' Commons, until 1717 [Wilson].

would only have made use of their power and authority to have introduced the Pretender the more easily.

Ormonde [1] is gone away, but whither is not known. Mr. Porter thinks he is gone into Somersetshire and Sir William Wyndham with him to head a party there and raise a commotion in favour of the Pretender. The Act for suspending the Habeas Corpus Act till the 24 January was read a third time to-day and ordered to be engrossed. They say there are several warrants sealed ready to be sent into the country upon the passing that Act to take up suspected persons. The Tories upon this report of the Pretender's design to invade us say that it is only a Court trick to gain a standing army.

Saturday, July 23. Found myself very indisposed to go on with the law and I could not apply myself to it and therefore read part of Boileau's tenth *Satire*. It is designed to expose the faults and vices and follies of women. I am extremely pleased with it.

Went to Uncle Marshall's, Kentish Town, more especially to see grandmother and carry her a bill of money. She received me with more kindness and freedom and good humour than ever she used to do at Hackney. I stayed with her an hour in her room alone with her. She was good company and seemed pleased with mine. How true it is that absence creates love. It surprised me to see so sudden an alteration in her temper and her manner of behaving towards me. Saw Uncle and Aunt Marshall, neither of my cousins, himself nor his wife. Talked with my aunt about politics. She is extremely violent and cannot tell how to keep her temper. Was forced to say what I did in very mild terms and alleviate it with some sort of concessions or else by the way of raillery. She still keeps to the old way of saying the most absurd and shocking things that silence one at once unless one may venture flatly to contradict her. They are indeed all violent Tories and by their actions, though deny it in words, show that they are really for the Pretender.

From thence went to Hyde Park where a camp was formed consisting yet only of two regiments.[2] The regularity and order

[1] James Butler, Duke of Ormonde, was so alarmed by the Parliamentary proceedings on 20 July that he fled and joined the rebels in France.

[2] The camp ultimately consisted of the Life Guards and Horse Grenadiers, and three battalions of footguards, together with their artillery, under the com-

of the tents and the disposition of them make a very pretty show. I never saw a formal camp before and I was very well pleased with this. A great number of people were continually going and coming to see it. A great deal of gentry in coaches appeared in the camp. As was going home met father with others in a coach going to Hyde Park, so went back with them. When we came to the place in which the camp was they would not let the coach go in, and my father therefore took his horse which I rode upon. I was very much to blame in my behaviour towards my father upon this occasion, by not seeming so willing to let him have it because I had my boots on and looking discontented upon it. It was foolish as well as undutiful in me, as I knew I must let him have the horse.

Sunday, July 24. Rose at between 8 and 9. Read the end of our Saviour's sermon upon the mount. Went to breakfast, dressed myself and went to the Temple expecting to hear Dr. Sherlock,[1] but heard one Mr. Smith. He made a very good sermon from these words of Our Saviour which he quoted out of one of the prophets and applied to himself. 'I came to heal the broken hearted.'

Went to Somerset House Walks. Very good company. There was Judge Tracey's daughter[2] there: she is a celebrated beauty but a mighty coquette. Puts on a great many airs that are affected and can never become any woman.

Monday, July 25. Rose at 7. Spent an hour in mending my stockings and breeches. Went to John's Coffee House. Saw Mr. Jackson and Mr. Witnoom. Had some talk about the public affairs. Mr. Witnoom thinks we must call in foreign forces to assist us if the Pretender makes an invasion, that we cannot depend upon our English troops, the common people are so

mand of General Cadogan. The camp was situated along the wall by Knightsbridge and Kensington Acre. Similar reviews became a feature of London entertainment. In the 1722 display 7,000 men were in camp and a fair rivalling Bartholomew Fair was held on the edge of it.

[1] Dr. Thomas Sherlock (1678-1761), later Bishop of London, was Master of the Temple.

[2] Robert Tracey, judge in the court of common pleas, had two daughters, Anne and Dorothy. The latter married John, the son of Judge Pratt.

poisoned with Jacobitism and so much set against the present government.

Went to the British Coffee-house. Stayed there an hour, looked over many of the *Examiners* [1] : I never met with an author so very bold with truth and so impudently asserting falsehoods in my life, and yet his paper must do a great deal of harm at least in hardening the Tories against any possibility of conviction.

At 8 went by water to the Park. I had a mind to have talked to the waterman about the King and recommended him. Began just to speak of him but had not assurance enough to go on because the waterman seemed not to be of my mind. I am sensible this is a great defect in me that I have not freedom enough to speak what I would.

Walked in the Park and then to the Drawing Room. A great crowd of people. I met with Mr. Haddon. He seems a little to affect the air of a courtier, but I don't think it much becomes him. Saw Mr. Paulet [2] there. Had the courage to bow to him and speak to him, though I did it very awkwardly. Saw the King very plain a great while. I could not help looking smiling and pleased when I looked at him. His countenance is so full of good humour that it naturally communicates that temper to them that behold. I am sure I showed a peculiar cheerfulness and joy in my countenance when I looked at him. Heard the princess talk a great while together. She talks English very prettily, is mighty familiar and good-humoured. Talking of the English parties, she said she was always very angry with the English when she was reading their history to see how violent and raging they were against one another.

Tuesday, July 26. Rose at 8. Began upon the law. My mind ran pretty much upon the letter I intended to write to Aunt Stevenson, that I could not finish one case. Inclinable to sleep. Read Boileau's tenth *Satire* against the women. He has an admirable talent in describing the characters of persons and hitting all the circumstances that are proper to let a clear and strong light in upon it. There a great many of the characters of wives which

---

[1] *The Examiner*, 1710–12, was started by Swift, Bolingbroke, Prior and others.

[2] Charles Paulet (1685–1754), Lord of the Bedchamber to the Prince of Wales: he married Lavinia Fenton, the creator of Gay's Polly.

the *Spectators* and *Tatlers* have so well described. It is done with a great deal of humour, spirit and just observation and knowledge of mankind. I think I cannot too often read his works: they are the most proper to form one into a polite natural way of thinking and writing of any modern writings whatsoever. I should be glad if I could get the habit of thinking in his way and manner.

Came to brother's again about 8 o'clock. Stayed and supped there. Mrs. Henry and young Mr. Henry supped there too. She is a woman of good sense and good breeding but, I don't know how, carries a face of too much dejection upon her. Seems to bear her misfortunes upon the loss of her husband [1] with too low a spirit and is too submissive in her behaviour by bearing too great a distance and using too much ceremony in her salutations. Came home to bed at past 11.

Wednesday, July 27. Rose at 6. Studied the law all the morning till between 11 and 12, when I went to brother's to go to see the great ship at Woolwich. About 1 o'clock we set out from the Tower, mother, Aunt Lomax, brother and sister, and brother William and Cousin Dudley and myself, in a pair of oars, but it was fitted up in the manner of a pleasure boat with awnings, which are iron posts to make a covering, much more convenient than the ordinary tilt, with curtains and a cloth to cover it. We got to Woolwich a quarter to 3. Took a little refreshment there and went to the ship which is called *The Royal George*. It has been building two years and half and was designed to be called *The Royal Anne*. It was indeed called so before, for though in effect it is entirely new yet it is called refitting or rebuilding an old ship when any old plank or board of the former ship is made use of. And this they do, as our waterman said, to avoid the necessity of having a new Act of Parliament without which they cannot build a new ship. This ship is the largest that was ever built in England and it is indeed of a prodigious bulk. When one walks within it and views the massy size of all its planks and the vast capacity of it and the prodigious strength of it, one is apt to think one would be mighty secure in the midst of the sea in it.

[1] The Rev. Matthew Henry had died thirteen months before. Young Philip Henry (1700–60), who later took his mother's name, Warburton, was M.P. for Chester from 1742.

At the forecastle is a large figure of King George a horseback trampling upon the Turks, carved very well in wood. The King's Yard there is very full of large timber. There is, besides another man-of-war, a third-rate making in the same dock and abundance of men at work.

We returned to Greenwich, where we got some wine and cakes &c. into the boat which we drank by the way. One of the watermen was a man of good sense and pleasant humour and talked well. He seemed to be a Tory but seemed to be very much for the King. He diverted us very well with his stories and humorous talking to the company in other boats. Came home to brother's. Supped there off fish that we bought upon the water. Came home, went to bed between 11 and 12.

Thursday, July 28. Rose at 8. Studied the law till about 12 o'clock. Then began to write [a] letter to Aunt Stevenson but could not go on with it. Went to dinner at 2. From thence went to the camp. It is crowded like a fair but with better company, for the best of the nobility and gentry in England go to see, and there is constant line of coaches going and coming all the afternoon long. I saw abundance of pretty women there. There are 12 piece of artillery there which stand before the camp about the middle of it. There are about 3,000 soldiers, horse and all. The horse are at each end of the camp. There is but one line. Met Mr. Mills there. Went with him into General Robinson's tent. He was not at his tent. The generals have everything mighty neat and convenient.

Friday, July 29. Went to Cousin Billio. I went to see his wife at her lying-in and pay her a formal visit. Found her and her mother Jeffries alone. Sat there a great while: no material discourse. Went away and gave the nurse and maid half-crown each. Cousin has a very fine boy. He has the most cleanly and agreeable look I ever saw a child of that age have. There is nothing that is disgusting or unpleasant in the sight of him as I think there generally is in a child of that age.

Went home in the coach with Mr. Burgess where there were two strangers. I thought I made some kind of figure in the eyes of the strangers by talking as I did with him about Leyden and

A PAGE OF DUDLEY RYDER'S DIARY, ACTUAL SIZE

the affairs of the college there. I talked pretty well without any of that bashfulness that extremely takes off from the gracefulness of speaking. Indeed I observe I then speak best when I am in strange company that don't at all know me, that I don't think have any mean opinion or of whom I have not already conceived any awe and distance, but when I am excited to speak out of a little vanity and desire of appearing of consequence.

Saturday, July 30. Mr. Burgess came to breakfast with me. Talked about the affairs of Leyden. There are many English there. It is likely that the University will be very much frequented by the English, ours having so little advantage for learning and besides extremely corrupt in principle, that the Whigs will be afraid to send their sons there.

To Change where I dined upon mutton chops. Went to our friends at the Crown[1] where there were Mr. Witnoom, Jackson, Crisp and several others. One Mr. Wadsworth who was there and is a Whig too was complaining of the dissenters and railing at them very vehemently. It seems he says he has been cheated by one of them and his prejudice seems to proceed from thence. There are indeed too many of the churchmen who are not Tories nor for downright persecuting them and yet think they have no right to have anything to do with the government. Even the Whigs themselves that are churchmen have not all got over their prejudices. They look upon themselves as persons in a higher rank, of a superior degree and therefore grudge them all the privileges that they have. Think that they are born to something above them. However, Mr. Wadsworth was sufficiently answered both by myself and Mr. Crisp who spoke very warmly upon this occasion.

Went to Mr. Smith who walked to Hackney with me. We had no discourse material till we almost came there, and then we talked about Mr. Berkeley's notion of abstract ideas. I proposed the objection Mr. Porter made to me against it, viz. that unless we had a[n] abstract idea of entity or being we could not have any idea of God or ourselves, because it is by adding our abstract ideas of entity to his attributes that we make up our notion of God. He could not satisfy me in his answer at all, and so it dropped. Came home, supped, went to bed at 11.

[1] The Crown Tavern in Ironmonger Lane: kept by Tatnall.

Sunday, July 31. Rose at past 8. Did nothing but eat breakfast and dress myself. Went to church. Heard a stranger that Mr. Newcome [1] had put up. I was extremely angry with him that in his prayer when he came to pray for King George he said, ' I desire you to pray for the King &c.' One would think if those priests that used that method of praying for the King had any regard to the reputation of sincerity they would not make use of such an equivocative, prevaricating way with God Almighty. He made an indifferent sermon.

Monday, August 1. Rose at little past 6. This is the day of the King's accession to the throne when the Queen died. The bells have rung very thoroughly and continued a long time.

Played upon the viol and read part of a play of Regnard, *Le Distrait,* wherein the chief character, and from which the play takes its name, is that of an absent man, one who forgets what he is doing of, who is with him, continually mistakes one thing or person for another, and is held distracted. This is what my brother Richard [2] is very apt to be guilty of. When you have been talking a good while to him he will stare at you all of a sudden and look as if he did not understand you before or did not hear you.

Dined at Hackney with father and sister only upon eggs and bacon and cold beef. Came to London on foot about five o'clock. I called at brother's where wrote a letter to Uncle Marshall about grandmother's affairs. Perplexed about what title to give him: at last called him ' Honoured Sir ' and subscribed myself his obedient nephew and humble servant.

Came home, dressed myself in best clothes and laced ruffles and went to St. James's at 9 o'clock. There were several bonfires in the street as I went along in the coach and vast crowds of people in the streets to look at them but no tumults or disturbances at all. The Rioters Act began to take place to-day. When came to Court got an easy passage through the bar by following another that went before me. The Drawing Room was extremely full of company dressed very fine, scarce any without gold or silver trimmings to their clothes.

[1] Peter Newcome, M.A. (d. 1738), was appointed rector of St. John-at-Hackney on 5 February 1703.
[2] His elder brother, the draper.

Tuesday, August 2. Went to dinner to brother's where were Mr. Merreal [1] and his brother and his wife and Mrs. Lee. Sat with her by ourselves at a separate table where we laughed together all dinner time. She told me upon the occasion of marrying without parents' consent that she thought it very imprudent in any young woman to entertain any man under the character of a courtier before he had made his applications to her parents and gained their consent to court her. That for her part she would never do so, much less marry any man without her father's consent.

After dinner sat with the men. I can make no judgement of Mr. Merreal by the little conversation I had with him. He said he was going to see the machine invented to perform an equal at sea [2] and offered me to go along with him. I did so. The machine is such an one as is not affected by the tossings and motions of the ship. It is by the means of a pendulum which will keep its regular exact motions notwithstanding all the shakings of the ship and also is such an one as is not affected by the difference of air and climate, the heat or coldness, moistness or dryness of it. It could not be judged by what we saw of it whether the thing would do or no, but he says Mr. Flamsteed [3] has seen it and is extremely pleased with it.

Supped at brother's. In the way home had a great mind to have met with a whore and talked with her, to give me an assurance and confidence, for it has put me sometimes into a strange kind of condition when a whore has taken hold of me and asked me to go with her. Came home at past 10.

Wednesday, August 3. Went to dinner between 1 and 2. Carried Sallust with me and read the beginning of the *Catiline Conspiracy*.

We had nobody come to Sue's to-day, except myself. Mr. Witnoom and others of the club would fain have had me gone with them to it, but I had engaged myself before to Cousin Watkins in the dancing bout at his house.

[1] Alexander Merreal was overseer at Hackney in 1715.
[2] One of the many attempts at the discovery of longitude encouraged by Parliament. In Nichols's *Anecdotes* a similar device is credited to John Harrison, to whom Parliament voted £5,000.
[3] John Flamsteed (1646–1719), the first Astronomer-Royal.

At about 9 o'clock we met. There were two ladies well dressed and looked like gentlefolks. The others (who were called in through the disappointment of other company of which Cousin's mistress was to have been one) were but ordinary dressed and seemed to be ordinary sort of folks. When the two ladies came in I was there and behaved myself but awkwardly towards them, till at length I became familiar with them in dancing, and I was pretty tolerable company. One of these two ladies was Mr. Barker's [1] sister. I suspected it when I saw her closely, but not being certain, when I asked whether her name was not so she said no, and she was born in Holland, I did not think it was her. But it seems she did that only to conceal herself from me a while. At last I found her out. She is very pretty but very short, and no breast. She is a good sensible brisk girl. We had a great deal of dancing and I performed pretty well by the help of a partner who understood country dances very well, though seemed but an ordinary person. I danced a minuet with Mrs. Barker before I knew her. Did it but indifferently, but nobody else would dance a minuet but myself, and I believe it passed off pretty well, though I did not keep the time at all.

At length we finished our dancing and I and Mr. Hayward, for he and his partner Mr. Hulst [2] were there, sat by Mrs. Barker for a great while talking together with her. He is a man of a good, lively, brisk fancy and says abundance of things to the ladies with a great deal of freedom. I behaved myself pretty well upon this occasion, though I did not say near so much as he did. At length got a coach and I handed Mrs. Barker into the coach and Mr. Hayward the other ladies. He went in after her and when I was going in another gentleman who danced with us desired he might come in for he had a particular reason. And Mrs. Barker approved of that, thanked me for my civility, and I desisted and went home a-foot. There were five couples of us in all. We had wine and cakes besides some wine that Mr. Hayward and Hulst sent for from their own house. We passed the time very merrily and I came home about 3 o'clock. Went to bed presently after the writing of this.

Thursday, August 4. After dinner went to Tom's Coffee House, where met with Mr. Whatley, who came home with me

[1] Cf. note, p. 43.   [2] They were in business as druggists.

and stayed [with] me till 6 o'clock. Our discourse turned chiefly upon philosophy. He told me of the faults which I am sensible I am a little guilty of, and that is when he proposes anything that is new I rather look upon it with a design to find objections against it than with a desire to see it in its full light, when perhaps all the objections would vanish of their own accord. He told me (what he says he never told any one before) that he once sent his philosophical discourses, which I have seen, to Mr. Addison with a long letter to him directed to him at Button's Coffee House but with a feigned name, and desired that he would read them and send again. At length after a fortnight's time Mr. Addison sends them again with a letter to him wherein he thanks him for the confidence he had in him and says it is full of such an air of honesty that he should be very glad of the author's acquaintance. He afterwards sent him his printed speech and returned him his own letter with another writ on the back side of it to thank him for the honour he had done him. He returned him his only that he might be satisfied that the speech came from the same hand that the philosophical discourse did. This gave Mr. Whatley a wonderful deal of pleasure and I don't wonder that he is so well satisfied with himself after this. However, he has not got an acquaintance with Mr. Addison yet, though he says he can whenever he will, and that Mr. Addison knows him. He was telling me also of his acquaintance with Lord Chief Justice King,[1] how free and familiar he is with him. I have often wondered at this, that such a man as he should admit him into such an intimate familiarity with him.

Friday, August 5. Met in the street Mr. Smith. Went with him to hear him play with Mr. Demodore.[2] He plays much better than he did. While they were playing I sat by reading a *Spectator* which gives an account of the story that is told of Seneca who was an old man and his young wife Paulina who was so extremely fond of him that when Nero sent to command him to die she resolved to die with him and did so. But what was observable in it was an epistle writ by Seneca when he was absent

[1] Sir Peter King (1669-1734), chief justice of common pleas, later Lord Chancellor. His Nonconformist sympathies led to the advancement of a number of young lawyers, among them Dudley Ryder and his friend Bowes.
[2] The music master.

from his wife to a friend of his concerning his wife and the concern he was under for her. This is a letter commended by the *Spectator* and by Montaigne from whom he tells the story. But with submission to such men I think that letter is exactly agreeable to the general of all Seneca's letters, that they have the air of epistles writ by a philosophic mind at ease and reflecting upon the affairs of the world without being himself concerned in them. They don't seem to come from the heart and the passions that are design[ed] to be expressed in them have not that face of nature upon them that they should have, particularly this epistle.

Saturday, August 6. To Mr. Smith, where played two or three sonatas upon the flute, and then came in a cousin of his with his wife, but lately married. It seems he has been a wild spark and passed through a great many adventures in his life. He is now married to a very pretty agreeable woman but seems very indifferent towards her. I did not behave myself with that ease and freedom of carriage that is becoming. I don't know how, I am mighty apt to be uneasy in the company of strange ladies and don't know how to compose my mouth, my eyes or settle my hands or legs. Every part of me seems to be in a restless posture and I am at a loss how to dispose of myself.

Came home, found Mr. Denn [1] here with father. Mr. Denn is a man of a very pleasant conversation. He is mighty cheerful, has abundance of agreeable stories to tell *à propos* and tells them very well without the common digressions and with the little circumstances that often make them agreeable.

Played upon my viol. Read some of *Catiline Conspiracy*. It seems to be something like the case of England about the time of the rebellion when the Irish were sent for by King James.[2] Everybody were in a terrible consternation for fear of a massacre, the whole nation was in an uproar and news was spread about that the Irish were within a mile or two of them and were destroying everything they met with. Went to bed at almost 11.

Sunday, August 7. Rose at almost 8. Did nothing till break-

---
[1] Mr. Allard Denn (d. 1732), an eminent brewer and Nonconformist of Clapton.
[2] In August 1688: this caused great public outcry—and the publication of *Lillibullero*.

fast. After that read some of Sharrock, *De Officiis*, his third chapter wherein he discourses upon the first of his seven laws of nature which he says are written upon every one's heart which are the first principles of all other laws of nature. The first of these which he here treats of is that no hurt ought to be done to an innocent man.

Went to church, heard Barker. Went afternoon with Cousin Billio to hear Mr. Oldsworth. I don't much admire either his delivery or sermon. Afterwards went to hear Bradbury at Salter's Hall. Heard him make his prayer. He has strange way of running over a multitude of texts of scripture without connexion or design. He has a most admirable voice and a fluent rolling tongue that everything he says comes off from his mouth very clean and easy.

Monday, August 8. After dinner about 4 o'clock went to Aunt Bickley's [1] where was for two hours. Cousin Abigail was there besides my two aunts and a young lady that lives there, one Mrs. Loyd. I held out the conversation pretty well and committed no blunders. Talking of the camp I invited the two young ladies to go with me there and offered them my services. It was pretty difficult for me to manage this affair so exactly as it should be because Aunt Bickley seemed inclined to go. However, I invited her also but she refused it and so we agreed to go to-morrow.

Came to London. Called upon Mr. Smith to lend him some music I promised. He came with me to John's where met Mr. Witnoom, Jackson, Potter, Crisp, &c. We went at last to the tavern. We were exceeding merry, full of good humour. Mr. Porter sung us some songs. He seems to have good judgement but his voice is very indifferent, it is not clear nor loud.

Came from the tavern at near 12. As I came along Fleet Street had a mind to attack a whore and did so: went along with her a good way, talked with her tolerably well, and at last left

---

[1] The will of John Bickley, citizen and upholder, of Mare Street, Hackney, which was proved on 25 February 1701-2, refers to 'my wife Abigail' and 'my granddaughter Abigail Ryder (the daughter of my wife's daughter Abigail)'. These appear to be Aunt Bickley and Cousin Abigail. The same will refers to 'my niece Anne Harding and her children'—presumably the diarist's aunt and cousins.

her. Did so with another girl. It makes me a little uneasy for fear somebody that knows me should have seen me, though with the first I went down another street and with the second did but just speak to her and went a little way with her. Asked her whither she was going, and came home. Went to bed a quarter to one.

Tuesday, August 9. Rose at past 7. Studied the law. Left one long case without reading it. Was a little uneasy this morning about what I did last night with respect to the whores. However, I have this advantage from it, that I intend never to attempt such a thing again by way of frolic as I did then.

After dinner went with Mrs. Loyd and cousin to Kensington and the camp. At Kensington, not having been there before, we did not know the way into the garden nor how to find the man that shows the house. A little perplexed about that. However, at last we got to see the rooms. There is nothing very fine there. We saw several rooms, a few pictures, though no great matter, a gallery where Charles 1st is painted on horseback at the farther end and at the other he is painted with his Queen. There is some pretty good paintings on each side but they don't stand in a good light. The man that showed us the room could not tell us the masters that painted them. All the painting that is there is almost nothing for a palace. We saw but one bed in all the house and that was Queen Anne's in which she was sick and died. Gave the man 2s. It rained a little: however, we went back again to the door next the street into the garden, where we walked about a great while. I was but very dull company all the while and the ladies seemed to be sensible of it. It rained more or less all the while we were in the garden, that we had not time to see all of it, being obliged to sit down under a tree for a great while. The gardens are well kept and very pleasant. There is a greenhouse, done in the inside with pillars of wood and arches that looked very grand. At last we came out at half an hour after six.

Came back again into the camp. It rained all the while. However, they were for getting out to see an officer's tent, so we got out and it began to rain faster. However, Mrs. Loyd went on apace directly out of the way, till coming by an officer's tent he invited us to take shelter in his tent, which we accepted and sat down by his bedside. The officer was not a man of a sprightly wit and genius, did not say anything that was agreeable to the ladies and in too heavy and dull a manner. He asked us to drink a dram of rack, which we refused, and I thanked him for his civility. It rained very hard and we were in terrible concern for our coach, but he sent his man to call it, and at last it came. I offered his man a shilling which he refused.

Now we were got into the coach in the way home and the ladies told me their design was to go [to] one Captain Hutchinson's [1] tent if I had not stopped there. They began to banter the officer that had received us into his tent and criticized mightily upon the dull heavy air he had. This furnished matter for discourse for a long time, and I talked pretty agreeably in the way of raillery upon that subject, and their avowed design to visit the other captain. I began now to be better company to them than ever and from henceforth we were very merry in laughing and bantering all the way home. My cousin and the other lady are mighty critics upon the behaviour and air of the men and their conversation, and nothing but a free, very familiar pleasant kind of conversation is agreeable to them. Cousin has the least of that herself for she can scarce speak a word in conversation, much less become familiar and brisk. The other talks more, and more wittily, is more genteel, and has less of that bashfulness which cousin has. They vexed me two or three times by their sudden bursting out into laughter and then whispering together. It looked as if they laughed at me. I am sure it was very unmannerly and ungenteel. I luckily got into a vein of mirth and raillery which I kept up, I think the best I ever did in my life.

Wednesday, August 10. Went at past 6 to Cousin Watkins, who invited me to dance at a friend's house of his, but I refused because I should stay out too long and I am afraid the company is not very good.

Went to Change and from thence to our club where were Mr. Witnoom, Jackson, Smith, Porter, Hide, Street and one I never saw before, Mr. Marten, who is a person of a pretty agreeable conversation being very free and familiar. He tells stories, but does not utter himself with ease, but stops and hems. However,

---

[1] Edward Hutchinson, Captain of Horse in the second troop of Horse Grenadier Guards.

because he does not seem much concerned about it himself, it passes off pretty well.

It is very credibly and assuredly talked that the King of France is either dead or very ill that he is not expected to recover. Talked upon that, what would be the consequence of his death with respect to France. Orleans seems to bid fair for the crown having the Jansenists and Protestants on his side. There is an alliance made between our King, the Emperor and the Dutch which has caused stocks to rise considerably.

Thursday, August 11. At past 12 o'clock Mr. Powell [1] came to me. I inquired about the University of Oxford. He says they are so busy about the church and politics that nothing else goes forward with them: learning or politeness has nothing to do there, and they are so infected with their Tory principles that a Whig is a kind of a monster to them and carries in its ideas with them the worst of characters, everything that is ill. They will scarce keep company with a man of that character. Swearing and drinking and railing is what completes an Oxford scholar at this time of day. They are bred up there in the most narrow, confined, ungenerous principles in the world and go out from thence possessed with the notion that religion and good sense is to be found nowhere but among their own party or sect: are prejudiced with malice or ill-will to all the world besides, that the Whig gentry and nobility are afraid of sending their sons there and begin to take them from thence and send them to foreign parts, particularly to Holland, for education.

Mr. Powell I perceive affects the character of a genteel, careless, negligent gentleman and behaves himself especially to his familiars with a strange kind of jaunty unconcerned, merry, laughing air. This is a character that is much affected now and men think it genteel. Sat together till about four in the afternoon at the tavern: cost me half-crown. I find I am very apt to use the word 'I profess' very much at almost every sentence. I believe it must be taken notice of by other people. And this I take to be the account of common swearing. By custom an oath becomes necessary to a sentence, it looks to him bald and bare

---

[1] Samuel Powell, son of Thomas Powell of Clapham, was admitted to Queen's College, Oxford, in 1714, aged 16. He was called to the bar, at the Inner Temple, in 1720.

without it. I am resolved to endeavour to avoid the frequent use of any word. One may in time come to be known by a single word as a man is by a peculiar suit of clothes that he has wore a long time.

Went to my closet at 9 o'clock. Read to the end of *Catiline Conspiracy* by Sallust. It seems to suit our present case mighty well here in England. It is a sad case when criminals are so powerful that the State is afraid to take notice of them and punish them. Went to bed at half an hour after 11.

Saturday, August 13. Rose between 7 and 8. Began to write to Aunt Stevenson. It takes up a great deal of time to polish the style and turn of a phrase: the writing down the sense and thought take up but very little. If I could bring myself to let my thoughts pass as they first come out of my head it would save me a great deal of time and pains and perhaps be better.

Going to Hackney met Mr. Swain who was going there, so went together. Talked of the Hackney ladies, of Mr. Gould,[1] his strange impudent manner of behaviour, of Mr. Newcome and Smith, Mr. Moreland's usher [2] who has lately a living given him of above £100 per annum.

Sunday, August 14. Rose between 7 and 8. Read some of Mr. Locke's *Reasonableness of Christianity* where he gives an account of the advantages and benefits the revelation by Christ brought into the world. He writes with the greatest clearness I ever met with [in] any man. His style is pretty diffused and prolix, it seems to have come from him without any study or choice of words, but to have writ his thoughts down as they presented themselves to him in different lights, much such a language as a man that is full of a subject and has a command of words would use in conversation.

I have made now a serious resolution and promise to God that I will make it my duty to obey his laws in opposition to anything

---

[1] This was probably John Gould, son of the very rich J. Gould, who was a director of the India Company. He later became Inspector of the Outport Collectors' Accounts. His brother Nathaniel became deputy-governor of the Bank of England.

[2] Mr. Benjamin Moreland was head-master of Newcome's School at Hackney. From 1721 until his death in 1733 he was head-master at St. Paul's School.

that may come in the way of it. Methinks I feel an unusual kind of gladness and pleasure within me now, and yet I cannot but fear that the next temptation that comes in my way will overcome this resolution.

Monday, August 15. Fitted myself to ride out in the afternoon with Cousin Joseph Billio. Met him in the street. He went home with me. Prepared things for journey to Court at night. He was telling me what a happy couple Mr. Borrett [1] and his wife are together. He says he thinks they are the best example in the world of that happy state of matrimony that is described in the *Spectators, Tatlers* and *Guardians,* and their life together seems almost to be regulated from those rules that are there laid down and is the best comment upon them and illustration of them.

Went to dinner at brother's. After dinner stayed till brother had dressed himself accordingly and we went together to Hampstead. When we came there I was concerned to find out Mrs. Lee who is now there. At length brother and I went to her lodgings and she was just then come to the Walks, so came back and found [her]. Took two or three turns upon the walks with her and another lady that accompanied her. She seemed very glad to see me and I believe has a kindness for me. Then we went home with her to her lodgings and she treated us with wine and received us very kindly. Our conversation was free and familiar and good humoured, very merry. It was now 7 o'clock and we left her. I kissed her very sweetly two or three times and she seemed to receive it very willingly.

Came home in haste: were in London about 8. Made haste to fit ourselves for Court. Came home and cousin after having borrowed a coat and wig came to me. We were shaved and dressed out as well as we could, and after a good deal of hurry and confusion, for cousin is strangely perplexed upon such occasions, forgetting something or other, about 9 o'clock we set out in the coach for Court. Before we went in we went into St. James's Coffee House, because he was thirsty. There were several noblemen there which we took no notice of, though the place

---

[1] The Borretts were related to the Powells: the will of Samuel Powell, grocer, of Hackney, proved 20 February 1714, mentions a nephew John Borrett and his sons Samuel and Thomas, 'under age'.

appeared more like a handsome parlour than a coffee-house. Just drank a glass of cool liquor and went into Drawing Room. There was a very small appearance, only prince and princess there, and not the King. Met with the Brerewoods there, who seemed to have been scarce ever there before, though they endeavoured to look as if they were mightily acquainted and accustomed at Court. Saw my lady Townshend,[1] as fine a face I think as ever I saw.

About 11 o'clock came away. It rained and there was no coach. At length a coachman comes and asks if any gentlemen were going to the Temple, because there was a single gentleman had taken his coach and gave him leave to fill it, so we got this coach, and thanked the gentleman for his humanity in being concerned for others such a night. I don't know who he was, but he was a man that seemed to be of an extreme good humour, very pleasant, told us some stories. We came to Hand Court. We got out and cousin was hungry, so went to an eating-house that was shut up and got some cold lamb, which he ate heartily of. Sent for my cloak and coat and came home about 12. He then smoked a pipe and we sat together till past 2, talking upon different subjects but never without conversation. Went to bed about 2.

Tuesday, August 16. To dinner by the Temple because it rained. After dinner went home, took my cloak, changed my wig at barber's and went to brother's. From thence to Clark's shop,[2] where we looked over the books and I bought a miscellaneous translation of most of Horace. Came back to brother's. Stayed there to see the Venetian ambassador's[3] entry. His coach of state was the finest I ever saw in my life : it was very large and almost all covered with gold, scarlet velvet in the middle of the top.

Received a letter from Mr. Leeds.[4] Upon reading it thought

[1] Dorothy, second wife of Viscount Townshend : she was Sir Robert Walpole's sister.
[2] John Clarke, publisher at the Bible and Crown in the Poultry.
[3] Signor Tron : appointed November 1714.
[4] Edward Leeds (d. 1758) of Croxton, Cambs. Admitted to Inner Temple 1710 : King's serjeant 1748. Cole says he was ' a heavy, dull, plodding man, but a great lover of antiquity '. His daughter Henrietta married John Howard, the philanthropist.

it wrote very well with some spirit, which gave me some uneasiness. I am concerned to find I am so inclined to envy that I cannot bear my friend should write so well as myself. I have read the letter a second time and an illnatured envious pleasure rises in my mind to find that it was not so good as I thought it had been.

Read when came home some of Horace's *Odes* and the translations of them. They are full of admirable sense and excellent turn of humour. One cannot read any book I believe more fit to learn one the polite way of writing and conversing than Horace, and one cannot be too familiar with him.

Wednesday, August 17. Went to Button's where met with Mr. Gore.[1] He is a very handsome man and his chief study and care seems to be to be a fine gentleman and make himself as polite as possible to fit himself for the conversation of the ladies and appear a man of distinction among them. He talks pretty smoothly and well but has little of learning or deep judgement. There was one Mr. Brian, a gentleman that is known by writing several little pieces of poetry in manuscript and politic ballads and songs. Mr. Gore was telling me he had got some verses of his upon the Richmond beauties and we were willing to get into his company, so sat at the same table with him, and at last conversation was entered with him and we soon became pretty familiar, and mentioning the former verses he took them out of his pocket and showed them us. There is very little that is good in them: the ladies mentioned have nothing particular in their characters or distinguishing. He presented us too with a new ballad upon the Duke of Ormonde's running away of his making. He seems to be a man of a good memory, talks pretty freely.

Came to John's and so to the club with Witnoom, Smith, Jackson, Milley. At length Mr. Porter, Heathcote and Street came also. Our conversation was part of it upon Mr. Berkeley's notions. Mr. Street was a little fuddled and took a thing very ill which Mr. Smith said. I never saw him so angry before. Indeed Mr. Smith is too apt to be suspicious and fancy everything that is said is done with a design to reflect upon him. This was the occasion of what he said that affronted Mr. Street. However,

[1] Possibly Thomas Gore, fourth son of Sir William Gore, entered at Inner Temple 18 June 1711.

he was pacified at last and he got into his usual way and now indeed his company became nauseous and very disagreeable. He has a most strange way of keeping all the discourse to himself though he says nothing that is useful, diverting or improving. Mr. Heathcote is a man of a good deal of humour and talks with a great deal of freedom and familiarity and sometimes with judgement, but he gives himself too great a latitude in talking obscene things which he utters without any manner of reluctancy. Mr. Milley is a man that says but little but seems to be a person of good judgement and reflection. I am mightily pleased with Mr. Porter, who is certainly a man of very good sense and thought, very modest and says what he says with a great deal of submission and modesty, though very just and strong. Mr. Witnoom has good sense too, but is a little too full of his own opinion and warms himself in disputing for it that his stuttering grows upon him very much in the dispute or answer. Mr. Jackson's talent lies entirely in raillery and being merry with what is said and turning it into ridicule. Came home at past 12 o'clock.

Thursday, August 18. Rose at 7. Mr. Whatley knocked at my chamber door and called me up when I was in bed. He came to go with me to the cold bath. Went with him not fully designed to go in. When came there there was company. He undressed and went in first. It appeared a very small matter as he performed it. When he came out and was dressed I resolved to go in too and went to the brink of the bath and jumped in head forward with a great deal of resolution and swam about and went out and went in again. It is indeed a very small matter, the cold does not affect one at all and is scarce perceptible while in the water. I applauded myself mightily when I came out for my resolution and courage. Gave half-crown, 6*d.* of it to the man, and we took a walk to the New River-head.[1]

About 7 o'clock went to Grecian Coffee House [2] where met with Mr. Goodall. We entered into conversation about the club of free-thinkers that meet there. He says they are set of men who laugh at the prejudice of mankind in favour of the revelation and talk with the utmost assurance as if they had the clearest demonstration that the Christian religion is an imposture. Mr. Goodall

[1] At Islington.
[2] The resort of the learned in Devereux Court, Strand.

does not entirely come into their notion but is rather a sceptic, sees difficulties that regard the revelation that are inseparable to him but yet cannot but think the miracles of our Saviour to be true. Stayed with him there till past 10 o'clock and then came home. Ate a plum cake on the way.

Friday, August 19. Between 8 and 9 went to Mr. Whatley's to go to see the review of the soldiers in the camp. He was not ready. We talked of a case of law that he had read. It will be very serviceable to talk over what we read, it will fix it in our memory and give a greater light into it. There was a dissenting parson, a young man, with him. We went out together to go to the camp but were informed that the review was put off: however, we took boat to Whitehall and from thence walked to the camp. There were many people going there.

When we came into the camp, it was about prayer time and at one place the captain's tent was made use of for the church and all that could come in were admitted, but we saw several other assemblies of soldiers and others at prayer which were in the open air. Each regiment had one and it was by the ensigns' standards and kettle-drums, which last were made use of for a desk for the parson and the soldiers made a ring about him. As we went further into the camp there was a whole regiment exercising. It was divided into two parts each of which had several words of command. General Tatton [1] exercised one and he is remarked to be the cleverest man at exercising an army: he is on horseback before the soldiers drawn up with a large front about four men in depth. He gives the word of command twice and it is then obeyed. I was mightily pleased to see how such a body of men moved with an exact regularity: it looked like a huge machine in motion. It was surprising to see in how many different shapes and appearances they put themselves upon the words spoken and how exactly they divided into distinct bodies and made a face this way and that way, how they wheeled round like a mass of wood fixed upon a centre.

There were a great crowd of people on foot and horseback and in coaches to see these exercises. During them we lost Mr. Whatley in the crowd and though we looked for him a good

---

[1] William Tatton (d. 1737), appointed Major-General 1 January 1710; later Colonel of the Buffs and Governor of Tilbury Fort.

while did not find him, so we walked homeward pretty well tired, the weather being hot. When we came to Charing Cross the dissenting parson, Mr. Whatley's countryman, and I went to an eating-house and there eat our dinner. After this we came together to the Temple and in the way he asked me where I lived, that I was forced to invite him to come to see me. I was not very fond of his acquaintance. I left him to turn into the Temple and then came home.

Saturday, August 20. About 9 o'clock from thence to brother's and breakfasted there of bread and butter and birch wine. Stayed an hour with sister. She is a person of very good natural parts and sense but not having been used to reading her knowledge is confined within the compass of a very few things, that it is very difficult to maintain a conversation with her for any time.

Father says it is certain the King of France died last Thursday and has left the Duke of Orleans among others guardian to the Dauphin.[1] Everybody thinks the Pretender will still make an attempt. Read some of the translations of Horace's poems. I don't think they come up near to the spirit of the original.

Sunday, August 21. Mr. John Emmett[2] called me in the afternoon. Walked in the garden together. He is pretty good company, talks pretty well upon news and other matters. Went with him to meeting. I was not so attentive as I should have. Was a little uneasy about Mr. Hammond[3] in the next pew.

After prayers saw Mr. Hudson[4] at the door. He was telling me how lonely he lived without any of his family with him. I told him he must find out a way to get some of the ladies at the school[5] to visit him now and then, and I promised him to assist

---

[1] Louis XIV died on 1 September 1715 and his nephew Orleans became Regent. The Whigs feared he might strongly support the Pretender. But he proved more concerned to exclude the Spanish Bourbons from the French succession than to retain the Stuart succession in England.

[2] He and his brother Morris were sons of Henry Emmett of Dalston Lane.

[3] The schoolmaster.

[4] Young Hudson became clerk to Peter Marsh, the attorney.

[5] Hackney was famous for its schools. The girls' boarding-schools included those kept by Mrs. Wallis, Mrs. Hammond and Mrs. Elizabeth Hutton. The latter may be that described by Strype in 1720 : 'there is a fair house near the church called the Black and White House ... now a school for young

him in that if I might receive some of the benefit of it by coming to see them at his house. So we went together to the back gate and there they were. He after a little time of silence spoke to them. They took him at first for a servant of the house but afterwards they discovered he was not so they seemed very much inclined to have a correspondence with him, but they told him Mrs. Hutton was coming and desired he would go and come again half an hour afterwards. I came home and stayed longer at supper than half an hour, that when I came they were gone. However, Mr. Hudson called to them at their window and asked them to come down. They told him they could not but seemed very much inclined to it. I did not discover myself to them.

Came home, went into my closet, read Mr. Locke's *Letter of Toleration*. It is admirably well-[writ] and the whole affair about toleration in religion is put into so clear and strong a light that I think it cannot but convince any man that reads it. He is for a universal unlimited toleration and that a magistrate has nothing at all any more than any other man to interfere or meddle in religious matters.

Monday, August 22. Entertained myself with the viol till dinner time, but first went into Mr. Hudson's and walked several turns in his garden and talked about the method of getting into an acquaintance with the ladies at the school. I began to condemn myself that I should be so very familiar and concern myself with one so much beneath me in age and learning.

There came in then a letter directed to Mr. William Ryder. It looked as if it had been opened and the wafer was scarce dry. I opened it and found a copy of verses to him in praise of his friendship and kindness and charity. It surprised me exceedingly, there is the appearance of something very ill at the bottom. I am apt to think it came from one Bragg because he asked twice for my brother to-day and would not leave his business with me. It intimates some very close and intimate acquaintance between him and some woman to whom he has been extremely kind. I

gentlewomen': this house belonged to the Ryder family later in the century. Its site is now Bohemia Place. Mr. Hudson had a worthy forerunner in Mr. Pepys, who on 21 April 1667 visited Hackney chiefly ' to see the young ladies of the schools, whereof there is great store, very pretty'.

dare not communicate it to my father till I have made some further discovery: his temper is to be very hot and tempestuous at first but then to grow cool, remiss and negligent as soon as the first shock is over. My mother saw the letter come and me open it so that I could not conceal it from her, but what I wonder at was that she seemed to be very little affected with it, whereas it affected me so much that it perfectly took away my stomach. How glad now should I be for some prudent friend to consult with what to do. I am afraid he is got into a way of robbing the shop to maintain some woman or other.

Mr. John Emmett came to me to play together upon the flute about 9 o'clock. He brought one flute and we had ne'er another. I played two or three tunes upon the viol and we went into the long walk, and he there played over a great many tunes. He plays chiefly by ear and seems to have a very good one. He plays pretty well, but a little confused as persons that play by the ear only generally do. At past 10 he went away. Went to bed at a little past 11.

Tuesday, August 23. About 8 o'clock went to Mr. Hudson. Inquired of him of Bragg's character. He says he is a silly intruding fellow, very poor. My brother was acquainted with him but seemed to despise and often affronted him by kicking him and throwing stones at him. This made me think the letter did not come from him.

Came to brother's. Did not know what to do, all my thoughts and care was about brother William, how to manage that affair. Went into brother's parlour all alone, sat there thinking on it. At length came in Aunt Billio and Mr. Overall's brother.[1] They soon perceived that I was troubled. However we talked a little gravely upon the subject of communicating secrets to friends and the advantage and ease it gives to the mind. I talked pretty well with them. At length Mr. Overall went away and I communicated the matter to Aunt Billio. She could not tell what to advise me but was very much concerned at it. About 7 o'clock we went together to Hackney. As soon as I came here I went immediately on foot in the dark to the postman to inquire who gave him the letter for brother William and he told me it was

[1] Aunt Billio's daughter Sarah married Edmond Overall of St. Andrew, Holborn, on 17 April 1707: she died in the following year.

young Bragg. This was a mighty ease to me to find I was like to make a discovery.

As I came home went to the back door of the schoolhouse in the field and there found Mr. Hudson, Milbourn and Gould at the door. The girls were at first very merry at dancing but presently comes the schoolmistress and reproved them very severely for their having held discourse with a man and entertaining them upon the wall. One of the Lancashire girls talked very smartly to her again. However, the mistress was very angry and took away from thence. I came home, supped and am still very thoughtful about brother William, how to go with the discovery. Aunt Billio was afraid he might have been engaged in taking a purse upon the highway [1] and that letter was sent by one of his partners. Played upon the viol and went to bed at almost 11.

Wednesday, August 24. Went to the shop. Took brother into an alehouse, began to talk to him very seriously. Told him how much I was concerned for him and promised him to be his friend in everything, and acquainted him with my suspicions, and then with the letter. He told me he knew nothing of it nor from whence it came, that he was engaged in no intrigue, no ill thing whatsoever. He told it me in such a way and manner that it entirely convinced me there was nothing in it. Dined at chophouse. Went home, lay upon the bed a while finding myself very faint and heavy by reason of my walking so much and so fast. Went to Cousin Watkins, bought some sal volatile of him, drank some of it in water there; very much restored me. Stayed with him for almost an hour. Talked about dancing, his courtship and several other things, particularly he would have had me gone with him to-morrow to visit the ladies Pilkington.[2] I should have been glad to have gone, but did not know whether it would have been proper, but what prevailed with me most not to go was that I had not a mind to be taken notice of as a great acquaintance of Cousin Watkins, and one that keeps much company with him.

[1] The violent fears aroused by this letter were caused by William's having been caught out in stealing from his father's shop on a previous occasion.
[2] The widow of Sir Thomas Pilkington (Lord Mayor 1689–91) and the wife of Sir Lyon Pilkington. They had Hackney connexions, but were then living at Streatham.

Went to our club. I was very well pleased with our conversation. It began to turn at first about the inclination of women to venery. Mr. Porter thinks they have twice the inclination to it that men have, which I cannot entirely come in with. We had indeed more bawdy now than ever before. I think I behaved myself pretty well and talked my share tolerably. We talked also about polygamy, which Mr. Porter thought lawful and that it is not necessary that a marriage contract be perpetual and for life. I was of another opinion, because I take it to be more for the interest of the world in general that one man should have but one wife.

Came home between 11 and 12. I was so raised with our discourse about women that I was extremely inclined that way and I looked for a whore with a resolution not to lie with her but to feel her if I could. However, I am very glad I did not find one. Went to bed at almost 1 o'clock.

Thursday, August 25. It began to rain and I went into a coffeehouse, where stayed till 11 o'clock. Read some of Steele's *Englishman.* Was very well pleased with his paper about Tom Harley's examination and the character of the Duke of Marlborough. Got to Hackney little after five. Walked out into the fields. Met Bragg and asked him what he meant by sending that letter to brother William. He said he did not send it. When I charged him here with it he said he did not write it, but would not tell who gave it him. He appears to be a very weak, foolish fellow and given very much to lying and extremely impudent. Brother William came here on horseback with a design to talk with Bragg about the letter. Went to him and he begged his pardon, but he did not write it but one Sherbourn did, who is gone into the country.

Friday, August 26. Rose at 7. Did nothing this morning because Mr. Henry being here I was forced to be with him. Had Mrs. Loyd's and cousin's company all the while, but not much of it alone. Mrs. Loyd is a good sensible girl, talks pretty well, but both she and I tainted a little with the humour of criticism and reflexion. Read some of the translations of Horace aloud and came into my closet. Mr. Henry and I exercised ourselves not long before a-jumping. I found the bones of my legs ache by so unusual a motion of them.

Saturday, August 27. To the Crown Tavern where Mr. Witnoom and Mr. Wadsworth. Mr. Wadsworth was telling us he had been at Norris's [1] farce at Bartholomew Fair and saw there the Duchess of Bolton [2] and several other nobility, who were come there to entertain themselves with low life. The performance was very indifferent. However, it made them laugh.

About 5 o'clock went to Mr. Smith. Stayed there a little time and then he walked with me to Hackney. He is now making a professional sermon upon these words: 'Wisdom's ways are ways of pleasantness and all her paths are peace.' He was complaining that not having used himself to write down his thoughts he was at a loss to make this sermon. We talked upon the subject and I said some things that were very good.

Sunday, August 28. Rose at past 7. Found my leg pained me, thought it was a strain by jumping. Had it rubbed with Hungary water. Found it easier. Put on a piece of flannel and so went to church with it. Mr. Gould and Skinner overtook me in the way. Gould affects very much an airy, unthinking brisk manner of behaviour, as much of the rake as possible. Mr. Skinner behaves himself more soberly and gravely.

After church stayed with Cousin Ryder and Mrs. Loyd. They had their house robbed last night of about £30 of plate. Mrs. Loyd put on strange airs when I first came up to them and looked another way on purpose till I spoke to her. She is a good, brisk, lively girl. Went home to dinner. Young Mr. Henry dined with us. About 2 o'clock Mr. Denn came in and told my father what they had done with the governors of the St. Thomas's Hospital in order to get a lease of some of their ground to build a meeting.[3] The Grand Committee manages their affairs and he

---

[1] Henry Norris (1665–1730), a trim little man with a squeaking voice, generally known as Jubilee Dicky, was one of several eminent actors who performed in booths at Bartholomew and Southwark Fairs.

[2] Henrietta, wife of Charles Paulet, 2nd Duke of Bolton: at this time she was Lady of the Bedchamber to the Princess of Wales.

[3] Many of the Hackney Nonconformists remained hostile to the new minister, John Barker. The unsuccessful candidate, Richard Mayo of Kingston, continued to officiate at meetings in Hackney, and the anti-Barkerites decided to build a new meeting-house for him. The foundation was laid on 12 September 1715 at the gravel-pit near the old bowling green in Mare Street (opposite the present St. Thomas's Square).

had met it and proposed it as a thing advantageous to the hospital. Went to Aunt Bickley's. We viewed the place where the rogues came in at. Then Mrs. Loyd came down and I was alone with her a little while. Talked of nothing with her but the robbery. When Cousin and Mrs. Hiot were there with us she said something privately to her aunt and laughed. I could not help being uneasy for fear it should be at me; in short I behaved myself but awkwardly that I soon went away, being uneasy within myself at the thought of having exposed myself to her. What a fool am I that I cannot be satisfied with the esteem of men of sense but must be uneasy if I am not esteemed by weak women too!

Monday, August 29. Began to read some of Perkins's law, but it came into my head to make my pen that belongs to my pocket book into a fountain pen, which took up all my morning and I did it at last. After dinner played upon my viol and read Horace. I begin to understand him better than ever. I like his manner of writing extremely. There is something so very polite, his connexion is very agreeable and surprising and his turns of thought very pretty. Cannot but take notice that in his descriptions he takes notice of the most obvious things of all and what to an ordinary eye would appear to be no great matter. He never seems to search very deep or refine upon things to enliven a description but always follows Nature in her greatest simplicity. About 6 o'clock Cousin Billio came in and brought me two music books he had of mine. We played over one anthem and sung with it to the bass: it sounded mighty well.

Tuesday, August 30. Between 8 and 9 Mr. Henry came down and we breakfasted together and were together all the morning. It is a very tiresome and uneasy thing to be obliged to have any person's company all day long for several days together. We had, however, a great deal of talk about his grandfather, who was brought up at Court and afterwards at Oxford, was a very good scholar and a very witty ingenious man, given to poetry. He told me he kept a constant diary from his going from Oxford to the end of his life which was writ in longhand and is now with him. He says it is very diverting to read the younger part of his time, for he used to take notice of many little simple trifling occurrences in his life, especially in the time of his courtship of which there is a very particular account.

Mr. Henry gave me an account of his relations by his mother's side,[1] particularly of two uncles, his mother's brothers that are now living, one a great Whig and a very sensible and learned man, the other a Jacobite, a prodigiously covetous man. Their names are Warburton, the first was a counsellor and was offered a judge's place in King William's time and other honour, but refused them all and thought to live a country, retired life, being rich. Young Mr. Henry is his heir. The other lives in the country in a large house, himself and a single servant-maid. He was a doctor of physic and a man of good sense and an agreeable conversation, but fallen in love and surprised with a declaration from his mistress that she was married to another man, he was entirely changed, his temper altered and turned a perfect miser.

Mr. Henry came here again from London : brought some of his grandfather's compositions in prose and poetry, both Latin and English. There are some very pretty turns of thought. I like his Latin the best, perhaps it is because the English is not so agreeable to the modern style.

Wednesday, August 31. As I was going to the club about 6 o'clock met Mr. John Emmett. Went with him to Tom's Coffee House by the Change. We talked about music and painting and prints. He is a great admirer of painting and prints and has some collection but does not seem to have any great judgement that way. He is to come to me to-morrow to see my prints. Went to the club. Our discourse turned upon politics and especially upon bawdy.

Thursday, September 1. About 10 o'clock Mr. Kennedy and Campbell came to breakfast with me. Our discourse turned upon public affairs and great men. I observe the Scotch are very much employed now at court and in foreign parts by our court. They seem to be men very fit for business, intriguing, cunning, tricking sort of men that have not much honour or conscience, but that are ready to comply with the court in anything. Went

[1] She was Mary, daughter of Robert Warburton of Hefferstone Grange, Cheshire. The most eminent member of the family was William Warburton, Bishop of Gloucester.

to dinner and then to Whatley's. He was going to meet a foreigner from Bâle that was recommended to him. Met Mr. Whatley and the foreigner at British Coffee House.[1] The foreigner told us something of the state of religion at Bâle, that none used to be admitted into the church government but Calvinists. They have an University at Bâle. Mr. Bernoulli,[2] a great mathematician, is professor there. They have very few students there. Finished my letter to Aunt Stevenson and gave it to the bellman.

Friday, September 2. Rose at 7. Went into the cold bath. I found myself in a greater hurry and confusion now than I did before. However, I jumped in twice but stayed in but very little time. I cannot say I find much benefit by it. Went to John's. Thence to London Coffee House, where Mr. Smith was playing with Demodore. Jackson came in and played a little. I don't find that he plays so extraordinary well. He has very little judgement and cannot play in time. Bought some tea and coffee for sister at Mr. Hulst. He invited me to drink tea with him. There was Doctor Tindal.[3] He is not a man that talked much. Had very little discourse there.

There is a report that the Highlanders have formed camp in favour of the Pretender on the pretence of a hunting match. It is yet uncertain what is the meaning of it. My Lord Strafford was to-day impeached at the bar of the House of Lords of high crimes and misdemeanors.[4]

Saturday, September 3. At little past 8 brother's man came to tell me father desired me to go to the Hay [5] with brother and

[1] In Cockspur Street; a house of call for Scotchmen (Timbs).
[2] Jean Bernoulli (1667-1748), a member of a famous Bâle family of mathematicians. His chief work was in calculus and integration of fractions.
[3] Dr. Matthew Tindal (1657-1733), Fellow of All Souls'. This 'Christian Deist', as he called himself, was a strong opponent of the High Church party. He wrote numerous pamphlets on religion and politics, one of which, *Rights of the Christian Church Asserted*, 1706, was distinguished along with Sacheverell's sermon by being publicly burnt by the common hangman in 1710.
[4] i.e. his share in the Treaty of Utrecht. The proceedings were dropped in 1717.
[5] Westbrook Hay in Bovingdon, Herts. The manor was held by the diarist's brother Richard, through his wife Anne. The property had originally been purchased by old Joshua Lomax in 1656 and 1667.

sister. Dressed myself immediately and went to brother's, but considering there was not room for me to lie at the Hay resolved not to go quite through, so went with brother to Hampstead where went to see Mrs. Lee. She was very glad to see me.

I don't know how, I am the worst person in the world to entertain a lady in conversation. Though I can be free with Mrs. Lee yet I cannot tell how to maintain an agreeable discourse with her : I am presently at a stand and at a loss what to say. Went with Mrs. Lee to Watford, when the coach was got just into the inn before us. I wish I could arrive at that talent of appearing indifferent in the company of the ladies. It is this that chiefly gives that life and spirit to a conversation which is agreeable and which the women especially universally like, and indeed what enters very much into the modern character of a gentleman.

As I came home, met a gentleman at the slough in the way to Hampstead. He was thrown by it. I made what haste I could to help him, because I had found out the way of passing it before. I came through it and directed him how to go but his horse was afraid, so I went back again myself into the hole to lead the way for his horse to follow, which it did. I was pleased with myself for this act of humanity in me. As we came near Hampstead saw a man with a footman behind him at some distance. There were some circumstances in their manner of riding &c. that made me suspect they had a design upon us and I was really very much afraid. However, I believe now they were honest men.

Went to father's shop where I was told Cousin Richard Ryder died about an hour before. I had heard in the morning he was very ill of the fever, but had no thought of his being so near his end. It surprised me but did not touch me so sensibly as I should have expected.

Sunday, September 4. Went to church in the afternoon. Overtook young Mr. Gould in the way : he was waiting for the girls from the school. However, he went on softly with me. I was ashamed to be seen in his company at church time, lest people, who all take notice of his manner of behaviour in relation to these girls, should take me to be of the same company.

Monday, September 5. Was not very much inclined to study this morning. Played upon the flute and viol a great part of it.

Went to dinner, where two women that looked tolerably well that came to see our maid. I invited them into the parlour to dine with us. It was a little difficult for me to behave upon this occasion. However, did tolerably well. After dinner employed myself in reading some of Horace's *Odes*.

Tuesday, September 6. Rose at 7. Studied the law all the morning. Read 5 cases in Coke about leases. Was pretty well inclined to the study of the law. About 12 o'clock, Mr. Whatley came to ask me to go with him and two of his friends to see the great ship at Woolwich, but I denied him because I have seen it before. He is one of the strangest unaccountable tempers in the world; sometimes he is the most pleased and satisfied with himself, hugs himself in the enjoyment of himself and thinks everybody else inferior to him. This morning he was very cloudy, dissatisfied with himself, says he cannot fix his mind to the law. It is certainly a very unhappy disposition and frame of soul to be so very unconstant. He can never continue his pursuit of one thing but is always diverted from his business. He was a little while ago pleased with the thoughts of setting hard to the study of the law and was mighty hot in reading Coke's *Reports*, but it seems he has left off that before he had got through twelve cases. I don't see how it is possible he should ever do anything considerable in any way or profession.

Came to brother's and so to father's where I stayed till he and brother and I and Mr. Gregg went to the funeral of Cousin Richard Ryder. When we came there we sat down in the room where the coffin was, looked as grave and sad as we could, scarce any conversation at all. I was very much displeased with myself that I could not be much affected with such a posture of affairs, that the death of a relation made so little impression upon me and I did what I could to raise a little concern in me. There were several young men of his acquaintance that came to his burial. We were all equally furnished with favours and white gloves excepting two cousins and brother Ryder and father, who were the mourners with cloaks and hatbands and black shammy gloves. We accompanied the corpse to St. James' Church where prayers were said in the church by Mr. Wigget's son. He was buried in the yard. We then presently got into the coach and came home.

I went to Tom's Coffee House, where I read a French paper from Holland.

Wednesday, September 7. At 6 o'clock received letter from Cousin Watkins to have a dancing to-night. Met Cousin Watkins and two ladies, with whom went to the tavern in Cornhill. We had only two other ladies, so that we had but four couples in all, Mr. Hulst and Hayward, cousin and myself. Presently after we began to dance, by the looks of my partner (who was no handsome woman at all) and some secret whispers between her and another, I could not but suspect they disliked me and talked about. This gave such a turn to my mind that lasted with me all the night. I could scarce venture to speak a word and was indeed very ill company to them. The company to be sure could not but observe it. Mr. Hulst and Mr. Hayward made all the diversion for the ladies. Mr. Hayward is a man cut out to please the women in conversation. He is so very familiar to them as to do that to them which would be very rude in another man. He was indeed the life of our company, for he is never at a loss to entertain the ladies with discourse and yet he scarce ever tells a story, but does by making a thousand little remarks upon them, kissing them, laughing at them, appearing angry with them in jest, not confining himself within any of the niceties of good breeding or the rules of compliment, but breaking all these laws in the way of raillery. I was astonished to hear how a man could sit, as we did after dancing for above an hour together, without being ever silent for half a minute together. I could not help envying him the pleasure of being agreeable to the ladies, and being uneasy with myself that I was so very dull company to them. We had a supper of fowls and tarts and fruit. It will be, I am afraid, a chargeable night to us. Went to bed between, 3 and 4.

Thursday, September 8. Rose at 9. Captain Cumming called me up out of bed. I had his company all the morning. Our conversation was upon Mr. Berkeley's notions, which we talked of a great while. Read some of Sallust's *Jugurthan War*. Mr. Henry came to see me : we talked chiefly upon his school affairs and what books he had learnt. He is a young man of good parts and a good scholar, understands Latin very well I believe.

Between 6 and 7 went to walk in the piazzas in the Temple. Went to the Gill House. Met there with Mr. Bowes.[1] We went together upstairs and a friend of his. After supper we took a walk in the street and towards Ormonde Street and in Lucas Square the gentleman his friend [2] sung us several songs. I was extremely pleased with his singing. He did it admirably well with a great deal of judgement and a good voice, but was surprised when Mr. Bowes told me he had never learnt of a master nor knew anything of the notes.

Friday, September 9. Read several cases and began to make use of my artificial memory to retain them and I find it has been of service to me that I have by that means recollected all the cases read to-day and thought of them as I went along the streets.

Between 9 and 10 brother William came to me and breakfasted with me. He is mighty fond of the company of the ladies and is now got into an acquaintance with Mrs. Loyd at Aunt Bickley's. He has the assurance to go there and talk with her for an hour together, nor is ashamed, though he says the most silly things imaginable and she banters him extremely. I wish I had that happy talent of being unconcerned and indifferent in my conversation with the ladies. About 7 to John's; met there Mr. Witnoom, Porter, Isles and Serjeant. We went together to the tavern where we sat till near 11. Our discourse at first turned upon Mr. Berkeley's notions. Mr. Porter's objection still continues, that upon Berkeley's principles you have no reason to believe that there is any other reasonable being in the world besides God and one's self. I could not clear that difficulty, but I did not conceive it so great an objection as he makes, and believe it may be answered, though he thinks it cannot. We talked of politics and the state of England, the advantages of its government and how much preferable it is to that of Holland, wherein the liberties of the people are not so great and secure as ours are. The rest of the company were saying that the Act against rioters

---

[1] John Bowes (1690–1767), of Hackney, studied law with Philip Yorke (later Lord Hardwicke). Called 1718, to Irish Bar 1725. Solicitor-General in Ireland 1730, Attorney-General 1739, Chancellor 1757, created Baron of Clonly 1758. Acted as Lord Chief Justice in Ireland 1765–6. The friendship begun at this time endured, and Ryder did much to advance his friend's career.

[2] Mr. Suly, a solicitor in Chancery.

had put too much power into the hands of the Crown, that if ever an ill prince should have a mind to oppress the subject and make himself absolute that Act would put it out of the power of the subject to redress themselves. I said what I could to justify the Act (which they would have had to have been only temporary and not as it is perpetual) but I did not sufficiently answer their objections and I think they were in the right of it. We talked also about poetry, my Lord Roscommon's translation [1] and the sublimity of David's psalms and the book of Job, and also upon Mr. Addison's genius, which I said I thought was extremely correct and fine, but not so quick an imagination, that is so soon and easily struck as many others. I was very well pleased with myself in the share I bore in this conversation and find I have got over that awe and concern I used to be under in Mr. Isles' company. The conversation goes on mighty agreeably and pleasantly when it is so managed as to make every one easy and satisfied with himself, and this is an excellent talent to be able to converse so as not to seem above the company but to make every one have a good opinion of himself.

Came away between 11 and 12. In the morning brother was saying he was going to write a letter to Mrs. Loyd and showed me part of it. I persuaded him not to send it, was very indifferent. When he was gone it came into my head to write a letter to her myself as from an unknown person: immediately wrote in shorthand a long humoursome letter enough, but did not send it and I believe shall not.

Saturday, September 10. Went to Mr. Smith where we played upon the flute together the greatest part of the time. Talked of Mr. Berkeley, borrowed his *Principles of Human Knowledge* of him. When I left, read the rest of the way in that book which has almost already convinced that there are no such things as abstract ideas in Mr. Locke's and the common sense.

Met with Aunt Bickley in Mare Street and, walking along with her, brother William overtook us, so we went to Aunt Bickley's together. Brother got with Mrs. Loyd and stayed with her in a separate place from the rest of the company. I had no talk with her at all, but she seemed to be mighty fond of conversing with brother. I came away and left him and could not help being

---

[1] His translation of Horace's *Ars Poetica*, 1680.

vexed to think that a person of so little sense as he is should be so welcome only because he is bold and impudent and is not ashamed to say the most silly foolish things to her.

After supper went into my closet. Played upon my viol and sung some of my Italian songs which I am in hopes I shall be able to presently sing agreeably with my viol, though never without some other music to guide my voice and ear.

Sunday, September 11. Went to church after dinner. Mr. Greenor preached. He is a man that affects a sort of pretty fancies and little puns and that gives a thing a pretty air of novelty and imagination. I could not help thinking him like those gentlemen who in conversation with the ladies that they may keep up an agreeable vivacity and spirit say a thousand little things and fancies as they come into their heads without any regard to their being just.

Came home and finished Mr. Berkeley's book. I am mightily pleased with the greatest part of it, and though he has not yet fully convinced and made me see his notions in a very strong light yet they have gone a great way [to] clear up the objection against them that Mr. Porter makes. I am in great hope thoroughly to conceive Mr. Berkeley the next time of reading and that that difficulty will entirely disappear.

Brother carried a letter from Mr. Humphreys to Mrs. Loyd upon the occasion of her suspecting him to be the author of the letter sent to her in which a great deal is taken from the *Tatlers*. It seems he was mightily concerned that she should suspect him of stealing thoughts from others.

Monday, September 12. Rose at 8. Mr. Emmett came to me immediately after rising to play together upon the flute. Did so and breakfasted together till 10. Then read Mr. Berkeley and then played upon the viol. Did very little this morning. Read some of Horace's *Odes*. After dinner did the same, expecting Cousin Billio to come, which he did not till almost 4 o'clock, when we played together upon the viol and flute till past 5 o'clock.

Tuesday, September 13. At between 12 and 1 went into the city to brother's. Cousin Robert Billio was there and told us that we were robbed at Hackney last night of some of our pewter and other things below-stairs of no great value. Dined there with Cousin Billio and Mrs. Jeffries.[1]

After dinner went to father's to desire his horse to-morrow to go with Cousin Billio to the Hay. He did not know whether it was proper to ride him because his eyes were not good, but went with me to the stable to see how it did. In the way there my father told me he heard it was reported that Mrs. Lee was to be married to me. I told him there was nothing in it at all, that such reports arise from a young man's being seen in a young woman's company but that I had no such design nor would entertain a design of marrying without communicating it to him. He said he heard Mrs. Lee was very deeply in love with me and took all opportunities of getting into my company. I said I did not know that, nor did I ever see her but by chance at brother's or so. I cannot well tell indeed whether she is in love with me or no. I believe there may be something in it and what confirms me is that her father met me the other day and asked whether I would not come and see him upon the bridge. I shall be sorry if she is in love with me, because I have no design to marry her.[2] I shall therefore take care not to be so frequent in her company.

Went home, dressed myself for the riding. In the meantime Mr. John Emmett came in. He looked over my pictures. He has no great judgement but is mightily taken with my prints that are of a fine neat work and does not like such as are more gross, though much better done, as the Sacrament of Poussin he does not like so well as the fine sort of French prints. Our conversation turned almost entirely upon prints and a little upon news. He drank some green tea with me.

Wednesday, September 14. Rose between 6 and 7. Got myself ready for my journey to the Hay with Cousin Billio and his wife. Talking with father about keeping house and the charge of it with respect to parish duties, he said if he continued to keep house it would cost him £12 more in parish duties. I said I thought that was a small matter. Upon that father immediately said, 'How can you tell how long I shall live?' I answered nothing, but I was extremely troubled that my father should put such an interpretation upon my words which were indeed spoke only at

[1] Robert's mother-in-law.
[2] She married Mr. Utber the goldsmith in the following year.

random without any the least thought of my father's life or death.

At 7 o'clock cousin and his wife came. They would not stay to drink chocolate and so left me to follow them after having drank some myself. Cousin Billio was extremely careful of his wife lest she should endanger herself by going fast; she was mighty fearful and timorous. We had no diversion upon the road nor adventures to entertain us. They had almost done dinner when we came to the Hay, were very glad to see us and we eat pretty heartily.

Soon after dinner there came in Mrs. Cowley, a young widow, and her own mother Mrs. Jermyn. The widow is very handsome and genteel and I made bold after my sister to salute them, though I find since, Aunt Lomax thinks it not genteel to salute them that I never saw nor knew before. The afternoon passed away in walking about the garden and these ladies' company. The young widow is indeed a fine lady. What troubled me most was a fear I had a stinking breath and it was perceived. This makes me of late very uneasy in company. I am resolved as soon as possible to find out the truth of it, and though I think to ask my mother that question it sounds so odd to ask whether my breath stinks that I don't know how to ask it. Aunt Lomax has a very odd turn of thought and is very apt to make us laugh by the ridiculous light she sometimes puts a thing into.

Thursday, September 15. Rose between 7 and 8. Read the 1st epistle of Boileau to the king. He writes with an admirable spirit and wit. Went then to Hemstead to be shaved. Saw Mr. Birch [1] and his son there. There was a mountebank in the town that for above two months every market-day exposed himself upon the stage. He had to-day given a hat to be cudgelled for. I don't well understand how these fellows can afford to do as they do, go attended with two or three servants, a fiddle and sometimes tumblers, &c. I wonder the selling their packets should answer that charge especially when all the people generally know what sort of men they are and that they are little to be depended. But this same mountebank keeps most of the

[1] Possibly Joseph Owen Birch, the father of Thomas Birch (1705–66), Secretary of the Royal Society; he was educated at Mr. Owen's School in Hemel Hemstead.

markets within a few miles of this place, these markets being upon different days. To-day was market-day at Hemstead. There was a great crowd of people and a great deal of corn to be sold, it being one of the greatest markets for corn in England for so small a town.

Came home about 1. Here was Mr. Boyd the parson. He had a sad stinking breath that made me very uneasy to sit by him at dinner. He is a strange scrupulous man, will never drink above one glass of wine, though if that one be full he will make no scruple to drink it, nor will he drink any health. He does not pretend to give any reason for his singularity in these matters. We were very merry, my Aunt Lomax saying abundance of comical things that cannot but make us laugh.

After dinner between 3 and 4 we went to Berkhamstead, cousin and his wife and my sister and I, by the way of Mr. Essington's; the country is very pleasant that way. His house is admirably situated in the midst of several woods that look very agreeable. We called at an inn, Mr. Finall's, where we drank our pints of wine. I chose that inn because he has some pretty daughters whom we saw. The mountebank had a stage there and he had given a pair of gloves to be cudgelled for that night, so that a crowd of people were gathered about the stage.

As soon as we got out of the town it began to rain and after some dispute about it I went back to borrow two riding hoods for the young women and so we came to Goody Butler's where my mother and Aunt Lomax were. We were received mighty kindly by the good woman. She entertained us with cold pork and bread and butter and admirable good ale. This provision was very neat and good and we eat heartily. The old woman was mightily pleased to see us like our entertainment. I was indeed very well pleased with the hearty welcome that we had at the farmer's house. At length her husband came in and he was as kind as his wife and glad to see us. He is an honest hearty man for King George, and is mighty glad to talk about him and politics. We came away after we had been extremely merry and pleasant about 7 o'clock. It was very dark and we came home; we were all a little tired and sleepy and at length, little past 9, got upstairs to bed.

Friday, September 16. Expected young Mr. Birch betimes to hunt or set. He came at about 8 and we went out with three greyhounds a-coursing and after a long time seeking and beating about the fields we started a hare, but we lost her and could not find another. I was soon tired of this sport. I wonder how any persons can divert themselves in this way to go round the fields for a long time in vain. The great difficulty in the country is to find matter of entertainment and how to employ one's self.

After dinner we were all to ride out to my Lord Bridgewater's Park.[1] As we were going out it began to rain and we turned back and did not go out again. Mr. Birch was then for going home and as he and I were going out I don't know how he had a mind to try my strength, fancying I was very weak, so we wrestled together, but I threw him six times following. He is indeed very weak that he could scarce move me. This striving ruffled me a little, made hot and put my spirits into a hurry, but it went off and we went to cards, sister and I and Cousin Billio and his wife. We played at whisk. His wife is mighty apt to fret upon the having ill cards and losing and says herself she cannot bear to lose, and therefore does not care to play. When it grew dark sister dressed up the servants in odd strange dresses and brought them in to divert us. We all laughed heartily, but they had nothing but their dress to entertain us. Then sister came herself dressed like a student of the university and she acted that part very prettily. We talk with her in that character and she did it mighty well. We are all glad of any such whimsy and fancy to divert us. I don't wonder those that live in the country are driven to take up with any such kind of sports and play to employ themselves.

Saturday, September 17. Rose about 8. Went into the fields where they were ploughing, followed the plough and ploughed myself. It is no difficult matter to guide the plough at all. They were now ploughing for wheat and it was a new farmer. It seems it is a custom of the country when a stranger comes into a farm for the neighbours to come and assist him with their ploughs to plough his ground for the first time. They sow two bushel and half of wheat to an acre.

We went to dinner at 11 o'clock because we were to go to London to-day and Aunt Lomax would make us stay to dinner because she had provided us a delicate dish of trouts. We all admired her fish, as indeed they were excellent. After dinner we

[1] Ashridge Park, Little Gaddesdon.

set out for home about 12 o'clock and sister went part of the way with us. Aunt Lomax had charged us not to ride fast when she was with us and to get her to return as soon as possible because it would be dangerous for her to ride much. So when we were got about 3 miles we would have had sister gone back, but she would not. She is indeed a person of a strong obstinate temper, the more you persuade her to do anything the more averse she is from doing it. However, she left us not far from Watford.

We got at last to London, but in the way we took a view of my Lord Carnarvon's gardens: from the end of them there is a prodigious canal at the end that takes up a vast deal of ground.[1] It seems my lord is very changeable and fickle. They told us at the inn in Edgware where we baited that my lord had just begun to destroy the form of his parterre after a great expense laid out upon it and that he had pulled down the whole side of his house that he had but just built up and has now built it up again because it did not please his fancy.

We got to London about 7 o'clock. The bells were ringing and there were illuminations and guns firing for the king's coming through the city. He was at Woolwich to see the great ship and came back through the City. Among the huzzas, that were very loud, I could distinguish some hisses: the fellows that dared to do that were very bold and impudent.

Sunday, September 18. Went with father and Mr. Lacy [2] to meeting. I was surprised to hear Mr. Lacy talk so candidly and mildly upon the building a new meeting-house now it was begun. He talked as if none of their side was sorry for it but wished them success and hoped they would have a popular minister to enlarge the congregation.

Monday, September 19. Went to John's, saw Mr. Witnoom and Crisp. Dined with them at the tavern. Our discourse turned upon the lawfulness of officious lies, as when a man tells an untruth to do his neighbour a service or when a man is robbed

---

[1] Canons, the magnificent house at Edgware, was built out of the wealth which James Brydges (1673-1744), 1st Duke of Chandos and Marquis of Carnarvon, acquired as Paymaster-General. Here Handel spent two years as organist. The 'Canal' was the lake (cf. *N.E.D.*).

[2] A Roger Lacy died at Hackney in 1738, aged 74.

and to save his life promises to give so much money without discovering the robber, whether such an untruth be unlawful or such a promise binding or no.

Went to Change to John's to go with Mr. Witnoom to Southwark Fair.[1] Mr. Porter came there and he and Mr. Crisp and others went with us to the Fair. We first went into Norris's booth and then into Penkethman and Bullock booth. They are both of them very mean and fit only to make us laugh. The farces are made up out of several very comical parts of other plays which are collected together. Penkethman and Bullock are a mere farce to look at them only; they have both of them so very simple a look, but yet in a very different kind. There was the Duke of Montague[2] and some company of fashion. There was rope dancing and tumbling at Penkethman and Bullock. It was very low life represented. There were now and then some good humorous turns came in that made us laugh with a just pleasure.

Came back to John's where talking about the actors and playhouse, and it was said that Booth[3] was the most low, vicious, debauched fellow of them all but a man of very good sense, but his conversation is full of nothing but bawdy and profaneness. The most virtuous of all the players is Mills,[4] he is a man of a good reputation in the neighbourhood, goes often to prayers and the sacrament and avoids ill and loose company and enjoys himself with his wife alone. Most of the rest are very debauched and loose.

Tuesday, September 20. Met Mr. Porter: he went along with me where soon fell upon Mr. Berkeley's notions and talked for

---

[1] Southwark Fair was held on St. Margaret's Hill immediately after Bartholomew Fair, to which it was very similar. Both were graced by theatrical booths in which some of the best actors played—Norris, Doggett, Simpson, the elder Penkethman, and William Bullock of Lincoln's Inn Fields Theatre.

[2] John, 2nd Duke of Montague (1688–1749). His chief delight, said the Duchess of Marlborough, his mother-in-law, was 'to get people into his garden and wet them with squirts . . . and such pretty fancies'.

[3] Barton Booth (1681–1733), who made his reputation as Cato in Addison's play, was joint-manager of Drury Lane.

[4] John Mills (d. 1736), one of the principal actors at Drury Lane. Colley Cibber said he was an 'honest, quiet, careful man, of as few faults as excellences'.

a great while about his difficulty, that upon his principles he has no reason to believe that there is any other finite spirit besides himself and God. Mr. Porter has promised to write down his thoughts upon this and send it me in a letter that he may do it more clearly and I have promised him to answer it in writing too.

From hence went to Cousin Watkins. There came in to him soon after some ladies to drink tea; one of them pretty enough, I sat down with, and behaved myself pretty freely among, though did not say much.

Wednesday, September 21. Went to dinner at between 1 and 2. Took with me some dialogues in French of Mr. Noble wherein he exposes several characters and does it very well. I take it nothing fits a man more for conversation than an acquaintance with the different characters in the world and being able to see the ridiculous side of them. This made me take a particular notice of those characters that I read. Saw Mr. Hudson at his door. Invited him to come and sit with me, which he did so for half an hour. We talked about the girls of Hackney. He is a good-humoured sensible young man. When he was gone went to grandmother and then played upon the viol.

Thursday, September 22. Went to Captain Cumming, sat with him from 5 till 7. He is a mighty obliging gentleman. Our conversation turned upon poetry and particularly Pope and Tickell's translation of part of Homer. He says Mr. Berkeley and two other gentlemen that are well versed in the classics read them over with the original together and compared them and they give the preference very much to Pope's translation and think it admirably done; that it is better than could be expected and shows the very great extensiveness of the English language. Mr. Cumming upon this mentioned an essay upon poetry by the present Duke of Buckingham. We read part of it together: it is admirably well and shows a great genius for poetry and judgement.

It is said there is a discovery of an association in favour of the Pretender. It is certain my Lord Lansdowne and Duplin [1] are both taken up and Jersey is sought after and six members of

---

[1] George Granville, Baron Lansdowne (1667–1735) and George, Viscount Duplin, Harley's son-in-law.

INCIDENTS OF THE 1715 REBELLION
Engraved by H. Terasson after Lud. Du Guernier

the House of Commons are ordered to be taken up by consent of the House of Commons, viz. Sir William Wyndham, Pakington, Forster, Harvey of Combe, Anstis and Kynaston.[1] It is said the Duke of Orleans has made this discovery to the King.

The Earl of Mar [2] has gathered a considerable body of Highlanders in favour of the Pretender and declared himself openly for him. The castle of Edinburgh has been attempted to be surprised by the Pretender's friends but miscarried. The Duke of Argyll [3] is gone down to assist the King but has not men enough yet to make a stand against the rebels who are making all the haste they can towards England. It is uncertain whether the Pretender is with them or no, but some say he is and others not. There is a camp formed at Stirling for the King, but they have but few men there yet.

Friday, September 23. Brother William came to tell me father wanted to speak with me, so dressed myself as fast as I could, went to father's about 10. He told me I must go on Monday morning betimes into the country with the commissioners. I could not help discovering that I had rather not go, which I was vexed at afterwards. However I promised to go.

Had a fire made in expectation of Mr. Bowes. Read in the meantime Tickell's translation of the first book of Homer's *Iliad* and compared it with the original. I think I can plainly see a greater beauty in the original than in the translation but I think it pretty well done. At length about 4 o'clock Mr. Bowes came. He looked over my prints and liked them pretty well. This made up part of our conversation. At length he came to talk of the miracles of our Saviour and says he thinks the heathens have

[1] Sir William Wyndham, M.P. for Somerset, surrendered but was liberated after eight months' imprisonment. Sir John Pakington, M.P. for Worcester, was acquitted ; Edward Harvey of Combe, Surrey, a kinsman of the Earl of Nottingham ; Thomas Forster, the Pretender's general, surrendered at Preston and escaped from Newgate to France, M.P. for Northumberland ; John Anstis, M.P. for Launceston, was acquitted ; Cuthbert Kynaston, M.P. for Salop.

[2] 'Bobbing' John Erskine, Earl of Mar, raised the Pretender's standard at Braemar on 6 September.

[3] Argyll, commander-in-chief in Scotland, took command at Stirling on 29 September. His troops, about 1,500 in all, were concentrated there to prevent the rebels, who had captured Perth on 14 September, from advancing into the Lowlands.

miracles as much to vouch for their religion as the Christians have for theirs; he said the Christian miracles have only one book, the New Testament, to vouch for them. This startled me and I could not well tell what to say to it. I fancy he is of the society of freethinkers, for he seems mighty ready to declare his opinion and fond of venting it and making proselytes. We had a good deal of talk upon this head and he urged a great many things against the Christian religion, as particularly that it could not be supposed but that there were many books wrote against it when it first rose in the world but they are all lost and that is the reason why we think now that it was so true that nobody could oppose it or object to the truth. He is a man of good sense and has every now and then a good thought and gives it an agreeable turn. His style is much better than one ordinarily meets with in conversation. He told me Mr. Suly, the gentleman that sang to us one night, was a man of a great deal of modesty and good sense, bred an attorney. When he was in worser circumstances than he is at present he had a very good offer of a subsistence upon account of his voice, but he absolutely refused it. He stayed with me till past 6 o'clock. I was well pleased with his company and hope he may be a useful and agreeable companion.

Read *The Merry Wives of Windsor*. There is a prodigious deal of humour and mirth in the character of Falstaff and it is impossible to read it and not to laugh by one's self. Went to bed between 12 and 1.

Saturday, September 24. Bought two French books in Moorfields, the *Dialogues of the Dead* [1] and another concerning the several interests of the princes and states of Europe at the middle of the reign of King Charles II.

Came to Hackney between 3 and 4. Cousin Joseph Billio came to me. We talked for some time about bashfulness in conversation. He was complaining that he does not know how to get over that concern and awe and uneasiness he finds upon himself in the company of elderly persons who knew him from his infancy. He said Mr. Dent was a man very faulty that way when he first came from Holland and he resolved if possible to break himself of it and therefore he used to go every now and then into unknown coffee-houses where he might meet with none but

[1] Fénelon's *Dialogues des Morts*, 1712.

strangers, and resolved to give a loose to his tongue and say whatever came uppermost as he was among who it was likely would never see him again. I am well pleased with the experiment and resolve to try it myself. We played upon the music and he went away and I went to the coffee-house with him, where saw several of the Hackney gentlemen, particularly Mr. Dawson.[1] I began to be a little timorous and afraid but Mr. Dawson with a great deal of seeming familiarity called me by my name and asked me whether there was any news. This in a manner at once restored my spirits and gave me a great deal of ease.

Brother William at length came home. He has been for above two hours at Aunt Bickley's with Mrs. Loyd, cousin and another young lady. He is got to a prodigious degree of assurance or rather impudence with respect to young ladies, seems to have no manner of regard to anything of decency on this side of downright bawdy. I am vexed with myself that I cannot help envying him, that I cannot rest satisfied with my own superior merit.

To-day a proclamation came out for the apprehending Wyndham with the promise of a reward of £1,000 to any one that takes him.[2] It seems papers of consequence about the Pretender's invasion have been found in his house. He himself was taken but made his escape.

Sunday, September 25. Rose at 8. Lay with my brother in the best room because young Mr. Birch came and he lay alone in our room. He was frightened in the night by a noise and raised the house for fear of thieves. Brother and I were surprised and got out of bed, but being in an unusual room we could not easily find the door. At length got out, went upstairs but could see nothing. It is very terrible to be disturbed so in the night and especially in the dark. I had a kind of terror come upon me.

Did nothing in the morning but read a little in Grotius' *De veritate religionis Christi* in order to find out what other histories there are that speak of our Saviour and his miracles besides the New Testament and the writings of the Christians themselves

---

[1] Probably William Dawson, brother-in-law of Samuel Heathcote: he was appointed churchwarden at Hackney in 1717. He was a director of the East India Company.

[2] He had fled to his house, Orchard Wyndham in Somerset; after various escapes he surrendered.

and I found that there is indeed no other history that mentions anything of it much to the purpose.

After sermon young Mr. Crisp asked me and my brother by his mother's order to come and dine with her. She and his sister were at meeting. I went in the coach with them and dined with them. I behaved myself with something of bashfulness and restraint. Madam Crisp was extremely civil and obliging to me. Our conversation was all upon different subjects, about news, &c. I talked I think pretty well upon these subjects but with a kind of awe and restraint upon me. I would feign have returned her thanks in a handsome manner and invited her to our house, &c., but could not bring myself to that freedom as to be able to do it well. Called at brother's about some writings that are to go with us to-morrow to Hertfordshire. Ordered the maid to call me at 5 to-morrow morning.

Monday, September 26. Rose at between 5 and 6. Had but an uneasy night of it being concerned lest I should not rise time enough. Went to Mr. Gregg's in Bartley's Buildings at 6. Drank some tea with him and the coach with Mr. Mears [1] in it soon called us. The morning was very fine and we were pleasant and good company. Our discourse at first turned upon the methods of stewards of manors [2]; particularly Sir Edward Northey [3] was mentioned as a man that had gained extremely that way, oftentimes by raising the fees and imposing upon the ignorance of the tenants. Mr. Gregg himself holds one manor as steward. He says it is a common practice of stewards of manors never to let a divided copyhold estate be joined again, but always to keep them separate that separate copies may be for each part which extremely advances the profits to the steward. We began to talk of law part of the way. I find by him that it is a thing more common than I thought it really had been for lawyers and attorneys to entangle and perplex a case on purpose to make more work for themselves. Serjeant Brainthwaite [4] is a man well

---

[1] A Hugh Meers, printer, died at Hackney in 1723.

[2] They transacted the financial and legal business of manors, held the manor-courts in the absence of the lords and kept copies of the rolls.

[3] The Attorney-General.

[4] William Brainthwaite of the Middle Temple: appointed sergeant-at-law in 1714.

skilled in that part of the law and generally engaged in those kind of disputes. It is, it seems, a practice common to some of the judges to encourage the bringing cases to a hearing before them at their chambers, by which very considerable fees come to their clerks, but which they are accountable to the judges themselves for by agreement. But yet these judges (as Littleton Powys [1] and Tracey who attend this kind of practice very much) will sometimes in favour to an attorney that is wont to bring matters before them go beyond their bounds. They don't do it directly, but when a judge advises a party to do so and so and one of them thinks it hard upon him, refuses to consent, the judge tells him if he won't he must move it in court the next term, but it had been better for him to consent. When a motion is made the judge tells the court he had heard the matter at his chambers and had advised them to agree so-and-so. The court is generally so partial to the opinions of a particular judge that instead of entering into the merits of the case they scarce ever fail to order the rule according to the judge's opinions and perhaps commit the attorney for refusing to comply before. This is a partiality that is very dishonest and unjust but such as almost constantly obliges the parties concerned to give their consent to whatever a judge proposes. The reason of the court's proceeding in this manner is to keep up the authority of the judges and not let an attorney or any other cry that the judge was ever in the wrong.

We came to Hemstead at between 12 and 1. There was father and Mr. Lomax and his son [2] with the witnesses on both sides to be examined ready at the inn. After dinner they began to go to work. In the meantime I went to young Mr. Birch and saw him ordering a straw hat. There was a shop maid with him and I began to jest and rally with her a little and did it better than I think I ever did such a thing before, but I find the girl of very good sense ; she answered me very handsomely and sometimes wittily that I was very well pleased with her talk.

[1] Sir Littleton Powys (1648–1732), judge on King's Bench ; for Tracey, cf. note, p. 61.
[2] Old Joshua Lomax (d. 1685) of Bolton, had acquired the manors of Westbrook Hay and Childwick between 1656 and 1667. He had two sons, Joshua (d. 1724) who was M.P. for St. Albans in 1708 (he and his son Caleb are referred to here) and Thomas (Aunt Lomax was his widow), who held the manor of Westbrook in 1694.

Tuesday, September 27. Rose between 8 and 9. Read the 7th epistle of Boileau to Mr. Racine where he rallies the criticism and censures of little mean poets that set themselves up against every [thing] that is well done and shows in a very agreeable light how much the most excellent writings are exposed to envy and censure. Went to breakfast. Afterwards entered into conversation with sister and Aunt Billio. She gave us an account of the censorious behaviour of young Mrs. Isaacs and Mrs. Stancliff[1] and how free they are to her in telling her the faults of her relations as well as others. Indeed she is a woman to whom all her acquaintance make no scruple to communicate their thoughts of the conduct and management of others and even her nearest friends. I intend to make use of her to that end to acquaint me with what other people say of me.

Went after dinner to Hemstead with Aunt Lomax and Aunt Billio and sister. When we came there they stayed to make a visit and I went to the inn to father and Mr. Lomax &c. Father thought it would oblige him to have my aunt and sister come and pay their respect to him. Sent for them immediately. They came, and old Lomax made a show of receiving kindly but he is of a temper that it is impossible to move by all the obliging things in the world. There is indeed no possibility of gaining him by favours and civility or any that one does to him; he will only make use of your civility against you if possible. He is a man of no natural affection: money is to him in the place of all relations whatsoever. The commissioners had now finished their commission and examination and they endeavoured to make up the matter and bring Mr. Lomax and father to agree. He would seem to be willing but it was all in vain; he would hear them talk and not be able to say a word against what they propose and yet be capable of standing it out and agreeing to nothing, though he could not but allow it to be reasonable. Such a man is not to be dealt with. All the overtures that you make to him he receives with no other view and design but in hopes of taking some advantage from them without any thought of agreeing or complying. There is one strange circumstance which my aunt told me afterwards. He came to her privately and told her he had lately gone to church and he found so much benefit by it and that their

---

[1] A Mrs. Elizabeth Stancliff was buried in Sikes' vault at Hackney on 26 April 1729.

worship and sermons were immeasurably beyond anything that ever was among the dissenters and desired her to go to church too. Afterwards he took his leave of aunt and sister and so did Caleb his son. Aunt and sister invited him to come and lie at the Hay to-night but his father would not let him.

We went then to visit Mr. Partridge [1] and his wife: we were treated at his lodgings with tea and fruit and chocolate. Thence we went to Mr. Birch's where we were very merry. I think I have now got more into the way of raillery than ever and do it with a better grace. When we were going to return to the Hay the coachman that brought them to Hemstead and went on purpose to fetch them refused to go back with them, it being too hard for his horses that had already been harassed about and were to travel to London to-morrow. This put us into a little hurry and confusion being contrary to our expectation. Father proposed to the coachman to bring us to the foot of the Hay hill and then to send for horses of Richard Clerk [2] to help him uphill, upon which I said he would not be willing to let his horses that had been tired at work in the ground all day go again to labour. My father upon this was very angry with me and expressed it more than I have known him a great while that I should be always contradicting him and finding difficulties to whatever he proposes. The coachman still refused to go and Mr. Birch then offered his horse to carry Aunt Billio and he got another to carry Aunt Lomax behind himself and another man and sister borrowed Mrs. Partridge's horse, so we rode to the Hay and got there very safe. We passed the night pretty merrily. Aunt Billio was extremely troubled with a palpitation of the heart. Went to bed between 11 and 12, having sat up longer than ordinary at picquet with sister.

Wednesday, September 28. Between 10 and 11 father and the commissioners and Mr. Marsh [3] came hither. The commis-

[1] Seth Partridge (1675-1748), a grandson of the famous mathematician of the same name, was a London goldsmith who lived at Hemel Hemstead, where he was buried.

[2] In 1741 a Richard Clarke conveyed the so-called manor of Buers in Boxhamsted.

[3] Mr. Ryder's attorney: probably the Peter Marsh, widower (a solicitor of St. Andrew, Holborn), who married Sarah Edwardes of Hackney on 17 April 1707.

sioners were well pleased with the Hay. We walked about the fields. Saw the well that was just dug to carry off the water from the Red House's cellar, it was 40 foot deep; the price of digging was 6s. a foot. It was to be filled up again so as to be left hollow at the bottom. They therefore filled it with timber and stones.

Went to dinner between 12 and 1. Aunt Lomax had got a very handsome dinner. Mr. Partridge, his daughter and wife came to dinner and some others, so that there was a large table. We spent the afternoon with the ladies. Mrs. Partridge is a pleasant woman in conversation and Mr. Partridge seems to be a very good-humoured man and of good judgement but does not talk much. His daughter is a pretty sprightly girl. Somebody in jest promised her for my wife. Mrs. Partridge said I would not stay for her. I could not help being pleased with the thought of it though all was merely in jest, especially when Aunt Lomax told me she was his only daughter and would be worth perhaps £10,000. We were very merry and we danced, sister, Mrs. Partridge and her daughter, some country dances. She gave us an account of the strange, familiar, extravagant temper of Mr. Moses Roper,[1] how his conversation was the most out of the way familiar, that he is prodigiously noisy and loud and takes all the strange ways of pleasantry and humour that he can think of to make diversion. He is the same man still now he is married, and with these talents he is accounted a man of a very agreeable conversation and good company. They went away at past 7 o'clock in the rain. Our conversation afterwards was but dull and we went to bed between 9 and 10.

Thursday, September 29. Rose past 8. Read some of Boileau. I am more and more pleased with him the more I read him. I find his poetry has a very different air and manner from the usual poetry. It is very much in the style and manner of Juvenal and Horace. His talent lies in a certain familiar way of thinking that makes whatever he says come into the mind with a peculiar kind of delight and pleasure. He does, as it were, give you your own thoughts and reflects the image of your own mind; whatever he says you have it as if it were your own and though you could not express it in so agreeable a manner as he has done, yet now he has once done it for you, you are apt to think you could have

[1] In 1720 the Roper family owned Berkhamstead Place and Park.

done it easily too. Boileau may very well be called witty, but then it is a humorous kind of wit that pleases me immeasurably more than all the lofty, far-fetched turns and high expressions and is a talent the ancients excelled in much beyond the moderns. I never read any poetry in my life please me so well as Boileau's. The humorous, pleasant characters in the *Tatlers, Spectators*, &c., have a being in his works. Indeed therein lies his admirable talent in drawing characters and describing the passions, humours, interests and fancies of mankind in the most natural agreeable light, and perhaps that is the reason why he is so very full of humour : it lies in seeing a thing properly and agreeable to the character and with an air of gaiety rather than in points and turns or lofty sentiments. And when Boileau writes, even to the King himself, he maintains the same character of humour and writes in a familiar style and with an air of gaiety. Indeed his poems are full of good sense more than any of the modern poets and will certainly bear the test of future ages.

Read the beginning of Burnet's *History of the Reformation* in his abridgement.[1] I don't much admire his style, it being too stiff and formal and too apt to run upon the same manner and his periods too long, but his thoughts are very good and the series of affairs that made way for the reception of the Reformation with so much ease are set in a full and proper light, both with respect to the people of England and the prince.

Spent all the day within doors, reading the *History of the Reformation* to the women. Spent the night before bed in drawing out a pattern upon canvas for a pair of shoes for Aunt Billio.

Friday, September 30. Rose before 7 o'clock. We were to go to Mr. Partridge at Hemstead to ride out with him and his family, but I was to get a horse, so sent for Mr. Birch. It came, but was so clumsy and like a cart-horse that father thought it not agreeable to my scarlet cloak and he rode upon him and I upon his mare. We were very merry upon it. Mr. Partridge was our guide. The day was very fine and he led us an extraordinary pleasant way. We rode to Lord Bridgewater's Park and at an house just by the Park we bespoke a dinner. These are some of the most pleasant delicious situations I ever saw, fine green grass with intermixture of little spots of wood and shade that the sun

---

[1] Published in 1682.

has not seen perhaps these hundred years. But the best part of our ride was to the top of a hill about two miles from the Park where there is a prospect of the largest extent I ever saw. And what makes it the most entertaining is that you see not only at a great distance but all the intermediate spaces lie open to your view, that there is nothing to interrupt your sight from the place where you stand to the uttermost extent of your view; you see over Bedfordshire, Oxfordshire, Buckinghamshire and other counties and a great many that lie within the compass of your sight. The Vale that you immediately look into is called Aylesbury Vale. The sheep upon the top of the hill and beneath in the steep valley added to the charmingness of the situation.

We returned to Mr. Greenwood's where we had bespoke a dinner about 2 o'clock. Had a piece of roast beef that was very good for dinner, and between 3 and 4 we went into my Lord's park. Rode about it and viewed the deer that is very plentiful. He has a great many red deer that are of the largest sort.

We went home another way than we came, through some little villages, the worst I have seen in this country. There was a statute[1] in one of them, which is a kind of a fair, but all that was to be seen was a little stall of toys at one of the houses and a few people got together about it. We came first to Hemstead, where we just lighted at Mr. Partridge's, drank some cherry brandy and went home.

Saturday, October 1. The farmers in the country seem to be generally mighty sort of grumbling people that are never contented but always complaining. This is the case of brother's tenants. Father can get no rents from them, though they are more than a year behind, and they are a sort of ungrateful, untractable sort of people; the more you oblige them the more imposing they are, and the more kind the less careful are they to pay their rent. I think a strict hand ought to be kept over them and not too gentle with them as father has been. They especially impose upon their landlords that live a distance from them and are ignorant of the affairs of husbandry.

Set out for London about 10 alone. Dined at Edgware. The landlord there I perceived was one led away by the last ministry but begins to be sensible that they were a set of villains. Had

---

[1] An annual fair where servants were engaged for the coming year.

some talk with him about these affairs and I explained them to him pretty well. There was a Sergeant just come in there to raise recruits. I had a mind to enter into a discourse with him and have his company but did not know how to begin it. Came to London between 3 and 4.

Sunday, October 2. After sermon I invited Madam Crisp and her son, who alone were at the meeting, to come and dine with us, which she did after some persuasion and I and brother went home in her coach. She has a very agreeable way in her discourse, her voice and manner is soft and engaging. I find she intends to make a figure in town at as little charge as possible. She has taken lodgings at London [1] also and her eldest son is to be with her and leave his chambers in the Temple.

Soon after went to prayers, performed but very indifferently. There is one great defect which I observe in my praying, that in it I have rather a regard to the company I am in all the while than to God, the object of my prayer.

Monday, October 3. Rose at between 7 and 8. Read some of Perkins' Law concerning deeds. Spent the rest of the morning at the viol and reading some French *Dialogues des Morts.* Am very well pleased with the humour of them.

Tuesday, October 4. Went to Cousin Watkins. Sat with him an hour, talked of his several courtships. He has made love and proposals of marriage to four several young women within this year and they have all failed. He showed me some letters that he wrote to and received from one of them. I wonder at the assurance he has to make so many attempts after having failed in the former but he has no sooner finished his affair with one but he is engaged in the pursuit of another. One would be apt to believe he thinks the more he courts the greater chance he has for gaining a wife and that it is hard if he does not get one out of so many. How he could find discourse enough to entertain them alone for two or three or four hours together I don't know.

Went from him to see Mr. Bowes between 5 and 6. He at last proposed to play at picquet with me which I agreed to. I was very much vexed with myself that I made some mistakes

[1] In Prince's Street.

that might be taken for designed cheats, but I am apt to think that he was convinced they were mere errors and not designed.¹ Came home. Read *The Chances*,² a comedy. There are now and then some good thoughts in it and the dialogue is natural enough, but there is no distinguishing or remarkable character drawn in the whole play. Went to bed at past 12.

Wednesday, October 5. Went to dinner between 1 and 2, took Molière's plays with me. Read Précieuses Ridicules. I was extremely pleased with character of the *précieuses* which make the whole foundation and design of the play.

Went about 6 to John's. Saw Mr. Jackson, who was reading some of *Tale of a Tub* to Mr. Demodore. I was mightily pleased with the wit and extravagant humour of it but it is too apt to give one a mean ridiculous notion of religion. Mr. Porter is a man of very good sense and talks with an agreeable air. Lent him Mr. Berkeley's *Of Passive Obedience* ³ and Tickell's *Homer* and the *Jew of Venice*,⁴ and he lent me Dr. Clarke's *Scripture Doctrine of the Trinity*.⁵

Thursday, October 6. Read several cases in Coke which I understood well and wrote down. Dined at the Marlborough Head in expectation of seeing Mr. Bowes there but did not. Read Molière's *Cocu Imaginaire*. There is nothing extraordinary at all in that comedy.

At past 8 Mr. Crisp ⁶ asked me to go and sup at an eating-house with him and another. Mr. Crisp is a man that affects to be a polite gentleman and gives himself the air of talking a little loosely. I find the entertainment of this kind of gentleman in conversation one with another is very trifling, a great deal of laughing, a little show of wit and humour, a comical turn to anything that happens, makes up the politeness and chief part of their conversation. Mr. Crisp's chief design and aim seems to be to gain the character of a polite gentleman and endeavour as

¹ The diarist later caught Bowes cheating him.
² Probably in Buckingham's version (first performed 1667) of Beaumont and Fletcher's play.
³ A sermon preached at Trinity College, Dublin, and published in 1712.
⁴ Lord Lansdowne's version, published in 1701, of the *Merchant of Venice*.
⁵ Dr. Samuel Clarke's book, published in 1712, caused great controversy.
⁶ Walter Crisp of Hackney.

much as possible to recommend himself to the ladies, being a man of a very agreeable face and person. Came home past 10. Went to bed at 11.

Friday, October 7. Studied the law all the morning. Remembered the several cases I read by the help of my artificial memory.

Went to the City about five o'clock to father's where I stayed till it was dark looking out for something to make a greatcoat of and did not do it at last. They have a vast trade for riding hoods and must get a great deal of money that way. Went to the play to see the last two acts. Came home and read some of Dr. Clarke's *Scripture Doctrine of the Trinity* and went to bed about 11.

Saturday, October 8. Went in the afternoon to father's after having paid my barber 12s. Came to Hackney with father in the stage coach. There was Mrs. Lacy.[1] She is a woman of good sense, fair spoken, that one would scarce believe what one hears of her horrid covetousness and ill management of her house.

The wine I drank at the tavern has not agreed with me and put me into an uneasy state of mind and nothing pleases me. Wine seems to have a much worse effect upon me than most people, it rather makes me dull and heavy than brisk or cheerful.

Sunday, October 9. Mr. Hudson dined with us upon our invitation. He and I begin to grow pretty familiar. He is a man of good sense, not much politeness, good-humoured. He has thought of going to study at Cambridge instead of serving a clerkship to fit him for the Temple. Advised him rather to go to Holland as a place much more advantageous for study.

Went to meeting in the afternoon, heard Mr. Barker. He has a good style and language and says a great deal that sounds well, but spins out the discourse to a prodigious length that one is in danger of losing his design before you come to the end. He seems to be a man not of much judgement but follows the sentiments and taste of them that went before him.

Brother William is seeking out ways to come at Mrs. Loyd. He went home with her and spoke to her in the morning, and in the afternoon after sermon went in with her and stayed above an hour. I find a particular pleasure within myself when I talk with

[1] Elizabeth, wife of Roger Lacy of Hackney; died in 1741, aged 76.

him about her and would fain find out a method of getting into her company. She is of a free and familiar temper and good sense and I could soon come to be familiar with her too. But I am ashamed to go there to meet with her because my aunt there would soon guess the reason of my frequent coming now, when I used so seldom to come before. However, I will bring it about if possible somehow or other.

Monday, October 10. Rose by 7. Read some of Perkins. I don't receive much benefit from this kind of reading because I cannot remember it nor write it down. After breakfast played upon the viol and flute and then read part of one of the *Prolusions* of Famianus Strada [1] wherein he gives an account of an entertainment made for the Pope by the academy of poetry. It had been a dispute among them which was the best and chief of the ancient Latin poets and they were divided into factions in favour of each of them, one becoming the patron of Ovid, another of Virgil, another of Lucan, another of Claudian, another of Statianus, another of Lucretius. They were now to have a kind of poetic contention or bet in which the patrons of each poet were to compose a copy of verses in imitation of the poet he admired, which were to be pronounced in a great assembly and the merits of each poet judged of by these compositions. The several poems writ in the style of the several ancient poets are there set down and seem indeed to be animated by the several authors which they imitate. Their peculiar excellencies or defects are so well copied that you have in them, as well as in the dissertation itself upon each, a complete and judicious character of each of them. It is very well worth reading over by any one that has a mind to have a clear notion of the distinct manners of writing and thinking of the several Latin poets.

After dinner mother went to see Madam Crisp. I would have gone with her, but my beard was too long and I had not time to get it shaved before she went, so went to see Mr. Powell. After this went to Cousin Billio and went into the house and stayed there till he dressed himself. He was going with me to our house when met Mr. Oldsworth, the parson. He was going to London but was persuaded to stay a while at Shore House, so

---

[1] Famianus Strada : *Prolusiones academicæ oratoriæ, historicæ, poeticæ,* etc., 1617. An edition was published at Oxford in 1631.

went there. He smoked a pipe. Our conversation turned at first upon the controversy about Mr. Barker. I spoke very well upon it in defence of our case.[1]

Tuesday, October 11. I had a great mind to ask my mother whether she had observed that my breath smelt strong but could not tell how to bring it out. Went to London with Cousin Billio. Our conversation was upon very indifferent subjects. Went home, got shaved and after having read Pope's *Essay on Criticism*, which is mighty well done, came back to father's where I asked father for some money. I expected to have found him speaking uneasily about his want of money, but instead of that he was mighty ready to give me money and perfectly good-humoured. I could not but be very sensibly pleased with it. He gave me 7 guineas.

Went from thence to Cousin Watkins, where sat an hour talking with him. He had this morning finished another courtship. The lady's mother would not consent because she thought her daughter too young to enter upon that state. He was recommended to the lady by some friends of his. He saw her as it were by chance, wrote to the mother his design and desired leave to wait upon her daughter.

Read a pamphlet, *Advice to the Tories who have taken the oaths.* I hear it is writ by Mr. Berkeley: it is not unlike him, it is writ with great freedom and ardour.[2] Read several *Spectators* from the beginning, having a design to read them all over again to improve my style and manner of thinking. I am well pleased with the characters he gives of the persons concerned in the club. Went to bed at 12.

Wednesday, October 12. Went to John's. Met our friends there. Mr. Porter gave me a letter he intended to write to me about Mr. Berkeley's notions.

Mr. Porter told us two remarkable things that happened in the illness of his sister of which she died. A little before she died Mr. Porter went just across the way to a friend. They asked him how she did and were drinking punch and desired him to give her a glass of punch. He went presently from them to his sister. She

---

[1] The Ryders were strong anti-Barkerites.
[2] This pamphlet, published in 1715, is still ascribed to George Berkeley.

had been asleep and waked as he came into the chamber. He asked her how she did. She answered 'very ill, but', says she, 'I have had a dream. What do you think I dreamt? I dreamt I was over the way (at the place where he had been) and they asked me to drink a glass of punch, and,' says she, 'give me some'. He told her it was not proper but was extremely surprised at it and she died in a few hours after. I verily believe the thing to be true; he is a person of admirable good sense and not in the least given to superstition or anything like it. Another thing happened also. The servant-maid came down in the morning and as she came into the kitchen saw the jack going very fast and stood still presently after she came in, all of itself. His brother and sister both of them saw it and very extremely surprised at it. A young physician that was there saw it; another did the same. He endeavoured all the while to ridicule it, and the morning on which his sister died, the jack and weights and ropes all at once broke and fell down in pieces, and now two or three days ago in his father's house both his father and mother saw their jack going and nothing to set it in motion, the weight lying on the ground which they went to see on purpose.

Thursday, October 13. Cousin Watkins and Mr. Opie [1] came to breakfast with me and after them Mr. Whatley came also. I was in a little hurry and confusion how to provide tea and bread and butter for so many. Went out with them at 11 o'clock to hear one Mr. Spering, a friend of Cousin Watkins, sing and play upon the harpsichord at the tavern, which we did at the Temple Tavern. I went after we parted to Mr. Loveits to buy a sword, which I did, a silver-gilt one for £3 4s., without the blade. My old one came to 4½ ounces of silver, which made £1 4s. 9d. at 5s. 6d. per ounce.

Friday, October 14. Thought of Mr. Porter's objections against Mr. Berkeley's principles. Began to write a letter but was not perfectly clear in my own mind and so did not go on with it. My mind is mighty apt to wander and forget itself or when a thought comes into my head I sometimes lose it again immediately by a sudden interruption, and indeed it is difficult to recover it again and be where I was.

Went after dinner to Aunt Bickley with a design to see Mrs.

[1] Mr. Opie: cf. note, p. 353.

Loyd and go from thence to London. Found only she and Aunt Bickley at home. I said a great many good, witty, handsome things to her, besides a great deal of good sense in more serious matters. We sat in the kitchen all the while.

Read several *Spectators*. There is a great deal of good sense shown in just reflections and observations upon the passions, tempers, follies, and vices of mankind. One of them was to expose the very trifling affections and inclinations of the fair sex, that are affected chiefly with outside of persons and distinguish them rather by their equipage, habits, &c., than the solid virtues of the mind and endowments of the understanding. I cannot but observe how much I am myself touched with external show; having a new sword on I could not help looking at it several times with a peculiar kind of pleasure. Sometimes it has made me uneasy to think that it was not so handsome as it might have been, that the carving is not well done. I am vexed with myself to find that my mind is too apt to be affected with such trifles.

Saturday, October 15. Between 11 and 12 Mr. Spering came to me. He sung some songs. I begin to be afraid he will be a little troublesome in his visits by coming too often in the morning. Went to Hackney. Intended to have gone to Aunt Bickley's to have carried some sal volatile to her in hopes of seeing Mrs. Loyd, but it rained and I did not. Came hither. I played a little upon the viol.

Sunday, October 16. Cousin Watkins dined with us. I had the toothache by reason of a hollow tooth that was wore so low as to touch the nerve. The pain is intolerable when anything touches it hard. I am fain therefore to be exceeding cautious how I eat on that side of my mouth. Cousin Watkins says the nerve may be seared and that will take away the pain entirely—as well as pulling it out. Brother had been at Aunt Bickley's. Mrs. Loyd asked him why I did not come. He told her I was bashful. She said she would tell me of it and seemed to like my company. It pleased me exceedingly to hear it.

The fear of the toothache made me mightily disposed at supper to be angry and fretful, every little thing that was done raised my anger, but I had prudence not in the least to show it.

Monday, October 17. Saw Mr. Ichabod Gould and Hudson and invited them to drink a dish of tea with me, which they did and I played my viol a little and he played some tunes upon the flute, though but indifferently. Our conversation was tolerable. They went about 5 and Cousin Joseph Billio came. We played together some sonatas upon the flute and viol and then I went to the coffee-house.

Tuesday, October 18. Read some *Spectators*. I observed the method in which every *Spectator* almost was writ. The discourse began with a little reflection in general and then, by pretty agreeable translations, the general proposition is illustrated by particulars which commonly extend to a considerable length. The art is to give them a pleasant humorous turn.

Went to dinner, then to Mr. Cynelum's. Had a lesson upon the viol. A great difficulty I find in that instrument is to draw a soft and fine note. Then to Uncle Marshall's. All at home but uncle himself. Our conversation turned a little upon news, but we had no disputing; things are now set in so glaring and full a light that they cannot tell what to say now to palliate them without harsh reflections upon the King, so that kind of discourse soon dropped. Cousin Marshall said he heard Cousin Allen [1] was going to be married. It struck me very sensibly, though I have no thoughts or inclination to have her myself, but because I have entertained a love and kindness for her that makes me so sensibly touched at the thoughts of her marrying another.

Wednesday, October 19. Dined at brother's. From thence with Mr. Samson and another to Stepney to see Mr. Warren. When came there, there was Sir Thomas Robet and several ladies. Mr. Warren is mighty thin and declining.[2] Sir Thomas came again in his nightgown and cap. He seems to be a man of a plain rustic kind of familiarity, pretty merry and laughs with the ladies.

We went to the club. There was Mr. Isles. He is a man that talks very smoothly and agreeably, tells a story well and makes a very good figure in ordinary conversation and is an agreeable companion. The rest of our company are men of very good

---

[1] Cousin Mary Allen, the daughter of Aunt Allen of Gresley.
[2] His death not long afterwards was ascribed to thwarted love (cf. p. 360).

sense and I don't know a set of young men that entertain themselves better and in a more improving manner for the generality. Mimicry is a most useful talent in this kind of conversation and a person that can repeat particularly what others have said upon particular occasions and imitate their manners never fails to be what the world generally calls good company.

Thursday, October 20. Went to brother's at 4. There were several ladies to see the procession of figures of the Pope, the Devil and the Pretender which were expected to be burnt. There was a great mob about the streets and much holloing for King George. It pleased me exceedingly well. The streets rang with huzzas for the King, but I could not but feel a great displeasure when I heard once a hiss mixed with the shoutings. The society of young men at the Roebuck [1] had prepared the effigies of the Pope, Devil and Pretender and some others to be carried in procession, but the Tories had spread about a malicious report that they intended to burn the Queen. It was therefore thought advisable not to prosecute that design, but they made a vast large bonfire over against Bow Church and burnt some images there with a prodigious crowd of people that were continually crying ' God bless King George ' and drank his and all the royal family's health. The streets were very well illuminated. I went home with Madam Crisp to her new lodgings in Prince's Street. She would have paid the coachman but I would not let her.

Read the 38th *Spectator*, was extremely pleased because I felt everything I read [in] it was designed against the fault that I find myself extremely guilty of, and that is a too great desire and love of applause in things which are in themselves the least commendable. I have continually a desire of pleasing in my eye and this gives birth and life to every pursuit or engagement, whatever I do carries an air of affectation along with it.

Read some other *Spectators* that please mighty well. I cannot but observe in what I have now read that the genius of Steele and Addison appears very distinct in them. There are several of the *Spectators* I have now read writ by Addison concerning tragedy, wherein he shows a great delicacy of taste and just relish of nature in its noblest and most exalted parts. He seems to be a man of a

[1] The Roebuck Tavern in Cheapside was the headquarters of the Williamite Club.

more serious temper and more elevated genius and higher thought than Steele and of a mind much more refined and improved with learning and knowledge of the ancients. Steele's character appears too in what I have now read. Those that are writ by him, as I discover by the letters at the end of each, are all of them upon lower subjects, generally upon the several characters of human life, remarks upon the behaviour of men in the world. His talent lies in a knowledge of the polite part of mankind, a perfect acquaintance with their humours and interests and designs, sees through the little arts and disguises that men put upon themselves and has a happy talent of putting them into a ridiculous and diverting light. Went to bed at past 12.

Friday, October 21. Father hears that Cousin Mary Allen is going to be married, I believe to him whom Aunt Stevenson calls by the name of Don Cholerick. Thought of writing a poem upon her marriage as an Epithalamium. Went to bed between 11 and 12.

Saturday, October 22. In Moorfields bought some pastorals by Fontenelle.[1] I remember Boileau gives him the character of writing very naturally in a simple, easy, natural style just as becomes the simplicity of shepherds, and I was very well pleased with some of these simple thoughts that I observed in his Eclogues.

After dinner went to Aunt Bickley's. They were all at home up one pair of stairs. Mrs. Loyd did not come in here because she was with her writing-master and I had not the assurance to ask where she was all the while lest it should be thought I came on purpose for her company. Unless I can have her company alone or with none but young ladies there is no manner of pleasure in it among Aunt Bickley and Lewis. So I left them about 5 and came very much vexed with myself for the awkwardness of my behaviour. It put me into an uneasy posture of mind just as if I had the vapours.

Played upon the viol. Did nothing all night but this and read some of Fontenelle's *Eclogues*. I think I never heard a more agreeable, simple, natural, beautiful thought than what he has in

[1] *Poésies Pastorales*, 1688, with a Discours sur la nature de l'églogue, by Bernard le Bovier de Fontenelle. They are indifferent specimens of the genre.

his second *Eclogue*. Speaking of the conversation between two lovers he makes one of his shepherds say to the other :

> Cieux ! quel discours charmans Silvanire entendit
> Devine les, Atis, toi qui scais comme on aime.

Sunday, October 23. Went after sermon with Cousin Joseph to Aunt Billio. He was telling me of the happy marriage of Mr. Borrett and his wife. She is a woman of the greatest prudence imaginable and of the strongest love and affection for him. Whatever he says and does makes a part of her happiness. The thought of him makes her neglect every other gratification whenever it comes in competition with him. He says he is sure if Steele or Addison had lived among them so long as he has done they would have wrote finer and given us a more complete perfect picture of that state than they have done. Where such a couple as these are met matrimony is certainly the happiest state of nature. But such a pair are, I believe, very scarce to be found. Prudence and discretion and good nature are qualities absolutely necessary to make that state completely happy, but these are seldom to be found among the female sex.

Monday, October 24. After dinner read some of Fontenelle's *Eclogues* and his discourse concerning the Eclogue. His *Eclogues* have every now and then some easy natural thoughts becoming the simplicity of a shepherd's life and pastoral, but sometimes too refined and has too much reflection.

Met Cousin Billio and Mr. Powell at coffee-house and went with them to the tavern. He told us of a duel that Mr. Dixon [1] fought, he and another, with two officers upon the occasion of their being cheated by them at cards. Dixon disarmed his man, but his friend was wounded by the other. We came at last to talk of love and gallantry. He is, I perceive, a man mightily inclined to that pleasure. He has got this turn of mind from a gay conversation with the gentlemen of Oxford and the young sparks about town. I must confess my own heart joined in with him extremely when he talked of the conversation with the ladies and the pleasure of their company and I began to resolve to apply myself more to the qualifying myself more for this kind

[1] A Mr. Henry Dixon was sidesman at Hackney in 1714.

of talk, and when he talked of dancing I had a strong inclination to improve myself in that qualification. I cannot but observe how apt I am to envy them that are successful in their address to the ladies and meet with acceptance among them, and yet it is but a foolish humour of mine.

Tuesday, October 25. Went to London in the 7 o'clock coach with mother, and Mr. Flemming.[1] He entertained us with several stories relating to public affairs and so is very good company especially for a stage coach. He told one story which I was very well pleased with, as it discovered the little tricks and evasions of the Tories. In Queen Anne's time, a knight came to dine with a friend of his in the city. The citizen was a Whig but the other a violent Tory. As they were talking of public affairs, says the knight to the other, ' It is none but you Whigs would bring in the Pretender.' The citizen, who suspected a fallacy in the word ' Pretender ', ' Sir John,' says he, ' tell me upon your honour and the word of a gentleman, who is it you really mean by the Pretender ? ' Upon this the knight answered, ' Since you put me to it, I will tell you, and I say Hanover and none else is the Pretender.'

Brother William came in and told me Mrs. Loyd had been last week in town at the Amsterdam Coffee-House[2] and lay there several nights without the knowledge of Aunt Bickley's family ; that she had been at the play in company of a cabinet-maker and wondered how she could condescend so low as to keep such company.

Came into the coffee-house where were Mr. Jackson and some others. We talked of more common affairs, but particularly of the beauty of Milton's poetry. I intend to buy a volume of his miscellaneous poetry in 12mo.

Wednesday, October 26. Dined at Temple Chop-House, where fell into a little discourse with a couple of men in the same room. The occasion of it was a strange kind of a story which was telling to them as I came in, which I asked of. However, we fell at last into some talk about politics and one of them I soon found was a

---

[1] Mr. Robert Flemming, a Scotch dissenting preacher at Founder's Hall, Lothbury ; died at Hackney, 24 May 1716.

[2] In Swithin's Alley, near the Royal Exchange.

Jacobite but I pressed him with the consequences of the Pretender's coming and also the very great improbability of his succeeding in his design. He had very little to say for himself but what was evidently nothing to the purpose. I was not at all displeased with myself for what I said upon this occasion, but I cannot but observe that I am not very fit to talk seriously to a Jacobite upon these affairs. I am too apt to be worked up into a kind of heat that makes me tremble all over and makes me speak with too much warmth and eagerness.

Thursday, October 27. Went to Mr. Samson to go with him to Westminster. Went with him to coffee-house where got two more and went in a coach. Walked about the hall, met young Defoe. Walked with him a little. Went into the court. Heard some motions, but little done. Came home on foot. Was at home all the afternoon till 7 o'clock. Read *Spectators* and play of Molière, *L'Escole des Maris*. It is very good.

Read some *Spectators* and then some letters of Voiture. He has a most agreeable turn of thoughts; a pleasant witty raillery is the talent the best in the world for writing letters.

Friday, October 28. Went to Westminster. Called upon Mr. Whatley in the way. We went together to my lodgings. Our conversation turned chiefly upon an amour that he has been lately engaged in. He was mightily taken with the lady where he lodged and she gave him reason to believe that she was no less pleased with him. In about a fortnight's time he thought fit to make a declaration of his love, which he did one afternoon when he was playing with her at picquet. She received his declaration with a sudden confusion and disorder that seemed to proceed from her affection to him. Her answer to him was such as gave him great hopes that he was not unacceptable, and a thousand tender things passed between them on her as well as his side. He at first told her frankly his own circumstances and that she could not expect much splendour or addition to her fortune by him. She made that no objection but still gave him hopes. She told him also her own fortune, that she had £500 year jointure. She told him also of a gentleman that made his address to her of a considerable fortune, better than her own, but that she had no design to have him. At length after several endearments had passed between them, when he one day pressed her to know whether he was to be happy or no, she told him suddenly and with a kind of a frown she wondered what should make him think of such a thing. This put into a great confusion and he answered: 'What, Madam, after what has passed between you and I!' This stuck with her and vexed her. He could not tell how to bear such an answer and he wrote to her several letters upon it and she began to look more kind upon him and treat him in a more loving manner, but every now and then took occasion to mention her own imprudence in her behaviour towards him but still gave him hopes, for though upon his still pressing her she used to tell him that it could come to nothing and that she would give him his letters, she never sent them him, which made him believe he was not quite forsaken neither. However, after he could get nothing certain out of her he began to think she had indeed quite cast off all thought of marrying him. He began to treat her in a colder manner, he wrote a letter to her and let her know that he was neither such a fool to be deceived by her kind of treatment nor so weak as not to let her know that he was sensible of it. After she had read it she came into his chamber and threw it down to him upon the ground. This was the finishing of this amour, for it was now grown to such a heat that they could not both be together in the same house, and Mr. Whatley left the lodgings, as she happened to do also soon after. He was very much perplexed with this amour. It was upon the account of the project of marrying her that he had resolved to study the law again, but this failing he has now resolved to lay it aside and apply himself to the public affairs and he is now seeking out for some place or other.

Went to brother's. There were Mrs. Loyd and Cousin Ryder. I was agreeably surprised to find them there and I entertained them pretty agreeably in conversation. We went at last to cards. I had a great many kisses of Mrs. Loyd and said a great many soft things to her, that I believe she is not displeased with my company. I invited her to breakfast with me to-morrow morning, which they promised.

Saturday, October 29. Rose between 6 and 7. Was in some little concern about the providing for the breakfast of the ladies that were to come to see me. I was not so brisk and gay and full of spirit now as I was last night. However, I was pretty tolerably good company. Lent Mrs. Loyd the 6th volume of miscellany poems and Steele's plays and two other plays.

Went to brother's upon the account of the ladies that were to come there than from any desire of seeing my Lord Mayor's show which was to-day. I was very merry and pleasant company to the ladies who were indeed very few at brother's. I said a great many prettinesses and humorous things that were gay and airy and savoured of a gay turn of fancy. Mrs. Loyd was not there till afternoon. When she came in I was mightily employed in conversing with her, was continually talking to her and taking opportunities of kissing her.

The show was but indifferent but we were continually backwards and forwards in the balcony and I generally followed Mrs. Loyd in her motions.

I then went to Skinners' Hall [1] where I got some good victuals. From thence to Plumbers' Hall [2] where I was told there was dancing. I went into the hall and the company seemed to be so very mean that I left and went to Ironmongers' Hall.[3] The porter would not let me in at first, but as I appeared like a gentleman and told them plainly I came only to dance they let me in. The hall was extremely crowded and it was so filled with dancers of country dances that it was a long time before I could get room to make one among them. One of the gentlemen had a very pretty lady that had the most engaging countenance I almost ever saw. I regretted it extremely that I did not take her for my partner when I had the first opportunity. However, I kept near her and had the pleasure of talking with her and looking upon her. I believe, though, she was a little coquettish by her manner of treating me, sometimes with a very seeming kindness, at other times looking with a frown. I must confess it made me uneasy when she looked unpleased at me and I could not help suspecting almost every gesture of hers as a reflection upon me. That is the great unhappiness of my temper, that I am too apt in the affair of love and woman to construe everything done by her I love to my prejudice. I behaved myself in dancing pretty tolerably and was not sensible of any considerable ungenteel, unpolite manner till the last dance which was *The Briton*, where a minuet step comes

---

[1] Dowgate Hill. [2] Chequer Yard (now Cannon Street Station).
[3] Fenchurch Street.

in unlikely that I could not do with that air and freedom that I did the rest and made me think that everyone looked upon me as a clumsy dancer. Both the dancing-places were so prodigiously crowded that it was scarce possible to dance in order and without confusion. However, the company grew thinner about 9 o'clock and we were glad we had room enough. We were now preparing to be set in for it till at least midnight and the musicians had gathered our shillings apiece to recompense them for their pains but at 10 o'clock the master sends word to the musicians to play no more and we were forced to break off. The gentlemen and ladies especially were extremely affronted at it as they are generally the most forward in this kind of exercise. Came home between 10 and 11. Went to bed at 12.

Monday, October 31. Rose at 7. Began to read Cicero's Philippic oration against Anthony. Cannot but observe in it that Cicero in answering the objection that Anthony had before made to him he dwells with a peculiar pleasure and satisfaction upon his own history and his glorious actions in the affair of Catiline and other parts of his life.

At 12 Cousin Dudley Ryder came. Went with him to Aunt Billio. When he was gone aunt asked me whether I had any design to marry Mrs. Lee. When I told her no, she said she was sure Mrs. Lee herself had thoughts of it and indeed I am apt to think so myself and shall therefore take care to avoid her company.

Tuesday, November 1. Rose past 7. Read some Cicero's Philippic oration. Played upon the viol. Went to coffeehouse, saw Mr. Crisp. I am not yet got over that foolish bashfulness that I have upon seeing him. Went to the play into the side-box. Stayed the first Act. Then to the new playhouse,[1] into the side-box, where stayed the first Act. Supped at the Gill House. Came home at 8. Read part of Molière's comedy *l'Escole des Femmes*. To bed at 10, being sleepy. It is to no purpose to come soon because I am apt to fall asleep.

Wednesday, November 2. Met young Defoe. Walked with him, talked about public affairs. He is a talkative sort of young

---

[1] The rebuilt theatre in Lincoln's Inn Fields, opened on 18 November 1714, under the managership of John Rich.

fellow, tells a story tolerably but does not seem to have very good sense, seems to be mighty superficial and talks the notions he has had from his father. Talking of Mr. Leeds, he said he thought he would never make much of it at the Bar, he might do well for a country gentleman but could not talk well enough to appear anything considerable at the Bar. Though I have no great opinion of Defoe's judgement yet I cannot help observing it immediately lessened my opinion of Mr. Leeds. I find I am very apt to join in with the sentiments of others concerning persons' characters.

Went to our club at Sue's. Dr. Avery,[1] Mr. Leeds, &c., were there. I was very well pleased with what Dr. Avery told us concerning the proceedings of Convocation. They have been lately engaged in the drawing up a form of prayer for the consideration of churches. The lower house made a motion that since there was none yet appointed it would be proper for the sake of uniformity of the Church. There might be one established whereas the bishops used before to make the prayer *pro re nata* as they pleased. The upper house of Convocation was against it and thought it a thing unnecessary. However, the lower house pressed it still upon them. A conference was appointed and Dr. Willis,[2] bishop of Gloucester, was to manage it on the side of the upper house when the lower house would not be contented to lay aside their design. Both houses were to draw up each a form and Dr. Willis drew up one which was communicated and it began in this manner, ' Almighty God, who has promised that where two or three are met together in Thy name there Thou wilt be among them and bless them,' &c. The lower house did by no means like this and said this was what would agree to any other meeting of Christians as well as their own and they would have something that should be peculiar to the Church of England. The bishop said he thought as they were the words of Scripture they were sound, but that would not do, and after a considerable time of deliberation they brought an amendment to it : ' Almighty God, who hast promised that where two or three are gathered together in Thy name in the place set apart and

---

[1] Benjamin Avery, LL.D. (d. 1764), assistant minister at Bartholomew Close, Smithfield. In 1720 took up medicine and became Treasurer of Guy's Hospital. He edited *The Old Whig Weekly* from 1735 until 1738.

[2] Richard Willis (1664-1734).

consecrated to Thy worship,' &c. The bishop was very much displeased with this amendment and told them it was very strange that the plain words of Scripture could not be used without their glosses and interpretation upon it, so the lower house set about making a form themselves which began thus : ' Almighty God, help us to take heed to our feet while we stand in Thy holy place,' &c. When this came before the upper house, Dr. Willis was still worse displeased with this than they could be with his and told them it was true this had some foundation in Scripture and he supposed they alluded to that place in the Old Testament where Moses is commanded to pull off the shoes off his feet, for the place where thou standest is holy ground. But, says he, ' I perceive you have not kept close to the text. I think if you would make use of this Scripture it would be proper to use the Scripture language and say, " Lord, help us to pull off our shoes off our feet while we stand in Thy holy place," but,' says he, ' to be serious, I am astonished and ashamed to find so many of your coat doing all you can to bring in all the superstitious rights and forms you can. I suppose the next thing will be to have a garment consecrated, too, and the Bible itself must not be read till it has had a sacerdotal benediction given it.' The lower house were confounded at this and so the matter has dropped.

Thursday, November 3. Mr. Leeds came to me at 8 and breakfasted with me. He is a man of not much spirit or vivacity and unfit to keep up the spirit of a conversation. At 10 went with him to Westminster, intending to go to the Exchequer where the Sheriffs were to be pricked, but that not being to be done till 1 we came back without doing anything at all, only in the meantime as I stood at the bookseller's shop in the hall I read some part of the *Persian Tales*. They are very entertaining and apt to lead one on insensibly till it is not without a great deal of reluctance that one breaks off reading, the story being continued through a variety of other stories or episodes, if I may call them so, which continue one's expectation and make one a little uneasy to get to the end of the original one.

Went into the glass warehouse over the New Exchange.[1] There is indeed a noble collection of looking-glass, the finest I

[1] A kind of bazaar in the Strand ; pulled down in 1737.

believe in Europe. I could not as I passed by there help observing myself, particularly my manner of walking, and that pleased me very well, for I thought I did it with a very genteel and becoming air.

Came home; went to dinner. Thence to father's to get a nightgown. When I looked upon silk satin to make one of my father was displeased at it and would have me have a calimanco. I did not like that and so let it alone. Went to my barber to be shaved. Received a letter from Aunt Stevenson. She writes very carelessly and sometimes obscurely that I don't well know what she means.

It is thought now very commonly and not without good reason that the Duke of Ormonde was in the ship that appeared at Torbay and sent letters on shore, but not finding things answer his expectation went back for France. The rebels in the North do nothing considerable and have yet gained no success. Went to bed at 11.

Friday, November 4. In the afternoon went to Aunt Bickley's to beg the favour of cousin and Mrs. Loyd's company to-night. There was Mrs. Hiot. She talks very agreeably and with an air of gravity and seriousness, without anything of that light kind of raillery that is frequent with your polite ladies. Went while the young ladies dressed themselves to Aunt Billio's where sister was, and to Mrs. Sikes. Mrs. Betty was not well. I bantered her pretty tolerably upon her having the vapours, &c. Went back to Aunt Bickley's, but the young ladies had taken the opportunity of the fine weather and were gone before. I came home, found them and was very agreeably entertained with them. We then went to cards, during which time I sat next to Mrs. Loyd, with whom I talked and even kissed her every now and then, that I was agreeably entertained. But as for the cards I did not much mind them but did not lose anything all the while, though we were at it till almost 12 o'clock before and after supper. When we had done cards and were going to bed I was a little sweet upon her and would have had her stayed a little longer. This I perceive gave offence to sister and Cousin Ryder, that they told us I should lie with Mrs. Loyd and spoke in a way that showed they were offended at the particular address I made to Mrs. Loyd. It seemed to me to be effects of mere envy.

Saturday, November 5. Heard Mr. Newcome. He preached a sermon full of Whiggish sentiments and expressions of charity and forbearance towards his dissenting brothers. He is very much altered since the death of the Queen, in whose time he was beginning to show himself a Tory.

Called at the coffee-house, where a gentleman brought word from London that an express from the North had brought word that Major-General Carpenter[1] had come up with the rebels and gained a very admirable victory over them. This is not certain but not improbable.

Went to my closet, read the history of one Psalmanazar,[2] a native of the island of Formosa. He gives an account of the methods the Jesuits took to convert him, but all their answers had no effect upon him till he at last fell into the hands of an English divine who convinced him of the truth of the Christian religion and made him an entire Protestant. Went to bed at 11.

Sunday, November 6. I was in a very ill humour all this evening, everything that was said or done almost disposed me to be angry though I had more prudence than to give it vent. I cannot but be concerned that I have such a disposition which may grow up in time if not checked to be very ill humour and make me extremely troublesome to all about me when I become the head of a family. While I was in bed remembered that I had left my sword below in the parlour. It made me uneasy all night and dream of it for fear that thieves should come in and take it away. I am concerned at this solicitous temper of mine, I am afraid it should grow upon me with age, and if it should riches and wealth will be always a burden to me for fear of losing them.

Monday, November 7. Rose past 7. Read Cicero's 3rd oration against Catiline. He is here the same man he always appears to be, greedy of glory and full of himself.

[1] George Carpenter (1657–1732), general of the Government forces which crushed the rebellion at Preston.

[2] George Psalmanazar was the pseudonym of a literary adventurer who died in London in 1763. In Germany he passed as a Japanese, living on raw food and speaking a language of his own invention. When he came to England in 1703 this language became Formosan. His *Historical and Geographical Description of Formosa*, translated from his Latin by Mr. Oswald, was published in 1704. This contains remarkable details of the 'Formosan' religion and customs. Even scholars were imposed upon for some years, but by 1708 he became a butt.

Read the account of the island of Formosa. They used to sacrifice a great number of young children, one 9 years old every year to their god. They worshipped the sun and moon but only as inferior deities in subjection to the superior one. Their laws were exceeding strict. Adulteries for the second offence were punished with death, but a man was allowed to have as many wives as he could maintain which was to be judged of by an officer appointed for that purpose.

After dinner went to Mr. Powell's. Cousin Joseph Billio was with us. The best part of our conversation was concerning the University of Oxford. As for the public lectures, he says nobody regards them, they are all looked upon as mere useless things and rather for form's sake than for any profit that the students gain by them, and as for the private lectures by the tutors, they are very little more profitable. His tutor indeed had private lectures to him in which he went through the book of logic and ethics, but he did not much regard them and they are little observed. So that they seem indeed to have no advantages for study there above any other place, and the young men go there rather for the sake of its having been said they have been at the University than for any advantages to improve them in knowledge.

Tuesday, November 8. Was just going to Westminster and Mr. Fernley [1] came to see me, which kept me at home to entertain him with tea, which I did. He is a man of good common sense but has nothing of learning or politeness, very ignorant of the affairs of the nation and knows very little of what is doing abroad. He is an honest, well-meaning man, but I believe was led away with the cry of the Church so that he was a favourer of the Tories but begins to see through it and is I believe heartily for King George. It is reported that the rebels are come into Lancaster. The English of them are certainly come back from Scotland into England again and marching towards Lancashire. Major-General Carpenter is pursuing them. To bed at 11.

Wednesday, November 9. Found myself out of order, a general stiffness all over me and a cough. Went to Westminster. Heard several trials there and by what I observed of them that spoke in the affair of the riot, in which there was little but good natural

[1] His dancing-master.

sense and parts to be shown, I could make as much of a case as any of them myself.

Read some of the translations of Horace's *Odes*; got some of the verses that pleased me by heart. My cold increased, I was stiff and sore all over me, and my cough was very troublesome. Went to bed and took some fever water with a design to sweat but did not.

Thursday, November 10. Rose at 9. Found my cold worse than last night. This is my birthday. Had nothing of rejoicing upon it. I was apprehensive my cold would touch my lungs. I read Horace's *Art of Poetry* by Lord Roscommon. It is a very exact translation and surprising he could find such good English language to express his thoughts in so few words. I could not help upon this occasion remembering a translation of my own when I was at school of some of the beginning of the *10th Satire* of Juvenal, which upon reflection I wonder I was able to make then, and I think very good now. It is this:

> From East to West, from Gades to Ganges streams,
> Scarce one among a thousand can be found
> Whose whole informed judgement does direct
> His will to choose what's good and scorn what's bad.
> For what's the cause of all our hopes and fears,
> Our love and hate, but groundless rash conceit?
> For when thou hast gained thy long-desirèd end
> And with success thy greedy cares are crowned,
> Then something often damps thy joy and makes
> All thy success thy disappointment prove.
> The gods themselves, that men might see their pride
> And by experience learn to ask advice,
> Have foolish men that hateful things desired
> By their too kind indulgence oft destroyed.

I have forgot the rest.

Brother came hither to-night. Played at cards. Was in a very peevish, angry humour that everything that occurred made my blood rise within me and though I was at the same time sensible that I was in the wrong and reflected upon it, I found it very difficult to restrain this temper and curb myself. My cold is very ill and I intend to sweat to-night by the help of fever water and a great many clothes upon me. Went to bed at past 10.

Friday, November 11. Sweated a little in the night. Was hoarse in the morning and it still continued to affect my head, that a little motion is apt to make it ache. Went to Mrs. Hudson with mother and sister to breakfast. Drinking tea and eating made my voice clearer. The conversation turned entirely upon the manners, behaviour, way of living, clothes, dress, &c., of their neighbours and though at the same time they were blaming others for prying into the secrets of families and talking about others.

Mrs. Henry and Mrs. Bunkley and Cousin Billio and his wife dined with us. We had a pretty handsome dinner. Went at night to coffee-house. The rebels out of Northumberland joined with some Highlanders, in all about 1,500, are come as far as Lancaster; make very great journies. Our troops under Major-General Wills are assembling at Warrington to oppose them and General Carpenter is pursuing them. The papists in Lancashire don't rise much to join them as was expected.[1]

Came home. My cold was ill and affected my head, making it giddy. Went to bed at 10 without supper, but drank some buttered ale.

Saturday, November 12. Rose between 8 and 9. Had a pretty good rest. Find my cold something better, but my nose runs and my eyes. At 10 o'clock Mrs. Borrett and Cousin Joseph Billio came to breakfast with sister. Mrs. Borrett is a very agreeable woman. Cousin Billio had all the discourse on his side which he carried on just in his usual way, saying what comes next without thought or consideration whether it is fit or proper to be said.

[1] On 22 October at Kelso, Mar, with 4,000 men, joined the rebels from Northumberland (under Thomas Forster, Lord Widdrington and the Earl of Derwentwater) and Galloway (under the Earls of Kenmure, Carnwath, Nithsdale and Wintoun). On 1 November the combined force, now about 2,000 and commanded by Forster, entered England. At Penrith a large force of militia under Lord Lonsdale fled before them. At Preston, which they entered on 9 November, they were joined by the first substantial reinforcement, about 200 Catholic gentlemen. On the 11th Major-General Sir Charles Wills arrived at Wigan in command of Preston's foot regiment and the cavalry regiments styled Pitt's, Wynne's, Dormer's, Stanhope's and Honeywood's. Next day he advanced to Preston, but withdrew his attack on meeting stubborn resistance. On the 13th he was joined by his superior, Carpenter, with three regiments of horse who had been pursuing the rebels from Jedburgh.

After dinner read Cicero's 1st oration against Catiline. I could not but observe what a difference there is between our present kind of oratory at the Bar and Cicero's. The Roman often makes use of rhetoric, brings in his country speaking, &c., whereas nothing of that nature would be tolerable at our Bar and a man would be laughed at and ridiculed that should make use of such a figure. We are much more plain and simple than the Romans, but then the pulpit oratory comes up much nearer to the Roman. There these kind of figures may be made use of with credit.

Sunday, November 13. Father came to Hackney. He told me three men from Oxford were to be tried to-morrow for high treason at the King's Bench and therefore I went to London after sermon. Came to brother's. There was Mr. Owen [1] of Warrington. I was very well pleased with our conversation. He is a brisk active man and is hated very much by the Tories in that country who do all they can to hurt him, his wife and brother, that are gone from Warrington for fear of the rebels. The rebels are now at Lancaster where the mayor and aldermen, when the rebels came towards the town, met them in their robes and when they came in proclaimed the Pretender at the market in formality. He says that when the rebels were coming towards Penrith there were gathered together upon the plain before the town 8,000 of the militia and volunteers with my Lord Lonsdale at the head of them to oppose them and the rebels sent out three men before them who came unsuspected among the militia and heard what they said among themselves and then came where my Lord Lonsdale and others of the officers were consulting what to do and heard them determine not to fight. So that they went back and told the rebels what they heard and they came up. First 400 horse with trumpets before them. Then came 300 Highlanders with the bagpipes before them, then another body of 400 horse as before, and then a body of 300 Highlanders as before. Upon this approach the militia all fled immediately and the rebels came into the town and plundered my lord's house there. I stayed and supped with brother.

---

[1] Charles Owen (d. 1746), Presbyterian Minister at Cairo Street Chapel, Warrington. He was one of the stalwarts of the Hanoverian cause in the North and published a number of anti-Jacobite pamphlets.

Monday, November 14. Went to Westminster at between 8 and 9. Read Mr. Young's poem upon the last day [1] in the court during the time of swearing. There are some good things in it but the style is a little upon the bombast and the thoughts very affected and stiff. He seems indeed to have strained his wit and genius to its uttermost reach and drawn it dry. I don't admire the poem at all. Three men from Oxford were arraigned at the King's Bench for high treason.

Went to the play. Stayed part of the first Act and went to Tom's Coffee-House. We heard from good hands and I believe it is true that Major-General Wills has cut the rebels to pieces in Preston. They had cast up an entrenchment to defend themselves which he soon broke through but then they barricaded themselves up and he set fire to the town that he might not fight at such a disadvantage and then the rebels were forced to leave the town and fight it and they were soon cut to pieces and no quarter was given by him. But my Lord Warrington who headed the company of volunteers is killed in the action.[2] This action has taken up the discourse of the coffee-house all this night till 11 o'clock. It is not yet printed, but we expect to have the particulars to-morrow. Came home at 11.

Tuesday, November 15. Mr. Fernley came to see me about dancing. I would have agreed with him to learn the rigadoon for a guinea, but he would not take under 2 guineas. I intended to give him that if I might learn the minuet perfect for it also, but he asked another half-guinea for all that so I thought fit to consider of it.

The news we had last night is not entirely confirmed but part of it is and there is a paper published by authority this night which says that Wills has come up with the rebels at Preston and had a little skirmish with them. They are gone into the town and defend themselves. He has surrounded the town in order to attack them. Three thousand Dutch troops are arrived

---

[1] *The Last Day*, by Edward Young, the author of *Night Thoughts*, was published at Oxford in 1714.

[2] The rumour was exaggerated. When Carpenter arrived on the 13th, Forster surrendered with 7 peers and 1,489 men. Stanhope put the rebel losses at seventeen. George Booth, Lord Warrington, did not die until 1758.

at Deptford to-day, the other three thousand are gone to Scotland.[1]

Wednesday, November 16. Went to the club at 'Change. Our conversation turned partly upon the news that are come to-day from the rebels and partly upon other subjects. Came home at 12. Met with a whore. Went with her into a corner. After she had asked me several times to go with her she asked me if she could do me any other service. She told me her name was Barker. She is a little black woman. I began to think she was the Barker I knew,[2] but by what I could see of her face it is not she. The action stings me with remorse after having done it. It was not pleasure to me and my inclinations were not raised at all. I don't know but it may give me a disgust for women a good while.

There is an express come to-day that General Wills had attacked the rebels, had several of his men killed in the town but had forced the rebels all to surrender.

Thursday, November 17. By going backwards and forwards to Mr. Samson's and the coffee-house forgot my dinner, that I had none all day. Began to learn the rigadoon of Fernley. Agreed with him to teach me that and perfect the minuet for 2 guineas and a half. Went to John's at 5 to meet Mr. Isles and others upon agreement to see the orrery at the India House. We went there, but the key not being to be found we put it off till Saturday at 3 o'clock. We went from thence to hear Mr. Demodore play upon the flute to the tavern. We stayed there.

As we came back there was a noise and a mob gathered in Cheapside. The Tories had designed to have burnt the figure of King William and some Whig noblemen which the Whigs having notice of got a warrant to take them, which they did and brought them to the Roebuck. When they were there the Tories gathered a large mob and came and were for pulling down the house and breaking in, upon which the gentlemen in the house fired at them several times and killed several. The mob

---

[1] These 6,000 troops were the number stipulated by the Treaty of Utrecht. By April 1716, General Cadogan pacified Scotland with them: they left nothing earthly undestroyed between Stirling and Inverness.

[2] The lady he met at Cousin Watkins's dance? Cf. p. 68.

still continued and my Lord Mayor came in his coach and the mob was dispersed.[1] Came home at 11.

Friday, November 18. Went to the coffee-house. Fell into some company, Mr. Hunt and others. Talked about news. There is an express come to-day from Duke of Argyll which gives accounts that he has had a battle with Mar and gained a victory.[2] The particulars are not very clear and the victory seems not to be very complete. Most people seem to be of the opinion that the Duke of Argyll would have done much better to have acted rather upon the defensive and kept them on the other side the Firth without giving them the opportunity of a battle because that is what must be that which they desire. As long as they can do nothing they lose and it is a victory to us to hinder them from making an ingress, but the Duke of Argyll is an ambitious man and perhaps was afraid lest the honour of conquering the rebels and reducing them should be given to others or shared with others if he had stayed till the Dutch troops came, which seems to have been the occasion of his going out of his camp to fight the rebels.

Saturday, November 19. Went to the India House with several friends, saw the orrery.[3] It is an admirable machine to assist and help the imagination in conceiving the Copernican system and the manner in which the several planets describe their orbits or other motions and explain the several phenomena that arise from them. One single turning of the instruments sets all the several bodies, the sun, moon and earth and the planets, in their several distinct motions, the earth at the same time moves round the sun and upon its own axis, the sun moves round its own axis, the planets of Venus and Mercury perform their motions round the sun and the moon hers about her own axis and round the earth also, and the several eccentricities of the planets and the different inclinations of

[1] This was the anniversary of Queen Elizabeth's birth, one of the four recognized days for riots. About 500 'Jacks' tried to rescue the effigies of William III, George I, Marlborough, and a Scaramouche, which had been intended for the bonfire in Smithfield.

[2] On 13 November Argyll, with 3,000 troops, fought an indecisive battle at Sheriffmuir against Mar's force of 8,000. This checked the rebel advance.

[3] Invented by George Graham, made by J. Rowley, and named after Charles Boyle, Earl of Orrery. Ryder later bought the specimen now at Sandon Hall.

the several planes of each of the planets, and all these are put in motion at one time, so that the several phenomena that appear in the hours are here exactly described and seen. The eclipses and phases of the planets and all the different regards of each to one another appear plainly and evidently. It is performed by above eighty different wheels. It is indeed a machine that must have cost a vast deal of pains and thoughts in the composure. It is finely wrought with silver and designed as a present to the Emperor of China by the East India Company. The author of it is Mr. Rowley, who himself was there to show it and explain it to us. There is not one phenomenon that appears in the sun, moon or earth or Venus and Mercury but what it shows, and at the same time discovers the reason of it.

There is another express come to-day from Argyll that gives further particulars of the action between him and Mar. It seems to have been a very bloody one and the loss of each side seems to be pretty equal, but the Duke of Argyll gained the field of battle and took prisoners and carried away the cannon and baggage of the rebels who seem to be dispersed. They have disappeared and are unwilling to come to another engagement.

Came home. Read some of Bossu upon the Epique Poetry.[1] I observed with respect to myself that my great fault in thinking or writing is the want of method and conceiving the subject in its several divisions and parts.

Sunday, November 20. Young Defoe came to the meeting in the afternoon and sat in our pew. He had some company with him. I was concerned lest he should go home with me. He would expect a bottle of wine, which I had not. However, I asked him but he did not go with me.

Monday, November 21. Rose at 8. Read part of Cicero's oration *pro Archia poeta*. I have intended to read over all his orations if possible to gain his way and manner of thinking, to teach me to talk handsomely and fluently upon any subject that occurs, to observe his transitions and manner of connexion that I may become as much an orator as possible. Went to London afoot. After while went to Mrs. Miller's concert upon London Bridge. There was no great matter of a concert.

[1] *Traité du Poème épique*, by René le Bossu (1631–80).

Tuesday, November 22. Rose at 7. Went to Westminster before 8. Heard the trial of one Dorrell,[1] for high treason for conspiracy to levy war against the King, to depose him and set the Pretender upon the throne. The evidence proved very sufficiently that he had with others conspired to raise a rebellion by going to Oxford and there joining others and setting up the Pretender's standard there, as it was to have been done at Bath, but that was prevented by the coming of General Popper with his dragoons into Oxford. He was found guilty of high treason and is to receive sentence the last day of the term.

Came back and dined at the Sugar Loaf [2] with two gentlemen students whose names I don't know but whom I have seen before.

Wednesday, November 23. Went to brother's and then to our club. I talked very well there and was mighty well satisfied with my own conversation both in what I said relating to the law and other subjects that occurred. I came away from thence in a very good cheerful brisk humour. There is nothing that puts one into a better humour than a cheerful well-kept-up conversation when one has especially bore a good part in it one's self and upon reflection applauds one's own discourse. I don't know how, I found myself in the most cheerful state of mind, which my sister observed by my look when I came to her from thence.

The Dutch troops that were in London marched out to-day towards Scotland.

Thursday, November 24. After dinner read some of the *Misanthrope* of Molière. I like the beginning of it very well. A letter came to me from Mr. Whatley with my cloak, wherein he desires my company that afternoon. I could not help looking upon it in an ill light and his begging my company methought looked a little mean, as if he was abandoned of others. It indeed gave a little kind of an aversion to him.

Friday, November 25. After dinner had my tooth drawn out. I was a little afraid at first to go but resolved upon it and it was

---

[1] The Jacobite captain Dorrell, an ex-hostler and brewer near Clare Market, was charged with Captains Gordon and Ker. He was hanged on 30 November.

[2] A tavern at the back of the St. Dunstan and the Devil in Middle Temple Lane.

drawn out without my crying out or moving at all. A little of my jaw was broke but not painful.

Designed to go to the country dancing at Mr. Fernley's school, but my cheeks began to swell by the drawing my tooth and I stayed at home. Read out the *Misanthrope*. It is a play well worth reading over often.

Saturday, November 26. My head began to ache very much and my cheek to swell more. Passed away the afternoon in doing nothing but playing a little upon my viol. Brother William came hither, talked a little with him about Mrs. Loyd. It is a very pleasant subject and I talk of her with a peculiar pleasure. Went to bed at 10.

Sunday, November 27. Rose between 8 and 9. My cheek was swelled as before. Could not go to church. Read some of Mr. Burton's discourse upon seeking first the Kingdom of God. I was mightily pleased with his manner of treating that subject. Have been all this day but in a kind of restless condition not knowing how to employ myself, uneasy for want of something to do. I think one ought to provide against this temper beforehand. I find myself too subject to this and dread illness upon no account more than its being likely to bring along with it a turbulency and perplexity of thought and want of fixedness of mind.

Tuesday, November 29. In the afternoon read the beginning of Cicero's oration for Milo and some of the *Tatlers*. Young Mrs. Hudson came in as it grew dark and talked pretty handsomely and familiarly to her. To bed between 10 and 11.

Wednesday, November 30. In the afternoon read part of Cicero's oration for Milo. I am resolved to read his orations often and the other ancient authors that I may if possible get a habit of thinking in their manner in such a turn and in such a connexion as they do. There is no one better than Tully to assist one's invention and give one a copiousness and extent of thought and fill the mind with ideas.

I cannot but observe in my conversation with my mother and

our own family how little I say that is worth repeating or hearing and that our conversation together is generally very dull. I attribute it as much as anything to this, that there is nothing to encourage or to excite oneself : a concern for one's reputation has no force or efficacy there to help to put oneself forward and make one desirous of saying or doing anything extraordinary. And it is the great advantage of an education from home that being conversant in the world raises the spirit of emulation and desire of excelling in persons, which forces out what they have within and excites them to improve and draw forth their talents, whereas an education at home keeps the mind languid and in an inactive state, does not put it upon action nor force it to try its strength.

At night read *Jane Shore's Tragedy*.[1] It is writ in imitation of Shakespeare and not ill done. There is a great many good things in it, not that I think it looks like a piece done by a masterly hand. The thoughts are many of them but vulgar commonplace ones, only transformed into Shakespeare's style have an uncommon aspect. To bed at between 10 and 11.

Thursday, December 1. Young Mr. Powell came to see me with Cousin Joseph Billio. He gave us some account of the vices that are most prevalent in Oxford. They are drinking and swearing, which are very common and so not scandalous, but as for whoring, that is not so common, at least not so public. But he has been told that among the chief men in some of the colleges sodomy is very usual and the master of one college has ruined several young handsome men that way, that it is dangerous sending a young man that is beautiful to Oxford.

I find Mr. Powell is a very loose young man. He has learnt to despise religion of every kind at Oxford by seeing every one but the Church of England continually ridiculed and contemned there and the Church of England itself yet more scandalized and vilified by the vicious lives of those that pretend most to defend and magnify it, so that he is very indifferent as to any religion at all, only thinks that the outward name and dignity of it ought to be kept up by an established church.

---

[1] Nicholas Rowe's *The Tragedy of Jane Shore*, 'Written in Imitation of Shakespeare's Style', first produced at Drury Lane in February 1713/4 and published in 1714.

Friday, December 2. After dinner went to my grandmother. Stayed with her till 4 o'clock, then went to coffee-house. The Parliament of Ireland is now sitting. They are a set of brave hearty men, zealous for the Protestant succession and haters of tyranny and oppression to Protestants in Ireland, are much more unanimous in their zeal for liberty and property than we are here in England, and though the number of papists there is vastly superior to that of Protestants, yet the Protestants are able to keep them in order and prevent any trouble or danger from them themselves, whereas we in England that have much fewer papists here are not sufficiently armed against riots, tumults and rebellions and popery. I can attribute this difference to nothing else but this, that those in Ireland having an enemy so near them makes them more upon their guard, keeps their zeal against popery hot and watchful, whereas in England popery has not so many professors and makes the less figure, that the Protestants are less united in their defence against it.

Saturday, December 3. Read *Timon of Athens* at night. I am very well pleased with the play. There is a great deal of good morality to be learnt in it. The chief moral of it is that prosperity creates abundance of friends and adversity drives them away again. The character of a rigid severe philosopher that was always condemning the world and speaking his sentiments of men freely is very humorously described. Went to bed at 12.

Sunday, December 4. Rose at past 8. Went to church. Resolved to apply myself to the remembering the sermon with a design to repeat it to my grandmother to accustom myself to speaking. Did so and came home and repeated the heads of it with my own enlargement upon it very handsomely. Went to meeting. Applied myself to the remembering the sermon which I did pretty well but would not repeat it when came home for fear of bringing it into a custom that it would be expected constantly.

Monday, December 5. Uncle Marshall came and dined with us. He is a man of no very pleasant conversation but understands good eating and drinking very well.

Went to John's. Met Mr. Witnoom and some other friends. One Mr. Page that knew Mr. Witnoom joined himself and after a little silence began to talk, but so as I never heard any man talk like him. When he began he spoke in such a grave and theatrical manner and with the air of authority that I expected something extraordinary, but after some time of discourse I could not conceive what he aimed at. His words flowed from him in a very easy manner, and a man that understood nothing of the subject would really think he talked mighty well, but to me he seemed to talk without having any idea at all, they were words that conveyed no meaning to me and I believe came from him without any thoughts affixed to them by himself.

And this I found to be his character by Mr. Porter and Witnoom's account of him, that they can never understand him.

Went with them to Tom's Coffee House to drink hot arrack punch. There was Mr. Kelly with us, a gentleman that had been in Spain. He told us the Inquisition there, according to the received opinion there, never took up any man for heresy but upon the oath of nine witnesses, nor convicted him but upon the oath of thirty, but it seems that a man that swears to a hearsay is accounted a witness. He himself was once called before a deputation of the Inquisition. It terrified [him] extremely when he came before them. They seemed to know nothing of his being called to them, bid him not be concerned or afraid, they should do him no hurt, and after some long introduction asked him whether he had done nothing that might give offence to them. He considered and told that he did not remember anything at all. Then they mentioned an English woman whom he had known and after several questions asked him whether he had never given her any book. Then he remembered and told them she came to him one day and borrowed a Bible of him and asked him whether he did not know she was going to turn Roman Catholic. He told them he knew nothing of it at all and they let him go and told him if they wanted him again they would send for him. But they never did.

Tuesday, December 6. Sister is very ill and the Doctor says it is the smallpox. I could not but observe the working of my own mind upon the occasion of a difference of judgement that happened between father and brother about something mechanic. Though I did not know myself which was in the right yet my mind at first sight gave it of my brother's side. When I thought of the reason why my mind so readily assented to what my brother said I found it to be this, that I had observed several times before that my brother has commonly been in the right in his judgement of things of that nature, which working insensibly upon my mind rose in it a kind of prejudice in favour of my brother's assertion of that matter and he was then in the right. I resolve therefore to be more cautious for the future in what I assert, and choose rather to be silent than say a thing that does not come into my mind with a pretty good degree of evidence, for this I find insensibly weakens a man's credit with others.

Wednesday, December 7. Called at brother's. Sister has very good symptoms yet upon her and the smallpox seems to come out kindly, the family looks very cheerful.

Went to our club. We had a good deal of talk before we entered upon our business, in a humorous merry strain, in which I bore my part very well, for I never as I think make so good a figure in any company as I do there, for I have a perfect freedom in it and I believe am well respected.

Thursday, December 8. At 12 Mr. Whatley came to me, seemed out of humour that I had not been to see him and, I believe, thinks I have a mind to break that intimacy that has been between us. Indeed I have no mind to continue very familiar with him, because he is apt to grow troublesome where he is intimate. He seems to think I ought to neglect all other friends to serve him or enjoy his company. Went in the afternoon to brother's. Saw sister. She was mighty cheerful; the smallpox came out very kindly and she is glad she has got them.

Read *The What D'ye Call It*.[1] They say it is writ by Pope, though Mr. Gay's name is prefixed to it. It is thought he had some design to reflect upon some authors by it, but to me it seems as if he had no design at all but to write something very new and out of the way, and those places in which some very grave things and fine thoughts are imitated seem to be only done with the design to heighten the farce and make the thing appear the more

---

[1] Gay's burlesque of the current style of tragedy, particularly of *Venice Preserved*; published in March 1715.

ridiculous by the applying such thoughts to so mean a subject and not with a design to ridicule those pieces which are imitated as is generally thought.

Friday, December 9. Brother Ryder breakfasted with me. I dined with him and Cousin Dudley Ryder. He is a man that has got a most strict notion of honour and thinks it the basest, meanest thing in the world to desert a cause after he is once engaged in it. This makes him speak of the rebels that are brought to town to-day with the greatest indignation and thinks they deserve hanging for their cowardice as well as their rebellion. The chief rebels that were taken at Preston, Lord Derwentwater, Lord Widdrington, Forster, Mackintosh and several other English and Scottish gentlemen, are come to town to-day under a guard of soldiers. They come in a-horseback in but an indifferent condition. They are disposed in several prisons, some in the Tower, others in Newgate, &c.[1] There are about 200 come up in all.

At 7 o'clock went to Mr. Fernley's dancing school. There were some pretty ladies. I danced myself at first with a very stiff air, but as I grew warm in it I danced much better and with a great deal of ease and freedom.

Saturday, December 10. Read Coke concerning the right of presentations and advowsons. Continued so long upon that one subject before I could clear it up to myself that my spirits and thoughts tired and I began to be weary.

The rebels that came in yesterday prisoners were carried some of them, as Lord Derwentwater, &c., to the Tower, others among whom were Forster and Mackintosh, into Newgate, and others to the Marshalsea. As they came into London they were very much insulted by the mob,[2] who reproached them, especially Forster, in a very provoking manner. The rebels looked very much dejected.

To bed at 12, after having read some of a French comedy.

---

[1] The noble prisoners were sent to the Tower; the rest, according to their rank, to the Fleet, Newgate and the Marshalsea. Derwentwater mordantly remarked that one house would hold them all . . . *Bedlam.*

[2] They preceded the prisoners with warming-pans: Forster, 'the man under the Rose', was chiefly hated for breaking his oaths to George I.

Was very well pleased with an epitaph that Mr. Smith told me was made by a Scotch man upon himself—

> Here lig ick Martin Abercod.
> Ha mercy on my saol lord God.
> As I would do gin I were God
> And ye were Martin Abercod.

Sunday, December 11. Went to the Temple Church. Heard Dr. Sherlock. He is a man of excellent sense and his sermons are generally calculated for that particular audience, who being gentlemen of the law and at present many of them inclined to Deism, he generally vindicates the authority and honour of the Scripture and the Gospels.

Heard Mr. Hunt in the afternoon. His congregation are some of the politest and richest persons among the dissenters, especially young men like him. He is a man that has formed his congregation himself and they follow him chiefly because he seldom preaches upon doctrinal points and handles any subject with an air of familiarity and freedom without seeming to confine himself to any set of notions or opinions that have been prescribed by others. He may be called a latitudinarian in preaching.

Monday, December 12. Went to the play at night called *Virtue in Danger*.[1] Cibber acted Lord Foppington. Part of the intrigue and plot of the play turns all upon fornication and cuckoldom and Lovelace carries out his mistress by force into the closet for that end.

Wednesday, December 14. Came to brother's in afternoon. Aunt Lomax gave me an account of the barbarous ill-treatment her husband had from his brother Joshua, even from their very first setting out into the world. When his father was dead he immediately began to play his game with his brother Thomas, who had had an estate settled upon him and his wife at their marriage. But Joshua now endeavours to ruin his brother, tells his brother's creditors that his brother was poor and had nothing, would not be able to pay them anything and would have persuaded them to arrest him, forbids his brother's tenants from

---

[1] Sir John Vanbrugh's *The Relapse, or, Virtue in Danger*, first produced in 1696, enjoyed great popularity in the eighteenth century.

paying him any rent, that the estate was his. And did all he could to ruin his brother that he might be at his mercy. But when this would not do he tells his mother, who had an estate to dispose of between them, that his brother had all the estate and he had none, tells a great many lies concerning him; and at last, when she was ready to die, makes a will for her wherein he gives himself everything. And though she desired his brother might see it before it was sealed and bid him send to him, he never did send to him not let him know of his mother's sickness, but tells her that he had sent and his brother would not come. The sealing of the will was prevented by her sudden death and so that mischief averted. Then he goes to law with him and though he was cast in every suit yet pursued his brother in hopes to make him so poor as to force him to comply with his terms. And though his brother treated him always with the greatest kindness, assisted him with money to gain interest for him to get into the Parliament, he could never be reconciled but always persecuted him with lawsuits. Nor was he thus a villain only to his brother; everybody that had to do with him found him one, endeavouring always to circumvent them. He forged a deed once and makes it his common practice to tell lies, so that in the relation of any matter of fact, especially relating to himself, there is not the least credit to be given to it. Indeed, he seems to have something of a fool as well as a knave joined together in him, for he tells lies sometimes only in sport when his own interest is not at all or at least very remotely concerned in it. His constant aim and design is to get money. To this tend all his dealings or actions. This engages him continually in lawsuits and makes him persevere to the uttermost extremity in them; if he makes any propositions or terms he does it with no other design but to make some underhand advantage by it and if possible catch you in your words or your actions, never designing to be bound by what he says or does himself. I never heard, however, of a man that in all his actions showed greater villainy and baseness of mind and at the same time greater folly.

Went to Club at 'Change. Our conversation was rather merry than improving. Some of the company told us of a man that has the art of speaking so as to make his voice come to one as if it came from any other side or distance than where he is himself. By this means he plays abundance of tricks and has been a common diversion to gentlemen at taverns by deceiving any of the company that are ignorant of it or the servants of the house, calling them from remote places, making the voice that speaks to them come as if it were from the bed or from the ground or from the stairs, that he has tricked many people into confession of their sins and prayers that they could not when the trick was told them be persuaded but what it was the devil, he does it so naturally. Particularly Mr. Martin told us of one gentleman that was by that means brought to think himself at the point of death, that he actually made a verbal will and made him one of the executors and said his prayers and was so persuaded that the devil was there that though his friends told him of it how it was done he could not be persuaded till a long time but that the house was haunted.

Friday, December 16. At between 12 and 1 went to Mr. Whatley's. He now thinks himself in the most happy state he ever was in being in the way of making continual improvement and resolved to fit himself to appear in the world in a public capacity in the state. He told me as what was a mark of confidence in me and friendship to me how he came to be first acquainted with Lord Chief Justice King. He says when he came from Scotland and was at Exeter Assizes, his own country, he began to have some thoughts of studying the law and one day when he saw Sir Peter King at the sessions house he went out into the Cathedral Church and immediately wrote a letter, though he had never seen him or at least spoke to him or any way knew him before. By this letter he was introduced into his friendship and from that time received into a kind of familiarity with him. This friendship he has ever since maintained with him, and it has been a great comfort and support in his life.

Mr. Whatley told me he was beginning to read mathematics. Advised me to do the same. It is a study in vogue among the great men and perhaps might be of service to recommend a man in the world. I would set about it if I could spare time and it was not better to apply myself to reading the ancients and forming my manner of thinking and judgement which seems to be of more immediate service for me in my character of a lawyer. I don't intend therefore to forsake that design of reading the ancients but if I can find time besides, I don't know but I may spend an hour or two in the day upon that study.

Went to dancing at Mr. Fernley's. I behaved myself better

than I did the last time, for I am sensible I acted with too much gaiety and gave too great a loose to a merry disposition. It is certainly more becoming a gentleman to dance with ease and sobriety than to affect abundance of odd unbecoming motions that are apt to proceed from a light mind that is taken with such extravagant flourishes. Came home between 11 and 12.

Saturday, December 17. Received a letter from Aunt Stevenson. I believe I have now gained their esteem entirely at Gresley that they have all a very great opinion of my parts and capacity, that I believe my Aunt Allen would be glad if I had an estate large enough to fit me for her son-in-law. Perhaps as it is she has some thoughts that way, because I have several times given them reason to believe by my words and actions that I have a very particular respect for Cousin Mary Allen.

Sunday, December 18. Mr. Swain told me that some of the young gentlemen of Hackney have agreed to have a dancing one night these holidays and Mrs. Wallis [1] has granted her room for it and I am desired to make one. I was very well pleased with the design but afraid its being at the school will look mean and low, but as we don't design any of the scholars shall be of the number of the ladies it has a better aspect, but then Mrs. Wallis's daughters and lodgers must come in, so that we can have scarce any of the ladies of the town.

Brother William had to-day a pair lace ruffles. I am very much concerned to find him so extravagant in what he wears; his gloves, his shoes and stockings are all of the finest sort and must cost a great deal of money. How he comes by it is what I cannot account for any other way but by robbing the shop or borrowing. Whichever way it is, it is not a little sum I am sure of, for he is always full of money and very extravagant in his expense. I am surprised to see my father take so little notice of it. I ventured to tell my brother of the extravagance and the folly and ridiculousness of his wearing lace ruffles in Mr. Swain's company and in general spoke against that vain foolish way of going fine as he does, but I don't find it had any influence upon it at all.

[1] Mrs. Elizabeth Wallis (wife and governess of the school in Church Street) died at Hackney on 16 January 1718/9.

Monday, December 19. Dined at Mr. Bailey's [1] with mother and Aunt Lomax. There was a tradesman of Leicester at table. He said that town is a very Tory town but as there were a few officers there when we obtained the victory at Preston they made a bonfire at which they drank the King's health, &c., and confusion to all his enemies. Upon this, one of the parsons of the town told it to several persons that this gentleman whose name was Mr. Craddock and another drank confusion and destruction to all the clergy of the Church of England. There is one thing pretty remarkable, that when this gentleman went to the parson by himself and told him he expected he should recant or be prosecuted, the parson bid do his worst; it was dangerous to meddle with the clergy and would only turn to his own damage in the end. 'Don't you know,' says he, 'what they got that prosecuted Dr. Sacheverell?' [2] This shows very plainly that the advantage he made by his prosecution has encouraged the clergy to do anything though never so vile from this precedent, that nobody would for the future dare to prosecute a clergyman again. It is certain the clergy in the country have been the greatest instrument in raising this spirit of rebellion through the nation and that have done by the most false and malicious stories. One parson I was told had the impudence in the time of Queen Anne to assure some of his parishioners in the country that the notion of the Hanover succession was all a fiction and a story and told them that there was no such place as Hanover in being nor such a manor as Hanover, that the Whigs only imposed them upon them with a design to set aside the right heir.

Went to the ball at Clothiers' Hall. I was denied entrance but with much difficulty obtained. Did not like the dancing there at all, neither the master nor scholars. From thence at almost 11 went to Mr. Fernley's ball to dance country dances. When came there there was a good deal of company but it did not seem to be good, that I did not care to dance and therefore, after having danced one country dance, came away at between 11 and 12.

---

[1] His father's partner: a poor man with a large family.

[2] The trial of Sacheverell in 1710 for sermons attacking the Whig ministers, evoked great demonstrations of mob sympathy. Dissenting meeting-houses were attacked, Godolphin and other Whig statesmen were turned out, and in the November elections the Tories won an overwhelming victory.

I saw to-day by Mr. Smith's means a pamphlet that was thrown about in the streets and laid at people's doors and in their pews in church about a week ago called an answer to the Bishop of Canterbury's and other bishops' declaration against the rebellion. I gave a transitory look over it and find it full of malicious reflections and bold impudent assertions that are directly contrary to truth.

Tuesday, December 20. Went to the Fountain Tavern.[1] There was Dr. Hollier. He was complaining of the folly of a great many of the dissenters in talking commonly about the Whigs at court, how little they regarded them, that they would serve them no further than their interest led them, and they had not virtue enough to take off the Acts of Conformity and Schism Act.[2] He said that the court found the necessity they had of the dissenters and would have taken off these Acts the last session of Parliament if the dissenters had demanded it. That it was not too late now, for they found the necessity of doing still in order to get public officers in the militia, in the common council, in the commissions of peace, &c., that might be trusted. For as the state of the nation is at present there are not churchmen among the Whigs enough to fill up these places and that it would be absolutely necessary to keep the peace of the nation either to take off these disqualifications of the dissenters or keep a standing army which is much the worst of the two.

He talked very well but as I thought with an air of authority, too much as if he knew a great deal of the mind of the court more than other people. He said my Lord Townshend and Secretary Stanhope[3] came about a fortnight ago into the City about the choice of common council and went among the dissenters and chief of the Whigs. He says my Lord Townshend is a man who acts in what he does for the good of the dissenters more upon politic views than any principle of virtue or honour to loose them

[1] Beside Inner Temple Gate.
[2] The Occasional Conformity Act 1711 allowed Nonconformist preachers and teachers to practise, upon certain conditions, outside the counties where they were originally qualified. The Schism Act 1714 made it compulsory for the schoolmasters to be licensed by the bishops. Both Acts caused profound discontent among the Nonconformists. In 1718 Stanhope proposed their repeal, which was effected in January 1719 despite the opposition of Walpole.
[3] James Stanhope (1673-1721), Secretary of State for the Southern Department.

of their burdens, but Stanhope is a man truly and heartily in their interest.

Went to the coffee-house; saw Mr. Gould and Swain there. Talked with them about the dancing which they had agreed upon but I found I could not bring Mrs. Loyd along with me and must be like to take up with one of Mrs. Wallis's daughters for a partner and therefore did not profess and don't design to go.

Wednesday, December 21. Went to our Club. Went through two or three titles. Mr. Leeds told us that he heard that Secretary Stanhope had by the order of the Privy Council, where it was devised, sent to Mr. Barrington Shute [1] to desire him to write down the reasons why it should be proper to have the Acts of Occasional Conformity and Schism taken off at this time and sent them to him as heads for the Lords and Commons to argue upon. Mr. Shute communicated it to Grey Neville [2] and they sent to Mr. [blank] a young gentleman dissenter of the Temple to desire him to write down his reasons for them which he communicated to Mr. Abney,[3] who told it to Mr. Leeds. So that we have reason to expect the Parliament will this session take off these Acts.

We had a dispute about the trial of Lord Oxford. Mr. Isles and Witnoom and Crisp thought that the articles against him would not amount to high treason and that it would be very hard to condemn him for this, that any minister of state might be condemned if he might, for he had the orders of the Queen for what he did and the confirmation of the Parliament by vote afterwards. I was against that and thought the confirmation of the Parliament signified nothing. However, the dispute ended without any proselyte. Mr. Heathcote was of my side and said he did not doubt but he would be found guilty, and that it is only a story raised by the Tories that the House of Commons intended to drop the impeachment because they cannot convict him of high treason.

To-day the Common Council were chosen and by what I hear

---

[1] John Shute Barrington (1678-1734), M.P. for Berwick, lawyer and author of works on the rights of dissenters.

[2] M.P. for Berwick.

[3] Thomas Abney of the Inner Temple; justice of common pleas 1743; died of gaol distemper in May 1750.

the Tories have the majority. Mungor, the brewer, who is now in the messenger's hands as a suspected person, is chosen common councilman and so are several that are known Jacobites but who have taken the oaths to qualify themselves. The oaths to the King are now administering through the City of London and Westminster, all the inhabitants, prentices and servants being summoned to take them. This was thought an impolitic thing by Mr. Isles and Witnoom because now abundance that would not else have taken the oaths and so could not get into offices to hurt the Government, by being in a manner forced to take them, have the opportunity of getting into places, business, &c., and so hurting the Government.

Friday, December 23. Went to the coffee-house. Saw young Mr. Gould there. He would oblige me to talk with him about the difference between Mr. Barker's friends and Mr. Mayo's.[1] His passion entirely overcame his reason and though I said nothing to excite his passion he by talking worked himself up to that extravagance that he fell upon Mr. Williams [2] and called him a rogue and villain and thought ne was a Papist and all this with a noisy loud voice.

At night when others were gone to bed I got Mr. Locke's works and read part of his second *Letter of Toleration.* I am resolved to be very conversant with Mr. Locke's works. I am told that my Lord Cowper [3] told some of his friends that asked how he came by that clear, close way of talking. He said it was from reading very frequently and attentively Mr. Locke's reasoning and Mr. Chillingsworth against the Papists.[4] The last work I therefore intend to buy and read also.

Saturday, December 24. Rose at past 8. Read some of Mr. Locke's second *Letter of Toleration.* I am persuaded if people would but use the same words always in the same signification they would very seldom differ in their sentiments. It is words that

---

[1] Daniel Mayo (d. 1733), Presbyterian minister at Kingston, where he also kept a school, was Barker's unsuccessful rival for the Mare Street ministry.
[2] Dr. Daniel Williams (1643-1716), the Presbyterian benefactor. He was minister at Hand Alley, Bishopsgate, and lived in Hoxton.
[3] The Lord Chancellor.
[4] William Chillingsworth (d. 1644) published a number of attacks on the Catholicism which he first embraced and then abjured.

perplex us and the difficulty is to get clear, distinct notions affixed to them. Read the beginning of his third *Letter of Toleration*.

After dinner went to the coffee-house. Mr. Merryweather [1] told us how Mungor, the brewer, who is in the messenger's hands, was chose common council-man for Aldgate Ward. Eight gunsmiths who belonged to the ordnance of the Tower voted for him and though they were told beforehand that he was a man taken into custody for treasonable practice against the Government and could not stand, and that besides they would disoblige the Government and lose their work, they said they would not damn their souls and betray the Church for any. These are Dr. Welton's [2] people.

Went to the other coffee-house where were Mr. Swain, Gould and Humphries. We talked about our dancing and I learnt by them it is a point of honour if a lady refuses a gentleman that asks her to dance and dances afterwards with another gentleman for the first gentleman to challenge the other, and therefore one should take care in mixed company how one behaves. Mr. Humphries [3] is a man of good sense and by what I find had some hand in writing *The Patriots* of which one Harris [4] was the chief author, a very young man who comes sometimes to the meeting with him. He has writ two or three other pamphlets by which means he has got acquaintance with most of the Whig nobility who encourage him and especially Stanhope who has commended him to my Lord Haversham,[5] who he says told him that my Lord Lansdowne [6] was put into a dungeon in the tower and that he will be tried for conspiring to assassinate the King which he intended to have done by inviting him to supper at his house and there to murder him.

[1] A Richard Merryweather died at Hackney on 22 February 1719.

[2] The Jacobite rector of St. Mary's, Whitechapel, on whose altar-piece Dr. White Kennett, Sacheverell's opponent, was portrayed as Judas.

[3] Samuel Humphries (d. 1738), author of a *Life* of Prior, 1733, *Peruvian Tales*, 1734, the librettos of several of Handel's operas and numerous translations. Handel had 'a due esteem for the harmony of his numbers'.

[4] *The Patriot* was a journal which ran from 22 March 1714 until 20 January 1715 : in No. 125 the author is stated to be John Harris, a man of not two-and-twenty.

[5] Maurice Thompson, 2nd Baron Haversham. His father, John, was a prominent supporter of the Hanoverian cause.

[6] George Granville, Baron Lansdowne, was imprisoned on suspicion of Jacobitism on 26 September 1715 ; released 8 February 1717.

Sunday, December 25. In the afternoon went with Cousin Joseph Billio to hear Mr. Smith at Dr. Williams's. He has a very good pronunciation which suits to the thoughts and makes use of a certain vehemence in his delivery that is very proper. He seems to imitate a little Booth, the actor.

Monday, December 26. I showed my father my letter from Holland [1] which tells me of a league between the King of France, Spain and Sicily to set the Pretender upon the English throne and that the Duke of Orleans has now agreed to perform his part in it by sending 20,000 men into Scotland, &c. My father was surprised at it and would have had me send it to the Secretary of State, though it could signify nothing, that I was sorry I had told it my father.

Tuesday, December 27. In the afternoon went to Aunt Bickley's where stayed about an hour and then came away with the ladies to the school, where we danced till past 1. There were no good dancers at all. I was surprised among all these seemingly gay and brisk young men there was so little of gallantry with the ladies. I had Mrs. Loyd for my partner and she was very good-humoured and I very free with her. Mr. Humphries was pretty sweet upon her and took opportunity of talking with her, but he does not seem to be very brisk in his talk with the ladies. Came home with the ladies to our house at 2 o'clock.

Thursday, December 29. Came to the coffee-house. There was young Mr. Powell, who told me how he was just come from London with Mr. John Tyssen [2] and one Mr. Henley, who quarrelled in the way and drew their swords and fought, but he interposed as much as he could and prevented them doing one another any harm. Mr. Henley was in drink and Mr. Tyssen behaved himself extremely prudently indeed and was very unwilling to engage in the dispute and much more to quarrel, but the other being in drink would force him to it. Came home. Went to bed at 11.

Friday, December 30. In the afternoon went to coffee-house where was Mr. Moreland the father and young Mr. Powell.

[1] From Mr. Potter.
[2] The brother of Francis Tyssen, lord of the manor at Hackney.

The quarrel last night had made a considerable noise and Mr. Henley had told his friends how he had been abused and that Mr. Tyssen reflected upon King George and upon Mr. Moreland, both which were false.

Went to the other coffee-house, where were young Mr. Samuel Moreland and Swain and others. We went together to the tavern and played at whisk till 11 o'clock at night. I lost 6s. I find gaming is a very bewitching thing and I could scarce tell how to be willing to leave off. I do not know how one is insensibly drawn in to play on in expectation of regaining what one has lost. And therefore I think I will endeavour never to game high but only for so much as will not disturb or make me uneasy any way. To bed at past 11.

1716*

* From 1 January to 25 April inclusive, the year is given as 1715/6 in the MS. For convenience, however, I have adopted new style numbering.

Sunday, January 1. Mr. Kingsford dined with us. The subject of his conversation generally turns upon himself and he seems to have it always in his eye to raise in you a mighty esteem for his riches and wealth, and though at the same time he is glad to get a dinner from any of his friends, he would fain make you believe he is worth a prodigious estate. A strange kind of ambition and vanity indeed to be thought a rich beggar! A man that appears like a poor fellow and yet is worth £40,000. He was complaining of the prodigious covetousness of his son-in-law Venner and setting him forth in very lively colours as a man that would sooner part with all his friends and relations than lose the least sum of money by them.

Monday, January 2. Came to London in the morning with mother and father, to brother's. Mr. Bayes [1] came there to assist my brother in returning thanks to God for my sister's deliverance from the smallpox.

Went to John's coffee-house, met Mr. Smith and Mr. Porter and Jackson there. We went to the tavern together and fell of talking upon the women and matrimony. Mr. Porter has no inclination to marry at all. We talked about the free will of man and the prescience of God and their seeming inconsistency to us.

Mr. Porter was telling us that most of the young physicians were Deists, as Dr. Hulse,[2] Mead,[3] Plumtre,[4] &c., and he wondered whence it should come to pass, for, for his own part, he thought the truth of religion was capable of the greatest evidence.

Came to brother's. Supped there. Played at cards. Lost a

[1] Joshua Bayes (1676–1741), assistant minister at the meeting in Leather Lane.
[2] Edward Hulse, M.D. (1682–1759), a famous Whig physician; first physician to George II; baronet 1739. At this period he lived at Hackney.
[3] Richard Mead (1673–1754), physician to St. Thomas's and later to George II.
[4] Henry Plumtre (d. 1746), later President of College of Physicians.

little money. I don't know how, the losing though it does not concern me much, yet makes me that I cannot be merry and look pleasant. Came home at 11.

Wednesday, January 4. Went to see the Thames which is froze over. I was extremely struck with the sight. It is all froze over, but by the snow and the tide, which has broke the ice and heaped it one upon another, it looks the most wild and confused sight I ever saw. It looks as if there had been a violent storm and it had froze the waves, just as they were justling and beating against one another, and the billows and foam and white froth were grown stiff just as they were at the height of their hurry.

Went to our club at London Coffee-House. Our discourse turned chiefly upon the management of the King since he came to the crown, in which Mr. Witnoom talked very much against it and thought it would have prevented the present rebellion to have passed over the fault of the last ministers in the Queen's reign in relation to the peace. But we all opposed this entirely and thought it was the best step the King could take to settle and secure himself upon the throne to do justice to them that had betrayed the nation, that had the King received the Tories into favour and into his ministry it would have been the ready way to set the Pretender upon the throne and dethrone the King. It is plain that the present rebellion is only the continuation of what was begun in the Queen's time and not at all an effect of the King's turning out the Tory ministers and calling them to account. Instead of breaking out in Scotland it would have begun at London and been carried on with much more success. However, he is still persuaded that he is in the right and still dreads the consequences. We talked also about Lord Oxford. He argues very much also against his being guilty of treason and thinks it impossible to prove him guilty of it according to the laws of the land, and is very much concerned that they should go about to prove it, for he thinks they will strain the law which which will be breaking in upon the constitution and acting directly contrary to the true and general principles of the Whigs themselves. Indeed he is pleased with nothing that is done by the present government and thinks the ministers act upon principles of revenge and not according to reason. He thus exactly argues as a Tory does and yet I believe he is a true Whig.

FROST FAIR ON THE RIVER THAMES, 1715-16

Thursday, January 5. Mr. Ward came and breakfasted with me. We talked about Criticism. He said that he believed the elegant conciseness and strength of the Latin and Greek tongues is almost wholly owing to their ellipses, viz. their leaving out some words which in our modern languages we are obliged to express.

Went in the coach with Mr. Moreland with whom I talked a great deal of politics and very well. He is himself mightily inclined to the melancholy side of affairs. He thinks the Parliament won't take off the Acts of Occasional Conformity and Schism against the dissenters, and the clergy will still get the better of the laity and perplex our affairs.

I was desired by Mr. Bunkley [1] to come and take part in a country dance at his house. I did so and had young Mrs. Gery for my partner. We were very merry and I danced pretty well upon the whole. Our conversation was nothing extraordinary and we had nothing of kissing.

Friday, January 6. Rose at past 9. Did nothing but dress myself and called at Mr. Henry's who was to go with me to Hackney where I was going to be merry with Cousin Ryder and Mrs. Loyd in choosing King and Queen, it being Twelfth Day. We passed that afternoon and evening at cards during which we were very merry and kissed Mrs. Loyd and cousin very much. At last brother William came and we played at blind man's buff and puss in the corner, when we had more kissing. We at 11 o'clock sat down together to the fire and had a pretty brisk conversation in which I maintained the chief part with Mrs. Loyd. Cousin Ryder sat silent all the while excepting a few observations and reflections which she would make upon [what] I said, taking notice of anything that looked like satire upon the Sex. They are both of them unacquainted with the world and have seen little of polite conversation and are therefore suspicious and mighty jealous of their honour and very captious at anything that seems to reflect upon their sex. To bed at 2.

Saturday, January 7. Rose at past 9. Was merry with cousin and Mrs. Loyd. They stayed to dinner and went away at past 4. Mrs. Loyd is a very smart girl, has good natural sense and reads pretty much, but wants something of good breeding.

[1] A parson.

Cousin Ryder had good sense but has not the talent of conversation, says very little, reads much and delights mightily in books of gallantry, romances and tragedies but her great defect is in her ignorance of mankind. My brother William talks with them with the greatest freedom but without any guard upon his words. His talk with them is prodigiously silly and sometimes a blunt thing comes out from him that is affronting and yet by what I can perceive, though they despise him for his parts, they love his company because he is free with them, kisses and tumbles them about and makes a mighty noise with them. So natural is it to women to like a man that rattles and talks with assurance, though never so much from the purpose.

Monday, January 9. Read Mr. Locke's third *Letter of Toleration*. Cousin Robert Billio came to me to go a-skating. We went together to the Marsh and skated a little. Dined with him at home and went to London in the afternoon.

Went to father to give me some money. Found him at the coffee-house in Aldersgate Street where was Mr. Freke.[1] I asked him how my Lord Chief Justice King did and after some little talk he told me he would introduce me to him and take me with him to dine with him, which I was very well pleased with. Began to write to Aunt Stevenson. In order to it read several letters of Voiture [2] to help me to fall into his way of thinking. I was extremely pleased with many of his thoughts.

Tuesday, January 10. I paid Mrs. Hawksbee her rent and asked her to drink some tea with me which she did. Talked with her about the present public affairs and the rebellion. I find she has been prejudiced by the conversation of Mr. Bunbury but does not seem to be very much so. I talked to her pretty well in the behalf of the King and his ministers. She could not tell how to deny anything but still seemed not satisfied.

Went out to the New River head with my skates where I diverted myself upon the ice till 3.

The seven lords taken in the rebellion went up to the House of

---

[1] Thomas Freke (d. 1716), pastor at the meeting in Bartholomew Close, Smithfield.

[2] Vincent Voiture (1598–1648); his letters are outstanding for their liveliness and wit.

Lords where they heard their impeachment read against them and were ordered to prepare their answers on Saturday and had the liberty of having any one person apiece to advise them about their counsel, because the Scotch lords especially pleaded their ignorance of the English lawyers and their unacquaintance with any of them.

Wednesday, January 11. Went to dinner and then to the Thames. There were multitudes of people walking in the middle of it, where a great many booths were erected [1]; but did not go on. Came to brother's. From thence to our club where we proceeded in our civil law till past 7 o'clock.

Went to our club at the Change where were Mr. Heathcote and others. Mr. Porter thought nothing would effectually prevent the power and mischief of the clergy as a law to hinder the parsons from preaching anything of their own and to revive the ancient custom of reading Homilies in the room of them. We were also lamenting the mischief that is like to come to the nation by the means of the charity schools that are erected about London especially, which are most of them in the hands of the Tories and the clergy. If a law was made that no charity or free schools should have clergymen for their masters it might be of great service to reform them.

Thursday, January 12. Rose at past 8. I intended to go out to Hackney betimes to skate with Cousin Billio, and therefore read what came next into my hands and that was an Italian book. Went to brother's at 11, then went to the Thames which was froze over and a great many tents set up, in which were coffeehouses and wine and ale and other things sold. I went across the river upon the ice in a path that had been worn out, it being all rugged and uneven. Came home, read in Virgil to the end of the first book. To bed at 12.

Friday, January 13. Cousin Billio came to me and we went to the Marsh and skated there till dinner. Came to brother's. John Dear, brother's tenant, was there. He is an honest cheerful man that does not grumble and be uneasy about his paying his money. He is, too, a man of very good sense and sagacity and

[1] On Prince Frederick's birthday, the Whigs roasted an ox on the ice.

talks well of the affairs in which he is conversant, viz. farming, and seems to have a great memory. He is not able to write nor read and yet keeps a very exact account of his money and what he pays and receives by his memory only. I am mightily pleased with the honest plainness and simplicity of the man. Came home. Read part of the comedy of Molière's called *L'Escole des Femmes*. To bed at 12.

Saturday, January 14. After dinner went to brother's. Bought some oranges and lemons to send to Aunt Allen. Stayed at brother's waiting for Mr. Hudson who promised to call me there to go to Hackney. We went to Hackney together on foot. He is lately become clerk to Mr. Marsh and seems already to understand some of his business well. I am in hopes by conversation with him to learn a good deal of the practical part of the law and the methods of beginning the practice of law from its first original.

Sunday, January 15. Nothing extraordinary. We went to prayers and my father read a sermon to the family instead of me, which made me very uneasy all the time. I could not but observe it, though I endeavoured to quell these risings and uneasinesses in me I could not do it. They proceeded from my vanity because I think I read very well. Went to bed at 10.

Tuesday, January 17. Went to brother's. Sister was brought to bed about 12 o'clock of a dead child. She was frightened the night before by a fire that broke out in the shop but was stopped. She is as well as can be expected in her case.

Went to the new playhouse to see *Dioclesian*.[1] There are a great many very good dances in it and singing, but as for the drama I think that is but very indifferent. The decorations are some of them very fine, but I think the Paris opera is much finer. There were choruses of singing just like the French operas. Came home past 10.

Wednesday, January 18. Went to dinner at the Marlborough Head. Met Mr. Bowes there. He promised to come and sit

---

[1] Henry Purcell's *Dioclesian or The Prophetess*, libretto by Betterton; published 1691.

with me till 4 o'clock. When I came home Cousin Dudley Ryder met me just as he was going to his ship for the East Indies. He came upstairs with me but was in haste. I wished him a good voyage, kissed him and he promised to write to me.

Mr. Bowes came to me presently, and we had no conversation that was considerable. At 3 o'clock we went together to the Thames and walked from the Temple Stairs almost to the bridge. It is very surprising; there is one continued road all along with booths built almost all the way, in which are all sorts of toys and eating and drinking sold. It is thronged all the way that sometimes it is difficult to get along for the crowd.

Came to our club. Did nothing there but converse together. On Monday Dr. Wake was consecrated Archbishop of Canterbury in the room of Dr. Tenison who died, who was made so by King William upon the death of Dr. Tillotson. Upon the death of Tillotson it was debated in council whether Dr. Stillingfleet,[1] or Tenison should have it and the council were for Stillingfleet as a man of learning and vigour, except Duke of Shrewsbury [2] who stood out firmly against him for Dr. Tenison. King William seeing one only differ and be so strongly against Stillingfleet privately asked him the reasons of it. He said he would tell His Majesty a story. When he was in Italy he had occasion to get into the acquaintance of a certain nobleman in Italy who could do him a great deal of service and was necessary to his affairs. In order to this he found there was no other means but by bribing his servants, but none of them would accept any bribe till he came to the parson and for money he introduced him into his lord's acquaintance. He afterwards became very free and familiar with the nobleman and it came into his head one day to ask him how it came to pass that he was first acquainted with him (for he had not observed the steps that were made use for it). Upon that he told him that all the rest of his servants were faithful and incorruptible but his priest, and wondered he would keep such a fellow in his house. Upon that the nobleman told him he had chosen him as a fellow that was just capable of performing the office of the priesthood and for that he did very well but was every way a very worthless, silly fellow,

[1] Then Bishop of Worcester.
[2] Charles Talbot, Duke of Shrewsbury (1660-1718). In 1694 he was head of the Government.

and if he could recommend him to one more silly and foolish than he, he would turn this away and receive him. 'For', says he, 'a man of sense will always be meddling in my affairs and will either be at the head of my family and concerns or else will certainly perplex or entangle them.' 'And', says Duke Shrewsbury, 'I leave your Majesty to make the application.' The King took his advice and made Tenison Archbishop, a plain, honest, well-meaning man who would have no scheme nor designs in his head. This story Mr. Bourroughs told me.

Thursday, January 19. Rose at past 8. Read several of Voiture's letters in order to give my mind the proper turn for writing to Aunt Stevenson. I am mightily pleased with these letters. I think this is the best turn of raillery and the best manner in the world of writing letters of gallantry and politeness that have nothing of business or matters of importance. They are writ in a very free, negligent way with ease and without anything of stiffness, but a certain agreeable familiarity runs through the whole, which are full of wit and humour. I think this is the best epistolary style and manner I ever met with.

At 1 o'clock Mr. Leeds came to see me according to appointment to go to the House of Lords to see the impeached lords come to the bar of the House and give in their answer. Went there and after some difficulty got into the House of Lords with a crowd of Parliament men. There is nothing like a good assurance and impudence to get in at such places.

The Lords Widdrington, Derwentwater, Nithsdale, Nairne, Kenmure and the Earl of Carnwath pleaded all of them guilty and laid themselves at the King's mercy and desired that the Lords would intercede with His Majesty for them. Some of the lords gave in their answers in writing. The Lord Nithsdale said he would not affect delay and therefore confessed himself guilty of the rebellion and was sorry for it but pleaded in extenuation of it that he was surprised into it and when he came at Preston was willing to save the effusion of so much blood as might have been spilt if they had continued obstinate, and that when he surrendered he was promised to be recommended to His Majesty's mercy, &c., to which effect most of them pleaded. But Lord Wintoun put in a petition to desire the Lords to assign him counsel, because the other counsel assigned him would not accept it and that he might have further time to put in his answer because he had matters of great importance that would be necessary for him to put into his answer. And in his petition he also desired he might have a clergyman, one Elliot, to come to him. It was debated in the House and Lord Harcourt said he thought his counsel could do him little good but God knows what the parson may do. It was objected that the parson was a Nonjuror but it was ordered that he might have him come to him upon this condition, that he should continue with him all the while and not be permitted to go and come backwards and forwards. And a solicitor was allowed him also.

The form of proceeding in the House of Lords is this. The Lord Chancellor [1] calls the prisoner who is kneeling at the bar and upon his answering bids him rise and then tells him that he was impeached by the House of Commons of high treason and that he had had all his time to give in his answer—'What is it you answer to the impeachment?' When the prisoner had answered that he confessed himself guilty of the treason, &c., the Lord Chancellor asked the House whether his plea should be received and upon the House's saying 'Yes' he says 'Ordered'.

I read the declaration of the Pretender's since he came to Scotland wherein he invites all his subjects to come in to him, gives a general pardon to all that should not be in arms after his coming against him and complains of the hard usage he has met with. It is writ with a good deal of spirit to gain the common unthinking people, but full of lies. Sir Richard Steele has published it with his answer to it, which he calls the subject's answer to the Pretender's declaration.[2] It is done very well.

Began to write letter to Aunt Stevenson but could not finish it before the bellman came. To bed at 12.

Friday, January 20. Went to the coffee-house. Read *The Freeholder*.[3] It is an answer to the Pretender's declaration in the way of raillery. It is writ with a great deal of wit and spirit. Supped at brother's. In my way home had a very ill fall upon my left side.

[1] William Cowper, 1st Earl Cowper.
[2] Published on 13 January as an enlarged Part 5 of the weekly *Town Talk*.
[3] Addison's journal supporting George I; published from December 1715 until June 1716.

Saturday, January 21. Went to Hackney with Cousin Joseph Billio. Found brother William at home. He had been at Aunt Bickley's. He had been there for above an hour and though the whole family were together in the same room he and Mrs. Loyd got together whispering all the while. She is indeed a very strange girl, but I can resolve all her behaviour into nothing so well as into strong desire to appear a wit and a beauty among men and the love of their company. There is one thing which she and Cousin Ryder are very faulty in and that is a manner of seeming never to be obliged by one : though I have spent money upon them, lent them books and given them several, I could scarce ever get so much as a single thanks for it all. They are mightily afraid of owning any obligation to a man, but I take it it proceeds from an ignorance of the world and polite breeding.

Had my shoulder which pained me still bathed with some spirits and took some Cucantellus's balsam. To bed at 10.

Sunday, January 22. Rose at 9. Neither father nor mother are at Hackney. My pain in my left shoulder is spread over my neck too and got a little into my right shoulder. Did not therefore go to meeting. Read some of Cicero, *De Finibus*, where he is disputing with an Epicurean about the *summum bonum*.

Read in the afternoon Dr. Bates upon the existence of God. I think there is nothing of greater use than frequently to run over the arguments for the being of God from his works and the evident signs and tokens of an immeasurably wise and powerful and good Being that are apparent in the formation of the world.

Father came home at night. Had a pretty long dispute with him about election,[1] against which I said a great deal more than I really thought I could have done before I was insensibly drawn out. And I don't know but those texts of Scripture which are applied to this doctrine of an absolute election of particular persons to salvation may be taken in a more general sense to signify the predetermination of God to save mankind by the death of His Son and to justify this without perfect obedience. My father could not tell what to say to this but seemed to be shocked.

---

[1] i.e. the Calvinistic doctrine. Nonconformity was split between this doctrine and the Armenian doctrine of salvation by works.

To bed at 10 after having drank some bottled ale with a design to sweat in order to remove my pains.

Monday, January 23. Had but a very indifferent night's rest, the pains about my shoulders were much more sensible in the heat of the bed and sweating than when I was up and has extended itself to my thighs, so that I believe they are rheumatic. In the afternoon read in Virgil and in Perizonius's *Universal History*, which I can still read, and this seems to be pretty good account of things.

Tuesday, January 24. Wrote a letter to Mrs. Loyd and Cousin Ryder but could not tell how to send it so as not to let any of their family suspect it. It came into my head to send a book with it and write a letter with that to Cousin Ryder in which I would enclose the other. I did so and sent it by John.[1] As soon as they got they laughed and ran away with it from Aunt Bickley, who saw them receive something from John.

Wednesday, January 25. Went to brother's and then to concert of music at Mr. De la Fond which he has every Wednesday night at 7 o'clock. There was pretty good music and a boy that belongs to St. Paul's of about nine year old that sung several songs to the Harpsichord and viol; he had the strongest and finest [voice] I ever heard in my life from a child.

Thursday, January 26. Mr. Horseman[2] came to me as he appointed yesterday to go together to Westminster. He seems to understand it mighty well for so short a time as he has been studying it. He told me Mr. Humphries is a man of very good natural parts, but has had nothing of education but only at school. He has a great memory and used formerly to read Romances very much, which has given him a very good style and he writes very well.

The King came to the House of Lords and gave his assent to an Act for continuing the suspension of the Habeas Corpus

---

[1] The Ryders' manservant.
[2] Oliver Horseman, son and heir of Oliver Horseman, physician of London; entered at Lincoln's Inn 27 June 1713.

Act and he made a speech wherein he told them he was further assured the Pretender was in Scotland and that he expected some foreign assistance. On Monday the Commons presented an address to His Majesty to thank him for his care of the public and promise all needful supplies for suppressing the rebellion and effectually his resentment against any foreign power that should assist him. The Earl of Seaforth has submitted to the King and the Marquis of Huntly is likely to do the same.[1] Lord Wintoun on Monday pleaded not guilty to the impeachment of high treason and said he was forced into what he did.

Read some of Spenser's *Fairy Queen*. I was mightily pleased with it and intend to read it over.

Friday, January 27. I hear the King has sent a very sharp memorial to the Duke of Orleans about his assisting the Pretender and desires he would tell him plainly whether he intends it or no and not to pretend friendship and to assist him underhand. It is said Mr. Iberville,[2] the French ambassador here, is going away and forbade the court and that the Earl of Stair has been ill-treated at the Court of France.

Saturday, January 28. Dined with Mr. Samson and Mr. Bowes. He is a man pretty ignorant of the world but a sincere honest man that is very prejudiced in favour of the Church and really thinks it the best in the world and is concerned for it, but he is also one averse to popery and in the interest of King George. We were talking about these affairs and Mr. Samson talked of the absurdity of an established Church and said some things of that matter that offended him very much, that he said, with a great deal of concern, that he was mighty sorry to see whither things were tending. He could not bear the thoughts of popery and living under a popish prince, and the Whigs were for subverting the Church, so that he thought the nation was in a pitiful condition. Went to Hackney. Read in Chillingsworth at night. To bed at 11.

---

[1] Seaforth escaped to France; Huntly submitted and was pardoned.

[2] M. D'Iberville, appointed Envoy Extraordinary to London in December 1713.

Sunday, January 29. Went to cousin Billio after sermon with father. Aunt Billio said she heard brother William was brought off his time [1] and told my father she thought he would do well to get him a wife and so settle him, that she could recommend one to him of a sweet temper, a great deal of prudence, meekness, and humility, and moderate fortune. Father said it was time enough. I don't know upon what account he said that, unless that he cannot part with money at this time to set him up.

Monday, January 30. Went to church, it being King Charles's Martyrdom, and I was mightily pleased to hear the parson, one Mr. Astor, make a very loyal sermon in which he very handsomely exposed the folly and villainy of the present rebellion. I remember there was a very different sermon preached this day last year, a very violent one against the dissenters, but Mr. Newcome I believe is now persuaded that the interest of the Whigs is so well established that he can expect no favour upon the account of High Church principles and therefore has put up a man of Whiggish sentiments to preach.

When I came home found Aunt Lomax and Mr. Owen of Warrington here and young Mr. Henry.

Mr. Owen told us with relation to our victory at Preston that the surrender of the rebels was gained by General Wills's bullying and swearing rather than anything else. After the first attack when Wills had retired and invested the town, Derwentwater comes out with a trumpet and was brought into Wills's tent and told him that they were willing to stop the effusion of blood and therefore offered to surrender the town in twelve days' time if they had no relief. Upon this Wills swore a great oath and pulls his watch out of his pocket and swore that if they did not surrender within twelve hours' time he would cut every man of them in pieces and swore he would not give them a moment's time longer. This he confirmed by the most bitter oaths, curses and execrations in the world, that Lord Derwentwater was perfectly terrified that his very lips trembled, and he desired that he would let him stay with him during the attack. But Wills told he would not let him. He should go into the town again, for he had a mind he should spread the terror among

[1] i.e. finished his apprenticeship.

the rest of the rebels. And sent him back again. Soon after McIntosh[1] came out and he being a man of passion and a terrible swearer as well as Wills they fell into a perfect passion together, and McIntosh told him he had a thousand of his Scotch Highlanders that would every man of them fight two of his troops. Wills swore by all that was sacred that he, if he would bring out his thousand men, he would only set Pitt's horse against them, and if they did not cut them all to pieces he would be damned and promised he would not let any other soldiers assist them. In short, he swore so violently and with such a terrible air that McIntosh went back into the town and before the twelve hours were expired they surrendered.

Mr. William Crisp gave us an account of the state of Liverpool and the country there, when the rebels came into that country. He says when they first heard that the rebels were come to Penrith and were going towards Preston, from whence they were to go either to Liverpool or some other way, they were put into a mighty consternation at Liverpool which is a place of trade and a majority of Whigs, the Mayor also being a strong active Whig. They immediately resolved in council to put the town into the best posture of defence they were capable of and immediately sent a crier about the town for all men that could work to meet together at the market cross the next morning, and accordingly there met there a great number of workmen, and they were presently set on work to dig ditches and raise batteries all about the town in the most convenient places, and in three or four days all the avenues were fortified and several little forts or batteries were raised and several pieces of cannon were mounted, that at length there were near eighty piece of cannon round the town. All the young men of the town that were on the side of the Government formed themselves into companies and were disposed of in a military manner. The ships that were in the port assisted them with arms and ammunition and the sailors were placed at the great guns to manage them. In this posture of defence they continued till he came away and are so still without

---

[1] Brigadier William McIntosh of Borlum, a tall raw-boned man, fair, beetle-browed, grey-eyed, and speaking broad Scotch. Wills's disposition is indicated by the fact that after Preston he was challenged to a duel by Carpenter, his senior officer.

any attack made by the rebels upon them but not without frequent alarms. Mr. Crisp was made a captain of one of their troops during this time.

Mr. Crisp went upon an expedition to search for my Lord Molyneux,[1] a very rich papist that lives within three miles of the town and known to associate with the rebels. He went one time and nobody would open the house till he fired into one of the windows, but then he found nothing but a very few arms. But then another time, one Sunday morning, the mayor sends to him to desire him to go to this lord's house, for he had intelligence that at that time there were to be a meeting of several popish gentlemen at his house. So up he got and with a few more they go towards the house. In the way they heard that some gentlemen were rid very hard to Lord Molyneux's as particularly Sir Roland Harley and his son and others. He could not overtake them before they got into the house but he comes to the door of the house and waits the arrival of his friends. When they were come they demanded entrance, which was granted them, but no gentlemen or men were to be found in the house, none but a few ladies who said that my lord was gone out and they were all alone. But this would not satisfy him and he said he knew my lord must be in the house and several other gentlemen and that he would not go away without them. By this time a vast mob of sailors and others were come from Liverpool and had beset the house and threatened to pull it down and burn it if they would not deliver up themselves, to prevent which my lord comes out and his son, but denied there were anybody else, till at last he forced him to bring out Sir Roland Stanley's son, but would produce no others. So they went back to Liverpool and these men were committed to custody with two gentlemen more that they took upon the road. This happened that very Sunday that the rebels surrendered themselves at Preston and it was universally believed and with very probable reason that Lord Molineux had agreed to join the rebels upon their approach to Liverpool, though whether there be legal proof of that so as to condemn him he cannot tell.

The county of Lancaster is now very well filled with good officers in the commissions of peace and militia, but it was a

[1] William Molyneux, 4th Viscount Maryborough (1656-1717).

long time before this was brought about. My Lord Aylesford [1] is Chancellor of the Duchy of Lancaster ; all the commissions for the peace, &c., must pass his hand, but he is a high Tory and suspected very justly of affection to the Pretender's interest. My Lord Derby [2] is Lieutenant for the County, an honest, true Whig and an active man and often pressed the court to have the commissions of peace changed but could never get it done till this rebellion. And when he was sent for to court and desired to go down to put a stop to the rebellion, he answered he was very willing to go down but he was afraid of being put into prison by the justices and that he would not go till they were changed. Upon this Lord Aylesford was sent for to court and a list of justices was given him to put in. He pretended he would, but put in but seven. In short there were several orders about it before it was done, till my Lord Derby told them he would not go down till he had the commissions all of them changed and sealed and signed in his pocket, which he at last gained but not without difficulty. The answer my Lord Townshend made him when he wondered at the delay was that the Nottingham family was not at that time of day to be disobliged, my Lord Aylesford being the Earl of Nottingham's brother.

Mr. Owen told us he put in that letter into the *Flying Post* which gives an account of the new-invented gag [3] of which there are two hundred-weight found in one papist's house.

It is a matter much talked of among the dissenters whether the Occasional Conformity and Schism bills will be taken off from the dissenters, but I don't find that they think they will be taken off now. The court Whigs are not in the interest of the dissenters but are mightily for the Church : besides their interest leads them not admit the dissenters into posts of profit of honour, for then as these were bought, by a greater number of men for them to be divided among, their particular share in them would be lessened, and the Church Whigs as well as Tories are willing to keep the preferments and advantages among themselves and within as narrow a compass as possible, however willing they may be that the dissenters should enjoy the liberty of

---

[1] Heneage Finch, son of the 1st Earl of Nottingham.
[2] James Stanley, 10th Earl of Derby (d. 1736).
[3] 'The Pretender's cross-bow', a metal gag which fitted over the victim's tongue and cut his mouth if he tried to speak.

worshipping God according to their consciences which is a matter of the least moment with them, that nothing but an absolute necessity is ever likely to prevail upon them to admit the dissenters into the preferments.

Mr. Owen lay at our house and at night he and I had some little dispute about predestination, but I don't [think] that he has so very clear a head in the way of arguing. To bed. Mr. Henry lay with me.

Tuesday, January 31. Aunt Lomax told me that Mr. Bunkley told her the reason why I was not invited to the last dancing at Bunkley's was that it had been talked of in Hackney, upon the account of my being there once before, that it was designed on purpose to give me an opportunity of gaining one of the young ladies Gerys and their mother did not think that proper, as I was only a student. If I had been at the bar and had business indeed there might be something more said to it. And therefore she was not willing I should have any more of these opportunities. It is a strange thing how tattling women will raise stories without any the least foundation, but no doubt the good mother was very prudent when she had such a thing put into her head not to hazard her daughter again. It seems the young ladies have £4,000 apiece left them by their father.

Came to brother's. There was Mrs. Lee. She is a lady of an admirable sweet temper, perfectly good-humoured and I am persuaded would make an excellent, prudent, discreet wife, much better than Mrs. Loyd, who is indeed better for a mistress to toy and play with than a wife.

Came home at 9. Began to go on with my diary from Sunday, which I continued hitherto. Till 12 o'clock.

Thursday, February 2. Mr. Whatley came to me at 12 o'clock and we played together some sonatas and went to dinner together. He told me he had just then been with my Lord Chief Justice King and he told him that there was a stop put to the new levies of soldiers because the King was very well satisfied now that the Pretender would not be assisted by France.

After dinner at past 3 o'clock we went to the Inner Temple Hall where the judges were at dinner and a play was to be acted before them. He got me in and I saw *The Chances* acted before the judges and the hall full of spectators. Went to brother's after this and supped there.

Friday, February 3. Went to Mr. Bailey's where brother William had a supper to treat his friends upon the account of his being to-day out of his time. Stayed there till past 12 o'clock.

Saturday, February 4. Met Mr. Porter in the way to Hackney and he turned back and walked with me to Hackney. Did not talk about Mr. Berkeley's notions.

Sunday, February 5. To meeting both morning and afternoon. I had a mind to have translated some of David's psalms into poetry which I attempted but could not make it do. To bed at past 11.

Monday, February 6. The Earl of Mar is gone from Perth and the Duke of Argyll has taken possession of it and is pursuing the rebels as fast as he can. Lechmere [1] made a motion in the House of Commons for a general Act of Indemnity but was opposed in it by Stanhope, Walpole [2] and others. Walpole said he had £60,000 offered him to make such a motion.

After dinner went to Mr. Bowes's chambers where were both him and Mr. Oxford. Our conversation at first turned upon Homer, whose translation by Pope they had been just reading and admire extremely. Then we talked of the women. Mr. Bowes, I find, as most other young men do now, looks upon women as only fit to be subservient to a man's lust and not to be an agreeable companion.

Tuesday, February 7. Went to cousin Watkins to see his wife. She is a good agreeable woman but not a beauty. We played at cards and cousin would have had me stay at supper, but pretended an obligation to go.

Came to brother's. Heard that there was a design formed for

---

[1] Nicholas Lechmere (1675–1727). He had been dismissed from the office of Solicitor-General in December 1715 because of his opposition to the impeachment of Oxford.

[2] Robert Walpole's chief activity at this period was discovering the plans for the rebellion and suppressing its leaders.

the escape of the rebel prisoners in Newgate, they having sawed through the iron bars that keep the windows but it was discovered and a guard of soldiers sent. And some of the principal men of them loaded with thongs and fetters. Came home at 11. To bed presently.

Wednesday, February 8. There is an express come that the Pretender was going away on board a ship at Montrose but his men would not let him.[1] General Sabine [2] is sent after them with a considerable detachment and our army is possessed of Dundee.

Went to our club at Change. Part of our discourse was entirely bawdy which Mr. Heathcote talks with a great deal of freedom.

Thursday, February 9. Mr. Porter came to call me to go to Westminster Hall to hear the sentence passed upon the six impeached lords that pleaded guilty. It was some time before we could find out a method of getting in within the scaffolding. At last we bought two tickets at a crown apiece and got into the gallery, where we had a full view of the whole assembly which was the largest I ever saw in my life, the Lords and Commons being there and a greater number of spectators than both together. I thought it one of the noblest sights my eyes ever beheld. The lords came to their places, which was on the bottom, in their robes, which was a very magnificent sight, and after them the Lord High Steward, who was my Lord Chancellor Cowper, came in attended with twelve maces. He first took his place upon the woolpacks where he usually sits as Chancellor and then the commission to make him High Steward was read. After which he rose out of his former place and had a white wand delivered to him and he went to the chair placed under the throne and sat down and then he commenced High Steward.

Then the crier spoke aloud that the lieutenant of the Tower should bring his prisoners to the bar, and the Lord High Steward after they were come spoke to them, told them they were impeached of high treason and the articles of impeachment were

---

[1] The Pretender and Mar embarked at Montrose on 4 February after sending their baggage with the army to avoid suspicion.

[2] Joseph Sabine (d. 1739), later Governor of Gibraltar.

read aloud by the crier, and then their several answers they had put in before were read also. Then the order of the day for giving sentence was read and the Lord High Steward asked the prisoners whether they had anything to offer in arrest of judgement why sentence should not pass against them. Upon which they each of them made speeches. Lord Derwentwater began first and so the rest. Being behind them I could not hear much of what they said but in general they pleaded for mercy and offered nothing in arrest of judgement.

When this was done, Lord High Steward told them and the House of Lords he thought he was obliged to make such observations upon the pleas and answers of the impeached lords as might vindicate the justice of the sentence that was to be passed upon them. My Lord spoke his speech with a great deal of temperance and with an excellent delivery and voice, and at last pronounced the sentence in a most solemn and tender manner.

Came away and dined with Mr. Porter at Charing Cross. We were very well pleased with our success.

Saturday, February 11. Went with Mr. Leeds to Westminster. I begin to understand a great deal more of the practice of the courts than before and the law clears up more and more every day that I am in hopes now to make a much greater progress in the law than before.

Uncle Dudley Ryder and Cousin Robert Ryder his son at Hackney to-night. When uncle was gone to bed my father talked with me about brother's estate which is so cumbered and the tenants so backward in paying their rents that it is not likely to bring him in any profit these many years. I advised my father to sell it and the overplus after debts paid would be so much in pocket and help my brother extremely.

Sunday, February 12. Went to church with Uncle Ryder. Young Newcome[1] preached. He is a man of but little sense. Went to church in the afternoon with uncle again. Heard Mr.

---

[1] Henry Newcome married Lydia Moreland, and joined with her father as schoolmaster in Newcome's school, which enjoyed considerable fame in the eighteenth century. His son Henry married a relative of William Cole, the antiquary and diarist.

Strype [1] who is an old man, preaches not politely but tolerably good sense.

Did very little that night, being obliged to keep my uncle company, who understands nothing at all but his own law affairs.

It came into my head to write to the occasional paper upon a subject that fell into conversation by chance concerning the advantage of encouraging foreigners to come into England and settle among us. It is certainly the policy of any government whatsoever to attract as many subjects to it as possible, both as their strengths and riches consist in the multitude of inhabitants and also as it is the means of drawing the trade of other nations to ourselves, learning their arts and manufactures and gaining their artists. Now there is nothing more opposite to this maxim of government than persecution or hindering people from enjoying their own religion with freedom and ease. The miserable effects of persecution in this respect are very sufficiently seen in France and Spain. It is to the refugees of France that we owe our silk manufactures and the chief of the stuff ones and multitude of other things which were formerly imported hither from France and now much better made at home than there.

Monday, February 13. Went to Mr. Whatley's in the afternoon. Then to the playhouse. Saw *The Spanish Friar*.[2] It is a very good play and well acted. I observed that most of the clappings were upon party accounts. There happened to be some reflections upon the priests which the Whigs clapped extremely and the Tories made a faint hiss.

The Pretender is certainly gone away from Scotland with Mar and it is said he is arrived in France.

Tuesday, February 14. Read Coke till 12 o'clock, then I looked into Waller's poems in which I was very much pleased with several thoughts that I light upon there. He seems to have been a man of the most lively ready genius.

Went to brother's where was Mr. Owen, who told me that the Government were well assured that several foreign princes had furnished the Pretender with £1,500,000 for his expedition into

---

[1] John Strype (1643-1737), historian and biographer, was lecturer at St. John-at-Hackney from 1689 until 1724.
[2] By John Dryden, 1680.

Scotland. The Pope had promised him £200,000 upon his landing and that he had already received the greatest part of the whole one million and half, the princes of Italy and the Emperor having concurred in making up that sum.

The Government seems to expect an invasion upon Ireland and therefore the Parliament there have qualified the dissenters there to serve in military offices and lest the dissenters should refuse to accept they have voted all to be disaffected to His Majesty who being qualified and capable of serving in the militia refuse to act. Mr. Owen assures me that the King has ordered ten men-of-war to go to Ireland.

The Pretender run away and left his friends in the lurch and has thereby so much exposed himself to his friends that they are ashamed to own him. Went to North's Coffee-House. It is said that the Earl of Stair [1] has purchased a letter or two of my Lord Oxford which will be sufficient to convict him. Came home at 10.

Wednesday, February 15. After dinner went to our club at Sue's. We were talking of some ingenious young men in the Temple that were counsellors but had not much business. I find indeed it is not the way to get business and have the character of a good lawyer to seem acquainted much with other things. Went then to our club at Change. We there immediately fell into discourse about the lords that had sentence passed upon them. Mr. Witnoom and Mr. Isles were pleading for mercy for them and hoped the Government would pardon them all. That subject kept us almost all the while, they two against all the rest of us, who thought justice upon them would be much more serviceable to the nation.

Thursday, February 16. After dinner Mr. Bowes, Mr. Oxford [2] and Mr. Tillyard [3] upon my invitation came to drink some tea with me. They desired me when they saw my bass viol to play

---

[1] Ambassador at Paris. Harley was impeached in June 1717 but acquitted when the prosecutors failed to appear.

[2] William Oxford, son and heir-apparent of Thomas Oxford of Southwick, Southhants, entered at Inner Temple 13 June 1712.

[3] Probably Joas Tillard, third son of Abraham Tillard of London, merchant, entered at Inner Temple 19 October 1710.

to them, which I did but was in a great deal of confusion that I played not near so well as I do sometimes. They looked over my pictures. When we sat down to conversation we talked about that manner of writing which was brought so much into fashion by the *Tatlers* and *Spectators* and which the town has by this means got a relish of. The *Freeholder* is writ now in the same manner, in which they say Addison and Bishop of St. Asaph and Hoadly and some of the greatest pens in England are engaged.

Friday, February 17. Went to see Mr. Horseman. Told me Mr. Humphries was one of the authors of the *Instructors* and wrote about half of them. He showed them me and I looked over two or three of them which he said were his and I was surprised to find them so well writ. They have the zeal and the spirit of the *Tatlers* and *Spectators* in them, a good deal of humour and wit. He is not above 20 years old now and is likely to become a considerable man in that way, but Mr. Horseman says that he has not fixedness of thought enough for a larger composure and begins a great many things and leaves them off and goes to others before he can finish them. He showed me some letters that were sent to Mr. Steele when he wrote the *Spectators* which he had not made use of, that came to him by Mr. Harris who was Steele's secretary and had all his letters that he did not use.

He told me my Lady Derwentwater went to court and would have been introduced to the King by some of the nobility, but they would not introduce her, and that she waited as the King came through the room and then fell upon her knees to him and presented a petition, but he could not accept of it and turned away from her. And she got admission to the princess and begged her to intercede for her husband, but the princess told her it was not in her power to do her any good, she could only mix her own tears with hers.

Went to the Gill House. Mr. Northey[1] came in. Mr. Bowes told me that he had a great deal of practice and that he had spoke before the House of Commons as counsel for the hackney coachmen who have petitioned the House. He seems to be but a heavy, dull sort of man and incapable of making a good lawyer. Came home at 11.

[1] Edward Northey, son of William Northey of Hackney and nephew of the Attorney-General; called to Bar, Inner Temple, 1709.

Saturday, February 18. Rose at 8. Read Coke all the morning. Was tired with one long case which I could not well comprehend. When that happens I am apt to think the law so difficult a study I shall never be able to do anything at it, and at other times, when my thoughts are clear and steady and my reasoning just, I am apt to fancy great things of myself and that I shall make a great lawyer.

After dinner went to coffee-house with Cousin Billio where was Mr. Dolins [1] with whom I conversed about the public affairs. He said a Bill for the easier and speedier trial of the rebels that are taken and shall be taken was passed yesterday, but it was very much opposed by the Tories and Mr. Letchmere, who when it was just ready to pass, after it was engrossed and himself was of the committee that prepared it, stood up and told the House he had found out a fault in the bill which he did not doubt but they would all be sensible of, and it was about the word *now*, but he was immediately answered by Mr. Vernon, Mr. Walpole, Stanhope and other of the principal Whigs who were very angry with him for abusing the House so. The chief answer the Tories made use of against the Bill was that it was against the liberty of the subject to take away the ancient law of the Kingdom in which every subject was entrusted and by which he was to be tried by his country among his friends and acquaintances.

The deed warrant is signed and sent for the execution of the six condemned lords next Friday.

Sunday, February 19. Brother William Ryder came into the meeting in a new black coat and laced ruffles and new white gloves. I have been so much concerned about my brother's extravagance that it has always of late put me into an uneasiness when he comes to Hackney so fine, but to-day I think I never was in a greater. I could not help reflecting upon the ill consequences of his folly and extravagance which I thought could not possibly be supported but either by robbing the shop or borrowing money, either of which is a fair way to ruin him.

Monday, February 20. After dinner Cousin Ryder and Mrs.

---

[1] Daniel Dolins of Hackney (d. 1728), knighted 1722; secretary of Committee for Promoting Christian Knowledge in 1714; a friend of Ralph Thoresby, the diarist.

Loyd came to our house with Aunt Lewis.[1] We walked together into the garden for half an hour, where we were pretty merry, but we had not much opportunity of being alone together there. I walked home with them and we three walked by ourselves about the fields till it grew dark, during which time Mrs. Loyd mentioned one Parry, an humble servant it seems of Cousin Ryder's, which made her a little angry and uneasy, and she mentioned one Woolridge, one that courted Mrs. Loyd. Upon this there grew a kind of diffidence between them, that the chief discourse was nothing but broad hints and intimations given by each of them, one against the other. When we came to their house we stayed at the door together about half an hour, talking about love.

Tuesday, February 21. Walked with Cousin Joseph Billio in the morning to Aunt Billio. It was extremely pleasant walking in the fields, the first beginning of the spring when the sun begins to warm the earth and gild the fields and wonderfully agreeable to the mind and I feel a strong kind of cheerfulness and alacrity diffuses itself all over me.

Walked to London in the afternoon. At 6 o'clock went to the Grecian Coffee-House. There is a great deal of the best company there. Stayed by some of them, heard their talk. The six condemned lords are to be executed Friday. My Lady Derwentwater was to-day at the Houses of Lords and Commons to have presented a petition to them in favour of the condemned lords, but it won't be presented to the Houses till to-morrow, when the Duke of Richmond[2] promised her he would present it to the House of Lords and they say Sir Joseph Jekyll[3] is to present it to the House of Commons. The rebellion in Scotland is almost at an end and it is expected there will be no more trouble there, and the Duke of Argyll is coming to London.

Wednesday, February 22. Went to our club at Change. The House of Commons have adjourned till to-morrow sevennight. Mr. Heathcote told us that Mr. Walpole and one Mr.

---

[1] Wife of Captain John Lewis (d. 1726), oilman, who lived in Mare Street.
[2] Son of Charles II and Duchess of Portsmouth.
[3] M.P. for Lymington and chief justice for Cheshire; Master of the Rolls 1717-38.

Fuller [1] stood up at once till Mr. Walpole carried it and the other sat down. And he then told the House that they could nor but be sensible that there were several ladies without that were for petitioning the House in behalf of the condemned lords, but as this would necessarily arouse some debates upon that which would be improper (meaning concerning the King's having the right or not right to pardon the lords) he proposed it to the House that they should adjourn for a week that they might avoid entering into these debates. He was then seconded by the Comptroller and Mr. Stanhope. Mr. Fuller would then have presented the petition from the Lady Derwentwater and others, but it was told him he could not enter into such matters till the former was determined and there followed some warm debates upon the adjournment. Mr. Steele was against it and after great deal of debating upon the division it was carried for an adjournment by seven majority, but he said he was well satisfied there were many voted against the adjournment that would have been for rejecting the petition. The House of Lords had the petition read to them and after a great many speeches and debates upon it it was carried to address His Majesty in favour of the condemned lords. This news very much displeased us of the club, because this would cast the odium of their execution if they should be executed upon the King, as it seems likely he will still execute them, because the prince stayed in the House and divided with them against the address.

The conduct of the Lords in voting for an address in behalf of the condemned lords seems strange, but is accountable either from their regard to the dignity of their House and the relation of the families of the condemned lords to some of them, who have to be sure made all the interest possible for them, or else the prevailing force of money. But the King does not seem inclined to pardon them by what he said to Lady Derwentwater last Sunday when she fell upon her knees to him and presented a petition. After he had read it, he told her in French he was sorry for her misfortune but he never sought the life of her husband, and could not help her. I think the King would show a noble resolution and steadiness of mind in spite of the Lords' address to execute them on Friday.

[1] Samuel Fuller, M.P. for Petersfield.

Thursday, February 23. At 12 o'clock went to father in order to ride out, but his mare was lame, which I went to Mr. Leeds to tell him of, and he offered me his horse and he would borrow another, which I took very kindly and accepted. So he and I and Mr. Horseman rode out to Edmonton. We came home at between 6 and 7 with one Mr. Bruet, Mr. Horseman's uncle at whose house we were and drank some wine.

The King answered the Lords' address to reprieve such of them as should appear to him to deserve it. It is pretty certain that the King is against saving or reprieving them himself and this address displeased him. It is thought there is no reprieve yet given and though people generally think some of them at least will be reprieved to-morrow, I am of another opinion.[1] It looks as if there had been a great deal of money given to procure this address.

Friday, February 24. Our maid told me that Mr. Bunbury brought home the news last night that the lords were reprieved for forty days. I could not give much credit to that, knowing the Tories love to deceive themselves with agreeable news. I resolved therefore to go immediately into the city and know the truth of it. Went to brother's and there heard that there was no reprieve and the guards were gone to the Tower. So went to Tower Hill and got a convenient place to see the execution.

The whole hill was full of people that I never saw so large a collection of people in my life, and a vast circle was made by the horse guards round about the scaffolds and a great many foot guards in the middle. At length Lord Derwentwater and Kenmure came in two hackney coaches from the Tower to the transport office over against the scaffolds. I saw them both. Lord Derwentwater looked with a melancholy aspect, but Lord Kenmure looked very bold and unconcerned.

Lord Derwentwater was executed first. After he was brought upon the stage and was saluted by several officers and others that were there, he prayed and spoke to them and told them, as I am informed, that since he was to die he was sorry he pleaded guilty, for he was an innocent man, for he knew no king but King James III. He was a papist and therefore had no priest along with him. He seemed to behave himself very well and make his exit decently

[1] Widdrington, Nairne, Carnwath and Nithsdale were reprieved.

enough, though with but a melancholy and pious aspect. Sir John Fryer, one of the sheriffs of London, attended both of them upon the scaffold. The executioner struck off his head at one blow and then held it in his hand and showed it to the people and said, 'Here is the head of the traitor. God bless King George!' His head and body were wrapped in a black cloth and put into the coach in which he came and carried back to the Tower.

About half-hour after that Kenmure came upon the scaffold and looked with all the courage and resolution of an old Roman. He walked about the stage with a great deal of unconcernedness. Two clergymen attended him upon the stage and prayed, he being a Protestant. When he was beheaded his body was put into a coffin. What he said I have not yet heard.[1] There was no disturbance made at all, while the mob were as quiet as lambs, nor did there seem to be any face of sorrow among the multitude.

It is very moving and affecting to see a man that was but this moment in perfect health and strength sent the next into another world. Few that die in their bed have so easy an end of life. But then what must be the thoughts of a man in that condition, that could count every moment before his death and reflect to the very last, it is impossible to conceive, because one cannot put oneself into that form and temper of mind which these circumstances will necessarily put a man into. The pain of dying is nothing. It is but like a flash of lightning, begun and ended in the compass of a thought. Life itself is attended in every one with much more grievous pains. Why then are we afraid to die? Is it the loss of the pleasures of life, of all the agreeable things in which we delighted? That cannot be all. No, the strange uncertain dark prospect that is before us terrifies us and makes afraid to be we know not what and go we know not where.

I was very well pleased to see that the King had resolution enough to execute these lords. I think he has given in this a greater proof than ever of his fitness to govern this nation, and I am persuaded it will have a good effect both at home to make the Tories partly despair and partly come over to the King, and abroad to raise his character in foreign nations, and convince them that it is not the clamour and noise of rebels or the mob that shall interrupt the course of justice or shake his resolute mind.

[1] He only prayed for James III.

Dined at brother's. There was Cousin John Ryder [1] come from Cambridge. He says the great majority there are against the King, though they all, except five or six, take the oaths to him. They are also much inclined towards popery and are introducing its several practices and doctrines by degrees. He says that a man in a disputation for the Doctor's degree had like to have lost it for maintaining that the absolution of the priest was nothing else but a declaration that God would pardon upon report.

Went at 6 to Grecian Coffee-House. There are a great many gentlemen of very good sense come there. I ventured to sit down among some of them and talk a little about the execution of the lords to-day. Heard them talk a great deal.

Nithsdale made his escape last night out of the Tower.[2] The other lords are reprieved till next Wednesday sevennight, the 7 March.

Saturday, February 25. Cousin John and Robin Ryder went to Hackney with me. He says when Dr. Sherlock was last year Vice-Chancellor of the University he was so far from discouraging the expression of disaffection and disloyalty in the students and those that belonged to the University that he encouraged it and if any information were brought of persons that drank the Pretender's health, &c., he checked the informers and refused to punish the criminals, and yet this man has by a University address which was nothing of extraordinary loyalty and by other insinuating arts found means of being made a Dean.

Monday, February 27. Rose at past 7. Continued all the morning with Cousins Ryder. It was very uneasy to me to be thus obliged to be always with them and have no time to myself. In the afternoon went to London with them and was glad now to have an opportunity of leaving them.

Tuesday, February 28. At 3 Cousin John Ryder and I went to see Cousin Marshall. Found them all at home. At first

---

[1] Uncle Dudley's son (1697?-1775), at this time a student at Queen's College; later Archbishop of Tuam.

[2] His wife, accompanied by Mrs. Mills and Mrs. Morgan (the latter wearing two sets of clothes), smuggled him out in the guise of the enceinte Mrs. Mills.

entrance we looked very silly at one another and could scarce go through the first salutations with a good grace. After we had been some time together we became a little more familiar. Cousin [1] told me he was now engaged in translating St. Cyprian's works and going to publish it with notes concerning the primitive discipline of the Church,[2] which I find he has very much studied, having read the Fathers. We talked also about some philosophical questions, about astronomy and the new system concerning the world in the planets, &c. We talked also about Mr. Locke, which subjects were started by Cousin Ryder. When we were got upon this kind of subjects, the conversation flowed on easily and naturally.

Wednesday, February 29. Rose between 6 and 7. Drank the juice of two Seville oranges as I have done for several mornings in order to remove the scurvy which I believe I have got and purify my blood and to sweeten my breath which I have suspected this good while has been very strong.

Went to our club. Read civil law. I hear Lord Nottingham is turned out of his place of President of the Council and his brother Lord Aylesford from being Chancellor of the Duchy of Lancaster, the occasion of it his being the chief of those that voted for the invidious address of the House of Lords to reprieve the condemned lords.

Thursday, March 1. Rose at between 6 and 7. Went to the cold bath (it was a hard frost) upon the account some rheumatic pains which I had upon, sometimes in my shoulders and arms and was now settled in my foot. I am persuaded it is the best remedy for the rheumatism and intend to go in often. Came home. Mr. Samson came to me about 10 o'clock and soon after Mr. Fernley, my dancing-master. I was very much concerned lest Mr. Samson should discover him to be a dancing-master but I believe he did not.

Friday, March 2. Uncle Dudley Ryder and his son John came to dine with us. We went to the tavern together. Uncle has nothing in him to make him an agreeable or profitable com-

---

[1] i.e. Nathaniel Marshall.
[2] Published in 1717 : *The Genuine Works of St. Cyprian*, 2 parts, fol.

panion, unless to his clients in his own business, but he has nothing of learning nor knowledge of the world nor politeness of thought.

Saturday, March 3. It is very much talked of that there will be a war with France who will declare openly in favour of the Pretender. It is said the Pretender had an audience of the Duke of Orleans for several hours when Earl Stair went to have audience and he was refused.

Went to Aunt Bickley's in order to see Mrs. Loyd. Found all the family at home, so was obliged to keep all company. At last took my leave and went downstairs, when I had an opportunity of getting the young ladies by themselves and being with them for quarter hour, but had been put into such a heaviness and dullness before that I could not talk with much spirit to them then.

Sunday, March 4. Went to church. Was very negligent about the service that was performed. Could not but blame myself for it, especially since my thoughts were chiefly employed about the ladies, how to get opportunities of looking at them through my glass. I could not help looking at Mrs. Alworthy, who has a strange roving eye.[1] I thought it was very comical to see her looking about her and seeming entirely unconcerned about what passed in the pulpit and at the desk, and yet to see her lips continually moving in the repetition of the prayers and joining in the forms of worship with her mouth.

Tuesday, March 6. Mr. Whatley came to me and went out together to the Change and dined there, and then walked in Drapers' Gardens, where there happened to be a couple of ladies walking, one of them very pretty. After having taken several turns and talked of philosophy and concerning the ladies, Mr. Whatley attacks them and begins: 'Ladies! The hours and everything about us smile upon us. How happy should we be if you would condescend to smile upon us too!' After this opening we joined them and walked along with them. The ladies seemed not much displeased. Mr. Whatley had now the task to keep up the conversation, for I could scarce speak a word which he did do, but with less spirit than I thought he could have done.

[1] According to a note in one of the Tyssen MSS., Susanna, daughter of Justice Alworthy of Clapton, was later seduced by Samuel Heathcote.

I could scarce forbear laughing aloud to hear in what a comical manner he carried on the dialogue. After one turn the ladies would have gone out but we pressed them to stay a little longer and they did though for my part I was so uneasy because I had nothing to say that I should have been glad if they had gone away. One of the ladies seemed to be of very good sense and talked very well, said some sharp things. At last they said they were tired and we let them go.

Came to Hamlin's with Mr. Whatley. Whatley was very merry and gay and talked in his usual manner, quoting upon every turn some Latin verse or sentence out of Cicero.

I went at 7 o'clock to the dancing at Mr. Fernley's dancing school. It cost me 2s. for wine and 3s. for Mr. Fernley and 1s. for a hautboy. I think this is too dear for the pleasure I had, the women not being very good company.

Came home at past 11. I found Mrs. Hawksbee and Mrs. Bunbury in great terror upon the account of a strange appearance in the air which they had seen. It was then gone but it soon returned. It was indeed very strange: all towards the north a pale light like smoke mixed with flame shot up and down through the air in great streaks. It was in a perpetual motion, sometimes here and sometimes there, that enlightened all that part of the hemisphere much more than the rest. At last it by degrees wheeled about towards the east. I stayed up till almost 1 looking at it, when it seemed to be almost gone. Mrs. Hawksbee was under a mighty consternation and trembled very much about it.[1]

Wednesday, March 7. Rose at 8. Read Civil Law all the morning till almost 12, when played upon my viol endeavouring to learn to play over the several keys and voluntaries upon each of them, which will give me a much greater relish of music and make me more fit to play lessons.

Dined at brother's. There was Cousin John Ryder. We talked about the appearance last night. He mentioned it as what was told him, that it might possibly be the approach of a comet.

---

[1] The phenomenon caused great consternation. Lady Cowper wrote: 'The Whigs said it was God's Judgment on the horrid Rebellion, and the Tories said it came for the Whigs taking off the two lords that were executed.' The Rev. Mr. Whiston lectured on the subject at Button's, entrance one shilling.

Dr. Avery told us a thing that he was very well assured of, that the King had promised Derwentwater his life if he would discover the conversation that passed between himself, the Queen, Duke Dumont and the Pretender when they were together for several hours in her closet, not long before her death, and that Derwentwater had promised to discover it to the King in writing upon condition that he should not let anybody see it besides himself, the prince and princess and the two secretaries, which the King promised and then sent him back to the Tower, who said he would write it down and send it next day to the King. When he came to the Tower his priest set upon him to persuade him from this and assured him that his life was safe and secure without it, that he had interest enough in the House of Lords to protect him and besides told him of the ill consequence it would be of to their cause, which would be lost for ever if that came to be revealed, that they persuaded him to send the King word next day that he knew nothing at all of the matter. Upon which the King said this was such egregious trifling with him that he could not bear it. And when he was upon the scaffold, the Doctor said he had reason to believe that there were persons that had power to bring him back to the Tower if he offered to make any discovery. And Mr. Ward [1] said a person upon the stage told him that Derwentwater was managed with all the art in the world to prevent him making discoveries. There were only three men in black that seemed concerned with him, but these took particular care not to say or do anything that might move him or excite him. When he spoke to them they would not answer a word to him nor scarce look at him when he looked at them, and when he was speaking, if he seemed to be in danger of over-shooting himself, they would pull him by the coat and give him notice. They managed him there till his head was laid upon the block.

Went to our Club at 'Change. Mr. Heathcote is a man who can talk of nothing but either public affairs, which as a Parliament man he cannot help taking notice of, or else dogs and horses and hounds and hunting. A war with France is very much talked of but not yet ascertained. Some think it will be only an underhand war carried upon the account of the Pretender.

[1] Possibly Knox Ward, son of John Ward of Hackney. Entered Lincoln's Inn 15 February 1714/15.

Thursday, March 8. Rose between 6 and 7. Immediately went to the cold bath, jumped in three times. It took away my breath so much that I could not tell how to stay in long at a time, but the last time I stayed in almost a minute.

I heard that a young woman relation of Mrs. Wallis's the school-[mistress] hanged herself on Sunday night last. The reason of it seems to have been a too sensible resentment of her unhappy circumstances which reduced her to the necessity of receiving her subsistence from her uncle. She had been a great while melancholy before and mighty uneasy within her own mind, but last Sunday she several times expressed her thoughts about self murder, that she thought it reasonable where a person was neither serviceable to the world nor herself, and that put the family into a great concern about her that they watched her continually, but at night she slipped away from them privately and shut herself up in a room, and though they pursued her in five or six minutes after she was found dead upon the ground with her garters tied fast about her neck.[1]

Cousin Billio's were there and after supper we went to country dancing or dancing minuets, having got a fiddler of the town. We had punch to drink of my brother William's gift in regard to his being out of his apprenticeship and oysters and cold fowl, it being brother Ryder's birthday. We were very merry. I had Mrs. Loyd for my partner. She seems to be of an amorous constitution enough and kind and loving. We went to bed at 1.

Friday, March 9. Rose between 7 and 8. Were very merry with sister and the two young ladies who lay at our house. It is said that Lord Nairne was yesterday with the King and has made discoveries very considerable.

Saturday, March 10. Went to John's Coffee-House. We talked of Sir Richard Blackmore's essays that are just come out.[2] He was said to be a man very much conceited of himself. That

---

[1] She was, according to Newcome, Martha Wallis, a mantua maker, niece of William Wallis. He adds that the same evening 'strange coruscations of bright and sometimes red clouds in violent motions like the smoke out of a great gun seen all over England'.

[2] *Essays on Several Subjects*, 1716; cf. Addison's praise in *The Freeholder*, No. 45, and Pope's attack, *Dunciad* ii, 259-68.

essay upon epic poetry Mr. Witnoom said Mr. Hughes told him Mr. Addison commended and approved, but as for the rest they were not so well liked.

Sunday, March 11. Cousin Billio preached in the afternoon. I did not much admire his sermon. There did not seem to be much of spirit or justness of thought in it.

Monday, March 12. Rose at 8. Took some cream of tartar as that which sweetens the blood. I took it chiefly with regard to my breath which I am afraid smells very strong and makes me very uneasy.
In the afternoon went with Cousin John to the bowling green. To bed at 10.

Tuesday, March 13. At past 5 went to the play called *The Drummer*.[1] There is a good deal of mirth in it and something pleasant and entertaining. The prince was at the play. An epilogue was spoken to recommend the cause of religion and liberty and loyalty to the care of the ladies, some part of which was very good. The beginning of it was but dull. However, I was very well pleased to hear it clapped by a full house and a general approbation of the sentiments. The Duke of Argyll stood with the prince talking with him.

Wednesday, March 14. I have had lately a great mind to dance well and as I stood to read I endeavoured to keep my toe out while I was reading, which took up my thoughts so much that my reading was not with so good effect as it should have been.
After dinner came home and read part of Burmann's [2] oration before the University of Leyden upon his accession there. He complains in it very much of the neglect of the Latin tongue and the little regard that is had to its purity in the professors of other sciences, and especially inveighs against the French, who by an ambition to spread their own language and cultivate that have

---

[1] Addison's *The Drummer, or The Haunted House*, first produced at Drury Lane 10 March—this was the second performance.
[2] Pieter Burmann (1668–1741), the great Dutch classical scholar. In 1714 he succeeded Perizonius, who occupied the chair of history, Greek language and eloquence at Leyden.

neglected the Latin almost entirely, which is the only means of correspondence among the learned.

Read some of Waller's poetry, in which I was mightily pleased with some things which were very just and fine, but sometimes a whole poem would be tainted and nothing but a whole series of unnatural and strained thoughts from one end to the other. I read his life also. He appeared under his misfortune [1] to be a man of but a mean spirit, guilty of the lowest humility and submission and flattery. Methinks it is but natural for a poet to be inconstant and ready to change and vary with every wind. Thus Waller when he was returned from banishment under Oliver flattered him to the highest degree and upon the accession of King Charles II equally flattered him, of which both there are now poems of his extant.

Thursday, March 15. Rose between 6 and 7. Went to the cold bath and agreed with the mistress of it for a whole year, for which I gave her two guineas and entered my name in her book. I intend to go in often. The reason of my design is that I think it will strengthen my body, purge it of ill humours, fence me against cold, prevent convulsions which I have sometimes been afraid of by reason of those sudden startings which I have sometimes. I have heard also it is good against the stone and gravel, which I have been afraid of upon the account of those sharp pains I have had about my belly. I expect also it will cure me those rheumatic pains which I sometimes feel and secure me against the gout, which I believe I have felt something of in my health. It will also cure the laxity of the nerves which is the occasion of what they call the vapours.

A little before 12 went to Westminster to hear Lord Wintoun's trial.[2] I found it very difficult to get in and almost despaired, but I resolved to endeavour to join the Lords' eldest sons as they went in and go along with them. I waited in the court of requests in expectation of the House of Lords coming, before whom the Lords' eldest sons I expected would come, but first of all came the company of gentlemen that waited upon my Lord High Steward. To them I joined myself and passed through the

---

[1] i.e. during his trial in 1643 for plotting to seize the City of London for Charles I.

[2] He had originally deferred his plea.

Yeomen of the Guard, who suspected that there were some among them who had no right. One of them stopped me but I looked as big as I could and said something which I have forgotten, and he let me go in. If a person has but courage and could put on a good impudent face he may always find out means of getting to any of these public sights.

When I came into the court, I found it full, just as it was upon the giving sentence upon the lords that pleaded guilty. I was in some pain for a good while after I was got in for fear I should be discovered and turned out, till I gained an assurance and was perfectly easy as to that. I took my pen and ink out and wrote down what I could, but the distance was too great between me and the prisoner and the managers of the House of Commons, that I could not hear perfectly, for I stood above the throne.

When Lord High Steward's (who was Lord Chancellor Cowper) patent was read the prisoner was called to the bar and Lord High Steward told him he had the advantage of being tried before those whose parity of condition in everything except those bonds and the high charge that is laid against him rendered them the more susceptible of mercy in his behalf. When my Lord High Steward had done and the impeachment and his plea to it was read, the manager of the Commons began. Mr. Hampden opened the charge. In the speech, which he read out of a paper he had in his hand, which I could hear only imperfectly, he mentioned the particular facts for which he was charged with high treason and answered the plea of the prisoner. Next Sir Joseph Jekyll spoke and opened the nature of the treason. He went on to oppose the several acts of Lord Wintoun to the plea that he was forced to join with the rebels but did not join them with a rebellious mind.

The Attorney-General, Sir Edward Northey, spoke next but I could not hear much what he said, only broken words and sentences.

When the witnesses were brought to the bar of the House, the first was a Scotchman [1] who came out of Scotland with the rebels to Preston and was examined as to the whole progress of the journey and marches, but could not hear the particulars. There were three more witnesses examined who were among the rebels,

[1] William Calderwood, quartermaster with the rebel army.

one of which was a parson [1] that was Forster's chaplain and came up to London with him bound. When he stood up to be examined there was a general laugh and noise through the whole court. I am very glad they have exposed him in this manner by making him a witness. When each of the witnesses were examined on the side of the House of Commons, the Lord High Steward told the prisoner he might then cross-examine them himself, but he did not [2] (his counsel stood on the other side of the bar, Sir Constantine Phipps and Peer Williams, but L.H.S. said at first that they were not to assist him in anything in relation to matter of fact, but if any matter of law arose it was then their business only to speak).

Then Lord Forester, one of the officers in the King's army, was called upon and he stood up in the House of Lords and was examined about the surrender of Lord Wintoun, who delivered up his arms to him, and whether he gave him any hopes of mercy, and he said he did not. Generals Carpenter and Churchill in the House of Commons and Generals Wills and Mundy and Colonel Cotton at the bar of the House were all examined concerning the surrender and whether any terms of mercy was offered them or whether they knew if any encouragement was given them to expect mercy of the King, to which they all agreed that there were none given. There were some questions asked of these officers by Wintoun, but I could not hear them. Then all the witnesses on the part of the House of Commons were examined. L.H.S. told the prisoner it was now time for him to make his defence. He then said he had not had time to bring up his witnesses, and desired that he might have further time given him, upon which Attorney-General and Steward Cowper spoke against it as a thing inconsistent with the usual methods of proceeding and the Lords adjourned to their own House to debate about it, and returned and L.H.S. told the prisoner that their lordships had considered of it and think it inconsistent with the forms of their House to make any delay ' and therefore you must proceed to your defence, whether your witnesses are come or

---

[1] Robert Patten, who soon after published a *History of the Rebellion*. Having sworn away several men's lives, he became a popular preacher.

[2] Wintoun's reply was a gibe—'I hope you will do me justice and not make use of *Cupar* law, as we used to say in our country, "Hang a man first, and then judge him."'

no'. Upon this Wintoun said that 'this is a form I am not used to (or as some understood him, ' this is a foolish form ') and I am upon trial for my life'. When he was going on it was moved for an adjournment and agreed to till to-morrow at 11 o'clock.

Friday, March 16. Went to Aunt Harding's and sent for some tea and treated them there. Met Mrs. Knot, our old maid when I was a child. She was extremely glad to see me and expressed fondness for one whom she had nursed and bred up.

At 7 o'clock Lord Wintoun came by. He had been at Westminster at his trial and was found guilty. He made no defence, said nothing to justify himself but what he said in his plea, nor did he bring any witness to be examined in his behalf nor did his counsel speak one word for him. So that when the question was put to each of the lords singly whether he was guilty or not they all, not one contradicting, said he was guilty upon their honour.

Saturday, March 17. At night read some poetry which I intend to do often in order to give a politer and more lively turn to my style and thought. To bed at 11.

Sunday, March 18. Going to meeting with father, Mr. Lacy overtook us. Father told him that I had discovered some mistakes in Mr. Barker's sermon and began to enter upon the question and difficulty which I had started at dinner. I was very much concerned to hear my father give such a handle to have it said that we went to meeting only to find fault, so I put it off as well as I could, but father, fond to show his son's parts and capacity, would still push it on. My father is too apt to be betrayed into great imprudences from the vanity he has to show my parts.

At night read a sermon of Tillotson about the work of life and improving time. He has a surprising way of laying his subject and design before you in the plainest and most convincing light. There is one thing which this sermon has convinced me of my folly in, and that is the neglect of secret prayers in set solemn times and my wandering of thought and inattention at the public worship of God, both which I intend by the grace of God to amend for the future.

Monday, March 19. Uncle Marshall came to see grandmother and dined with us. In the afternoon played at picquet till almost 5. Went together to the bowling green, where we were diverted with seeing the eagerness and earnestness of men in the pursuit of their bowls. It is something shocking to see a man of sense running after his bowl and with the greatest earnestness and seeming seriousness address himself to it and bidding it rub or run and then put his body into several odd motions and turnings and shrugs.

After bowls sat down with Mr. Skinner, Mr. Howard and others. Mr. Howard entertained us with two or three pretty stories which he told in a very agreeable manner something like Mr. Isles. Came home. Spent the rest of our night till we went to bed at picquet.

Tuesday, March 20. After I had been at brother's a little while went to Hamlin's with Cousin Joseph Billio. Met there Mr. Whatley and Mr. Smith. We four went to the tavern together, where Mr. Whatley showed us a paper which he had writ for the cure of the vapours. Mr. Whatley proposes that a man should fix to himself one determined end, whether it be riches or wisdom or whatever it be, that he should keep this habitually in view. Mr. Smith read it first over to us, but he did it with such an air of contempt and superiority that he did not do justice to the thoughts.

Mr. Whatley proposed to us that we should meet together in order to talk of some useful subjects and whatever occurs to us in our private reading or observation worth communicating. We agreed to meet together at Hamlin's next Tuesday at 3 o'clock, and that sentiment of Cicero's that a philosopher ought to be *totus aptus ex sese* [1] which Mr. Whatley quoted is agreed upon to be the subject of our next conversation. I don't much admire Mr. Smith as one very fit for this free conversation which we propose. He is too stiff and precise and too suspicious to be a very agreeable companion. Cousin Joseph Billio is a person also who I take not to be the fittest for such a society. One scarce knows when he is in earnest, and when in jest, he has so strange a way of asserting things with vehemence, when it is evident he does not mean what he says. And then he is very apt to con-

[1] *Tull. Parad.* 2nd.

tradict without reason and cannot make concessions. As for Mr. Whatley, I expect he will be the life of our conversation. He has perfect good humour and is free and open and unreserved.

Wednesday, March 21. Mr. Whatley called me to go to the cold bath between 6 and 7. As we went along, he quoted several Greek sentences and Latin, which is very constant with him. I observed to him upon that, that the quoting authors, Latin or Greek, looked so much like pedantry and ostentation of learning that I would advise him to use it very sparingly, never to do in company where he was not well known, because it would expose him as vain.

After we had been in the cold bath and were coming home Mr. Whatley said he would go another way than what we came, which was out of my way. I made some difficulty at it and he observed that a person should not for the sake of a little humour give way to the temptation of being unwilling to do what his friend proposes. But Mr. Whatley is indeed himself far from being of this temper, nothing is more common with him than to oppose the little trifling inclinations of his friends. I am sensible indeed that I am sometimes faulty in that respect, but this proceeds rather from a sudden turn than any ill design or ill humour.

We went to Gray's Inn Walks, where we read over together a pamphlet upon the nature of study. I was mightily pleased with it. There are some of the justest observations upon study and reading in the world. Particularly there is one which I am resolved to make use of in regard to the choice of books. He recommends it as a necessary thing to read but few books but those the best in each particular profession, especially those who have writ first in any science or art, who have introduced it into the world and are looked upon as the masters of it.

Met brother William. He went with me to dinner. He told me that Mr. Hampshire had a great inclination to Mrs. Loyd and that he had a mind to make his address to her, that he had desired his assistance. When this was told me I felt a sudden uneasiness arise within my breast, and, though at that moment I could not desire to have her myself for a wife, I could not help being concerned that she should be another's.

Went thence to our club at 'Change where were Mr. Isles,

Witnoom, Jackson, Porter and Crisp. Our first conversation was about the rebellion, the Triennial Act which it seems is a thing talked of and set on foot by the court.[1] Their end in it seems to be to secure a Whig Parliament which they are in doubt about upon the next election (since the King they say has resolved not to allow any money out of the Treasury to gain one) and also to give encouragement to foreign princes and states to engage in alliances with us, which the inconstancy of our affairs and the frequent changing of Parliaments and our factions make them afraid to enter into with us.

Another part of our conversation was upon the characters of men and Mr. Isles and Witnoom were observing in several gentlemen of good sense some defect or other that rendered them grossly blameable, as particularly that Mr. Serjeant was very much affected and strange in his conversation, that Mr. Hughes had vanity and would every now and then introduce a saying of his own which he had spoke before and intimate his conversation and familiarity with the considerable writers of the present age. Particularly once he said that it was he put Mr. Addison into the way of finishing his *Cato*, which he had despaired of doing.[2] I could not but observe that a secret though improper pleasure arose in my mind upon the mention of the faults in the characters of these men.

Mr. Isles told us a story of a young man that came to him to help into business and told him he was capable of any business that required application and industry and no great head, that he was very diligent and careful. 'I went', says he, 'and received £30 for a gentleman in silver the other day and did not take one bad piece among it all.' I was extremely pleased with this circumstance. I thought it seemed extremely natural.

Came home at past 12. Went to bed at 1.

[1] Originally there was no prescribed length for a Parliament. To prevent such abuses as that of Charles II when he retained one Parliament for seventeen years, an Act for Triennial Parliaments was passed in 1694. Under this, an election was due in 1718. To prolong their power the Whigs introduced a bill substituting septennial Parliaments. This was passed in May 1716 and continued in force until 1911.

[2] John Hughes (1677–1720), a minor poet, dramatist and essayist of whom Johnson wrote a short life. He actually did persuade Addison to put *Cato* on the stage, and undertook to write the fifth Act—even though Addison himself wrote it ultimately.

Thursday, March 22. Went to cold bath with Mr. Whatley at between 6 and 7. The most intolerable humour of Mr. Whatley is that he is assuming and too free and loves to lead the way and be the guide and director and governor. He came to breakfast with me, but was in great haste and because the maid did not come time enough with the things for breakfast, he went away without staying for it. It is strange that because he is pleased to call a man his friend he should fancy he has by that a right to do what he pleases with him and his goods.

Went to dinner to see Mr. Freke because he desired me to come and see him and promised to introduce me to my Lord Chief Justice King's acquaintance, but he was not at home.

Went to Hackney. As I was walking it came into my head to write a poem to Cousin Bibby and Mrs. Loyd about the symptoms of love in the room of a letter which I promised upon that subject. I composed a few verses upon that head, viz.

> As yet a tender mind unused to love,
> Wonders to feel so strange a passion move
> Within its breast.
> In vain the conscious Fair with distant mein
> And artful looks conceals her secret pain.
> The wondrous passion fills the charming face,
> Each feature warms and glows in every grace.

Went to see Mr. Skinner. There was his music-master with him who played upon the organ and sung to it 'Genius of England', which is a noble song: there is something very grand and sublime in it and fit to inspire courage. I sat with him from 4 till past 6. He seems to be a man of good sense and admirable good temper. Our conversation fell for some time upon the temper of the people of Hackney, which he was complaining was so reserved that there was no sociableness or familiarity kept up between families, especially that the women were very much got into the way of censure and scandal and deal in it very much.

Heard there was to be dancing at Mrs. Wallis's to-night, and determined to go there, which we did. I got Mrs. Hudson that lodges there for my partner. She is very agreeable but does not say much. Our dancing passed off pretty well but had too much company of the schoolgirls. Stayed till past 10. There was a French gentleman that danced, who could speak very little English. I had the impudence to venture to talk French to him and I think I did it pretty well. At the end we gave the dancing-master's apprentice for playing upon the fiddle 2s. apiece, which I thought was too much.

Came home. Found everybody but servants in bed, but I determined to sit up a while and read. My inclination led me to sit in the parlour by the fire because it was a little cold, though I was convinced it would be better to sit in my closet because I should be in danger of sleeping before the fire. However, I went into the parlour to sit down, and it came into my head that I was now a-going to break the very rule which I had laid down for myself to-day in some thoughts I wrote down upon *totus aptus ex sese*, viz. that I should habituate myself to submit to the determination of reason by taking care especially that in little matters where there is no greater temptation to the contrary but only the humour or sudden fit of inclination, I do nothing contrary to what I judge right and fit. This thought made me immediately resolve to go into my closet and sit there, which I did and I was mightily pleased with myself for this one act of resisting inclination. To bed at past 11.

Friday, March 23. Rose at 8. Read some of Cicero's Paradoxes in order to understand his meaning in this expression of his *totus aptus ex sese*.

Went at past 7 o'clock with brother William to the Ball. The dancing-master Mr. Lovel danced admirably well, that I almost envied his condition and a secret wish came upon me that I had been a dancing-master to have had an opportunity of excelling in that way. It came into my head then that I was well made for dancing and had I been brought up to it should have excelled in that way, whereas in the present way of life I did not think I should make any figure.

Saturday, March 24. Rose at 7. Went to cold bath. Came home. Read law. My foolish passion for dancing had got so much into my head that it interrupted my study and hindered almost every thought of law as I read it.

Went to John's Coffee-House: met Mr. Porter there. Talking about the ease of the death by beheading he said he thought immediately after the head was off he had his sensations all perfect as long as the circulation in the brain continued. He said that he has cut off the head of a viper which has been alive for some time after and would bite and wound as mortally then as before. The viper's body after its head is severed from it will move 24 hours after, and he has skinned a viper and 24 hours after that it has moved, and though he has cut the body in two parts it has moved still and when that motion was ended he has pricked each of the parts with a pin and they have both of them moved upon it and winced as if they had felt pain. He said this was an argument that there were two consciousnesses, because each part moved when they were separated. This was what we were disputing upon a good while, but came to no determination.

Went to Hackney. Mr. Leeds walked with me and Cousin John Ryder. Our conversation was nothing extraordinary. As we went to Hoxton we went into the place where they made cannon and balls,[1] where we saw the moulds in which the cannon were cast and the manner of casting brass cannon. The moulds are made of a tempered earth that hardens and are entirely spoilt after having made one cannon. Mr. Leeds went to our house and I sent for a bottle of wine and treated him.

Sunday, March 25. I was when at church in the morning extremely concerned to see my brother William so very fine and extravagant in his dress and clothes, that it interrupted my attention to what was said. I know my father does not allow him money enough to spend at that rate, nor do I think he robs the shop now; there are too many watchful eyes over him I believe to let him be capable of doing that. He must certainly then have somebody that makes an advantage of lending him money at vast interest. It will signify nothing to speak to himself about it: it is a misfortune that he has not sense enough to be capable of advice.

After sermon went with Cousin Ryder to Aunt Bickley's. I was pretty gay and lively in my discourse. Mrs. Loyd was there and mightily pleased with our company, but I was afraid to talk too near her lest my breath, which I am afraid is very strong, should offend her. To bed at 11. Took some cream of tartar in hopes of its purifying and sweetening my blood and thereby sweeten my breath also.

[1] This is probably the Foundry near Windmill Hill, St. Luke's, which John Wesley used twenty-five years later as the first Methodist chapel.

Monday, March 26. Father spoke to me about his circumstances, that they were but indifferent. He mentioned brother William, that he did not put himself forward in business and was afraid he would not be fit for business. I might have had a pretty good opportunity of talking with my father about brother William's manner of living and extravagance, but I was afraid to mention it before I had well considered the matter. I know it will be an inexpressible grief and concern to him to have such a thing put into his head and may perhaps do him a great deal of harm.

In the afternoon Mr. Porter came to see me. I sent for a bottle of wine to treat him. Our conversation was nothing extraordinary because Cousin John Ryder was there. Walked to London with him. Our conversation happened to fall upon disorders. He said that abundance of diseases are now mixed with the venereal one, especially the King's Evil very often takes its original from that. When any of the parents have had it and though outwardly cured yet has propagated itself to their posterity in the King's Evil,[1] and it is a sign that the King's Evil derives its original from the pox when it yields to mercury, for no other sort of the King's Evil will yield to it but that.

Tuesday, March 27. Rose between 5 and 6. Went to the cold bath. The morning was a hard frost, that I was almost afraid to go in, but I conquered my fear and did go on. Met Mr. Whatley there.

Went to Hamlin's in order to meet Mr. Smith, Whatley and Cousin Billio, there to go together upon our former design. Mr. Whatley brought us a paper with some thoughts upon *totus aptus ex sese*, and so did Mr. Smith a little upon the signification of the word *aptus*. Though I had writ down a good deal, I did not think fit to expose it.

When we had done talking of our appointed subject, Mr. Whatley read to us some occasional reflections of his own which he calls *pensées détachées*. One was that when he read such a book as Homer that had entertained the greatest men in the world, Plato, Aristotle, Cicero, &c., he was pleased to think that he was just so employed as these great men had been before. It was an entertaining thought to him to think that he now saw the same

[1] i.e. scrofula.

sun and moon which enlightened Plato, &c., and in them observed the wisdom and power and goodness of the Creator as they had done before him. We agreed the next Tuesday to bring in writing each of us a scheme of rules and methods for the better improvement of our society, and also to read part of the 1st *Satire* of Horace together.

I went then with Mr. Smith to a friend of his, who plays upon the bass viol very well, who is a silk weaver and works in gold and silver and makes the richest gold and silver stuffs that are made in England. We played, Mr. Smith and I, upon the flute and he upon the viol, and some time after a Frenchman came in who sung some of the French opera songs in concert with our two flutes and the bass. He sung particularly that part of the opera of *Psyche* [1] which we saw at Paris, in which the Vulcans come in and sing *Frappons*, &c. It pleased me very much as it revived in me the ideas I had when I was at Paris and filled me with that same kind of pleasure which I had when I was in the opera there. The French music has a very different air and manner from ours; it is extremely simple and easy, but there is a peculiar kind of harmony which touches me very sensibly. To bed at 12.

Wednesday, March 28. Went to our club. I talked very well upon our civil law. I find I have a very clear head and conceive a thing as quick and clearly as most. Mr. Leeds told us that Judge Blencowe [2] at the last assizes at Oxford made a very long charge to the Grand Jury, in which he said that the riots and tumults that were made here were the beginning of the rebellion in Scotland and therefore if that was just logic, Oxford was the first in the rebellion.[3] Upon his saying this several of the Heads of Colleges, who as usual sat upon the bench with him, went away and consulted together what to do as to this reflection of the judge. It was proposed by some of the hottest of them to bully the judge, but that was overruled by the rest who determined to depute some of their company to go next morning to the judge and desire him to explain himself as to what he had said. Accordingly they went

---

[1] Jean-Baptiste Lully's *Psyché*, 1678.
[2] Sir John Blencowe, judge of common pleas.
[3] The rioting at Oxford was quelled when General Popper and his dragoons rode into the town on 17 October 1715.

to his chambers and told him their errand and desired he would explain himself. He said he thought he had spoke plain enough upon the bench and so many as were there to hear him could not but understand what he meant and therefore he should not be at the pains to say it in other words. It looks as if the judge had notice of some design that the Parliament had to curb the power of the clergy and resent the insolence of the University.

Went to our club at Change. Mr. Heathcote talked a good deal about the repealing the Triennial Act which is so much the subject of discourse at present. He argued very much from the necessity of it in order to the having a good parliament which he said would be almost impossible the next time of choice if that Act be not repealed.

Friday, March 30. Paid landlady £3 6s. for quarter's rent and coals. Pleased myself with the thoughts of going to Aunt Bickley's and seeing Mrs. Loyd that night. Called there but nobody at home.

Saturday, March 31. Rose at 7. My physic worked very well with me. Cousin John Ryder and I exercised ourselves in jumping. Read by myself at the house of office Horace's 1st *Satire*, about the discontented humour of mankind in their present enjoyments.

After dinner went with Cousin John to Aunt Bickley's to ask the young ladies to walk out. We found them engaged at work that they could [not] go out so soon. I had brought an orange on purpose to give Jack Lewis but I was in a mighty difficulty how to give it him lest it should look like ostentation to his mother. It made me a little uneasy that I had like not to have given him it at all. At length at 5 o'clock I persuaded them to take a walk, it being a very fine evening, but Aunt Bickley said she would walk with us. I could not refuse to accompany her, but Aunt Lewis easily observed that we had much rather be alone, and so she put her off it and told her we were going to ramble a great way and would walk too fast for her.

We walked together towards the Marsh till we came upon the side of a hill, from which we had a very fine prospect of

MARE STREET, HACKNEY, 1731

This print is not contemporary and its source is unknown. Although it may not be authentic it is reproduced as the only available illustration that shows, with some accuracy, the part of Hackney where Dudley Ryder lived

the Marsh and the town [1] and houses beyond it. Here we sat down together upon the banks. Our conversation turned very much upon a book that they had lately read called *Lindamira*,[2] a kind of a romance which they very much commended and admired. This led us naturally into a discourse about love. They pretended to be mighty ignorant of that and careless about it, but at the same time discovered a peculiar pleasure in hearing it talked of. We sat upon the bank for an hour and half. Indeed as long as Mrs. Loyd is present there is no danger of being at a loss for discourse, for she loves dearly to hear herself talk. As we came home when it grew duskish and the sun was set, but the evening continued extremely pleasant, it came into my head to talk of gallantry and knight-errantry and enchanted castles and cruel giants who barbarously treated the Fair. The houses that we saw at the distance I suspected to be enchanted castles and the trees to be giants and ourselves knight-errants that were ready to vindicate the peerlessness of the beauty of our ladies at the point of our swords if any dared to deny it. I carried on this fancy as well as I could but I must confess did it but indifferently that I was glad to drop it.

Came home, found myself a little uneasy, my throat began to grow a little sore and my pulse beat and my hands grew hot that I suspected I had got cold and was going into a fever, so I went to bed. Drank some fever water and sweated.

Sunday, April 1. Found my throat pretty sore. Was afraid I had got such a cold as might bring me into a consumption because I had heard of a consumption being got by such a thing. Cousin John Ryder stayed at home with me. We walked in the garden together and read a sermon of Archbishop Tillotson together and talk about it, and what else it raised in our minds. The sermon was an admirable good one about the security from dangerous errors; that the good man, one that sincerely desires to know and do the will of God, shall be secured from any dangerous and fatal errors, both because such a man is better disposed to see and discover the truth, and the goodness of God is concerned to secure such a man from dangerous mistakes.

---

[1] Hackney.
[2] *The Adventures of Lindamira, A Lady of Quality.* Written with her own hand to her friend in the country; Revised and corrected by Tom Brown, 1702.

Upon the occasion of something in this discourse we talked about an established Church, and I convinced him of the absurdity and inconvenience and unreasonableness of it because it laid a bias upon the mind in the search for truth and a man ought not to have any bias, passion or interest given to him.

Went to meeting in the afternoon, and to Aunt Billio's afterwards and from thence we took a walk in the fields towards the Marsh. It was a mighty pleasant evening. Intend to go into the cold bath to-morrow morning a-horseback.

Monday, April 2. Rose at between 5 and 6. Brother William rose with me and told me he had been last night with Mrs. Loyd a good while alone and they talked about Mr. Humphries, that she could not help commending him and owned her esteem for him. It was with some concern that I felt within my breast a strong kind of uneasiness upon the mentioning that, and I am now very sensible of the justness and truth of what the *Tatler* had mentioned before with regard to the women, that even where they are not in love themselves the sense that other ladies are beloved and esteemed above them will make almost in love, at least uneasy and jealous. Though I am sure I am not in love with her and should not choose her for a wife, yet when it was told me that she had a mighty regard and seemed to have a love for Mr. Humphries I could not help being very uneasy.

Read some of *Lindamira*. There are a great many very natural thoughts and turns of humour and passion which I am well pleased with.

After dinner went to Madam Crisp's to see Mr. William who is very ill of the consumption and almost given over.[1] As I went along several serious thoughts came into my mind as proper matter for conversation with Madam Crisp, in relation to death, but when I came there the discourse did not turn that way. Mr. William himself was there and Mr. Read the parson and any that might discourage him or sink his spirits, I perceived, was avoided so that I scarcely condoled with her upon her son's dangerous illness, and the conversation turned upon news and other indifferent matters. Madam Crisp seemed glad to see me and did as generally she does, make me a compliment

[1] William Crisp, bachelor and lodger, died at Hackney 7 August 1716.

upon my being company, which I did not know how to take because I am but too conscious to myself that I am not agreeable company.

Came home, went to Aunt Bickley to wait upon the young ladies there to London. They were for going in the coach, but I persuaded and almost forced them to walk on foot, it being a very fine evening about 5 o'clock. When we were got a little way in our walk Mrs. Loyd appeared unwilling to walk on foot and said she had been blooded that morning and it would be dangerous for her. Upon this I immediately would have had her gone back and I would have got a coach for her because I was indeed afraid it might do her damage, but she then persisted in it, notwithstanding all my prayers and entreaties, to walk. At last we fell into gay discourse and *Lindamira* came into conversation, upon which I very handsomely rallied them upon their affected ignorance of love when they were so much delighted with that book.

I conducted them when I came into Moorfields in a coach to brother's where they stayed a little while and I went with them to her uncle's where I left them for a while, but came back to buy some snuff there for sister, and I went upstairs to them, being all alone, and stayed with them till past 9 o'clock.

Tuesday, April 3. Rose between 5 and 6 in order to accompany my sister part of the way to Bath. I had before pleased myself with the thoughts of having by that means the company of a very pretty lady, and I found my expectation not in the least disappointed. The lady was Mrs. Marshall.[1] She had something so very agreeable in the cast of her countenance and features of her face as touched me very sensibly when I first saw her. I therefore kept as close to the coach side as possible and took all the opportunities I could of looking into the coach and talking to her, and indeed I had more assurance than ever I had before, for I ventured to talk to her very soon. But my eyes were always fixed upon her and the more I looked the more I felt myself moved and pleased with her looks, and it was something of a pleasure to me now and then to meet her eyes and catch them turned upon me. I had the vanity to think that she was pleased with me at first, but soon my joy upon that account

[1] Sally Marshall, the daughter of a Highgate tailor.

was turned into uneasiness and a great many little accidents, the motions of her eyes or change of her looks or words made me think her approbation at best but very fitful. I think I never felt my heart more sensibly moved in my life than I did with the sight of her. She has some inexpressibly sweet in her countenance. She never said much but had as I thought a most agreeable modesty. I and brother went with the coach to dinner at Slough. All the way I took every opportunity I could to look at her and talk to her and express a tender concern and peculiar regard for her. I could not help wishing I was going to the Bath with her and told her so. At Slough I had her company nearer and was more and more charmed with her and did what I could to entertain her with discourse, but I was, as I am always, very deficient that way. From Slough we went a mile in the coach with her, our horse being led before us.

I thought myself very happy and expressed to her as much and seemed extremely unwilling to part, but we were forced to do it to go to Aunt Lomax's, whither we went that night, but it [lay] across the country. We found it very difficult to find the road, so that we did not get to the Hay till 9 o'clock at night. The latter part of our journey was very tedious and unpleasant, being very dark and in continual danger of losing our way, as we did often.

Brother Ryder and I soon after we parted with sister fell into conversation about brother William. I told him my sentiments of him, that his extravagant way of living could not possibly be supported by what my father allows, and therefore he must get either by robbing the shop or borrowing upon vast interest, and I thought this last was the likeliest, because being formerly discovered in robbing the shop the eyes of all the shop are upon him to watch him. I asked brother what to do in this case, whether to advertise my father of this. But my brother said that would be a very dangerous experiment; my father is strangely and unaccountably prejudiced in brother William's favour and thinks he knows his business.

Brother told me that father's affairs in relation to partnership are in a very difficult posture at present, the partnership being now out and to be signed again. Mr. West has refused to sign it with Mr. Bailey because he sees him to be a man unfit for business. My father is at a great uncertainty what to do in this case, whether to turn off Mr. West or Mr. Bailey. If he turns off this last it will be a great hardship upon him because he has a large family of small children. If he lets the other go he will be in danger of losing the greatest part of his trade. And how my brother William will be brought in I don't know. Our conversation broke off where it begun, for we remained still in an uncertainty what to do.

When we came to the Hay Aunt Lomax was in bed. We came to her door and knocked. As soon as she heard it was us she began to make a most hideous noise and crying, as if she was extremely sick, but it looked so much as if it had been done with design that I had not the least sentiments of pity. She was glad to see us, but full of complaints of her own case, though as our conversation increased she seemed to forget she was ill and talked as well and brisk as if not at all out of order. We went to bed, tired, at 10.

Wednesday, April 4. Rose before 6. Did not go out till past 7. Went the by-way through Bovingdon to Watford. The road was extremely pleasant, much more than the common road, but difficult to find, that we lost our way. At Watford we went to Mrs. Evans's. She is, it seems, an ignorant Tory and looked upon the strange appearance in the air as a prodigy that portended great things, and her sister said that the King would not have pardoned the rest of the lords as is talked of except it had been for that. So very ignorant are the people and so easy to be imposed [upon] by superstition.

Came to London at 2 o'clock after a pretty fatiguing journey through a great deal of rain and wanderings out of our way. When was at brother's Mrs. Byam and Mrs. Mesees came to brother to desire him to go with her to the Sheriff's Feast,[1] which was to be to-night. He could not go and after some consideration I offered my service which was accepted. When we came there we soon got to country dances. Mrs. Byam was my partner. The company was not so good as they said was usual at their feasts, though there was some of the nobility. Mrs. Byam was a little peevish that I had not that pleasure from her company that I expected, but she is a very sensible girl and talks well enough. There were some few pretty ladies enough but

[1] Sir John Fryer's feast at Skinners' Hall.

nothing very extraordinary. Came home at 12. Brought her home in the coach.

Thursday, April 5. Rose between 7 and 8. Began to write down some rules for our society with Cousin Billio, Mr. Smith and Whatley. When Mr. Whatley came in he was extremely dejected and got into one of his melancholy fits. The poor man could not put on one pleasant look nor speak a word. He told me now he expected never to be happy and cheerful more. I did what I could to divert him out of this humour, but all in vain. I did not know but reading over the *Guardian* wherein his case is exactly described might touch him and please him and therefore read it, but he was unmoved at the description of himself, when I mentioned Milton's poem upon melancholy [1] and endeavoured to change his melancholy into that agreeable one which Milton there describes. But all in vain.

Cousin John Ryder came to me and asked me to go with him to Uncle Marshall's to dinner. They were at dinner but we got a good dinner. Our conversation was nothing extraordinary, only Cousin Marshall, as we were talking of Dr. Bentley,[2] said that he was one of the greatest men living. He was acquainted perfectly with everything and talked of any subject that occurred with the greatest ease, but then he said with all this learning and parts he had not common sense in his behaviour and management of himself. He was so intolerably insolent that he treated everybody with whom he conversed as his scholar and had not the least deference or regard to the rest of mankind. This makes him hated by all the university of Cambridge and all that converse with him. His pride is so great that it is intolerable.

Friday, April 6. Went to Hackney on horseback. Walked the horse all the way. I had a mind to think as I went along, but did not much. It is a strange thing how vanity and love of being observed and esteemed mixes itself insensibly in our most ordinary actions. I could not help as I went along pleasing myself in hopes somebody or other that knew me would meet me

---

[1] *Il Penseroso.*

[2] Richard Bentley, Master of Trinity, 1700–42. His encroachments upon the privileges of Fellows led to his being twice brought to trial before the Bishop of Ely.

in that thinking studious posture. It might give them a notion of me as a great thinker, that knows how to employ myself alone and take pleasure in retirement. This is not the only time I have had that thought in my head and it has made me put on a more fixed countenance than ordinary.

When I came to Hackney my mother's house was almost filled with ladies. Some of the company stayed with us all night, and I was obliged to spend my time chiefly with them. I had the assurance to put on a certain air of familiarity and indifference towards them which I thought became me very well.

Saturday, April 7. Went to Hackney at 6 o'clock. Read two or three poems that I met with at Moorfields by the way.

Sunday, April 8. Rose before 8. Read a little of Sharrock's *De Officiis* [1] concerning the debts that children owe their parents and I was very well pleased with one thing that was mentioned, that children ought from gratitude to behave so as to make their parents as easy as possible and never to do what may render their lives troublesome or burdensome to themselves or make them uneasy. Methinks indeed children ought always to have this in view and act with a regard to that in all they do that may any way affect or concern their parents, to observe their humours and inclinations, and never give way to any desire or fancy of their own that may be displeasing to them.

To-day the new meeting-place was first preached in and Mr. Mayo began it. He preached both morning and afternoon. He dined with us. Among other things of conversation, the manner of pronunciation in preaching was talked of, and the way of making sermons. Cousin John Ryder being at table would now and then put in something of his in a way unbecoming a young man and I was mightily in pain about him for his too great forwardness, though perhaps I might be guilty of the same fault myself.

Mr. Mayo is a good, honest, sincere man that I believe has the good of people at heart as much as any man. He has also right notions of the manner of preaching, which ought to be done in familiar, easy way that is natural and like conversation

---

[1] *De Officiis secundum Naturæ Jus*, Oxford 1660, by Robert Sharrock, archdeacon of Winchester.

upon important subjects, but it is his misfortune that his voice tires before he gets to the end of his sermons. The meeting-house was pretty full in the morning, but very full in the afternoon, though the majority seemed to be strangers.

Monday, April 9. Rose at 6. Went with Cousin John Ryder to the Marsh River and there I jumped into the water and so did he go in. It felt colder than the cold bath, not that it is really colder but the cold bath is so cold that it makes glow again. We read Horace together by the way.

When we came home Cousin Joseph Billio came and breakfasted with us and as we walked home with him it came into our heads to go to the bowling green now there was nobody there and we did so and met Mr. Justice, who made up four. We went away about between 1 and 2 and promised to come again in the afternoon, which we did, and I won 4s. 6d., not only by the game but laying wagers upon my bowls being better than my antagonist. I played from 4 till 7, when I began to play very well.

At night Mr. Justice and myself and Cousin Billio and Ryder and Mr. Howard went into the house to break a bottle of wine that I lost to Mr. Justice. Our conversation immediately was turned by Mr. Justice (who is a very angry man) to the subject of the new meeting-house. It is a strange thing how this affair has soured the minds of people in Hackney, especially Mr. Barker's side, against their brothers that they cannot allow one man a good word that is against them. It was in vain for me to say anything, for I was presently overpowered by the torrent of words and ridicule of Mr. Justice.

Tuesday, April 10. Went to London at 9 with a design, my Cousin Ryder and I, to go to Putney to see Mr. Gregg. We took Cousin Watkins with us who was to dine at Madam Pilkington's. We together by water. Cousin Watkins is a man that has no idea of good company unless there is singing and merry stories. So to singing he went and though a very bad voice would go on. Thus our journey passed away upon the water, with very little other conversation than what was about music and singing.

We went to Mr. Gregg's, but he was not at home so Cousin

Ryder and I were forced to go to an inn. Our dinner there was but indifferent. I talked with my landlord about the gentlemen of the town, particularly Mr. Oldsworth, whom he said at first when he came into the town had scarce clothes to his back and those very bad, but when he got into his property was finer than anybody else, that all the ladies in the town fell in love with him. I talked with him also about the ladies and asked questions about them, that I believe the man believed we were fortune hunters.

We walked out into the fields to look about the town till 3 o'clock, when we went to Mrs. Pilkington's. My time passed away there in looking upon them at cards at ombre. I don't find among these fine folks that their conversation is better or more improving or diverting than others, only they have a certain genteel air of carrying it and saying very ordinary things without concern. It grew towards 5 o'clock and I was glad it was time to remove. We made our bows and went away.

We walked it all the way to Southwark, it being a fine day and very pleasant. We stopped at Spring Gardens [1] to refresh ourselves with a glass of wine, but were most sadly abused there by some of the servants when we went away because we told them the bottle in which they gave us our wine wanted considerably of full measure. They happened to know Cousin Watkins and bantered him about his pills and purges. However, we bore it all and look indifferent unconcerned philosophers at the noise and folly of fools. Went away with our pipes in our mouths and walked the rest of the way home, only crossed the water.

Wednesday, April 11. After dinner to father's to get a suit of clothes. I was very much in doubt what to have but after some talk with my father about it who was unwilling I should have cloth, I chose a stuff.

Went to our club at Change. Mr. Isles as usual told several stories mighty agreeably. I wish I could imitate him, but I am sensible my memory is not good enough for it.

Yesterday the Duke of Devonshire made a motion in the House of Lords for the repeal of the Triennial Act. He introduced it by telling them that he was the person that brought that bill into the House of Commons when he sat there. He thought

[1] New Spring Gardens, better known as Vauxhall Gardens.

it would have been of service, but the consequences of it have shown the contrary, that multitudes of inconveniences had attended which he enumerated in a very handsome manner. He therefore proposed that it might now be altered. It was read a first time in the House of Lords and ordered to be read a second time next Saturday.

Forster got out of Newgate this morning and is not yet heard of.[1]

Came home at 12. I was very warm with drinking wine and had a mighty inclination to fill a whore's commodity. I walked up and down the street in order to find one. At last one came behind me and clapped me on the back as if she knew me and when I turned she begged my pardon; she thought it had been one she knew. However, she soon recovered herself and asked me to go along with her. She had a very pretty girl at my service. I was a little confounded what to say to her and could not rally her as I would have done, so after some little discourse I parted with her and came home.

Thursday, April 12. Before dinner went to Gascoigne's the tailor's to take measure of me for a suit of clothes.

When came to Hackney went to the bowling green. After some time stay there, Mr. Howard who was playing at bowls came to me and asked me to come with Mr. Skinner and sup with him. I thanked him and did not refuse, but I began to repent of my being so easily brought to it especially since I was afraid I should be obliged to a return, which would not be convenient. So after bowling we went to his house. I soon found myself very unfit for their conversation which turned almost entirely upon the little trifling adventures of their lives, what they did such a time, what they met with when they went to such a place, what such a man said on such an occasion, &c. In this manner the whole time was spent without my having an opportunity of putting in a word, for I cannot tell how to make a story out of anything of that nature.

Friday, April 13. Aunt Billio dined with us. She told us how she was perpetually teased by Mr. Barker's friends with the

[1] Having made Pitt, the keeper of Newgate, drunker than usual, Forster locked him up and let himself out. He escaped to France.

stories raised upon the other side. The women that are for Mr. Barker are grown half-mad in his favour that they have no temperance nor are able to set any bounds to their tongues.

Came to London. Was in some perplexity what book to take in hand that I began to think of a method of study when I did not read law. I have a mind to read over the best classics and also gain a good knowledge of the history of England. And besides this would read over our most polite authors in order to form my own style and gain a good habit of thinking and speaking. The only time I can allow for this kind of study is the afternoon in London and sometimes the whole day in the country, for I have determined law for my constant morning employment in town. For reading the Roman authors I think the best time will be from about an hour after dinner till 5 or 6 o'clock and from that time till bed for English history and polite authors in English, because they are most proper to keep me awake, such as plays, romances, poetry, essays, anything of wit or humour or imagination. As for the Roman authors or any other author of note I intend before I sit down to read any such author to make me a little paper book in which I shall set down whatever remarks occur upon them. I intend to begin with Cicero's treatise *De Legibus*.

Saturday, April 14. Rose at before 6. Went to cold bath. Read law all the morning. Stayed at home in the afternoon till past 4 for a new suit of clothes, in which time I began upon Cicero's *De Legibus*, and wrote down some remarks upon it.

Sunday, April 15. Rose between 7 and 8. Read part of a sermon of Tillotson. I am more and more pleased with his manner of writing. I am only vexed with myself that what I hear or read in the way of religion has no more effect upon my life to assist my conduct, teach me to govern my passions, conquer my unruly inclinations and live by the rules of reason.

Read some of Chillingsworth against the papists. He carries on that controversy exceeding well, pursues the Jesuit through all his sophistry and tricks and exposes him very fully.

Cousin Robert Billio was at the House of Lords last Saturday when the Bill for the repeal of the Triennial Act and establishing a septennial Parliament was devised in the House of Lords upon the second reading. The chief speakers on the side of the Whigs who were for the Bill were Lord Cowper, Parker, Islay, and on the side of the Tories against the Bill were Nottingham, Anglesey, Aylesford, Peterborough. Some of the chief arguments that were used against the Bill were that it was a taking away the liberty of the subject, destroying our constitution, giving too much prerogative to the crown; the people chose their present representatives only for three years and they would be no longer the Parliament chose by the people if they are continued longer without their consent, and their mind and will ought always to be consulted in matters wherein the constitution is to be altered. That formerly by the ancient custom of the Kingdom the Parliament used to be chose every year and the Triennial Act gave the crown a greater prerogative in this matter than it had before by the custom of Parliaments, since he might now continue one three years. That this will alienate the mind of the people from the King and if they are now disposed to rebel will encourage that disposition. That we ought not for a present little necessity or conveniency alter the fundamental laws of the nation and give up the liberty of the subject, nor put a power into the hands of the crown which some future evil prince or counsellors or ministry may make use of to the quite destroying the liberty of the subject. That it is therefore a matter of the greatest consequence, at least to posterity, to have this Triennial Act kept in being, and besides the very same reasons that are now urged for making this a Septennial Parliament may be used at the end of the seven years to continue it still further, so that we don't see where this will end.

The arguments that were made use of chiefly for the Bill were: that the present necessity of our affairs require it; that there is a strong disposition in the people to rebel and the enemies of the government were waiting for such an opportunity as the choice of a new parliament would give them to rebel again when the nation is all in a ferment and disturbances and mobs and tumults were raised through the Kingdom and the people assembled; that the Triennial Act had been a great prejudice to the people as it had been the means and would be so still of keeping up the spirit of faction and disaffection in the nation, setting people's minds against one another and destroying all society and good neighbourhood; that it ruined the estates of country gentlemen who could not bear the expense of so frequent elections. And besides this present Triennial Act is but of twenty years' standing and therefore to take it away can be no breach of our constitution unless the making it had been one. That there had been a Triennial Parliament enacted in the year 1640 but was repealed presently after the accession of Charles II to the throne for much the same reason that it is to be repealed now, viz. it being just a rebellion in order to strengthen the hands of the prince against his rebel subjects. And as to the ancient custom of calling Parliaments every year that was for the convenience of the subjects themselves who wanted to be at their own houses in the country.

Monday, April 16. Rose at 7. Took some cream of tartar last night and this morning. I took it with a design to purify my blood and so remove those ill humours which I believe are the cause of my breath's being so strong as I find it is every now and then.

Went to the Drawing-Room with Cousin John Ryder. There was a pretty deal of company and well dressed. The King and Princess were there. They have both of them a great deal of good-humoured familiarity with them.

Tuesday, April 17. Went to Hamlin's. Cousin Billio and Mr. Smith and Mr. Whatley and I met together. Went to the tavern and there read the 1*st Satire* of Horace together. Mr. Whatley was in a strange impertinently merry humour that he often interrupted us with a laugh without any the least reason.

When we had done with Horace Mr. Whatley told us he had something to communicate to us and would desire our counsel and judgement. He had now an opportunity offered him of going to Constantinople with Mr. Wortley Montagu who is nominated ambassador there, and that he was extremely pleased with such an opportunity of being introduced into the public affairs which he had long desired and endeavoured to qualify himself for. Mr. Wortley Montagu being an intimate acquaintance of Lord Chief Justice King, he had recommended him to him and he had been now these three or four days employing himself in the thoughts of writing a letter to Lord Chief Justice in which he gives him the reason of his choice and the *ratio* of his life, and he desired we would read it and correct what faults there might be in the sense of it. Mr. Smith then read it to us, of about an hour long, in which he first gave an account of the reasons of his desiring this journey and post, and then his own qualifications for it. Under the first head he introduced his notions of human life and philosophy in considering himself in relation to the whole universe of beings and that place which he bore with regard to the great, the mighty whole which comprehended innumerably more worlds besides our little earth. And in this view of himself all the distinction of fortune, honour or grandeur between men here which make so mighty and so vast a figure in the eyes of the generality of the world disappear, they being only like the hills and mountains upon the earth, which when they are regarded near look very great and seem to destroy the earth's rotundity, but when looked upon in relation to the vast mass of earth which our world contains appear only like the little unevennesses in the peel of an orange and are as it were nothing at all. But as he not only bore a relation to the whole system of being but was more particularly related to this world and his fellow creatures among whom he was to live, he was to consider himself with relation to them and the particular post or station in which he was to be among them, and in this view of himself he had for a great while determined himself to apply himself to public affairs even when his chief design seemed to others to be the law. He was now therefore very happy in having such an opportunity as this of going to Constantinople where he might have both an occasion of being introduced into business and also leisure and opportunity of improving his mind in the knowledge especially of what the ancients wrote and the best of the moderns, enlarging his views of men and the world and acquainting himself with the several interests of the princes of Europe, their relations to one another and their several views. He there gives his reasons for desiring this post in a great many more words and some very good thoughts. Under the next head, viz. his qualifications for this employment of secretary to Mr. Wortley Montagu, it is a little shocking to hear him talking of himself and his own qualifications but it is his temper and he cannot help it.

As to the whole performance there are a great many good thoughts in it, but writ in too confused a manner and with too

great a prolixity. The worst of it is that there appears too great an air of vanity to be relished till he is well known.
    Went to supper. Came home. Writ this in my diary and grew very sleepy. To bed 11.

    Wednesday, April 18. Went to our club. I talked very well upon the civil law. The more I observe my genius I find it lies chiefly in seeing through an argument and being able to judge of truth clearer than most. It is my great misfortune that my memory is not good, that I cannot relate particular facts and embellish conversation with proper stories. However, as I have the talent of seeing into an argument and discovering truth pretty well, I hope I shall be able to bear a tolerable character in life as a lawyer, though I cannot expect anything extraordinary. And together with this good judgement I think I have also a genius for polite writing and just natural thoughts. I have no very quick imagination nor ready wit but my thoughts I think are generally good and natural and something strong and lively.
    The Lords read the Bill for the Septennial Parliament the third time to-day and carried it, 69 to 33.[1] They say the French court is mightily alarmed at it because they have made mighty preparation for the election of another Parliament and sent over great sums of money for that purpose.
    Came home about 10 o'clock. Read some *Spectators* and observed very carefully the manner of introducing their thoughts and how they lay in the mind of the author.

    Thursday, April 19. After dinner went to Mr. Cynelum's. Had a lesson upon the viol. I was never so well pleased with my own performance as to-day. I am in hopes I shall be able to play delicately upon it and touch it finely. I paid him a guinea for a month's lessons, which has been I believe a year in completing.
    The Bill for the Septennial Parliament was to-day sent down to the House of Commons and read a first time and carried by above 100 majority.

    Friday, April 20. Mr. Leeds came to see me. I talked with him about some law cases that I had read. He has no very

[1] Actually 69 to 36; 24 lords entered a protest against the Bill.

clear method, but has a great many good thoughts and notions.

My head ached very much that I began to be very intemperate at it and did not know how to bear it. I could not help thinking how miserable I should be if I had the prospect of a continuance of it all my life and how willing I should be to part with life upon these terms.

At 8 o'clock Mr. Whatley came to see me and stayed with me till 10 o'clock. Our conversation turned upon philosophy and the great benefit that a man who has an entire confidence in the Almighty and lives in constant reflecting dependence upon Him receives. I should be very glad indeed to have such an habitual sense of God upon me as to be able to perceive Him before me at my right hand continually. At length we came to talk of matrimony, and I said though I had often upon consideration thought that the miseries and inconveniences that attended that state were much greater than the advantages of it and a man runs a vast hazard in entering upon it, yet at the same time I could not suppose myself capable of being completely happy here without it. I cannot but be uneasy to think that my life shall terminate with myself. The having children is a kind of continuance and prolonging life into future ages and generations.

Sunday, April 22. Rose at 7. Heard Dr. Calamy [1] at the new meeting. He preached very well, but he has a stiff, affected manner of delivery, though a good voice and the delivery pretty good else.

At night when the rest were gone to bed brother Ryder and I stayed together in the parlour. We fell into a discourse about my father, and my brother complained very much of his manner of treating him especially in his own house, that he was continually finding fault and even before his own servants; that he would be continually inculcating good husbandry before my sister, which used to vex her and make her uneasy. And though he has told him of it and begged he would rather tell it him in private than before others, my father still continued the same

[1] Edmund Calamy, D.D. (1671–1732), minister at Westminster and lecturer at Salters' Hall. Most noteworthy as the biographer of the ministers ejected under the Act of Uniformity.

practice, observing upon every little matter and taking notice of a thousand little things. Indeed it is a mighty misfortune in my father's temper that he cannot bear to see anything though never so little amiss without taking notice of it. Prudence is most necessary virtue in those who have a superiority and the direction and management of others, and wisdom is shown in nothing more than in the proper government of the tongue and to be silent. This prudence my father seems to know nothing of. It is very difficult to account for my father's actions and behaviour in some things. My brother was concerned that my father should invite a woman out of the country that had but some few goods of him to make use of his house as her own whenever she came to town, as she does once a year, and stays a fortnight. My father did it with a great deal of generosity and all with a good design, but without consideration.

Monday, April 23. Aunt Billio dined with us. She took notice of my brother William following Mrs. Loyd so much as he does and thought it was not proper and might bring an ill reputation upon those girls themselves and do them damage in their marriage. I could not but agree with my aunt in that and reflected with some uneasiness and regret upon myself for having been guilty of the same fault. Young women should be kept at a proper distance and not allow themselves in too close and near a correspondence with our sex. Their beauty or other less qualifications grow familiar before matrimony and we grow tired and weary of them before they have gained the effect of them.

Tuesday, April 24. Cousin and I went to Westminster in order to get into the House of Commons to hear the debates which were to be to-day concerning the Septennial Bill. When we came we went into the lobby of the House of Commons and being ignorant of the methods of gaining entrance, we waited there to gain experience by what we saw of others. But though we stayed there till past 4 o'clock excepting a little time at dinner, we could not get in, but it was said that none were let in but such as were specially named by the Speaker.

Went to Mr. Bois,[1] to know about the entering into commons,

[1] Reader at the Middle Temple.

which I intend to do this week. Went then to brother's. He said my father told him he had sold £1,700 worth of goods the last week and that his trade increased vastly upon this. This made me presently entertain hopes of my having some considerable estate by my father.

To-day the House of Commons read second time the Bill for the Septennial Parliament. It sat till past 11 o'clock, and then it was carried by a majority of 122.

Wednesday, April 25. Read some of the book in which the grounds of the bass viol is taught and the method of playing divisions and composing. I am mighty pleased with it and hope by its assistance to be able both to understand music and the art of composing and fitting the bass and treble together, but also to play well and readily upon it.

Went to our club of civil law.

Mr. Leeds told me that Mr. Abney and Mr. Foster [1] had a mind to set up a club of dissenters about the Temple in order to encourage that cause and make those that might come to the Temple not ashamed to own themselves dissenters, and desired me to be one of them, and that they were to meet to-night. I was not willing to meet to-night because of our club at Change and spoke in general against all promiscuous clubs where the company had no proper business. However, I agreed to meet them to-night, which I did at 8 o'clock. There was Mr. Abney, Mr. Foster, Mr. Leeds, Mr. Horseman and self. Our conversation turned upon the state of the nation, the influence of the clergy, and law affairs. Mr. Abney seems to be a pretty good story-teller and to have a good memory to retain the sayings of other people, than which nothing seems to be more grateful to the generality in conversation. We agreed to meet every Thursday between 7 and 8 and to admit none but such as should be agreed by the company and none but dissenters.

Thursday, April 26. Went to Westminster Hall. Came home with Mr. Bowes and Leeds. Mr. Bowes upon the mentioning

---

[1] Michael Foster, admitted to Middle Temple 1705; Recorder of Bristol 1725; Judge of K.B. and knighted 1745. He published several pamphlets on Nonconformity. 'As Mansfield wise, and as old Foster, just', wrote Charles Churchill. For Abney, cf. note, p. 154.

a Scotchman took occasion to tell us that he hated the name and sight of a Scotchman, for it was the genius and nature of that nation to be tricking cheating rogues that have always a design to deceive and defraud you. I thought he was too general in his invectives, though I think that they have more generally a disposition to play the knave than the English. They have especially the art of dissembling and carry it with the greatest respect and outward deference. They have the art of address and flattery to a great degree of impudence, that they are generally never ashamed or afraid to intrude into company, but push themselves forward wherever they are.

After dinner went to meet Cousin Billio and Mr. Smith at Hamlin's according to appointment. We sat together some time there and then they came to my lodgings. We met Mr. Whatley by the way, who came with us. He was then in one of his melancholy fits, had no life nor spirit, and never expected to be happy. We all applied ourselves to divert this humour. I thought his distemper proceeded entirely from want of business.

The Parliament to-day passed the third time the Bill for septennial Parliaments by a majority of 140.

Friday, April 27. In the afternoon went to father to desire him to come and sign the bond for me in order to my entering into commons, and to desire him to get another person to be bond with him, because that was the custom of the house to have two. The bond was executed by myself, father and Mr. Bailey. It cost 4s. and 1s. to the clerk.

Supped at Cousin Watkins's. The night passed away pretty agreeably. Cousin Watkins's wife is good-humoured and tolerable good sense. Our conversation turned upon matrimony and courtship, which gave me occasion to rally him a little upon his courtships, and talk with him about the manner of it. When I was in his shop Mr. Budget came in who talked with my cousin about the course of physic he put him in and how much harm he had done him and rallied him upon his pressing physic upon him. And indeed this seems to be very much his fault. He is very apt to overload his patients with medicines, and, besides, the doctors themselves are privy to it and act in concert with them. Dr. Hulse came in while I was there about a patient of his. He said he was pretty well and in a fair way, but he would write him some little thing, which he puts into the most advantageous form for the apothecary. This has made me almost resolve to be my own physician, at least to come as little into their hands as possible. If one could get off only with the charge of the physic it might be tolerable, but to fill one's belly and load one's stomach with useless medicines is dangerous. Came home about 11.

Saturday, April 28. Went to Aunt Bickley's to see the ladies there. They walked out with me at 7 o'clock into the fields. I did not maintain the conversation with a great deal of spirit, but was very much dissatisfied with myself that I could not find matter enough to entertain them with discourse. Why cannot I be satisfied with the character of a man of sense and enjoy myself without the trifling inconsiderable reputation of a good tattler with a woman or a fine gentleman among the ladies? What I am now aiming at, the character of agreeable company to the women, when I have got it can be enjoyed by me but a little while, to lose the relish of it at last by matrimony. But yet I am strangely prejudiced in favour of this pleasure and I cannot tell how to exclude it out of my present ideas or prospect of happiness.

Sunday, April 29. Rose at past 7. Went into the garden. Began to think of myself and seriously reflect upon my manner of life and the end of my being. Resolved to read the New Testament in order to know the will of God more fully and clearly, with a resolution to practise it. Read the four first chapters.

Mr. Mayo preached at the new meeting and administered the sacrament. I had a great mind to have received the sacrament but did not know it was to be given till I came to the meeting, that I did not care to do it upon so sudden a resolution, but this put me upon thinking of its nature and the end of its institution. And I don't find that it is anything else than an institution of Christ in remembrance of His death and passion and love to the world. And therefore every Christian as such is obliged to celebrate it. It is a misfortune that divines have made so great a matter of it as they have done, requiring so extraordinary a preparation for it as to force people from it, whereas it seems to be no more than any duty which if not performed with a sincere mind and out of a regard to God is rather hypocrisy than religion and as hypocrisy affronts Him. So it is with the Lord's Supper. A man that receives it and thereby with thankfulness remembers Christ and his sufferings for the world condemns himself if at the same time he allows himself the practice of sin which destroys the effect of his sufferings. It is a kind of mocking God and Christ to thank him for his love and goodwill in procuring such blessings for us and yet to refuse to accept of those blessings. But I intend next time it is administered at Hackney to receive it.

Mr. Mayo dined with us and did not care to enter into any kind of conversation but what related to religion and was apt to introduce these. But before a minister who is supposed to know so much more of it than we, we did not know how to talk upon that subject, so that we could not tell what to say to one another.

Monday, April 30. Rose at 6. Went to cold bath. Met Mr. Whatley there. The poor man was deep in the melancholy. He said he had spent all his past time in vain, he had learnt nothing, and that he despaired of ever being happy again. I think his is the most extraordinary case I ever met with or heard for a man to be in such a variety of states, sometimes to be the happiest mortal upon earth and perhaps next day to be transformed into the most wretched miserable creature upon earth. I don't know how to account for these different states in which he is at different times any other way than this, that as he is unsettled in his own mind without any fixed steady view to pursue he is generally at a loss what to do next, and how to employ his present time. That this is the case with Mr. Whatley I judge very much from what I have observed in my own mind. He has been, since he was capable of reflecting, left to himself and his own management, to direct and guide himself in what way of life to choose. His father died too soon and he had none to conduct his steps. Hence he was forced to choose for himself, but not being able to make this choice for any good reason, he would naturally change his mind as contrary reasons came into his mind. Hence I think it is of vast service to children to have parents to choose for them what manner of life to engage in, and parents themselves ought not to leave it to the uncertain unsettled elections of children themselves, who it is impossible should be able to make any settled judgement at all.

Went into commons at dinner. It was a little uneasy to me to enter upon such a perfectly new method and mix myself among a company of strangers. However, I passed it off pretty well.

I bought a pamphlet entitled *Proposals for Easing the Nation's Debt, increasing our money, &c.* A hundred guineas are offered to anyone that shall bring a copy of a good answer to this. I believe I could answer the pamphlet well; my only difficulty is how to gain the hundred guineas if I do, whether the person that offers this will stand by it.

Tuesday, May 1. I have been thinking of going down to the Bath to see my sister, who is there now. Indeed what excites me to it the more is the prospect of seeing Mrs. Marshall who went down with sister. I think I never saw a woman who pleased me better and had something so very agreeable in her.

My brother is thinking to solicit and make interest to be the King's draper and my father asked me to solicit for him. I told him I should be very glad to do him any service if I could, but as I was not acquainted with the methods of doing that it would be impossible for me to go through it, and indeed I have not assurance enough for that.

Thursday, May 3. Went to brother's. There were two ladies. Drank some tea with him. He was extremely free with them in talk and action. He was merry and tumbled them about and did abundance of things that looked rude, but yet I find such a familiarity is extremely taking with the generality of women, though all the wit or humour lies in nothing but external familiar notions and actions.

Friday, May 4. Went to Uncle Marshall's. They have had a sad accident, being overturned in the coach, and aunt hurt, though not dangerously. Did not stay because neither uncle nor his son were at home and there was company.

Came back. Went to see Mr. Bois. Our conversation was about law books and very little else excepting a little about the exercises that we are to do in the Middle Temple which I inquired of him.

Saturday, May 5. Thought upon my design to write an answer to the proposals for easing the debts of the nation, increasing its riches, &c., wherein the author endeavours to confute Mr. Locke's opinion. Read Mr. Locke's discourse concerning the raising the value of coin,[1] in which there is such a fullness of matter and reasoning that it is sufficient to confute what the proposals say without any further application of the arguments. To bed at 12.

Sunday, May 6. Rose at 9. Found my arm very painful in bed, that I could not move it without a great deal of pain. I have had the same pain these four or five nights. As soon as I am well warm in my bed it begins and very much goes away in the daytime. I was very much concerned because it was greater than ever before. However went to meeting. Heard Mr. Wood,[2] a dissenting parson of a congregation 14 miles from Preston. He himself gathered together 300 men chiefly of his own congregation to assist the King's forces against the rebels at Preston and were posted at Ribble Bridge. To bed at 10. Had my arm rubbed with a flesh brush in order to remove the pain, but it continued in the night.

Tuesday, May 8. Father sent for me to see the horse he had a mind to buy, but did not like him, not being gentle enough. My father does not care to give a tolerable price for a horse and has no judgement at all in one, and therefore is afraid to meddle with any, that he is extremely indifferent. Dined in commons. Went to Hamlin's. There were Cousin Billio, Mr. Smith and Whatley, and Dr. Hollier and Mr. Read.

From the coffee-house we went to the Fountain,[3] all of us except Mr. Read. Dr. Hollier was here the life and spirit of the company and indeed he has a very happy way of talking, and full of witty turns and pretty thoughts and reflections, that he maintains the spirit and life in the conversation by giving

[1] *Some Considerations of the Consequences of Lowering and Raising the Value of Money*, 1692.
[2] James Wood (1672–1759), Nonconformist minister at Atherton, Lancs. His strangely armed force (cf. p. 234) was reinforced by detachments from the Nonconformists of Horwich and Preston. For this exploit 'General' Wood was granted a pension of £100.
[3] Beside Inner Temple gate.

abundance of new and lively turns to things. One time the conversation fell upon Dr. Ratcliffe,[1] who was both by him and Dr. Oldfield [2] said to be a man of no manner of learning at all and whose whole art was confined within a very few sets of prescriptions which by the help of experience he had brought to be of some service. He was introduced into the world at first by the Oxford gentlemen by joining in with them in their Tory principles and being a good bottle companion. They sent him to London with great recommendations but without the least skill in the theory of physic or any learning at all, nor did he ever give himself to thinking or indeed could think at all, but practised rather by rote than real solid judgement and observations drawn from experience.

Several of the rebel prisoners in Newgate broke out last Friday night, among which were McIntosh and his son and eight more Scotchmen.[3] People don't know how to account for these escapes of the prisoners and the Tories make an ill use of it by saying the Government let them go on purpose out of fear.

Wednesday, May 9. Went to coffee-house. Read the last *Freeholder* with a great deal of care and observation upon the connexion of the several thoughts in it and the manner of introducing them, and I could not but take notice that several thoughts there come in in such a manner as when I write myself I cannot suffer in my own writing. But indeed that is my fault; I don't give thoughts their natural play and freedom. Indeed the difficulty of writing well is to express thoughts and observations clearly and delicately.

Thursday, May 10. Dined at Hackney, it being my father's and mother's wedding day. Aunt and Cousin Billio's dined with us. I cannot help observing with not a little regret and uneasiness the confusion and disorder in which our entertainments are made. My mother is generally uneasy all dinner

[1] Dr. John Radcliffe (d. 1714), physician to Queen Anne.
[2] cf. note, p. 238.
[2] Nearly sixty prisoners were walking in the press-yard after a feast at which the guests included the Newgate chaplains and some lady visitors. They suddenly attacked the keeper and secured the keys. Most of them were caught.

long and things are managed in such a manner as to require a constant care and circumspection besides what the servants do themselves.

Came to London. My arm was painful and I had almost resolved to be cupped upon it in order to remove the pain, but did not care to venture yet without better advice.

At 9 o'clock went to our club of dissenters. It was proposed by some of the company as a thing that would be very useful, that the dissenters should have a general correspondence together through all the counties of England. The Quakers are the pattern of this general correspondence together. It was talked of as a thing very useful to take an account of the numbers and strength and riches of the dissenters in all the counties of England; that by that means they might know how far their interest went and of what service they might be. The court seems to regard only its own interest and to take care of the dissenters only so far as it was necessary for this. They cajoled them continually by promises for futurity but neglected to make them good. Mr. Abney said he knew that the dissenters were promised last session to have the Schism Act taken off this session if they would comply with the Government designs, join heartily with them, but it is all come to nothing. Came home between 11 and 12.

Friday, May 11. Went to brother's. Was cupped there in my arm in order to remove the pain which was settled there. Went to supper. Met Mr. Whatley there, with whom I went to the tavern. He is now disappointed in his designed journey to Constantinople and his new scheme of applying himself to public business is quite overturned.

Saturday, May 12. Mr. Whatley came to see me at 5 o'clock to go to the cold bath with him, but was in a very great sweat and therefore could not go.

Mr. Whatley and I seldom talk of anything together than the state and temper of his mind and what naturally flows from that. It is his misfortune that he has looked too much upon himself. He talks now of going down into the country to live there and keep within the compass of his fortune, but I know him too well to think he will be able to continue there long.

Sunday, May 13. At night went to London. Vast crowds of people were walking the fields. Met Mr. Abney and Mr. Foster, who not having supped I went with them to an eating-house. Mr. Abney's talent seems to lie very much in telling a story, which he does with a pretty good grace. Mr. Foster seems to be a man very well acquainted with our English history and to understand the law well. I intend to cultivate a good acquaintance with them, being very sober men and I believe will be of advantage to me in the law.

Monday, May 14. Went to Hackney upon the mare that my father had bought. I was vexed he had not bought a better that is more gentle. Mr. Mayo came to our house to inquire the way to Mrs. Crisp's and I went with him there. I was surprised when I came there to hear Mrs. Crisp tell Mr. Mayo her son, that was now in so deep a consumption, had not been so religious as he ought to have been and had fell from grace of late, but thanked God he had had such a lingering sickness that had given him time to repent and talked a good while in that manner.

Colonel Oxburgh,[1] one of the rebels, was hanged to-day. He died a papist, though he had taken the sacrament the two last reigns to qualify himself to serve the Government as an officer.

Tuesday, May 15. Went to the Fountain, where several young persons, among whom were Mr. Wood, whom they call 'General' because he brought under his command 300 men for the King against the rebels at Preston, and Mr. Winter, a young man that preaches where Mrs. Crisp goes in the country. He told us Mr. Wood, having a congregation that loved him extremely and who would follow him anywhere, he brought them to associate together when the rebels first were upon their march southwards and then led them out armed partly with swords and pistols and guns and partly with scythes fixed to the end of straight sticks.

Mr. Towneley of Towneley was tried to-day at the Marshalsea

---

[1] Henry Oxburgh surrendered at Preston. He was actually beheaded and his head was displayed on Temple Bar.

and acquitted,[1] though it is well known he brought to the rebels sixty men, several of whom were hanged in Lancashire, but they say the present jury at the Marshalsea is not a good one. Yesterday morning at Westminster Hall Macartney's outlawry was reversed by a confession of error by the Attorney-General and he is to take his trial.

Went to Mr. Rollison's [2] to advise with him about my arm. He tells me the Bath will do me more good than anything. He is to send me a purge to-night that is peculiarly good against the rheumatism.

Thursday, May 17. Rose at 7. While I was in bed I had some thoughts of the Deity, the supreme being of the universe, and the prodigious evil of idolatry never appeared to me in so strong a light before.

Came back to Hackney in the afternoon with Mr. Bailey on horseback. Uncle Marshall and aunt and Cousin Billio were at our house. When they were all gone I went to the balls that were here to-day. Stayed longest at Mrs. Wallis's because Mrs. Loyd and Cousin Bibby were there. At length these two ladies went out to cool themselves and I conducted into the garden, where Sam Humphries came also and I entertained them very pleasantly at first with merry discourse and good sort of gallantry and raillery enough. Mr. Humphries all the while was rather serious and like a lover could not tell how to be in jest in his mistress's company. We walked there till the Ball was done and Mrs. Thompson came to my cousin and Mrs. Loyd to desire them to go home with them in their coach and after we had walked together a turn or two they could not stay any longer and left my cousin and Mrs. Loyd with us. John Gould had now introduced himself among us and in his rattling had got Mrs. Loyd to talk with. I was vexed to see her so long entertained with such a rattle as he, but could not help it. Poor Cousin Bibby Ryder was almost neglected by the company while all the addresses and gallantry were made to Mrs. Loyd.

[1] Richard Towneley's acquittal was due to the horror caused by Oxburgh's execution. The judge summed up for conviction. His nephew, Francis, was executed for his part in the 1745 rebellion.

[2] John Rawlinson, the Hackney apothecary.

I know this must be a very uneasy task to her and create a very troublesome envy.

However, at length I got them away and one Captain Hilliard [1] (who came to the ball and being acquainted with Mr. Humphries was in our company and gallanted Mrs. Loyd) took her by the hand to lead her. Mr. Humphries could not tell how to bear [it] and endeavoured to get her away, till at length some words passed between him and the captain who seemed to be in jest all the while. But when Mr. Humphries pressed him pretty hard he asked him whether he was in earnest. Mr. Humphries answered he might take it as he pleased. This was the beginning of a quarrel and everything was in earnest. Mr. Humphries talked pretty big and high, so that I thought it better to take the coach. But the quarrel growing to some height I thought it proper to take Humphries in the coach with us to prevent mischief, but he told the Captain he would come again presently and meet at the tavern. Mrs. Loyd was extremely concerned at this and seemed to interest herself very much in Mr. Humphries' welfare, that she was out of order in the coach and sick.

After we had set down the ladies my brother William and I and Mr. Humphries went to the tavern. I would have persuaded him not to have gone but he was resolute and said he had such a value and affection for Mrs. Loyd that he was almost glad he had such an opportunity of discovering it. When we came to the tavern I endeavoured to pacify them but they would manage it themselves and talk it over. The Captain had a friend with him. They talked upon it more coolly than I thought they would, but the Captain talked very handsomely and peaceably and said he was concerned anything should fall out between Mr. Humphries and he, who had been very good friends together a great while, and seemed very willing to make it up, and Samuel seemed not at all unwilling to make it up. But seemed to have a mind to show my brother and I what a value he had for Mrs. Loyd and therefore kept off from accommodation more and would have matters explained.

However, after a great deal of talking I persuaded them to refer the matter to the Captain's friend and me. The Captain's

[1] A Thomas Hillyard died at Hackney in 1723.

friend though inclinable enough to peace yet thought that the Captain was injured, but after we had talked over the matter a great while together I persuaded [him] to let us determine that they should shake hands and be friends and put up all differences without anything more or acknowledgements of either side. Samuel Humphries indeed seemed to be the most in fault, but had a mind to show his courage and love for Mrs. Loyd, who, I believe, indeed loves him very much.

Friday, May 18. Rose at 7. Took physic. Employed myself in the several intervals I had for reading, in reading Buchanan's *Franciscanus*,[1] which is a very good satire upon the mystic way of living among the papists and he has there exposed their roguery and knavery and villainy in all its arts and parts.

At 5 o'clock Mrs. Loyd and Cousin Bibby Ryder came to our house. Mrs. Loyd appears mighty vain upon this quarrel upon her account and endeavours to shine more exceedingly in her carriage and conversation. Cousin Bibby envies her and she is sensible of it, that every now and then there are distant hints and rubs given to one another.

Saturday, May 19. Rose at 7. Went to London at 8 in order to prepare for my journey to the Bath. Packed up my clothes, sent them to brother's in order to be sent to the coach to Bath.

Father and I determined that I should go on Monday and take John with me. My arm was very painful and father would have had me go into the Bagnio. I was very much against it. Did not. Went to Hackney with Madam Crisp in her coach. Our conversation turned upon her son that lies a-dying. Mr. Porter told me that Mr. Thomas Crisp had a grant from the King, of an estate worth 20 or £30,000, but how true it is I don't know. I did not care to ask Madam Crisp whether it was so or no.

Hired a horse for John at Hackney for £2 6s. per diem and gave 1s. earnest.

[1] George Buchanan's *Franciscanus et Fratres*, c. 1538, an attack upon the morals of the clergy which was an important factor in bringing about the Reformation in Scotland.

Sunday, May 20. Went to meeting. Heard Dr. Oldfield.[1] He seems to me to be the most out-of-the-way preacher I ever heard. Both his manner and his delivery, his style and thoughts, are all very uncommon. He preached both morning and afternoon. In the afternoon walked with Mrs. Loyd as far as her house. The girl seems extremely pleased and satisfied with herself since Mr. Humphries' quarrel for her.

Monday, May 21. Rose at little after 3. Got myself ready. Set out at between 4 and 5. I was at first uneasy upon the account of my horse which seemed very dull and without spirit. It being to-day Whitsun Monday, the country people had put on their best clothes and were gathered everywhere out of their houses to their diversions upon the green. I baited at Colebrook for an hour and came into Reading at 12 o'clock which is 32 miles from London. At the Inn, which was the George, I met with a pretty girl for a maid. I did not know how at first to introduce a kiss but at last did and kissed her twice with a great deal of jest.

Came out from thence at 2 and got into Newbury which is 15 miles at 5. Upon the road hither a young man upon the road commenced an acquaintance with me. He seemed to have nothing extraordinary in him; however, we conversed a little but were often at a stand for conversation, that I began to be tired of his company and wished I was alone. Pleased myself as I came along with the hope of meeting with a pretty girl to kiss at the inn at Newbury. There was such a one as I could kiss but not extraordinary. I found myself very much tired and my arm grown painful. I supped upon the broth of a neck of mutton which I had got on purpose for me. Newbury is finest for crawfish and trouts, but I had neither for supper. To bed at 10.

Tuesday, May 22. Went out at between 4 and 5. I thought the journey very tedious in the morning. However, we reached Marlborough by 8 which was 15 miles. Upon the road to Marlborough I met with a country girl and fell into chat with her and asked her questions about her dairy, she being dairymaid

---

[1] Dr. Joshua Oldfield (1656–1729), Presbyterian minister at Globe Alley, Southwark.

to a farmer, and about her sweetheart, that I passed away two or three miles of the time very agreeably.

From Marlborough went to Sandylane which is 12 miles. The greatest part of the way is over the downs, a vast hilly place and not a house to be seen for several miles together, all uncultivated. There was one thing which pleased me very much and that was a well which I saw there surrounded with troughs and a bucket to draw water for the cattle that is fed upon the downs. It put me in mind of the wells that the patriarchs used to draw water out of for their cattle.

Upon the downs I overtook a man on foot who said he came that day from Newbury and was to go 40 miles to-night. When I wondered at it, he said he had gone 200 miles in a day, and told us that he was Queen Anne's cook, but turned out by King George upon suspicion of a design to poison him, upon which he said he prayed God he might get safe home into his own country. He had not sent for him and immediately gave a hint at his being a cuckold, upon which I told him he was a saucy impudent fellow. He said he did not fear any two men living and was pistol proof. Upon this our discourse dropped and I left him behind. I began to grow very tired and weary of riding. Came to Sandylane. Kissed the girl there. From thence went to Bath through several little towns 13 miles.

When I came into my inn I got myself shaved and put on a clean shirt and better wig and made the best figure I could in a riding dress and went to my sister, not finding her at home. Her maid conducted me into Harrison's Walks where I found her with Mrs. Marshall, with whom I walked several turns and was very agreeably entertained, and talked pretty briskly myself. Mr. Samuel Powell was there and had got acquaintance with my sister and Mrs. Marshall and was grown perfectly familiar and by that means seemed to be very company.

Harrison's Walks are very pleasant and filled with company. I was surprised when I came into Bath to see in a country town as I passed through it so many fine ladies walking in the streets and appearing at the windows. Mrs. Marshall is indeed extremely taken notice of and admired as the most celebrated beauty there, and indeed there is something extremely charming in her air and manner. She seems to be perfectly good-humoured, not at all grown vain or elevated upon the addresses and regards of the world. She seems also to have very good sense and a taste for gallantry and politeness. Sister and she are grown perfectly familiar and intimate and sister is mightily pleased with her company.

Gnash [1] is the man here that is the life and soul of all their diversions. Without him there is no play nor assembly nor ball and everybody seems not to know what to do if he is absent. He has the privilege of saying what he pleases and talking to the ladies as his fancy leads him and no affront is to be taken, though he sometimes puts modest women to the blush. His conversation and sayings seem to make a great part of the conversation of others and the repeating of what he does or says helps to fill up the conversation very much. Upon this account, though he is a very ugly man in his face, yet he is very much beloved and esteemed by the ladies as a witty and genteel man.

Supped with sister. I was under some difficulty what to do about my diet, but I have told my sister that if she will provide and let me know the entire charge she is at I will bear my share. At 10 o'clock I asked the ladies to take a walk by moonshine and they did and it was mighty pleasant. I am wonderfully charmed with Mrs. Marshall's company and should think myself very happy in her for a wife, but what fortune she has I don't know. Came home at 11. To bed at past 12.

Wednesday, May 23. Rose at 7. Went out with sister to the Pump room at 8 and drank some bath water. Went and saw the several baths, the King's Bath and Court Bath and Leper's Bath, in each of which we saw some persons in. The ladies and gentlemen go chiefly into the Court Bath and are therein at the same time, though at different sides of it. I thought the ladies made but a very odd figure as they stood up to neck in the water.

Dined together with sister and Marshall's family. Sister and Mrs. Marshall had a mind to go to Bristol to-morrow and Mr. Powell and I to wait upon them and we have accordingly hired a chaise with two horses for them for 30s. for two days, and I have given 15s. earnest part of it.

[1] Richard Nash (1674–1762) was *arbiter elegantiarum* at Bath from 1705, for over forty years. ' He had ', said Goldsmith, ' assiduity, flattery, fine cloaths, and as much wit as the ladies he addressed.'

Went to the play, where Mrs. Marshall and sister were gone before in chairs. It was a play called *Love Makes a Man*.[1] The plot and dialogue of the play put me into a very grave humour and I found myself more in love with Mrs. Marshall than ever. There were one or two of the low comic parts acted pretty tolerably well but the rest were acted very ill. But besides this there was acted the *Cobbler of Preston*,[2] which was diverting enough but the whole diversion lasted so long that it tired us. The play was bespoke by Mrs. Walpole and was very much crowded and the Whig parts of the first clapped pretty much.

We came home and found Mr. Powell at our lodgings and stayed with us till past 12 o'clock and he was very merry. I could not help upon this occasion reflecting upon every defect of my own and comparing them with his perfections. My littleness and want of beauty, ill complexion, not being merry company nor gay and diverting, crowded in upon me at once and made me very uneasy. To bed at 1.

Thursday, May 24. Rose at 6. We sat out for Bristol with Mr. Powell. The journey there was but very indifferent, the weather being very bad and raining, but it was agreeable to me as it gave me the company now and then of Mrs. Marshall. The road is full of stones and the worst I ever went. When we came there to our inn and had dined we walked to see the College Church.

I began now to be extremely uneasy, finding myself incapable of entertaining Mrs. Marshall as I would do and Mr. Powell so much more diverting and, as I judged, agreeable to her. Mr. Powell is a strange, merry, rattling young fellow in the company of the ladies. His conversation consists very much in joining together the most odd contradictory ideas in order to create a laugh. It is my misfortune that I cannot talk to the ladies with that indifference that is necessary to make me agreeable to them. This is the reason why they are always upon their guard towards me, and though Mrs. Marshall will take a thousand freedoms and play abundance of little tricks with Mr. Powell she never said a familiar thing to me once or did a familiar action. I don't know how it is but there is

[1] By Colley Cibber, first produced at Drury Lane 13 December 1700.
[2] By Christopher Bullock, first produced January 1715/16.

I believe in me something of a forbidding reserved air in me that makes the ladies especially afraid to be familiar with me. And yet I remember I have sometimes been able in ladies' company to talk very freely. Mrs. Marshall is of a pretty gay temper and loves nothing better than to laugh and be merry. They were continually complaining that we were dull and desired Mr. Powell to make them laugh.

It rained so much that we were fain to stay at home from 5 o'clock all night. Bristol is but an indifferent city. The generality of the houses are not good and the streets very narrow, but there is one square which is extremely handsome and pleasant and is equal to most of our best squares in London.

Friday, May 25. Rose at 8. We went into the ladies' chamber and there were merry till breakfast. Between 9 and 10 we went out to the Hot Wells, about a mile out of Bristol by the waterside. The Hot Wells are just so hot as to take off the rawness of the cold, but in hot weather a person would scarcely think them warm at all. My sister and I walked up the rocks, but we could not persuade Mrs. Marshall to be at the pains. All the way up the rocks I had a great mind to communicate my passion for Mrs. Marshall to sister. I looked very heavy, pensive and concerned, that she took notice of it and thought me not well, but I could [not] venture to tell her the reason. I only talked to her about her and told her I heard she was in love with Dr. Avery, which she said she had heard but was unwilling to own she believed it. We met my Lord Perceval [1] and some others upon the rocks. They are very high but we could not see the sea, other rocks and hills prevented a very extensive prospect. As we came home a sudden gleam of light came in upon my mind and my thoughts grew more calm and I found myself more cheerful and easy. I don't know well how to account for it unless it proceeds from some small favour or other that Mrs. Marshall showed me. Perhaps she asked me a question or seemed more kind and favourable.

In the afternoon our landlady who had been lying in and her month not yet up invited us to drink tea with her, which we did. She gave the tea first to Mr. Powell and myself and

---

[1] John, 1st Baron Perceval (1683–1748), one of the founders of the colony of Georgia.

told us it was the custom in Bristol always to serve a man first, whatever women are at table. I ventured to discover the features of the father in the child and said also that the features of the father and mother were both blended together in it.

Our coachman was very impudent and told us we must set out at 2 o'clock: if we did not he would go without us. This vexed us very much that we resolved to go the later for it. In the afternoon we went to see Rackley Church, which is a very neat pretty Gothic building. There was the Father, Son and Holy Ghost in *basso relievo* upon the top of the ceiling. The Father looks a very old man, the Son with the crown of thorns and the blood at his nails and side, and the Holy Ghost looks a middle-aged man. While we were in the church the coachman came to us and told us we must make haste and go on, else we must lie by the way short of Bath to-night. This was so insolent that we could not bear, and I scolded at him and Mr. Powell took him by the collar. When we came to the coach the young fellow was very insolent and when Mr. Powell had spoke to him called him 'rascal', upon which Mr. Powell struck him with his whip. The father of the young fellow now began to be sensible that it was in vain to pretend to impose upon us, began to be calm and willing to appease us and said his son was in drink. However, the young fellow was so sullen and impudent that we were almost afraid to let him drive the ladies to Bath, but he did it very well.

Saturday, May 26. Rose at 7. Drunk four glasses of the Bath waters. Mr. Powell invited me to go to the breakfast given by Mr. Dormer of whom Mr. Powell won it. I went there but was extremely bashful and did not know how to behave myself nor care to speak with anybody. I was heartily vexed with myself that I was so foolish and did nothing but think Mr. Powell and Mrs. Marshall and sister must be ashamed to be known to be my acquaintance.

Came home, wrote letter to father after dinner. Found myself very weak and languid, my spirits failing, that I could not tell what to do about it. I sent for Dr. Baire and talked with him about my constitution and was well pleased with his account of bathing and the cold bath, wherein he perfectly agreed with my notions of it and the use of it, except that he said one might be in danger of overdoing it, and besides that it is very much in vain by cold bathing to contract the vessels unless the blood be diluted and made thin and the deleterious ill particles that are got among be dissolved, that the blood may be easy to flow. And therefore the cold bath is very proper after having drank the hot bath waters, to strengthen and confirm the vessels. He told me it might do me harm but could no good to drink the waters for so short a time as till Monday seven night, but three or four weeks would be of service to me. Upon which I wrote to my father the state of my health and desired him to determine my stay or return.

At 10 o'clock Mr. Powell came to us and Mrs. Marshall. She said when we were talking about love that she could never be in love with any man unless she lived with him constantly for half-year and so fell in love with him by degrees and knew his temper and liked his conversation, and then she did not know what might be.

Sunday, May 27. Went to the meeting with our company. Some thoughts of raillery came into my head during the sermon for conversation with Mrs. Marshall and put me into a gay humour that I never conversed with her in so pleasant and gay a manner as I did when we came home. My only concern was lest my breath stank and she should smell it, but that did not prevent my talking merrily to her.

The meeting is but a very small one and that not full. Went to church in the afternoon. Heard a very indifferent charity sermon for the benefit of the charity school. The church was extremely full.

Stayed at home after sermon all the rest of the afternoon with Mrs. Marshall and sister and Mr. Powell was with us. His company is strangely agreeable to them and Mrs. Marshall seems to have a peculiar love of it. I found myself very deeply affected with her, and I could not help at night telling my sister of it. My sister took it all in jest and I could not get her to talk with me in earnest about it, but I think I never was more deeply in love in my life. But indeed what makes me the most uneasy of anything with it is that I am conscious I am not agreeable to her. Nothing aggravates my circumstances so much as the acceptance Mr. Powell meets with from her and the joy with which she receives him. I am far from having a mean opinion of Mrs. Marshall. I admire her extremely, her beauty, good nature and good sense, but these I believe would not have that effect upon me which they have and make me so very uneasy if it was not that she favours Mr. Powell much more than me and delights in his company while she neglects mine. And yet he is not a rival properly, for he seems very indifferent about her himself. It was some kind of consolation to me and struck me with pleasure when he told me, talking about her, that he would not give 6s. for a kiss of her. How hard and unhappy is our fate that love must be bestowed where it is so little valued. And yet I don't know neither. If I was as much beloved, perhaps I should not be so much in love. Absence creates desire and inflames and excites it. I might be cloyed perhaps if I enjoyed it and grow cool and indifferent as he is. As long as I continue in my present condition I don't find I am likely to be easy all the while I am here, and therefore intend to go away with sister. It struck me to the very soul to observe her in his company doing everything to keep him with her and make him stay, when she neglects my company. I read two sermons to Mrs. Marshall the mother and daughter, of Mr. Hoadly's. They are writ with so much strength of reason and clearness that I intend to buy his sermons that are printed.

Monday, May 28. To-day being King George's birthday the gentlemen here have subscribed for a ball and entertainment to-night, and I have done so too, a guinea, for which I had three tickets which I gave to Mrs. Marshall and we went to the Ball at about 6 o'clock. There was very good company and good clothes. Mr. Gnash was the director and manager of it, and began it himself with a minuet. He asked my sister and Mrs. Marshall to dance with him, but they refused. There was but little French dancing, there being but few gentlemen that cared to dance. There was my Lord Conway,[1] in scarlet velvet. He is a great Tory, but it is thought appeared there on purpose to clear himself from suspicion of being concerned in the rebellion which he lies under. There were several officers

[1] Francis Seymour, 1st Lord Conway ; his third wife was Charlotte Shorter, Walpole's sister-in-law.

there and particularly Colonel Molesworth,[1] who danced very well, and is admired by Mrs. Marshall for gallantry and a fine leg and foot. There was Mrs. Walpole[2] and her sister Mrs. Shorter danced there very well. I gave my sister and Mrs. Marshall a favour of purple and orange knots, such as Mrs. Walpole wore herself as being the colours of Hanover and the Prince of Orange. And I wore one of the same myself in my hat. A great many gentlemen and ladies wore the same, though there were several that wore none at all, but some wore gold ones.

The French dancing was soon over and country dancing succeeded. At about 8 o'clock we all went upstairs to supper and there was a handsome entertainment of cold dishes. All the ladies that could, sat down at several tables that were spread and the gentlemen stood waiting upon them and eating what they gave them. After supper we went down again to dancing and I desired Mrs. Marshall to dance with me, but she would not. I then asked her to recommend me to a partner and she spoke to the youngest daughter of my Lady Shaw, so I danced with her till 12 o'clock, and was very merry. I am afraid I was too much so. I went pretty often to Mrs. Marshall and spoke to her and seemed so gay that I am afraid I was taken notice of for it. Came home at 12.

Tuesday, May 29. Mr. Powell breakfasted with us. I am in hopes I shall learn by Mr. Powell's example and conversation how to entertain the ladies better. The greatest fault in Mrs. Marshall seems to be that she is of too gay a temper and loves company and mirth too much to make a good wife. I used to think her of an admirable temper and perfectly good-humoured, but I have observed some cross behaviour towards her little sister that makes me suspect she is not so very good-humoured as I imagined.

In the afternoon I stayed at home with them till 6; then walked with them upon the Walks and Harrison's Walks. Mr. Powell came to us and then immediately all the conversation

[1] Richard Molesworth, colonel of a regiment of dragoons which served against the rebels in Lancashire.
[2] In 1700 Walpole married Catherine Shorter, ' a woman of exquisite beauty and accomplished manners'.

was turned to him and whatever he said or did was laughed at and made them merry and pleased, especially Mrs. Marshall. The worst of Mr. Powell's conversation is that he is apt now and then to make use of *double entendres*, which shocked me very much and I wonder Mrs. Marshall seems so well pleased with them and so little shocked at them.

Mr. Powell and I left the ladies and went and drank a bottle of wine together. Among the rest of our conversation he gave me an account of his life when he was in London after he just came from Hackney. He said he had been very loose and lain with abundance of girls, but never got any harm by them. But he spoke of it as of a thing that has no harm in it.

He said he had lived a much more regular life at Oxford, though he spent a great deal of money.

We talked of Mrs. Marshall. Her name happened to be writ upon one of the glasses we drank out of and Mr. Powell broke it. It shocked me very much to think of her name's being handled by the officers and her charms talked of there by them with the desire of their being prostituted.

Came home at past 10. Found Mrs. Marshall at her mother's and Mrs. Moore and the rest in sister's room, while the candles were set up at the windows, it being King Charles's restoration. When I saw the candles I immediately began to rally them upon their cowardice, which held us a good while and I have not talked and rattled so much since I came to Bath. But at the same time I could not help taking the opportunities I could of telling Mrs. Marshall how much I loved her. When her mother went to bed, Mrs. Marshall would go herself to bed also, and I took it very unkind of her that she would not be persuaded to stay at all, when she stays up much longer to have Mr. Powell's company. I could not help complaining of this to sister. To bed at 12.

Wednesday, May 30. Stayed at home all the morning. In the afternoon went to the coffee-house with Mr. Powell. There happened to be a dispute between a priest and some Whig gentlemen about passive obedience. As the dispute went on and one put in one word and another another, I could not help engaging in it myself, and I think got very much the better of him, till he was forced to go away. Indeed the whole coffee-house full of gentlemen were against him, but he argued very ill, and had very little to say for himself.

We came then to the ladies and sat with them all the evening, partly cards and partly conversation and other plays that were diverting. Mrs. Marshall's unkindness to me in denying me some little trifling familiarity which she granted to him made me extremely heavy and dull, that everybody could not but take notice of it. I think Mr. Powell takes and she allows him too great familiarity, as throwing her upon the bed with himself upon her, &c., but all this is in jest and pleasing, whereas the least freedom taken by me is frowned upon.

Thursday, May 31. I have had very little regard to the diversions of the Bath and scarce ever go out of doors but when they go along with me. Indeed they are all very insipid to me and I could be very well content never to go among the company. As Mrs. Marshall is very unkind and shows a disregard of me I have thought to endeavour to show at least a neglect of her and appear unconcerned about her. Indeed I have taken more notice of her little sister than usual on purpose because she seems to slight her and does not care to have her with her. There is one trick I find that has a very great efficacy towards making her attentive and willing to hear and that is to say a great many things in the form of a secret, to tell it in her ear. This raises her curiosity and she is willing to hear anything you would say in such a manner.

After dinner I walked with the ladies in Harrison's Walks, but they walked first alone, and Colonel Molesworth spoke to them as they were all alone in private, and told them it was a pity such fine creatures should conceal themselves from the world. But his conversation did not please them so much as his person, which Mrs. Marshall thinks very agreeable.

Friday, June 1. Mr. Powell and I prepare matters for our journey to-day to Mr. Blathwayt's [1] with the ladies. Hired a chaise and a pair of horses for which we gave 10s. and 4s. for the chaise. We set out about 11 o'clock. Upon the road I

---

[1] The gardens of William Blathwayt (M.P. for Bath 1693–1710) at Durham Park were famous; they were constructed in the Dutch style by Le Notre in 1698.

was very uneasy to see Mr. Powell so much taken notice of more than myself. Mr. Blathwayt's house is a very handsome one very well furnished with pictures and good rich beds, but the gardens are the most pleasant. The situation of them is upon several hills that entertain the eyes with a variety of prospects. The parterre runs along between them with a pretty canal in the middle at the end of which there are several fountains and a cascade from a very steep hill of 224 steps, the finest in England except the Duke of Devonshire's. We saw all the waterworks play which were very agreeable and delightful. At one side of the gardens there is a wilderness of high large trees in which there are a great many agreeable shades.

In one of them we made our dinner of some cold things we brought and sat down upon the grass for two or three hours. In this time Mrs. Marshall showed a great disregard of me and love for Mr. Powell; particularly she refused me a kiss when she gave him one immediately after. This put me into such a confusion and uneasiness that I could not bear it and was forced to take a walk by myself among the trees. Nor could I prevent the tears gushing out, that I was forced to be absent almost an hour. During this time Mr. Powell and the ladies were very uneasy what was become of me, but I came at last and my eyes I believe betrayed what I had been doing.

We gave the gardener 5s. and the woman that showed the house the same. We had a pleasant journey in going home as far as the fineness of the weather and prospects, &c., could contribute to make it pleasant, but my heart was sad.

Saturday, June 2. Rose at 7. Rode out in the morning after having heard from my father. He is concerned at my ill state of health and refers it to me to stay here longer or return and go to Epsom or Tunbridge as I please when I come home. I thought about it when I rode out and could not readily determine. I thought my health might be promoted by staying here but I was afraid to stay any longer with Mrs. Marshall.

Came home. Met Mr. Powell, told him how much I was concerned about my behaviour yesterday in the garden. He said he was surprised at it and thought I was almost mad. However, I told him the reason of it and begged he would never mention it. He offered me his service to assist me in my affection to Mrs. Marshall and promised me to promote my interest while I was absent. However, I told him it could never be and therefore I did not desire him to speak anything for me to her.

I was walking with Mr. Powell and Mr. Whatley sent for me. He was just come into Bath in order to go to his brother's. He was in a very sad state all over deeply in the vapours and despairing of a cure. I thought in a much worse condition than myself.

After supper I took the opportunity to speak to Mrs. Marshall and tell her how much I was concerned for what I had done in the gardens and begged her pardon, but she neglected it and said she did not know what I meant. I thought this was extremely cruel but she refused to hear me and went away.

Sunday, June 3. I went to meeting both parts of the day. My thoughts run upon Mrs. Marshall. I wanted an opportunity to talk to her and discover something of my passion. At last she came into sister's room and I longed for an opportunity to speak to her and sister went out, but her maid was in the closet. However, I could not help taking the opportunity of speaking to her, of begging of her to forgive all the rudeness I have been guilty of in her company, especially that in the garden, but she put it off and said she did not know anything of the matter. I was so confounded that I could scarce speak a word to her and I was fain to sit mute and silent, speaking only a word now and then. I find I have run myself further into the mire, and the more I endeavour to get out the more I get in. I think I never felt so great a pain in my life before; I could almost have been willing to die, my anxiety and trouble was so great. But I find myself something better now I have writ this. I will endeavour to drive her out of my thoughts. To bed at 12.

Monday, June 4. Rose at 5. Prepared for journey to London. Was very uneasy about taking leave. Did not dare to kiss Mrs. Marshall, though I kissed all the rest, but she was to go part of the way with us. Gave the two maids 5s. apiece and Mrs. Marshall's maid half-crown. Gave the pump woman half-crown. Mrs. Marshall rode in the coach to Sandylane and Mrs. Jane [1] rode upon the horse that was hired for her to come back upon,

[1] His sister-in-law's maid.

Mr. Powell upon the road asked me about my love for Mrs. Marshall and seemed surprised at me for being so much smitten with any woman, but I told him I was very sincere and should think myself extremely happy in her for a wife. But when he put it to me whether I had a design in reality to court her and promised he would do me all the service he could, I told him I was sensible she could never like me, and I desired only he would, if I happened to be mentioned, give as favourable a character of me as he could. There was a great deal of crying, both sister and her, at parting. I took all the opportunity I could of inculcating my passion and intimating my love, but I don't find it made any impression. I had been pretty easy upon the road but now her sight revived my passion and I longed to declare it to her, but I did only by remote hints and very soft sayings, but, alas, I could get nothing from her, but she seemed perfectly tired of any discourse and said so herself. I left her at past 4 and found an opportunity of kissing her.

I was very much concerned to part with her, but when I was got some way on my journey the thought of her began to vanish and I was longing for a young woman that I overtook upon the road on foot. I came all alone from Sandylane to Marlborough very fast, that I came in before the coach. At length the coach came and I immediately began to be merry and easy: thoughts of humour and mirth flowed in upon me and I talked in a very humorous strain to the ladies that came out of the coach. We all supped together and I was perfectly good-humoured. A customer of brother's came to see sister and invited her to her house whither we went after supper. I think I never was in a more merry, gay humour in my life. There were some young girls at her house, and I soon began to talk to them in a very merry, humorous strain, which held for above an hour all the time I stayed there. I wish I could always be in the same strain.

Tuesday, June 5. Thought upon the road about Mrs. Marshall. It came into my thoughts that I had in my parting with her at Sandylane talked to her in such a manner as must make her think I had a design to make my addresses to her. But then on the other hand I thought my circumstances were not proper at all for matrimony at present. If she has but a small fortune it would ruin me to marry her, keep me low in the world and prevent my rise. And if she has a considerable fortune her father would never consent I should have her without a proportionable fortune. I cannot suppose my father can or will give me enough to answer £2,000 fortune without the addition of a business or employment, but then here comes in the balance of my love and inclination to her and I did not find that so strong as to be an equivalent for all the rest. It ought therefore to be my endeavour to conquer this passion I have.

Came to Reading at 5 o'clock. It happens to be the day before the election for members of Parliament. There does not seem to be any great noise or hurry in the town upon this account.

Wednesday, June 6. Rode to Slough with Mr. Spragg. I talked with him about the Turkey Company and trade, he being a silk man and dealing with that company. At Slough we met father, mother and brother, come to meet us in a coach and four horses. We were very merry and I was peculiarly free with Mr. Spragg's daughters and very merry with them, that I believe they think me very good company.

Nurse [1] happened to be at brother's and I asked her about Cousin Allen, whether she was married or no. She said no, my Aunt Allen's sister had told her so, and said that they looked too high above their fortunes and expected greater things than reason would gratify them in. But it was owing to Aunt Allen, who affected an air of quality and yet at the same was guilty of abundance of very mean low things that exposed her to the country and made her the talk of it.[2] She was afraid it would spoil her daughter's marriage. For my own part I have entirely given over all thoughts of having Cousin Allen and grow very cool in my correspondence with Aunt Stevenson. I have not writ to her since I went to Bath and don't know when I shall. Supped at brother's. To bed between 10 and 11.

Thursday, June 7. Rose at 9. Was going into the City and met Mr. Emmett and another gentleman going to spend the day at the other end of the town. Went along with them. Heard

---

[1] Mrs. Knot.

[2] Among Aunt Allen's idiosyncrasies was the practice, recorded in a later diary, of not going to bed for three consecutive days and not getting up for the next three.

a sermon at Common-Garden Church [1] by the parson of it. It was extremely loyal and Whiggish. From thence went to the King's Chapel and heard music performed upon the account of the thanksgiving to-day for the success of His Majesty's arms against the rebels. The King and Prince and Princess were there and the Bishop of Salisbury preached a very good honest sermon full of abhorrence of the rebellion and all popish principles. It was not a very extraordinary polite sermon but good and substantial. We dined at a tavern at 4 o'clock. At 6 we took a coach and went to Kensington Gardens. I was mightily pleased with the disposition of these gardens, especially the wilderness part of it, where the wilderness of nature appears.

Came back and after having been half-hour in the coffee-house went to the Drawing-Room, where there was a very great assembly and very finely dressed. But Mrs. Marshall was still the same to me. All the gaiety and finery there could not fix my attention to them or call off my thoughts from her.

The day has been observed very considerably. A great many gentlemen and ladies wore orange-colour favours to distinguish themselves and there were very great illuminations at night, I think more than ever I saw, especially at the Court end of the town. The Tories were a little insolent in the morning, hissing those that wore the orange-colour favours and by wearing some of them rue, thyme and rosemary in their hats and breasts, signifying that the King should rue the time that he ever beat the rebels and the rosemary intimating his death. And there were little nosegays of these sold together in the streets. But the loyal party prevailed in the whole and they did not do any mischief nor appear in any great company.[2]

Saturday, June 9. Came home and set about finishing my letter in order to send it to London. Though I think I am deeply in love with Mrs. Marshall and that was the subject of my letter, yet I was more concerned to give Mr. Powell a good opinion of

[1] i.e. Covent Garden.
[2] At Hackney, Newcome wrote, 'in the Evening, the Gentlemen of the Parish, having club'd, erected a great Bonfire on the Bare at the Old Bowling Green and had Kettle Drums, Trumpets and Music, danced and drank loyal Healths, guarded by about 20 or 30 regular Soldiers and 60 or 70 Constables and their watch, to keep the Peace, it having been given out that a Mob would attempt the new Meeting house'.

my sense by my letter than to express the real sentiments of my mind, though I think I did that too.

Mr. Lewis came in and according to his manner gave me some hints and intimations of some irregular things my brother William had been guilty of concerning the ladies that had displeased them very much, and I find it was by taking them out one day and bringing Mr. Humphries into their company who pretends love for Mrs. Loyd. This was taken very ill by my Aunt Bickley and Aunt Lewis that he should joy to carry on intrigues between them and promote a thing that would tend very much to the dishonour of Aunt Bickley, who having Mrs. Loyd in her charge and under her care would be extremely blamed by her relations if any mischief should happen to her and she should marry against their consent.

Came home and sister and brother Ryder were come. I am grown more familiar with sister since I have been at Bath than I was before, and she seems more fond and desirous of my company than ever, and I cannot help desiring hers that I may talk of Mrs. Marshall. At supper we talked of Mrs. Marshall's family and were commending it extremely, that father gave a kind of a hint in a jesting way of her becoming my wife. This gave a kind of new life and vigour to my passion and I found myself all of a sudden more in love than usual.

Sunday, June 10. Rose between 8 and 9. Went to the old meeting to hear Cousin Billio. He made a very good sermon. I thought his delivery was something mended. Several merry, diverting thoughts came into my head to speak to Mrs. Loyd, that I could not but think that talent of mirth which I observed in Mr. Powell and others is very easily got.

At dinner was got into a very full humour, the thoughts of Mrs. Marshall overcame me and I could not get rid of them nor was able to talk about indifferent things. This fit of love held me all the while at meeting that I could not mind any that the parson said, though Mr. Mayo preached.

This being the Pretender's birthday it was given out before that his friends would wear white roses and green favours to distinguish themselves. A great many soldiers patrolled about the streets and were ordered to take away any white roses they saw. The constables also were ordered to do the same, and abundance were taken away and many quarrels happened upon it. Particularly an officer, one Mr. Musgrave, saw a gentleman walking in Gray's Inn Walks with a white rose on. He took it away from him, upon which they drew their swords and the officer wounded him that he was taken away. And a great many were taken up by the constables and carried to the counter for it.

Monday, June 11. Went to Uncle Marshall's. There was aunt and cousin and some Tory ladies with her. They were reflecting upon the insolence of the Whig mob. It is a strange thing how they are prejudiced. All the mischief that the Tory mob did in pulling down so many meeting houses, breaking open people's houses, insulting their persons and endangering their lives were nothing at all in their account, and they made light of them but now the least mischief or damage that the Whig mob do is aggravated and become intolerable. However, for my own part I am extremely glad to find that the mob can be raised for the Government and that a popular show is made on its side. If the mob for the Government grows strong and makes a noise and show people will naturally fall in with it. The Duke of Newcastle [1] is the man that promotes these Whig mobs more than any one. He gives away a vast deal of money upon that account. This has made him become the hatred of all the Tories, who are continually cursing him and wishing all evil may befall him.

I have been pretty much all this day free from the uneasy pains of love and kept myself pretty quiet. Aunt Lomax who came to town to-day, upon talking about Mrs. Marshall, said it was well known that she was worth £30,000. This made me a little uneasy because I could not expect that she would ever have me with such a fortune.

When I and my father and brother walked to London in the morning my father mentioned brother William and was very much concerned at his behaviour. He said he had no head for business nor thought about it. He said he was continually out at night, but what he did or where he went he could not tell, and if he asked him he always had a lie ready to tell. He said he heard also that there was some intrigue carrying on between

---

[1] Sir Thomas Pelham-Holles, Duke of Newcastle (1693-1768), a master of political corruption in an age which excelled in the art.

him and Mr. Keniston's (a man that works at the shop) daughter.

My father mentioned also a difficulty he was under with respect to partnership, for Mr. West had said he could not stay any longer partner with Mr. Bailey because he did not mind business. Now my father thought it would be hard upon Mr. Bailey to be turned out, because it would be difficult for him to settle in business and he has a great family. But then if Mr. West went off he would not be able to maintain the trade, the labouring part would lie so much upon him. I told my father I thought it not necessary to consult Mr. Bailey's interest in this case. They might give him time to find out another place and settle himself, but in this case I am at a loss how they would dispose of my brother William.

Tuesday, June 12. Went to Aunt Bickley's in order to meet with Mrs. Loyd and have a little merry brisk conversation with her, but she was not at home. Some thought or other put me in mind of Mrs. Marshall and I could not help being in a dull heavy mood. Indeed I could not but almost wish my father would take notice of it. But I am sensible this would signify nothing but merely gratify my passion in discovering it. For I cannot expect she will ever stay for me till I am called to the Bar. And yet I don't know how to bear the thoughts of losing her for ever. It cuts me to the soul to think that I must never be happy in that charming creature's possession. Methinks I could for ever abjure the sex if I may not have her, but I am in hopes time may conquer it and alter my mind.

Wednesday, June 13. Intended to go to Dr. Wadsworth [1] about the pain in my arm, which is not yet gone, and also to talk with him about my whole constitution, but meeting with sister and brother and talking about Mrs. Marshall I could not leave, till it was too late to go to the Doctor's.

Dined in commons. Went to our civil law club in the afternoon after having been at brother's and seen sister, who had received a letter from Mrs. Marshall. It revived my passion in

---

[1] Thomas Wadsworth, M.A. (d. 1733), later physician at St. Thomas's Hospital.

me to hear from her, especially since she mentioned Mr. Powell in the letter without mentioning me at all. This cut me to the heart, but I must bear it. She sets out from Bath to-day. How shall I be able to bear the sight of her or how shall I behave towards her? If I can I will endeavour to appear as indifferent as possible and be as good company as I can. But I cannot promise myself that I shall be able to do that.

At our civil law club I was pretty good company, as I am there, more than anywhere else. Went to our club at Change. There were Mr. Isles and Heathcote and others, but Mr. Witnoom was married yesterday to Dr. Scoley's daughter and therefore could not be with us.

Macartney was tried to-day for the death of Duke Hamilton.[1] Colonel Hamilton who was the Duke's second was the chief evidence against him. But he was brought in by the jury guilty of manslaughter, which is done as is said on purpose to prevent an appeal by the Duchess, or else they would have brought him in not guilty.

Thursday, June 14. Went to brother's. From thence to Cousin Watkins. I am the most free and familiar in my conversation with him of any one. He went with me to Dr. Wadsworth's about the pain in my arm, which I am concerned at. I intended to talk with the Doctor about my whole constitution, about the cold bath and Tunbridge and Bath waters. But when I came to talk with him I was at a loss what to say. I told him, however, of my use of the cold bath, and I believe the Doctor has a good opinion of it enough, but did not care to recommend it before the apothecary. He ordered me a vomit and a blister, besides an electuary and diet drink. Cousin Watkins sent me a vomit and came and attended its working himself. It put me into a great faintness and lowness of spirits that I was almost ready to faint away. I drank about six quarts of cardus tea with it. Then he laid on the blister, which he cut the next morning. Went to bed at past 10.

---

[1] This is a sequel to the duel described in *Henry Esmond*. James Douglas, 4th Duke of Hamilton, fought a duel with Lord Mohun on 15 November 1712. Both were killed. Colonel Hamilton, the Duke's second, accused General Macartney, his *vis-a-vis*, of attacking the Duke. The Tories thereupon maliciously fabricated a Whig plot. Macartney fled, but surrendered in 1716.

Friday, June 15. At 9 o'clock Cousin Watkins came and cut my blister. It is a very painful thing to have the new plaster put on upon the raw flesh but I bore it without the least motion or crying out.

Mr. Colebuck came to me this morning with a new wig, which I gave him 5 guineas for. Read some of Boileau's satires. I think I cannot read his satires over too often.

Dined in commons and agreed to do the Inn exercise tomorrow and had a case given me, but it was so much out of the way of anything I had read in law that I have desired Mr. Samson to make me an answer upon it, which he has promised.

Came home. Read a French book and translated part of it into English. I find I am apt to be at a loss for words to express my thoughts and I thought it would be of great help to me in this respect to translate polite authors: it would give me a *copia* of words and make them flow easier from me.

Saturday, June 16. At 12 went to Mr. Samson who made me an answer upon the case given me for my exercise at New Inn. At 3 o'clock went in our gowns, four of us together, with the Reader to the New Inn, where we read our answers one after another before him, and he at last read his opinion and reasoning upon it. He seems to be but a very dull fellow. It is all mere formality and signifies nothing. Not but that the other gentlemen that made the exercise seemed to have taken some pains upon it.

Sunday, June 17. My arm was more painful than it has been these two or three days, that I don't find the blister does it any good. Mr. Mayo preached the funeral sermon upon Mrs. Little. It is a strange thing how very little people think of their own death, though they are daily warned of it by the decease of their friends or neighbours or acquaintances. I wish with all my heart I could bring myself more to think of it.

Mr. Mayo preached in the morning upon these words in the 25th Psalm, 'The paths of the Lord are mercy and truth to such as keep his covenant and his testimony.' I could not but think this thought if well considered and meditated upon would be sufficient to excite a man to the practice of virtue and make him always easy and cheerful, to be fully possessed with the belief that whatever happens to him, how cross or adverse soever in outward appearance, will yet have a happy issue and tend some way or other to his advantage in the whole and indeed this is so just and agreeable to the natural sentiments we have of God that we cannot but believe it.

Mr. Mayo after sermon in the afternoon came and drank some tea with us, and so did Mr. Brookbanks [1] and Kingsford and others. It was said that it is thought we shall soon be engaged in a war with France when the Emperor is engaged with the Turks as he is likely to be by the means and interest of France, which is done chiefly in favour of the Pretender, and that a new rebellion is ripening apace.

I came to London in order to go to Westminster to-morrow morning, but what influenced me very much was that I had a mind to talk with sister about Mrs. Marshall whom she had been with yesterday. But when I came I had very little to say about her. Came home at 10.

Monday, June 18. Rose at 7. By the maid's assistance dressed my blister. Went to Westminster Hall. Sir William Wyndham came to the King's Bench to pray to be admitted to bail and Duke Somerset, Lord Rochester, Lord Jumont and Lord Gower came with him to be his bail. The curia took time till Wednesday to consult the cases stated and he is to be brought up on Wednesday again. Sir William Wyndham when everything had been said by the counsel made a speech himself. I was a little surprised to find him hesitate and hurry in his speech because I thought he had been a very good speaker in the House of Commons.

Went into the city to speak to Cousin Watkins about some breakings out upon my head which I was afraid was the itch, but he told me it was natural for the physic which I took to make me break out. However, I am not perfectly satisfied that it is not the itch, because I have had several times these breakings out at this time of the year, which I am afraid are the remains of the itch I got in Scotland.

Met with brother William. He told me Mrs. Loyd was not

---

[1] A Mr. Joseph Brooksbank was fined £20 for three parish offices at Hackney in 1714.

at all in love with Mr. Humphries though he is in love with her to the highest degree and he believes would marry her though she had nothing at all of fortune. It was some satisfaction to me to hear there was a man in my case.

Went to see Uncle Dudley Ryder who is come to town. Found at the tavern with father and Sir Richard Newdigate.[1] Sir Richard seems to be a very weak man and knows very little. Came home at past 11.

Tuesday, June 19. Went to brother's at past 4. Found Mrs. Marshall there and Mrs. Stancliff and Cousin Joseph Billio. I came in with a pretty brisk [air] and talked very briskly at first with Mrs. Stancliff but not so much with Mrs. Marshall. She went with us to the Park where we walked several turns. I behaved myself not very gay, not very dull. She did not seem much averse to me, but carried it civilly as indeed she could not do otherwise. I made her several compliments upon occasion which she took in a very careless manner. We came together, brother and sister and I and she from the Park and set her down at the Gate of Bartholomew Close from whence I walked with her to her house. I thought she might have asked me to go in but she did not.

Thursday, June 21. Came home after dinner. Did very little but sleep away the time till 4 o'clock, when set about a letter to Mr. Powell which I writ before but wanted to mend and polish and this was a much greater difficulty than the first writing it. I was puzzled at every sentence and after a great deal of thought and turning of it I was often forced to let it stand as it did at first, that I am persuaded it is better to let one's thoughts as it were clothe themselves with words such as first occur.

Went to our club. There were several new members in it since I was there. We talked chiefly of public affairs. It was taken notice of that the Government went on in the most surprising manner in the proceedings against the rebel prisoners. They are brought to town in great pomp and solemnity, kept in prison for a great while after special commission is made on purpose for their trial, and they are at last brought to trial. They have witnesses brought up and they have all the liberty m

---

[1] Father of Sir Roger Newdigate, the antiquary and benefactor of Oxford.

the world to insult the government and Court at their trials, they are found guilty and in a very solemn manner have sentence pronounced against them to be hanged, and then the scene is shut up, the curtain is drawn and we hear no more of them. It looks like a perfect farce to treat them in such a manner and at last let them escape or else do nothing to them.

There is a talk of an Act of Indemnity and indeed methinks that is much better than to pretend to try them and at last do nothing with them. This proceeding of the Court gives offence to abundance of the King's friends. Came home at 12.

Friday, June 22. Mr. Fernley came to see me. He is a man of no manner of education. Happening to lay his hands upon *Hudibras* we read some of that together and I explained the difficult words or allusions in it. I am mightily pleased with the wit of *Hudibras*.

Went to Hackney with uncle and Cousin Baxter.[1] Cousin Baxter seems to be extremely heavy and dull without any spirit or briskness, that I wonder what should make Cousin Katherine[2] in love with him, but this is some consolation to me and gives me hopes that though Mrs. Marshall cannot love me some other pretty girl may.

Mr. Child dined with us and we sat after dinner together to drink wine. Mr. Child was extremely merry and brisk and talked with a great deal of good humour and gaiety. I could not but be surprised to see a man of his age so free from the impertinencies and odd peevish humours that they are generally troubled with. He invited me very kindly to come and see him but though I would willingly go yet I don't know how to bear him company in his conversation and mirth.

At 7 o'clock Cousin Joseph Billio came, when the rest of the company was gone. I talked with him about Mrs. Marshall, but he does not admire her so much and told me that Mr. Baker,[3] the dissenting parson, knows her very well and talked of her as one he was extremely intimate with and had kissed very often. This indeed was the most powerful antidote against my love I have yet met with. He called her by the name of Sally Marshall

---

[1] Michael Baxter of Nuneaton.   [2] Uncle Dudley's daughter.
[3] Possibly Samuel Baker (d. 1748), who was concerned in the Salters' Hall controversy in 1719 and was later successor to Bradbury there.

as a familiar appellation that he was used to. I did not give the least intimation as if I had really an affection for her and desired her for a wife, though I could have been glad to have had the pleasure of communicating it. But I could not help keeping up the discourse about her, it being the most pleasing subject in the world to me.

Saturday, June 23. Intended to go to London this morning but did not because of the rain.

Went to London presently to see Mrs. Marshall who promised to be at brother's. Came to London and was extremely concerned to find she had been there yesterday with her mother and sister, but Cousin Bibby Ryder and Mrs. Loyd were there. I was very merry with them both but especially Mrs. Loyd, with whom I talked very freely and familiarly. If I could talk in that manner to Mrs. Marshall I believe she would think me very good company, but I don't know how to do that.

Sunday, June 24. Went to Cousin Watkins, with whom went to church to hear Mr. Massery. He has the most of impudence in his air and manner of any man I ever met with. He reads the prayers very well with respect to his voice and emphasis he lays upon the words, but he does in such a manner as discovers a superior opinion of himself. At dinner I was exceeding merry. My raillery went chiefly upon the subject of matrimony and my good disposition and inclination towards it, and I was very free with Cousin Watkins's wife upon that subject in asking her questions about it and her courtship, &c.

Heard Cousin Marshall in the afternoon. He preaches admirably well and uses very strong emphatical expressions that his sermons are really very well composed.

Went to brother's. Talked with sister about Mrs. Marshall and was put into a very melancholy and grave posture of mind. When I came hither I looked dull and heavy: I was even willing my father should take notice of it and ask me the reason of it, that I might by my answer give him ground to guess the true cause of it, and yet by this I should only expose myself. He has suspected me of love to Mrs. Lee and Cousin Allen and now for me to discover myself to be in love with Mrs. Marshall, what thoughts must he conceive of me?

Read some of Dr. Bates's discourse upon the immortality of the soul.

Monday, June 25. In the afternoon went to Mrs. Crisp's. Her son that is sick in bed of the consumption and past hopes of recovery conversed with us. He is very serious and loves to talk of another world and to prepare for it. It is indeed a happy state when a man is got so far into religion and so far above the world as to think of passing out of it without terror and distraction, to be able to be calm and serene under the assured expectation of death and leaving whatever is dear and pleasant to him. What a strange, what a surprising change will death make upon a man! And yet I don't know, perhaps death is a less alteration than we are apt to think. Men only disappear upon this stage when they die. Whether a man himself is altered or no, whether his mind is put into a different frame and posture, its temper and constitution, its sense of things varied or no, is not so easily determined.

Went to London at 6. Read part of *Cato* [1] : in relation to the love part I could scarce help crying at those tender passages, they being so like my own case. Came to town about between 7 and 8. Was in hopes to have seen sister who had been at Mrs. Marshall in order to have heard some news about her and therefore went backwards and forwards till she was come. She told me she would not come to see her till Thursday. I could not help indulging my sorrow and melancholy and desire of her, and yet my reason tells me it will never do.

Tuesday, June 26. Went to Hamlin's with Cousin Joseph Billio, talked with him about Berkeley's notions which he is now thinking of and reading. Went to the Fountain Tavern with him and Cousin Robert and Mr. Baker. Mr. Baker talked pretty much about Mrs. Marshall as if he was perfectly free with her. But when I came to sister and talked with her about him she said Mrs. Marshall had told her that she did not care to see him, he was so apt to be impertinently free and familiar that she was always afraid to speak to him. This gave me a great deal of ease.

Read some of Mr. Wotton's *Reflections upon Ancient and Modern Learning* [2] and find some very good and just observations in it. He goes a kind of middle way between Sir William

[1] Addison's heroic tragedy, 1714. [2] First published in 1694.

Temple who entirely gives the preference to the ancients and Perrault and others who give the preference to moderns in everything.

Wednesday, June 27. Went to father's. He was very glad to see me and spoke extremely kind to me about my health and told me he would spare no charge to recover me. I was vexed with myself that I could not make him some proper answer in return for all this goodness, but, I don't know how, I cannot tell how to express my sense of it to him as I should.

Went to our civil law club. From thence to brother's where I found Mrs. Marshall. She seemed very civil and kind, as far anything of words and looks could go, and I dared not to attempt to kiss her. I told her of Mr. Baker, that he mentioned her name with a great deal of pleasure, &c., but she said she was not well pleased with him at all, she disliked his conversation and thought him a very unmannerly rude fellow. I did not observe that Mrs. Marshall ever said anything that was bright or extraordinarily witty. What supports her is her beauty joined with a cheerful pleased look that is good-humoured and full of smiles. This makes her perfectly charming and makes me delight to keep my eyes upon her and hear her speak, though she says but little. I am extremely obliged to brother and sister and wish I knew how to make a return. I should be extremely glad of a proper opportunity of making a present to my sister to the value of three or four guineas but I don't know what to make a present of. I waited upon her home in the coach between 10 and 11. She just asked me to walk in, which I refused and she offered to pay the coachman, but I would not let her. Came home.

Thursday, June 28. Went to Hackney in the coach. Intended to have gone to Aunt Bickley this afternoon but it rained so that I could not go. Therefore stayed at home, read some French comedies and some of the translation of some of Horace's *Odes* and got some of them by heart. I endeavoured also to translate some of Virgil into English verse, but could make nothing of it. I find I have not a command of words and phrases enough to make a poet.

Read at night some of Chillingsworth's controversy with the Papists which I admire more and more I read it.

Friday, June 29. Went to supper and to coffee-house where met Mr. Abney. He says he had a letter from Mr. Grey Neville [1] in the North that says there are risings in Northumberland again and that some hundreds of men met in the night upon the heath. Came home, wrote part of a letter to Mr. Leeds in a merry style of raillery. To bed at past 12.

Saturday, June 30. Rose at 8. Finished my letter to Mr. Leeds. Paid my landlady for her quarter's rent.

Went to Aunt Billio's. There was a lady visiting there that lodges in Shore House. She had a fortune of £5,000 and married a man who broke in five weeks after the wedding. He is now beyond sea and she is here with three young children. She is an extremely agreeable woman and seems to bear her misfortunes with a great deal of cheerfulness and temperance.

Cousin Joseph Billio walked home with me and played upon the viol with me. I received a letter from Mr. Whatley in the country. He writes just as he talks, is grown happy all of a sudden and by his expressions of satisfaction in it one would think he was never to fall into the vapours again.

Sunday, July 1. Rose before 8. Read some of Tillotson's sermons.

At breakfast my father took occasion to complain to my mother of the want of money, as he very often does to me when I desire any of him, that it makes me sometimes wish I had not been brought up in the study of the law which requires more money than if I had been of my father's business. Heard Cousin Billio in the afternoon. I am always in pain for him while he is in prayer. I am persuaded he might make himself much more acceptable in prayer if he would take more pains about it, but, I don't know how, he is sensible he is not acceptable but attributes it to his want of that manner of praying which is peculiar to the dissenters and which he thinks not so good. But I think he is mistaken. He has nothing at all in his praying that justly deviates from their manner. As to his preaching that is much better, but even his sermons I think are not extraordinary. There is not that clearness of thought and good judgement in them which I should have expected from one who is a mighty admirer of Tillotson and

[1] Cf. note, p. 154.

the best of the Church of England divines. He affects a familiar air without anything of a tone, but does not succeed in it.

Went to Aunt Billio's and part of the way with Mrs. Loyd. She was very good-humoured and received my conversation very civilly, but she put on several airs which looked a little proud. Mr. Humphries followed us at a little distance but would not come up with us.

Came home. Read some of Mr. Flavel [1] of the immortality of the soul to the family. When I read such things as this I am apt to be convinced of the reasonableness of them and am apt to wonder people can, notwithstanding all the reasoning in the world, still persist in a course of sin and neglect of another world. And yet at the same time they make no impression upon myself. Indeed the world makes such strong and deep impressions upon my mind that I don't know how to conceive I shall ever be able to grow indifferent about it and lay aside an inordinate affection to it, only the assistance of the spirit of God is promised to my own endeavours.

To bed at past 11.

Monday, July 2. Dined with Mr. Samson at an eating-house. I don't know what Mr. Samson sees in me but I perceive he has a great value and friendship for me, and I believe would be very willing to do me any service, and indeed I take him to be a very honest, sincere, plain man.

Went from him to see Uncle Ryder at his chamber. He told me two observations which he had made. One is that men that cannot bear to be plainly contradicted and their judgements directly opposed may yet, by softening the matter, be brought over to act just as you would have them. Another was of Sir Richard Newdigate, the father of the present Sir Richard, that as he was a very cunning man he had a mighty art and trick of drawing persons into anything before they are aware of it, by beginning at a vast distance from what is his principal design and so bringing it on by degrees till he surprises you into the acknowledgement or concession or doing something which you would wish undone.

Went into the City to John's, where met with Mr. Witnoom, Mr. Porter and Crisp and Atkins. We went all to the tavern

[1] John Flavel (d. 1691), Presbyterian divine.

together and I wished Mr. Witnoom joy of his marriage. He seemed mightily pleased with himself and his wife and had a mind to appear as if the fatigues of it had not the least hurt him.

Sister came home and I longed to speak with her about Mrs. Marshall to know when I am likely to see her, but she is to go to-morrow into the country and there is no prospect of my seeing her this good while unless sister and I ride to Highgate to see her. Dr. Avery was at Mrs. Marshall's and they mentioned my name. I was mighty curious to know in what manner I was mentioned. It cut me to the heart the most sensibly when my sister told me the Doctor upon occasion of talking of me said I was very grave, because this would encourage her ill opinion of me and make her think that it was nothing peculiar to my circumstances at Bath that made me so dull as I was there, but my common temper. I almost resolved to give over the thoughts of her, never desire to see her more. But, alas! how shall I be able to do this? My thoughts run out to her whether I will or no.

Duke of Argyll is turned out from being captain-general of His Majesty's forces in Scotland. He is of a proud, hasty, insolent temper and very covetous and debauched, and it is said was endeavouring to change the present ministers, as Stanhope and Townshend, &c., and bring in Nottingham's party. He is said to have been very much the cause of the mercy which the Government has shown the rebels, which he did in order to make himself popular. It is thought also that he favoured the Pretender's cause in Scotland and gave them advantages on purpose. However, the Scotch are in general mightily for him and take it ill that their great general should be turned out. They are indeed apt to be jealous of the honour of their nation which makes them resent anything that seems to reflect upon one of their countrymen who has made a figure. It is said he offered to surrender up his place of Groom of the Stole to the Prince but the Prince would not accept of it and desired him to consider of it.[1]

Tuesday, July 3. Went to Mr. Samson's to breakfast. Borrowed Quintilian's *Institutio Oratoria*. He is very willing to lend me any of his books.

[1] When George I proposed to visit Hanover he wished to restrict his son's power during his absence. The Prince's resentment was ascribed to the influence of his adviser, Argyll, whom the King ordered to be dismissed.

Dined at brother's where Cousin Joseph Billio dined also with us. He talked very much of Mrs. Marshall and admires her extremely. He suspects that I am troubled very much at her going to Highgate, as indeed I am.

Went to Hackney with sister, Cousin Joseph and Aunt Billio in the coach. Aunt Billio told me somebody told her they thought I was in love with Mrs. Marshall. I rallied that fancy a little but it was a very true guess.

Wednesday, July 4. After dinner went to Aunt Bickley's to take my leave of Mrs. Loyd who is going to Bristol and perhaps will never return again. It was with some difficulty that I could bring about my taking leave of her in a good manner. However, I did at last, but in such a manner as that we laughed all the while.

Went to London. Cousin Watkins went with me to Dr. Wadsworth's. I asked his opinion of the cold bath and Tunbridge, but he put off these questions with slight answers and after he had ordered me some things, he told me after I had taken them he would talk with me about the cold bath, so that he has cut out another fee for himself.

Went to father's and he was vexed I should go into courses of physic. It would ruin my constitution and told me of a medicine for the rheumatism which had done very great things in the cure of it, and that is nothing but mustard seed bruised and steeped in wine. I was the better pleased with this prescription because in the things the Doctor had ordered me mustard seed is one of the ingredients. Went to Hackney on foot. Read in the way some of the French *Cato*,[1] which is preferred by the French critics to our English one.

When came to Hackney sister was at Aunt Bickley's taking leave of Mrs. Loyd. There had been a great deal of company there. She won't part very good friends with my Aunt Bickley's family. Cousin Bibby especially is no great friend of hers. She cannot tell how to bear to see all the respect and compliments paid her without any to herself. I went to meet sister coming home. In the way Mr. Rollison met us and would have us go home with him and he gave us some admirable good wine. He is a mighty generous man and I believe by that means gains very much upon the affections of people and promotes his trade.

[1] *Caton d'Utique*, 1715, by François Deschamps.

Brother William who had been also at Aunt Bickley's to take his leave of Mrs. Loyd told me that she wanted to speak with him mightily in private, and because she could then get an opportunity she appointed him to meet her at 12 to-night at their house. She received him at the back door. The servant-maid is her confidante and assisted her. Her conversation with my brother was chiefly about Mr. Humphries. She is of a strange temper, sometimes she gives him hopes, at other times destroys them all again. However, she tells him she will never marry below herself and therefore he must at least equal her fortune if he expects to have her. Mr. Humphries is, I believe by what I hear from my brother, really in love with her and intends to pursue it by proposals to her father as soon as he comes to age, which will be in a year and half. I am afraid she will make but an indifferent wife. I am surprised she should make my brother William her confidant as she does and entrust him with all her secrets, but perhaps it is because Mr. Humphries was very much by his means introduced to her and he acquainted him with his love for her first. Brother told me that she told him that Aunt Bickley has a mind that he should have his Cousin Bibby. By this I believe I can account for the civil treatment he has met with at Aunt Bickley's.

Took some physic to-night. To bed at 12.

Thursday, July 5. The physic I took last night made me very sick in the night and vomit three times. That put me very much out of order and made me afraid to take the purge this morning lest I should bring it up again, but after my stomach had been settled awhile I took it, but in half an hour brought it up and vomited several times. However, I had four or five stools, but it made me extremely sick and out of order till 10 o'clock.

At 12 o'clock my father came hither on purpose to see me having heard that I was very sick this morning. He came with a great deal of concern and told me everybody told him I was going into a consumption and begged me to take care of myself and ride out and use exercise, and he would buy a new horse very speedily for that end and would not grudge any charges for my health.

My sister and I were pretty merry and we romped together upon the bed and played as Mr. Powell and Mrs. Marshall used to do at Bath, that my sister told me she thought I could not have romped so well. Indeed it went pretty much against my temper, but she forced me upon it.

Read the French *Cato*. The plot of it is I believe more regular according to the rules of the Dramatic Poetry but I think the characters of the persons are not so well observed, and the Cato of Mr. Addison is a much greater person and more agreeable to the Cato in history than the Cato of Mr. Deschamps. I think also the sentiments in the English are much preferable to those of the French and have an air of grandeur and majesty becoming such persons as Cato and Caesar, far beyond what appears in the French. Read some of *Hudibras* and am mightily pleased with the wit of it.

Friday, July 6. Rose at 7. Took my pills. Spent the morning with sister. Was very merry with her and played and jested and romped with her. My sister [said] that Mrs. Marshall said she thought the officers were the most agreeable sort of men of any whatsoever, but being generally rakish and debauched she should never choose them for a husband. I found fault with this taste of the ladies, that they despised and neglected all the qualifications of virtue and good sense in comparison of a rakish air and a gay merry rattling conversation. I thought this was the reason why so many young men become rakes and coxcombs. My sister on the contrary said she did not value any extraordinary good sense or learning ; if a man was but good company this was sufficient and more than everything else. I have been in a great perplexity what to do about Mrs. Marshall. If I should declare my passion and avow a design to make my address to her, what hopes can I have of success ?

Received a letter from Mr. Powell at Oxford. He rallies a little in the beginning but grows afterwards serious in advising me to open my mind to her father and begin with gaining his consent, and he does not doubt but hers will soon follow. But what I shall do I cannot tell.

Cousin Joseph Billio came to see me. We talked about storytelling and the necessity of it for conversation and the difficulty of doing it well. He has to this end thought over stories and wrote down hints of them, but he finds it is to little purpose, his memory does not suffice for all the little circumstances that are necessary to the giving life and spirit to the story.

Saturday, July 7. Rose at 8. Took my pills as before. Spent the morning partly with sister, with whom I am grown very familiar, and partly in reading *Hudibras*, which is exceeding full of the most comical wit, which consists very much in odd similes and humorous turns such as are very fit for conversation with the ladies of a gay lively complexion.

Dined at Cousin Billio's with sister, Aunt Lomax and mother. Had a little dispute with Cousin Joseph Billio about established Churches. Cousin Joseph has a talent of introducing a kind of bawdy discourse which indeed generally shocks me so much that I don't know how to go on with it.

Went all to Aunt Billio where Mrs. Oileman came also. She entertained us exceeding agreeable with some songs which she sung as finely as ever I heard a woman sing in my life. She is a woman that is perfectly agreeable, talks in a most soft tender manner and mighty good sense and with cheerfulness, is of an admirable good temper. I was almost charmed with her.

The King went this morning through the City in his journey to Hanover. The Duke of Argyll is turned out of all his places at court both under the King and Prince, so that it appears that all the stories that were raised of the difference between the King and Prince about the Duke of Argyll are false.

Sunday, July 8. Rose at 8. Read some of Tillotson's sermons. Went to meeting. My thoughts ran all the while upon Mrs. Marshall that I could not mind what the minister said. Had a mind my father should take notice of it. One thing that made me the more desirous of this is that last night, talking with Mr. Child's daughters about me, he said he thought he must get me a wife, that that would cure me. Though this was said in but a kind of a jesting manner yet I cannot but fancy my father has had some thought of it seriously.

Passed away the evening in a strange, lifeless, inactive condition without speaking scarce a word. I don't know what my father thinks of me, but he seems cautious of speaking to me about it.

My mother grows extremely peevish and fretful, that she is angry at everything and my father can scarce say or do anything but she immediately snaps him up and takes it all in an ill sense. She never goes to dinner but is always out of humour at something or other, and nothing is done to please her. My father is far from being of the best temper in the management of himself towards my mother and the servants. He is very hasty and apt to give a loose to his sudden thoughts without consideration of the prudence of uttering or not uttering them, but yet I think my mother is much more intolerable and to blame. She will often misinterpret words or actions even the most plain and clear only to have an opportunity of blaming and fretting, so much it has possessed her. If she goes on to increase in this humour all her friends will grow weary of coming to see her and for my own part I shall come as seldom as possible.

Took my pills as usual.

Monday, July 9. In the afternoon at past 5 o'clock we went to Highgate and there happened to be some strangers visiting there, so that there was little freedom passed between sister and Mrs. Marshall. For myself, though I was in great concern and almost trembled to think how I should meet her, yet I behaved myself pretty well and with a great deal of cheerfulness. Mr. Marshall himself was there. I am mightily pleased with him and I think I talked in such a manner as must give him not an ill opinion of me.

Came home and sister was in a very brisk, merry humour and played and laughed and romped with me extremely. I am not unwilling to engage with her in this kind of entertainment because it may help me to learn that kind of merry, gay air which is so necessary in order to become agreeable to the ladies. My sister is naturally of a very brisk, lively temper and good smart sense. If she had had a polite education and been used to reading and cultivating her mind she would have made a very fine woman.

Tuesday, July 10. Rose before 8. Began to read some of Quintilian of Oratory, but was interrupted by breakfast.

Came to Hackney at 8 with Cousin Billio's. In the way talked with Cousin Joseph about Mr. Powell. He seems to begin to have a disrelish of the follies of youth though he is now but 19 years old, and has passed through those scenes of pleasure and gaiety and got to an end of them at the time when others scarce begin to have any relish of them. He is never ruffled or disturbed by any passion and acts with ease and tranquillity. Indeed I think he is of a make very fit to become a great man. He has a taste for gallantry, but enjoys it without any of the disturbance and difficulty that attends it and can leave it off when he finds it inconvenient ; even in things that have an air of debauchery and are less justifiable he appears in them as if he acted from judgement and consideration.

Came home. Met sister and Mrs. Hudson, who supped with us. I was very merry with them and talked in a very gay strain that I believe they must think me good company. And yet when I was in London I began to think I could not bear up under the present uneasiness and troubles I feel upon Mrs. Marshall's account.

Wednesday, July 11. Mrs. Marshall and Mrs. Phelps came in a borrowed chariot to see sister. It cheers my spirits very much to see that she carried to me with respect and a proper familiarity. I begin to have more hopes of her love than ever. I was pretty good company, though not extraordinary. I cannot yet be so familiar with her as I would be. As I am now in no business it would be madness for me to go to marry under a considerable fortune. I could indeed myself be contented with a little and so agreeable a wife as her, but I don't see how it is possible for me with what my father will give me and her fortune, which I don't find is likely to be above a £1,000, to maintain as genteelly as she has hitherto lived and will expect still to live if she marries.

Thursday, July 12. Went to London to father about buying a horse. Father told me he was extremely concerned about brother William. That a gentleman came to him to-day and told him that his son William had been engaged in the company of young men who had to do with a whore in Drury Lane and she was now with child and had like to have laid it to him, but has laid it to another of them. My father talked of him in a very angry manner and wished anything was become of him so he had but lost the sight of him, that he intended to send him beyond seas. I asked my father how he came by the money he must spend upon these occasions. He said he must steal it out of the shop. I said I thought he had another way of getting money, by borrowing it. My father said if he had he would not pay a farthing of it ; he should die in the gaol before he would pay his debts.

Friday, July 13. Went to see Mr. Hall [1] and Paul [2] the clergyman go to be hanged for rebellion and treason. There was a vast crowd of people stood all along Holborn to see them go by that it was difficult to see them in the sledge. The women were all in tears and were mightily concerned for the clergyman.

Dined at eating-house. Went to Smithfield with father in order to buy a horse, but could not light of one that was handsome and sound and such as my father liked. Talked with brother about brother William. He is mightily concerned but cannot tell what my father will do with him.

Went to John's. Talked with Mr. Jackson about public affairs. He is mightily pleased as well as myself that the parson is hanged for an example and warning to other priests that they may not fancy their cloth will be a protection to them against the justice of the law. It is said Paul talked in the cart at Tyburn very insolently and traitorously so as to acknowledge the Pretender and deny King George's title.

Supped at eating-house. At 10 o'clock I had a mind to walk about the streets and have some talk with the whores and go the furthest I can without lying with them. My chief end in this was to learn something of a boldness and confidence in addressing myself to persons, for indeed I am under a strange confusion and hurry when I attack a whore and cannot tell how to talk to them freely. But I could not attack them with that freedom as I would have done.

Saturday, July 14. Dined at eating-house. Went to Hackney. Hearing father and mother talk about brother William and being sensible that neither father nor mother were capable of thinking and determining well what to do about him, it came into my thoughts that it would be one very good qualification in a wife if she was a person capable of advising with and consulting upon any difficulty or occurrence. I found myself very weary and faint and out of order with walking to Hackney, and I observe

---

[1] John Hall, J.P., of Otterburn. Although he proved that he and his man were carried off by the rebels, he was condemned on the principle that to be with the rebels was to be of them.

[2] William Paul, vicar of Orton-on-the-Hill, Leicestershire. Captured at Preston, he was freed by Wills, but was apprehended in London by a J.P. of his own county.

in myself that upon any little affliction as this was my mind presently flows to Mrs. Marshall. All the little sorrows are lost and swallowed in my love.

Sunday, July 15. Rose at 7. Read some of Derham's *Astro-Theology*.[1] I think there is nothing more sensibly convinces a man of the being of God and impresses the sense of Him upon one than observing the testimony of His works and that plain design and contrivance that appears in them. I wish I could bring myself to this full and strong view of God Almighty. The more the world and the beings that are in it and in the heavens are searched, the more narrowly they are looked into, the more of wonderful art and wisdom and design appears in them, that one would think those who search into the works of nature most should be the best men and the most fully convinced of the being of God. O Lord, do Thou impress this great truth, the sense of Thy being and continual presence with us upon my soul, make it abide there and have a constant influence upon my whole life : oh, never let the world and things of sense be so powerful and strong as to deface Thy image in my heart or drive away the sense of Thee from my mind.

Father this morning at breakfast seeing me very dull and heavy told me he could not tell what was the matter with me unless I had lost my mistress. I only laughed at it and it passed over, but this shows my father is not without suspicion of the cause of it.

Heard Mr. Mayo both morning and afternoon. He is a man that talks mighty freely to the people and so as to make them very attentive and serious. It came into my thoughts to receive the sacrament of the Lord's Supper next time it is given by Mr. Mayo. I confess the chief thing that induced me then was that I was old enough and it might be expected from me, who have so long lived under the Gospel ministry and am supposed not to be ignorant of the doctrine and design and precepts of the Gospel. I am sorry indeed I should not have had better motives to it than merely the regard to men.

Read a sermon of Tillotson's [2] about the wisdom of religion.

[1] William Derham's *Astro-Theology*, published 1715.
[2] Fourteen volumes of Tillotson's sermons were published by Ralph Barker, 1695-1704.

It is an admirable good one, which one cannot read over too often. I observed immediately I had eat some milk at supper I smelt my own breath much stronger than before, which continued for some time till I brought up some phlegm, which I believe was occasioned by the milk, and then my breath was not so strong. I am apt to think milk is apt to create phlegm and therefore improper for me, that I intend to inquire of Cousin Watkins about it.

Monday, July 16. Father this morning at Hackney told me he would give me some certain allowance out of which I should keep myself entirely with clothes and everything, and asked me what he should allow me, whether £50 a year would not be enough, and after some time said he would allow me £80 per annum, which I thought full little enough to provide clothes and everything.

Read to the end of Wotton's *Reflections upon Ancient and Modern Learning*. I am very well pleased with the book, it is writ in a good style and a good spirit runs through it. I think to read some parts of it over often, for I find I am very apt to forget what I read.

After dinner went to Cousin Marshall's about this man who has got the medicine for the rheumatism. He thinks that my case is as much hysteric as rheumatic if not more and therefore questions whether this man's remedy is proper for me. But, however, he would have me talk with this man about my case and he will meet him with me. Accordingly I went from thence to find this man out. He lives in Derham Yard in the Strand. His name is Fowles. He was not at home, but I intend to go or send to-morrow and appoint him to meet Cousin Marshall and myself at Tiltyard Coffee-House over against Whitehall on Wednesday, 5 o'clock in the afternoon.

Cousin thinks the cold bath very proper for me. He talked in general about the practice of physic and said that the *materia medica* lay within a very narrow compass and that the business of a physician required the least time to be perfect in of any profession. He talked also about empiric medicines, which he said he began to have a much better opinion of, for he recovered his daughter by one of them given him by a gentlewoman, after all that the doctor could prescribe had proved useless and ineffectual.

But the doctors had made it their business to decry all this kind of receipts which are in the hands of private persons and thereby made persons of good sense and thought afraid to use any of them, though no doubt there may be very good receipts lodged in private hands.

Went to brother's. Father met us. He seems to grow careless and negligent about brother William and to let all pass again. I wonder how he can be easy under the apprehensions of my brother's continually robbing the shop as he believes.

Parson Paul's speech at Tyburn is printed [1] and also two letters which he sent to the Archbishop of Canterbury to intercede for his life, and another to Lord Townshend for the same end. I am told that the speech of Paul and Mr. Hall, which is much to the same purpose, were laid before the Council before they were printed and they thought it proper to print not only them but also the letters of Paul which might be compared together and so the justice of the Government more clearly evinced by their comparing. The speeches themselves are full of prevarication and lies and plainly appear not to be the genuine sentiments of a man at the last extremity going to leave the world so much as an artful contrivance to advance the party and cause.

Tuesday, July 17. Stayed with sister alone for above an hour. We talked about Mrs. Marshall. I was talking in a style of raillery and said Mrs. Marshall would have been glad to have had Dr. Avery. This my sister took very ill. She is strangely self-willed and obstinate and the more one endeavours to vindicate one's self the more perverse and stiff she is. And this I think the beauty in Mrs. Marshall's temper; she does not seem in the least inclined to that headstrong passionate temper, nor to be violent and rash in nothing.

At night sent to Mr. Fowles, the person who has the medicine for the rheumatism, to meet me to-morrow, but he was not at home.

Wednesday, July 18. Rose at 6. Went to cold bath. From thence to Fowles who was not at home. Then to Uncle Marshall's in order to acquaint cousin with it and we agreed

[1] In the *Daily Courant*. Cf. p. 274.

to go according to our appointment to meet him and to run the hazard of his coming, though he did not say he would. Breakfasted there. We talked about my pain in my arm and cousin said rhubarb he believed would do me good, that it was almost the only purge that the doctors themselves took and they chewed it as they went along the streets without confinement. For my present pain he advised to wrap some blue flannel about my arm, which Aunt Marshall has experienced to do a great deal of good in the very same case as mine.

Stayed at home in the afternoon reading law till past 4.

Went then in the coach to meet the man who had a cure for the rheumatism at Tiltyard Coffee-House. Cousin Marshall also met me there. The man is a very plain, rough man that has nothing of the appearance of a cheat, nor of one that has a design to get your money. He does not seem to have any skill in distempers, only having by experience found that his medicine has cured a great many persons of all sorts of pains in the body. He does not doubt the success of it at any time. His accounts of his cures agreed very well with what my cousin told me before, that I have no reason at all to doubt that he has performed very great cures of rheumatic pains after the patients have tried all the physicians could do to no purpose. The worst thing I like in him and that which is the only suspicious thing about him is that he pretends to cure other distempers as well as the rheumatism, as the venereal disease and the stone and gravel, but even in these cases he speaks of them in such a manner as does not look at all like a man designing to impose and cheat you of your money. He had got the names of abundance of persons he had cured and their dwelling. So that upon the whole I am resolved to try what his medicine will do for me, as he says it will cure me, though my pain may not be so much rheumatic. He said he could not get the medicine ready for me till Saturday night, when I shall send for it. It is to be done in wine which makes it much dearer, it being now £1 2s. whereas if done in ale it costs but 7s. 6d.

Thursday, July 19. Rose at past 6. Read law all the morning till 10 o'clock, but my mind run so much upon Mrs. Marshall that I could scarce mind what I read or comprehend anything. But there was one thing troubled me extremely and lay heavy upon my mind, and that was the apprehension I was under that I was not capable of getting my wife with child if I had one. I find myself not very powerful that way and it makes me very uneasy to think my wife should have reason to complain, that I could almost resolve not to marry, but I don't know how to conceive of being happy in this life without one.

Young Mr. Henry came to see me. Our conversation passed partly upon the University of Edinburgh where he is going in a little time and about classic authors and the manner of teaching school. He is a lad of good parts and a good memory and inclinable to study, that I believe he will make a considerable man.

We went to see Mrs. Bailey that lies in. I was pretty merry and brisk in conversation with them. Somebody told me I was in love. This made me talk of myself in a style of raillery, as I was in love and desperately so.

Friday, July 20. After dinner went into the City. Bought some cloth to make me a suit of clothes, 5 yards cost me £4 10s. Went to sister in hopes to see or hear something of Mrs. Marshall, but sister was gone there and had been there ever since the morning.

Went to the coffee-house and at the Gill House met with some company that asked me to go with them to the Mug-House in Salisbury Court [1] and I went with them to see the manner of it. I like the design of this institution very well. It is to encourage the friends to King George and keep up the spirit of loyalty and the public spirit among them. They have a president who proposes the healths. Between every health some of the company sing a song that is composed against the Tories and Jacobites. There is something in their manner of singing, which is generally attended with a chorus at the end of each stanza of the song, which has an effect upon those that hear it, something like the

[1] Read's Coffee-House, the most famous of the mug-houses because of the riot, described a little later, in which Read shot a man. This establishment was later called The Barley Mow Tavern, and in 1871 it became the headquarters of the Cogers Debating Society. A new building designed by Lutyens was erected on the site in 1937. The mug-houses which became popular at the beginning of the eighteenth century were politico-social clubs. At the Whig mug-houses the members drank loyal toasts from mugs adorned with portraits of George I and his ministers.

drums and trumpets in an army, to raise the courage and spirits of the soldiers. Methought it put me into a very brisk intrepid state to hear them huzza and clap hands and sing together. There is something I believe mechanical in this. It puts the spirits into a hurry and makes them have a swifter motion, as we put spirit into a dull horse by spurring it and hurrying it. I am persuaded these mug-houses are of service to the Government to keep up the public spirit and animate its friends, and I believe in time it will gain over the populace and make King George become popular.

There was a mob gathered about the door and we heard that there were some of the Bridewell boys come to attack us. This came to the ears of the society at the Roebuck and they sent some of their members to inquire into our circumstances and offer their assistance if we needed it and others came from the Tavistock Mug-House, so that our room was quite full. But we were not attacked and I came off very peaceably. The worst of it is I find some of the members of these societies are apt to be too flushed with their strength and attack persons whom they suspect before they are insulted themselves. However, I believe they do service to the Government in keeping its friends in countenance and dispiriting its enemies. There were several gentlemen among them but many as I guess only prentices and ordinary tradesmen. However, we are all upon a level there and those that can entertain the company with the most songs is the most taken notice of, his health being always drunk after he has sung a song. But between every song the public state health is drunk, which the President composes, who is elected new every night.

To bed between 11 and 12.

Saturday, July 21. Rose at 7. Read law. At 9 sister sent for me with a letter to let me know that Mrs. Marshall was to come to breakfast with her. I made all the haste I could and came there before 10 o'clock and presently after came Mrs. Marshall. She appears to me more agreeable every time I see her. I gave her a kiss which she took very temperately, but I was so much struck with the sight of her that I could not talk of indifferent matters or put myself into that merry, gay humour which she is so much pleased with. Mrs. Marshall behaved herself with a great deal of outward civility to me. Her agreeable smiling manner of talking to one or taking notice of what one says cannot but give one a little encouragement and flatter my hopes. I took notice that she every now and then threw her eyes upon me. I was pleased to see her take so much notice of me, but I cannot think it was with any design. Only I cannot but hope she took notice of my languishing look and deep concern that sat upon my brow.

Came home. I wanted my riding wig, but the maid having sent it to London instead of my father's for his journey, it put me into a great deal of concern and I never spoke so angrily to a servant before. I was vexed to find the passion had so much power over me. I begin to suspect my own temper more than ever and afraid lest it should betray me hereafter into some unlucky hit.

Sunday, July 22. Rose at 7. Expected Fowles to have brought his medicine to cure me of my pain in the arm this morning, but he did not come. The pain in my arm was very violent when I was in bed this morning.

At dinner I was taken with a fit of uneasiness and deep concern and all my thoughts were directed to Mrs. Marshall. I longed to see her and languished for her. It came into my head that I should pine away for her and grow very ill upon it. Perhaps this might move her pity. She might be willing to rescue me from death by her love. What ravishing joy and comfort would this bring! Methought this would at once revive and recover me.

Went to prayers in the family. Set myself with an intent to think and meditate upon what I have heard this day and make it of use to my practice, but it is very difficult for me to keep my mind long upon any such subject. I am too sleepy or I forget what I was thinking of. I wish I could be more watchful and solicitous about the concerns of eternity.

Monday, July 23. Rose at 7. Read law in Dyer's *Reports* till breakfast. Spent the rest of the morning chiefly in music.

In the afternoon Cousin Joseph Billio came to see me. Our conversation turned about the manner of delivery in the pulpit and about conversation.

I find my cousin takes a great deal of pains upon this head to make himself fit for conversation and gain the reputation of an ingenious man that way. I believe a person may be eternally at pains improving himself in this faculty, but I am apt to think it is impossible to bring it to any perfection where nature has not furnished a man for it. A good memory is necessary for it and a quickness and vivacity of spirit and temper. I cannot help very much envying those men that have this talent and can tell stories well and it gives me a great deal of uneasiness when I hear persons shine in this way. But as I said to Cousin Billio, we should consider that our silence is as necessary in general as their talkativeness. It is as needful there should be temperate hearers as those that tell stories and we should have a strange kind of a world if all were tellers of stories. Indeed it is a very necessary thing when persons that have this talent heap up stories one upon another. It must be a strange kind of a head that is heaped up and filled with a multitude of impertinent trifling matters of fact without making one useful reflection from them all, as I am persuaded is generally the case of those who are constant tellers of stories. And indeed I am apt to think a good memory does oftentimes more harm than good, it more commonly confounds and perplexes the judgement and mind than helps or enlightens it by the multitude of ideas that are heaped together. And therefore no people are looked upon as more trifling and thought of with more contempt than your lower rate of story-tellers, all they know is historical. A multitude of incoherent matters of fact are crowded together in their brain and no useful reflections or observations made from them.

Mr. Fowles came to me this afternoon and I have given him 22s. for his medicine which I am to have to-morrow at 8 o'clock. It strangely encouraged me to take this medicine and even raised my spirits with the thought of it to hear him talk of its virtues and the cures it had performed. He says it is good to purify and purge the blood and remove pains of all kinds.

Came to London chiefly with a design to see sister and talk about Mrs. Marshall. Did so. I was extremely heavy and melancholy about her. I could not tell how to conceive that she could ever love me when she was so much admired and she so much loved Dr. Avery. It made me so grave that I could not help crying. Sister gives me all the encouragement I can expect by telling me she thinks I have no reason to despair but I think indeed myself it is impossible for me to succeed.

Came home at 11 o'clock. There was a mob got about the Mug-House in Salisbury Court. There had been some fighting there before to defend it and they dispersed the mob, but then one of the Mug-House men was taken into custody by the constable and his friends were resolved to rescue him and broke the windows of the house where he was and made a great deal of noise and a vast mob was gathered about. However, they dispersed soon after. To bed at past 12.

Tuesday, July 24. Rose at 8. Read law all the morning. When I went out to dinner I saw a mob gathered together about the Mug-House. The Tory mob were resolved to be revenged for what the Whigs did to them last night and therefore to-day assembled against the Mug-House and broke all the lower part of the inside of it in pieces, quite destroying all the furniture and goods in it and beat and wounded some that defended it, but those few that were in the house defended themselves and killed one man of the mob and wounded several others. At length the soldiers came and dispersed the mob and the officers and some Whig gentlemen that were there were extremely enraged and searched several houses thereabouts that had encouraged the mob for those that had assisted in the pulling down the house, but they took but five or six of them. One of the sheriffs and several of his officers came to the place and were employed in searching the house and seeking about for any persons that had been concerned in it.

Went to Hamlin's. Talked with Cousin Joseph alone a great while. He tells me Samuel Powell is now at Epsom and that he intends in a short time to take chambers in the Temple and study the law but he fears he can never apply himself to study, that he will fall into the gay debauched company of the Temple that will prevent his making anything considerable in the law.

Wednesday, July 25. Rose at 6. Sent to Fowles for his medicine. Received it and took a glass of it at 7 o'clock.

Went to our club at night. Part of our conversation turned upon bawdy, a subject that is with difficulty parted with and what we all fell very naturally into. Mr. Witnoom was there and is grown thin upon matrimony. He works too hard and is too vigorous. It was some encouragement to me when it was said by Mr. Porter and others that in order to get healthy that a man should not do it often. I like Mr. Porter extremely for an apothecary. He seems to be a perfectly honest man and would in every respect prefer his patient's health before his own gain, and I believe he has a great deal of judgement. He advises me against too much reading and seems to be very much against my purging.

I found my pain in my arm much less to-day than it has been a great while before. It gave me encouragement to hope for good success from the medicine I have taken but I shall see more to-morrow morning.

Thursday, July 26. Rose at 7. Found my arm much worse than it was yesterday that I began to suspect the success of my medicine. However, I will go on to use it a little longer. It cannot be expected that I should feel the effects of it already.

Went to brother's in order to go to Hackney at past 11. As I went through Fleet Street there were two clergymen standing the pillory for a very notorious forgery. A vast mob was got about them but nothing was thrown at them. The people in general did not seem extremely displeased at their being put into the pillory.

Was very merry at dinner with sister and a woman at table who told me she perceived I was in love. I was not ill pleased to find it could be discovered. I had a great deal of bantering discourse about it and I think I never talked better in this manner. In the afternoon Mrs. Gorthan [1] and Aunt Billio came to see sister. I stayed with them all the while and was pretty merry with them, more than I usually am in company. I intended to go to Hackney to-night but Aunt Billio asked Mrs. Gorthan that I might go in her coach and she said I might but said she did not use to allow any man to go in her coach and spoke of it in such a manner that I thought she would not like it so well, so that I resolved not to go to Hackney because it would be looked upon as an affront if I went and not in her coach.

[1] A Mr. John Gawthern was present at the Hackney vestry meeting on 19 April 1715.

Friday, July 27. Went to Mr. Smith's at 11. It was very difficult for us to find matter of conversation, that we were forced to have recourse to music to entertain us. Dined with him and after dinner went to backgammon to help to pass away the time. Went to Hackney in the evening. Read some of Blount's [1] Characters. There is a great deal of wit and justness of thought discovered in them, that I am wonderfully pleased with them and resolve to examine them more narrowly.

Saturday, July 28. Rose at 7. Took my physic. I don't find this medicine does me any good or in the least removes my pain. Had some new clothes come home which I put on. Dined with sister. She mentioned Mr. Powell that he would go and see Mrs. Marshall if he should come to town. This cut me to the quick to think of the opportunity he has of seeing her and her regard to him while I am in a manner forbid visiting her. It puts me into a great deal of uneasiness to think of his coming to town as I hear he intends to do and take chambers in the Temple.

Sunday, July 29. At dinner a wasp stung me and gave me a great deal of pain that my hand swelled. However, I bore it with a great deal of patience on purpose to have it taken notice of by Aunt Billio who dined with us and I laughed it off pretty well.

Aunt Billio talked with me about brother William and told me that Ned Harding [2] was seen one Sunday morning with boots and spurs on and at night riding with brother. We are afraid he makes use of him to his pleasures and will introduce him also into a life of idleness and debauchery. I wish by what I said to her concerning him she does not think that I have a mind to undermine him, for God knows I should be extremely glad if he would take up and become sober and frugal.

After the sermon Mr. Bulkeley [3] and Henry came to our house

---

[1] John Earle's *Micro-cosmographie*, 1628, &c., published under his initials, had a preface by E. Blount. I can find no book of characters written by Blount, and it is quite likely that the diarist actually read Earle's characters.

[2] The Hardings seem to have been related through the Bickleys. John Bickley in 1702 made a legacy to ' my niece, Anne Harding, and her children '. In 1713 the Hackney vestry paid £1 16s. 6d. for the relief of Ned Harding and his wife.

[3] Thomas Bulkeley, a London silk merchant, married Esther, fourth daughter of Matthew Henry.

and stayed all night with us. Among other parts of our conversation we talked of Mr. Jeremiah Burroughs. He is pretty much offended with him and speaks against him and his preaching, but he seemed to speak it a little out of prejudice, I believe because he did not buy his wife's wedding clothes of him nor none of his congregation.

To bed at 11.

Monday, July 30. Went to coffee-house. Wrote down some thoughts about conversation and studying the art of it. Did not take my medicine to-day, because I have not yet found any benefit by it and I am afraid lest it should purge me too much. Put on a blue flannel that has a very deep dye upon it. This is what Aunt Marshall recommended from her own and others' experience to be extremely good in any pains. To bed at 11.

Tuesday, July 31. Rose at 8. Began a little book concerning conversation wherein I design to collect whatever matter of conversation occurs to me and read it over often.[1] Read some of *Nouveau Voyage to the Levant*,[2] wherein there are several things worth remarking, which I wrote down in my book for conversation.

Dined at brother's. Was in hopes I should have met with Mrs. Marshall there but did not. Cousin Joseph Billio came there, as I believe in expectation of seeing her also. Sister was preparing to go out and we were talking of Mrs. Marshall when she came in. I was not extremely merry, but pretty tolerable good company. Cousin Joseph did not show any great deal of readiness of conversation and was as much at a stand I think as ever I knew him among the ladies. I must confess this gratified my envious temper a little. When we had been together some time Mrs. Lee came in. I was concerned to think that she would perceive that sister had almost lost her former respect and familiarity with her upon her new acquaintance with Mrs. Marshall. At length we happened to see Dr. Avery go along the street and beckoned to him and he came to us and sat with us till

---

[1] Some surviving sheets of shorthand notes of books, anecdotes, &c., apparently belong to this little book.

[2] Jean Dumont: *Nouveau Voyage du Levant*, 1694, &c. ; translated into English, 1686.

past 8 o'clock. She has a very good opinion of him and likes his company extremely, but what was pretty extraordinary I perceived he is a kind of a confidant to her and he is advised with upon any proposal of matrimony to her. Mrs. Lee was pretty much rallied upon her affection to parson, whom she commended for good sense and good company, but said he should be the last man she should choose for a husband. It gave me a great deal of discouragement in my love for Mrs. Marshall that upon talking of the charges of keeping house and living genteelly she said that £400 or £500 a year would but just maintain a family handsomely in London. And I believe Mrs. Marshall is one that will never marry unless she can be maintained genteelly and handsomely.

Her behaviour to me is perfectly civil and sometimes I am apt to fancy she likes me, but it is a difficult matter to distinguish between her obliging manner of civility and real esteem and value and I dare not encourage myself in the belief that she has this for me.

Wednesday, August 1. Rose at past 7; took my physic. Read law till past 11 when read some *Spectators*. There are abundance of very just remarks upon human nature and the customs and manners of people. Read also in some *Travels to the Levant* and took notes of some things that would be proper for conversation.

Came to Hackney. It being the King's accession to the throne there was a bonfire before Mr. Alworthy's house [1] and I walked with Mrs. Hudson's to see it. I was very merry with them. There was young Mrs. Alworthy at the fire and young Mr. Heathcote talking together.[2] I stayed out with Mrs. Hudson's walking in the fields till near 11 o'clock. They don't say much themselves. I think the youngest of them is the most agreeable and I believe much the best humoured. She seems to have most of nature in her and nothing at all that is affected or proud in her, whereas the eldest I think has something of an air with her that is not so natural.

Thursday, August 2. Rose at 7. Read some of Quintilian in the morning. After dinner went to Aunt Bickley's. I was

[1] At Clapton. Mr. Alworthy was J.P. for Hackney.
[2] Cf. note on p. 191.

pretty merry with them and grow very free with them. Went to speak with Cousin Joseph and young **Mr.** Powell was there, come from Epsom. He says he would marry very soon if he was not so young, but does not know how he can possibly live till 25 virtuously without a wife. He has one of the best talents for gaining company and acquaintance of anyone I ever knew.

Came to London. Wrote letter to Aunt Stevenson at brother's, a pretty good one I do believe. Was uneasy about Mrs. Marshall. To bed at 12.

Friday, August 3. Rose at between 6 and 7. Went into the cold bath, stayed in 2½ minutes. Thought I found my arm something better upon it but it did not appear so in the day, for it was as bad as ever.

Went to Hackney with Cousin Watkins and his wife and my sister. I was pretty merry and talked with sister in a pretty familiar merry style all day, though now and then my spirits sunk and I found it difficult to keep them up to a pitch.

Saturday, August 4. Rose at 7. Began to take my quack medicine again in order to take it quite out to see whether it will do me any good or no. Went to Mr. Powell's to breakfast.

Our conversation with his father and mother was nothing extraordinary, but I find young Mr. Powell treats his parents in a very familiar way and talks to them as his equals and upon a level. After breakfast Mr. Powell and I walked in the garden alone and then we soon began to talk of my passion for and concern about Mrs. Marshall. He thought she was of a nature very easy to make an impression upon and it would be no difficult matter to gain her affections, that she was of a very extraordinary amorous disposition and intimated as if he thought her sufficient to tire a man at that sport. He then advised me to be resolute in conquering my passion and go to Tunbridge now in the height of company and divert myself out entirely from the hopes of seeing her. We talked about her father's circumstances and he says he is informed by one that deals with him that he is worth £4,000 or £5,000 only. His manner of living would make one think that he was worth more than that.

Dined at home. Sent for Cousin Billio. He came and we

played together upon the music. Went with him to Aunt Billio's. Had Mrs. Oileman's company. She took Cousin Billio and me into her apartment and showed us some pictures that her husband had sent over from Holland. She has a very handsome collection and some very good pieces. Aunt Bickley was there and talking of her son's having got a very good place in the East Indies by mere favour.

Came home. Read some of Fontenelle's pastorals. He affects a mighty simplicity in his dialogues and discourse of his shepherds and shepherdesses, and every now and then you meet with something very pretty and natural, as when a lover talking of his mistress being admired by all that see her says, ' et qu'on m'eut rendu fier en la trouvant si belle ? ' This is much more natural and simple than if he had made this reflection : ' how apt is a lover to be proud when his mistress is admired and praised by the rest of the world.'

Sunday, August 5. The reflection came into my head as I was dressing my wig concerning troubles and afflictions or grievances of any sort, that it would be a very good method to make one bear them with patience and less disturbance of mind to possess one's mind with the prospect of some desirable good thing or other that is like to follow from it. The prospect and good hopes of any good thing is a mighty help to mind under the pressure of any calamity.

After dinner Mrs. Marshall came into my thoughts and I was full of love. I could not get over it but went and laid me down upon the bed to soothe it. Fell into sleep and waked very easy as to that.

Monday, August 6. Rose at 7. Read some of Fontenelle's pastorals. I read them with a design to collect some little hints for conversation with the ladies.

Went to London in the coach with Mr. Ward. The conversation happened to turn upon the imprisoned lords in the Tower. Earl of Wintoun made his escape last Saturday night out of the Tower.

Went to father's to speak with him about a horse. He is a man of a very fickle unsteady temper and very unfit for action. He has no skill in horses and therefore is exceeding distrustful and difficult in buying one, though he has those along with him who do understand them.

Went home. Read some letters of the *Turkish Spy*.[1] They are admirably well writ, very diverting and in a good style.

After dinner went to brother's in hopes of meeting with Mrs. Marshall there, as I did. I was pretty good company to them at first and was brisk and gay, but Mr. Powell soon came and then the conversation was soon taken into his hands.

When he was gone, she and sister went upstairs for a while and I was left alone to meditate by myself and it came into my thoughts how I should address her if I was resolved to pursue my love. I thought I would talk to her in this manner— 'Madam, when a man is really in earnest and serious in his addresses, it is all in vain to make a great many protestations and use many words to declare his love. I come now to tell you that I think you the most agreeable woman living and have ever since my acquaintance with you been extremely touched with your beauty. I have had an opportunity of not only seeing your person which has all the charms that one could wish or imagine, but I have often with a great deal of delight and pleasure observed an extraordinary prudence and good humour and good sense in you, and whatever other qualifications are useful to make a man happy in your affection and possession. If it is possible for you to like me, don't make me miserable in a repulse. I don't now, Madam, expect you should answer me. Indeed, I dare not hear it now, I only beg you would allow me the liberty of waiting upon you. I am very sensible I cannot pretend to merit sufficient to expect it and indeed how few, very few are. But I must say this, that you saw me in the worst light at Bath. It was impossible for one so deeply in love as I was to act and speak and behave with that ease and indifference which gives a grace to one's actions and sets off one's whole person. Alas, Madam, was it not enough to strike the deepest melancholy and damp upon my spirits to see another continually before my eyes entertaining you with a seeming delight on your part, to observe you hearing his discourse with pleasure and playing and toying with him, while I was almost unobserved, disregarded? Surely,

[1] *The Turkish Spy*, a famous series of letters, translated from the Italian of Marana by William Bradshaw or Robert Midgeley, begun in 1687.

Madam, you won't wonder that I appeared so strange and seemingly unaccountable at that time.'

She stayed and supped at sister's and father supped with us. I believe he was not well pleased. However, he went home with me and Mrs. Marshall in the coach.

Brother Ryder told me that brother William had been with him and told him that he had begun to court a young lady lately come out of Lancashire.[1] The young lady has about £1,500 and I don't know but it may do very well for him. I believe it is the most likely thing if not the only thing that can settle him. If my father can but make matters agree with relation to his coming into the shop I shall be glad.

Tuesday, August 7. Read the law all the morning. I had great many thoughts about myself, what kind of a lawyer I should make and I could not but fear I should scarce make anything of it and almost wish I had been brought up to a trade, when I might have been upon a level with others, whereas now I am apt to think I shall make a very mean figure in the law.

Went to Hackney with Cousin Joseph. Overtook father going to Hackney also; he told us Mr. West was taken ill to-day. It put me in mind of some young men that I knew who died lately. I could not help looking upon myself as in the same kind of condition and could not think of the pleasures or enjoyments of life with any tolerable relish. It struck a damp upon them all and made me fancy myself near my exit too. If persons were seriously to observe the deaths of their friends or acquaintances it would have a mighty influence upon them, to win them from sensible enjoyments and make them grow very little fond of life. I think I have not been so cold and careless about what became of me this great while as I was when the thought of the death of my acquaintance came into my head. Methought death was now come home to my very doors and was nearer me than ever when those whom I used to see and converse with are taken off.[2] I began to think to what purpose should I take pains, lay out my care and concern for a future subsistence here, and be providing

---

[1] Mrs. Walker of Manchester.
[2] This morbid concern with death was soon to become a feature of the poetry of the Graveyard School.

for my profit or pleasure, when death methought just looked me in the face and I was soon going to leave the world.

Wednesday, August 8. At past 7 went to our club. Nothing extraordinary. Mr. Porter told me he wondered I did not study physic for my diversion, it is a very pleasant and delightful study and proper to begin it with anatomy. That I might go and hear lectures upon bodies every month in the winter at Surgeons' Hall in Wood Street twice a day about 1 and 5 in the afternoon; that they are worth hearing and well performed by some of the best physicians. I intend to make use of them at least as a method of spending my vacant time in the city.

Came home at 11. Had a mind to fill a whore's commodity and went about the streets in order to it, but could not conveniently do it without hazarding my reputation by exposing myself to the danger of being known. To bed at past 12.

Thursday, August 9. Came to father. Brother William seems mightily concerned about this project of his to be married, not that he is in love but he seems to be sensible now of his former past errors and would make use of this method to retrieve himself. I wish it may succeed.

Friday, August 10. I have been all this afternoon with father in Smithfield in order to buy a horse but could not get one. He is extremely afraid of venturing upon any horse and distrusts his own judgement and suspects everyone he sees, whether he has reason or no.

Went to brother's. Talked with sister about Mrs. Marshall. Sister told me she told her she could come and see her when she was at the Hay. It gave me a mighty joy to have a prospect of going with her there. I have directed sister to promote that as much as possible but I doubt whether she will let me wait upon her such a journey. Brother William is very uneasy about his mistress. He has told my father of it, who promised to inquire about her fortune, but I don't know my father has done it yet. He is strangely dilatory.

Saturday, August 11. After dinner went to brother's in hopes of seeing Mrs. Marshall. Did so. Stayed with her till past 7. They talked of going to Hampstead Wells next Monday and

I asked her whether I should not wait upon them. She did not say I might but said her brother would be willing to go out, she believed. I have too much reason to fear she would be glad to be rid of my company.

Sunday, August 12. Rose at 7. My father this morning took notice of some very little trifling things. I have sometimes wished I had been brought up in my father's business when I look upon the difficulties that meet me in the way of a lawyer, but then it has presently come to my mind that I could not tell how to have led a life constantly under my father's eyes. It would have tired me of life to have had him always teasing me with faults in trifles. It has been much happier for me to be absent. I have enjoyed all the pleasure and love and affection of a kind and loving father without any of the uneasiness that arise from his peculiar temper. If ever I shall have children I will endeavour to guide them with a much more even and steady hand, never to regard very little faults or, if they are such as may be of ill consequence, to do it in such a manner as not to be disagreeable to them. It wearies out a child of spirit to be always blamed.

Reading Tillotson's sermon about regeneration, it put me in mind of the advantage of a good and sober education. I don't know but the religion of people and their sobriety is much more owing to that than anything of their own reason. I that have had so many opportunities of being vicious both abroad and at home should, I verily believe, have fallen a sacrifice to them if it had not been from my sober education and modest bashful temper.

Heard Mr. Mayo both morning and afternoon. Mr. Walker, the young lady's brother whom my brother William has a mind to for a wife, dined with us. Mr. Walker is a man of good sense and talks well. Nothing at all in relation to brother William's love was mentioned by any nor did my father talk of it to him.

At night father talked of it with mother. He would be glad if it would do, but is in some concern how to give my brother a portion to set him up, he not having money enough at command, that he must either sell some of his houses or give him some of them.

Monday, August 13. Came to brother's. Talked with sister about going to Hampstead with her and Mrs. Marshall this afternoon, but I plainly see that she has no mind I should be in her company. It made me extremely melancholy and sorrowful to find myself so little regarded by her. She told me that she had another gentleman courted her that keeps his chariot and two footmen, but she believes she does not like him. I wish I could be easy under her disdain and neglect. I have thought several times of going to Tunbridge if possible to wear it off, but I don't know how to exclude myself at once from the hopes of seeing her so long. Alas, what an easy courtship has my brother William ! He is entertained by his mistress with all the civility and outward show of respect and esteem in the world. And yet, I don't know how, methinks when I think of his case I would not be without some of the difficulties neither. One is apt to fancy what is easily gained is not worth much, and besides there is a kind of secret pleasure in this longing and desire. It gives a sort of an extraordinary air to one's love to have it meet with difficulty.

Came home. Read some of the *Travels to the Levant.* After dinner read some of the same, then went to father's and to Mr. Freke's, but he was not at home. Did not well know what to do. The thought of going to study at that time of day did not enter into my mind with a relish. However, went home, read Mr. Locke's fourth *Letter of Toleration* and his memoir of the life of my Lord Shaftesbury.

Stayed in the coffee-house till past 8, then walked for near an hour under the Piazzas of the Temple and reflected upon myself concerning my love, how vainly and foolishly I acted in it. Of how much greater moment is it to make God my friend, live up to His rules and precepts. I reflected upon the nature of happiness. How wrongly do we judge of people's happiness by their external appearance. I was apt to envy the condition of every poor creature that passed by me whom I thought happier than I, though perhaps they were thinking how happy they should be if they could make such a gay appearance or put on such clothes as I. I thought what a miserable life it would be to pass away a whole eternity in such restless desires and longings and despair as I was in. Methought death was a little pleasant to me and gave me some consolation to think that this time would not last always. And yet, I don't know how, even under this view I could not help fearing lest I should carry the same temper and frame of mind along with me.

Came home. Played upon my flute: that composed me a little.

Tuesday, August 14. Rose before 6. Went to the cold bath and after that went to the Islington Spa[1] where drank a quart of the waters. I had a mind to drink them because I thought it might purge my blood and be a means of curing my strong breath. Stayed there till half-hour past 7.

Came home. Read law all the morning. After dinner read some of Mr. Locke's letters to Molyneux[2] and his to him. There is a mighty friendly way of writing shown in them and a great many things worth observing, several of which I wrote down in my book of conversation. He has a happy copiousness of style that expresses his thoughts clearly and sets them in a very strong and full light.

Went to brother's at 6. Saw there Mrs. Brown, the parson's wife. Did not know her at first. We fell into talk about matrimony and we had some pleasant conversation upon that head. I was pretty merry till she went and then my thoughts had free liberty to think of Mrs. Marshall. It was some little relief to me to hear sister say, when I was talking how willingly I could live in a solitary wild desert with her, that Mrs. Marshall herself had rather live with one person in a wood all alone than in the best company in the world beside. Sister told me that her sister Mrs. Deison was a woman extremely nice and delicate in all her clothes and furniture, that everything was of the finest sort and her manner of living was extremely chargeable. This made me think it would be impossible for me ever to have Mrs. Marshall who would expect to live much greater than I could possibly afford.

Prince Eugene has beat the Turks, routed their whole army, killed and taken near 100,000 men, that they are not likely to do

[1] Islington Spa, or New Tunbridge Wells, was opposite the New River head in Clerkenwell. More of a spa and less of a pleasure resort than its neighbour, Sadler's Wells, it was at this time a little out of fashion.

[2] Locke's letters to his friend and disciple, William Molyneux (1656-98), were included in *Some Familiar Letters between Mr. Locke and several of his Friends*, 1708.

any more against the Emperor and the war with the Venetians also is in a fair way of being ended.¹ This Turkish war is looked upon very much as a contrivance of France begun by the late King and carried on by the Regent in order to embroil the rest of Europe, that they might be at leisure to execute their own designs on England and the Emperor and in favour of the King of Sweden. This will likely make a considerable alteration in the affairs of Europe and the Pretender is like to lose all hopes by it; though it looks in England as if his friends were preparing for another attempt in his favour.

Wednesday, August 15. Rose at half an hour after 5. Went to cold bath. From thence to Islington Wells where I drank the waters. I found out new wells to-day where there are multitudes of people come every morning to drink the waters. They have a coffee-house there where the company meet altogether to hear the news read and some notable politician or other read one of the papers in a sad tone.

Came to sister's at between 8 and 9 in great expectation of seeing Mrs. Marshall, but was disappointed. I cannot tell how to express my sentiments and what I feel, so that I express it more by dismal melancholy looks and broken sighs and accents than in any continued discourse. What troubled me most was that I thought Mrs. Marshall did not come hither because she did not care to meet me.

I received a letter from Mr. Powell with the verses made at Bath upon the pump woman. I wanted to see her that I might give them her with my own hands. I don't find I am so very uneasy and concerned anywhere as when at brother's with sister. It revives it in me to see her who sees her so often and I cannot help almost bursting out into tears upon it.

Father has been with Mr. Walker, my brother William's mistress's brother, and he says her father left her £1,000. Brother William is very hot upon it and would fain have it done out of hand.

---

¹ Prince Eugene of Savoy was commanding the forces of the Emperor Charles VI, who early in 1716 made an alliance with Venice against Turkey. On 5 August he vanquished a Turkish army more than twice the size of his own at Peterwardein. His victories against the infidel were consummated in the battle of Belgrade in the following year.

Thursday, August 16. Rose at before 6. Went to drink the waters at Islington. Met Mr. Suly there. He inquired of me about Paris and the places there, and I could give him but very little account of matters there. My memory I find fails me very much. I should indeed get some book of travels to France in order to refresh my memory. I asked him to breakfast with me, which he did. He at last sung me several songs which he did admirably well and exactly in the Italian manner. He stayed with me till past 12, whereas I was to have been at sister's at 11 in order to go to Hackney and meet Mrs. Marshall at brother's.

Went there at between 12 and 1 and Mrs. Marshall and Dr. Avery were there. I showed her and gave her a copy of the verses Mr. Powell sent me made upon the pump woman at the Bath. She also desired to see Mr. Powell's letter and seemed mighty curious about it, but it being about my love to her I could not let her see it. It grieved me much that I could not oblige her by granting what she desired and I was afraid she took it ill.

Friday, August 17. Mrs. Hudson's and their brother breakfasted with us. Our breakfast was not managed well at all, that I was perfectly ashamed.

Went to North's Coffee-House. There was father. I heard there that the Pretender had sent over another declaration within eight or ten days, wherein he promises to settle the Church lands upon the Protestant clergy and give the rebellious Whigs' estates towards the repairing the damages his faithful subjects suffered by their late efforts in his favour. I heard also that some of the doctors of the Sorbonne at Paris have sent over to the Archbishop of Canterbury to advise with about the Reformation. It is pretty certain that matters run pretty high in favour of a breach with Rome.

Saturday, August 18. Rose between 5 and 6. Went to the cold bath. From thence to drink the waters at Islington. Met with Mr. Dry, with whom I walked and talked part of the time. His brother also, whom I knew before by sight but did not know who he was, spoke to me and I gained a new acquaintance of him and also with a doctor of physic, who told us that these waters were very good for leprosy and that several persons were there drinking it upon that account and were almost cured. He says they are better than Hampstead waters and extremely good for obstructions and also the scurvy. He told us also the original of these waters, that they were first found out in the Popish times and the monks of the minsters thereabouts had these waters conveyed to their house through pipes, which they made use of in curing diseases as the scurvy, but took it only as holy water sanctified by their priests, which gained them a great reputation till Queen Elizabeth, finding it made an ill use of, ordered the wells to be stopped up and the pipes broke. But about thirty years ago the father of the present possessor of them, Jones, was going to build upon that spot of ground when he found this well covered over.[1] He then sent to the physicians who tried the water and gave it their approbation as a very good chalybeate and they have continued ever since in good reputation. They were formerly, about twenty years ago, much more in vogue than now. This doctor says he has seen 200 coaches there.[2] It was frequented as Tunbridge and people went there for pleasure as well as their health.

After dinner went with sister to Aunt Billio's. Mother went part of the way with us but she went in so scandalous a gown that I could not help taking notice of it to her and in such a manner as made her a little angry and she would not go. Indeed I do think I did not do well in talking so much as I did about it to her in something of a harsh manner. But my mother is very much to blame in wearing clothes that make her friends blush for her and ashamed of being seen in her company.

When I came home and happened to see Pufendorf's *History*[3] in my closet it came into my head to make myself master of his account of England as a kind of an introduction into the study of our history. Began to read it.

The Prince and Princess dine every day in public at Hampton Court and all sorts of people have free admission to see them

[1] The newly-discovered wells are referred to in a poetical puff, *Islington Wells*, published in 1684. In 1685 they belonged to John Langley.

[2] The wells enjoyed one other period of fashion following on the visit of George II's daughters, Amelia and Caroline, in 1733. The site was built upon early in the nineteenth century.

[3] Samuel von Pufendorf (1632–94) wrote several modern historical works (in Latin) while historiographer-royal at Stockholm.

even of the lowest sort and rank in their common habits and the Prince and Princess are so affable and courteous to them that it gains upon the people's minds extremely and it is likely will be a means of making the King's cause grow popular.

Sunday, August 19. Heard Mr. Smith at our meeting. He has a good delivery though it is not yet perfectly agreeable. He lays too much stress upon the words that require the emphasis. After sermon in the afternoon he came to our house and drank a dish of tea with Mr. Denn and Neve and Cousin Joseph Billio. Mr. Smith is very well liked.

Monday, August 20. Mr. Kingsford came to our house and father asked him to breakfast. He said that money did everything now at Court, that the Hanoverians abused the King, particularly Madame Kielmansegg [1] took money for places and nothing was done without it. He said also that there was a great falling out between Mr. Walpole and the Duke of Marlborough. He said also this Parliament will be dissolved. It grieved me to think that the Whigs should fall out among themselves, but indeed I did not much believe Mr. Kingsford. I know he loves to appear a man acquainted with the affairs of the court and public matters, and I am apt to think would not scruple to make or at least improve a story to exalt his character in that way.

Went to Mr. Denn's to breakfast. After breakfast Mr. Burroughs and I played some music set for two viols. There seems to be a very good loving pleasant family at Mr. Denn's that is very happy within itself.

Mr. Smith came home and dined with me. Was pretty merry with sister. After dinner talking about love he told my sister that I was always in rapture when I talked of Mrs. Marshall. Upon this sister took occasion afterwards to be angry with me for exposing Mrs. Marshall by talking of her in company. Joseph Billio came and she fell upon him upon the same head and though we both endeavoured to pacify her it was all in vain. The more we talked the more hot she grew

[1] Charlotte Sophia von Kielmansegg, the chief mistress of George I; created Countess of Darlington in 1722. She 'drove a lucrative trade in vending small court favours'.

and vowed and swore she would never let either of us see Mrs. Marshall no more if she could help it. She is of one of the worst tempers that is upon that account. She is enough to tire and tease a husband to death. Whatever she once sets upon she harps upon so long till she has fatigued you out and worked herself almost to a pitch of madness and fury. She runs over a multitude of circumstances which inflames her the more. I went to bed in an ill humour enough which my sister put me into.

Tuesday, August 21. Rose at past 6. Spent all the morning with sister playing and romping with her. She delights in it as the most delightful entertainment in the world. I am only sometimes concerned that the servants and people in the house should see us so free together and take notice of it.

In the afternoon went to see Mr. Blundell and his wife. Mentioning the persecution of the Protestants in France, Mr. Blundell told us that some time ago when several of the Protestants came over to England he dined with them one day, and they told him that the greatest part of those that suffered for religion among them were students of the law. One told him he had been in the galleys for 30 years confined to the oars and living upon bread and water.

Went to John's. Met Mr. Porter there and others. He is very much puzzled about Mr. Berkeley's book of passive obedience. Mr. Porter mentioned it to me that he thought it would not be amiss if I wrote a letter to the occasional paper about Mr. Berkeley's principles in order to draw him out to answer his objection. But I refused to do it myself and told him he was the fittest person.

Wednesday, August 22. Read some *Spectators* and also the *Rape of the Lock*, which is a very witty poem, I think one of the best we have had come out these many years.[1]

Went with brother to buy a coach for Aunt Lomax which he did for £40 10s. It is a new coach and the maker, one Howard, seems to be a mighty honest, civil man. There was to be a crest embroidered upon the hammercloth, which we came to my landlady to have done.

[1] It was first published in 1712.

Thursday, August 23. Rose before 6. Went to drink the waters. My arm pained me extremely. It went off almost all of a sudden and I thought it was as great pleasure as I have felt a great while. It made me almost forget the pain I had before. It is almost worth while to be in pain a little while to feel the pleasure of going out of it.

All my Uncle Marshall's family came to our house in the afternoon and I with my uncle and cousin and his son went to Mr. Rollinson's upon my uncle's proposal. Mr. Rollinson entertained us very nobly with five sorts of wine and the fruit of his garden. My uncle and cousin were got into their element and wonderfully pleased with such entertainment and drank wine very plentifully. No extraordinary conversation. The goodness of the wine made amends for any deficiency of that nature. He has a very large garden, mighty well furnished with fruit of all sorts and very pleasant. He seems to have a good genius for improving ground and making it pleasant and delights in it very much and is glad to entertain his friends. When Cousin Marshall saw his wife, a very humble disagreeable woman, he said he did not now wonder he was so well pleased with the enjoyment of his friends.

Came home. The wine I drank had a little disturbed my head but not so much as to be very visible. My brother William brought his mistress in her way to London to our house. She seems to be of good sense but I think not a genteel person at all. She gave us a song, but does not perform extraordinarily that way. Went to bed early, not being fit for study.

Friday, August 24. Met Cousin Joseph Billio at brother's. Talked with him about Mrs. Marshall. He is very much touched with her, I believe, and comes to brother's on purpose in expectation of meeting her. Asked sister about Mrs. Marshall. She is to be with her to-morrow but I am in great concern whether to go to meet her or no, for I believe she takes notice that I am there always when she is and sister does not like it.

Saturday, August 25. Rose at before 6. Went to drink the waters at Islington. Met the clergyman [1] again there with

[1] Dr. Tilly.

whom I walked and talked a good while. Happening to talk about Charles II's reign and the popish concerns in it, I said I thought he was murdered by them, but he said believed not, for he was taken with an apoplexy not long before he died and when these fits come a man seldom holds out long. He said that when he was upon his deathbed a popish priest was sent to him who gave him the sacrament and the viaticum and he believed he died a papist rather because no other parsons were allowed to come to him than because he was persuaded of the truth of that religion, for he had been a perfect atheist and a very profligate man, and upon the deathbed was willing to take up with any religion that promised the fairest for a future happiness to him and made the best offers to him. He told me also about the Popish Plot against Charles II, that a friend of his first discovered it to the King by himself in private in his closet, and when he had gone through the several particulars of it, how it was to be managed and by whom and came to tell him the King of France was engaged in it, the King said he could not believe that, for he been such a friend to him that he could not believe he would engage in any conspiracy to take away his life. Oates, who was the chief man in the discovery of it, was a man of but an ill life though he really discovered a great many things that were matters of fact and in general revealed the whole plot; yet he was pushed on to bear some false witness which gave a discredit to his testimony in general and was, he believed, done on purpose to lay a blemish upon him.

It came into my head that sister and Mrs. Marshall were gone to have my sister's picture mended and I went to Mr. Van Blope's and found them there. Mrs. Marshall did not seem very well pleased with my coming and though I began to talk with them in a very merry noisy strain, yet it could not please them.

Came to Hackney. Received a letter from Mr. Leeds. I am vexed with myself that I find a disgust and a kind of uneasiness within myself upon finding him to write well, that I seem to keep up the correspondence with him rather with a design to feed my own vanity by an advantageous comparison than with any hopes or design of getting any advantage by it.

Sunday, August 26. Rose at between 5 and 6. Went on horseback to the Wells.

In the way I thought of the question which we talked of at Mr. Blundell's about the condition of mankind without a saviour, whether nature would not dictate that God would be merciful to and forgive repenting sinners, and this appeared to me very clear from the nature of God and His attributes, which we are to judge of by the perfections that we observe among men.[1] Whatever would be unbecoming a good man, whatever a good man would not do, we must to be sure take care not to attribute to God. If therefore it is derogatory to the character of a good man to be obstinate upon revenge and to be implacable, inexorable and not to forgive those that have injured him upon their confessing and being sorry for it, certainly it must be contrary to the nature of God, in whom all perfections are, to be so to the returning sinner. But then I thought of the objection which Mr. Blundell made, how shall the justice of God then be satisfied? He is just and perfectly so, but if He forgives sin without any satisfaction made to that, any recompense, you destroy His justice. But the weakness of this objection is plain, if we do but consider the nature of God's attributes. The reason of our attributing justice, mercy, wisdom, &c., to God as so many distinct perfections is from our weakness and the narrowness of our understandings that cannot conceive of God as He is in Himself but by the deduction of particulars. God is a simple, uncompounded, undivided being and these attributes of His cannot be so many distinct qualities or beings (as I am apt to think some conceive). They are all in Him conjoined, united and harmonizing. Whereas, according to our notions and ideas of justice and mercy, they will oppose one another if they are extended to those limits and bounds of each which our ideas have fixed to them. So that God could not be perfectly just if He was merciful. We do therefore an injury to God when, because we have made justice a perfection but at the same time our narrow minds don't take in the adequate ideas of it, we judge that unless that justice be fully answered according to our inadequate ideas He is not

[1] The diary contains several lengthy 'sermons'; the following passage is quoted in full to represent Ryder's reasoning and his aptitude for the Church, for which he had originally been intended, according to Hughes.

perfect. Whereas I think we ought to conceive of God's moral as that which makes Him do whatever upon the whole appears to be the fittest and best to be done without any regard whether or no this comes up to that strict notion of justice which we have fixed in our minds. It is a common maxim *summum jus summa injuria* and I think it may be very justly applied in the present case. The view of justice that we have fixed in our ideas is not such a one as admits of no exceptions, as will hold in every case and be always fittest to be done. Our minds are too narrow and limited to be able to settle such a notion of justice. Shall we then say anything is contrary to God's justice (if by justice we mean the real perfection in Him) which, though it does not exactly correspond to the ideas we have fixed to the word 'justice', yet is best and fittest to be done upon the whole? Now that mercy is a perfection, that it is good and becoming and proper to pardon injuries upon a sincere repentance of the offender, the common sense of mankind teaches, that always commends and praises this disposition in men, that blames those who will accept of no submission but retain their malice and anger and hatred notwithstanding all the marks of repentance in those that submit. Certainly then we don't conceive aright of God to suppose that He would be this inexorable malicious being. If it be said that the offence against God is vastly, immeasurably greater than any injury can be to man, I think it is a sufficient answer that the greatness of the offence is not to be considered in this case at all, or, if it is, it is looked upon among men as more commendable to forgive a great injury than a small one—and that any one can be too great to be forgiving upon repentance I cannot imagine. Repentance is the chief thing to be considered, that is, not only the sorrow for it but the return to duty and obedience, the return to allegiance and submission to His laws. And where that is, let the original offence be great or small, it is then fit, it is becoming and laudable to forgive. And as to those who say God could not consistently with His justice have forgiven mankind upon repentance without the sacrifice of our Saviour, let me ask them how was it consistent with His justice to provide a saviour for them, whence came that original motion of compassion towards mankind, what was it that was the cause of that? For that in effect is but the very same mercy that I am pleading for.

From hence it is plain that in the nature of things it is fit and becoming, worthy of God and agreeable to His nature to pardon sinners upon repentance. This original design of God to provide a saviour for men upon repentance shows that it was fit they should be pardoned upon repentance, for that was all that could be done by them to make amends and reparation, and if it was not fit, how came God to do it? But, say you, yet it shows that it was fit they should be pardoned upon the satisfaction made to His justice by the sacrifice of Christ, but not without it. I answer, since men could do no more themselves than repent and amend their lives and God thought fit to pardon them, it showed it was fit they should be pardoned. What way God would take to do this, with what form and ceremony, in what pomp and solemnity to strike awe and give a dread of sin, was entirely in God's own breast, and though He made use of this way by sending Christ into the world to die, &c., this is no proof that it would have been inconsistent with His justice to have done it any other way or to have made use of no outward method at all but forgiveness upon repentance, especially since it is the very same thing with respect to the sin and sinner, either to promise a pardon upon repentance only or upon that and any other condition which God Himself will take care to perform.

Came home at 8. Father took notice of me that I looked much better, of a more healthy complexion and not yellow as I used to do of late. I can attribute to nothing but the mineral waters which I have been drinking for almost a fortnight.

After sermon in the afternoon walked with Cousin Billio in the fields. Came home and found Mr. Mayo with Mr. Neve at our house and they were just got a-talking about the choosing Mr. Smith to our meeting here for every other Sunday, Mr. Mayo being to preach the rest. My father mentioned the concern he was under upon the account of Cousin Billio who might expect such a choice sooner than another, but Mr. Mayo talked very well upon that, that it was his misfortune not to be so acceptable in preaching. All the congregation had a great esteem of him but thought he would not keep up or increase the congregation and therefore were not willing to choose him. So that my father determined not to be present at their choice but to let them do as they would, thinking that better than to mention him in vain. Mr. Mayo has a great mind I find to have Mr. Smith chosen and he is then to supply his place at Kingston in his absence. Mr. Smith, I believe, is very well liked here and I believe will be chosen for every other Sunday.

Monday, August 27. Rose at between 5 and 6. Went to drink the waters on horseback to Islington. Conversed with Dr. Tilly, the parson I got acquainted with there.

Found in the morning all of a sudden a sort of swooning and giddiness in my head come upon me. It did not continue above quarter of a minute but it surprised me very much. I attributed it to the fumes of the waters of which I drank five pints and ate soon after this.

Came to brother's. Sister was all alone. At length Cousin Joseph Billio came, but he came in expectation of seeing Mrs. Marshall and he seemed extremely concerned that he did not find her there. It gives me a great deal of uneasiness to find him so mightily taken with her and so fond of every opportunity of seeing her. I am very much afraid lest she should like his conversation, as I am apt to think she does.

Tuesday, August 28. Rose between 5 and 6. Went to drink the waters. Got into conversation with Dr. Lee.[1] He asked me what I drank the waters for. He told me they were as good at least as Tunbridge waters and said three pints in the morning was enough for me.

Went away at 7 to sister's to take leave of her. They did not go till almost 10. She was very uneasy and peevish because the coach did not come so soon as she expected and was a little cross with me.

When they were gone I went to Paul's to view the City from the top of it. It was a fine sight, but I had a great curiosity to see the inside of the scaffolding of the Dome upon which Mr. Thornhill[2] is painting and the man that keeps the keys

---

[1] Possibly Francis Lee, M.A. (1661-1719). In 1691 he was deprived of a fellowship at Oxford for being a nonjuror, and took to medicine. He became a licentiate of the College of Physicians in 1708.

[2] James Thornhill (1675-1734), knighted 1720, sergeant-painter to George I. Hogarth, who married his daughter, was his pupil for a time. The monochrome decorations at St. Paul's (done against Wren's wish) had frequently to be restored, but some of Thornhill's sketches are in the British Museum.

of the whispering gallery told me that nobody ever went up there. Mr. Thornhill would not admit of it. However, I desired him to show me the door into it, which he did, and told me if I would ring the bell and ask for Mr. Thornhill they would admit me up and I must then make my excuse to Mr. Thornhill. This shocked me a little at first. However, I thought it could be no such great crime to beg the favour of seeing his painting and design. Accordingly I ventured and was admitted up by his servant. When I came I made my bow to Mr. Thornhill and told him I had a great curiosity to see so extraordinary a piece of painting as that of the Dome of St. Paul's, and begged the favour of being allowed the liberty to view what was done of it. He told me this was a liberty which he did not usually allow to anybody, because if it was people would come in so great crowds that they would interrupt him in his study and painting. However, since I was come, I might go about it and view any part of it. I thanked him for the liberty and began to look about me, and then told him we should now be able to vie at least with Paris for history painting which we have been so deficient in before. He told me he had been about this a year already and expected to finish it in a year more. All the architecture is already done, only the gilding and enriching the great part of it remains yet to be done, but then the history part is not begun yet. There are three models hung up with different designs, one of which is chosen, and all the models are divided into eight columns or pieces of architecture, in each of which some one story of St. Paul is described. There had been indeed a design once proposed to have the whole Dome all in one without the divisions into several stories, but one story of St. Paul would not have been enough and then to have put more together within one arch would have only confounded it. The models differ partly in the different stories that are described in each and partly in the different postures and manners of describing the same story. There is the story of St. Paul's escape out of the city by being let down in a basket described in two of the models, but in that which is chosen that story is not put in and I think with judgement because the being let down in a basket I think is but a trifling story. In the model chosen there is the story of the viper at Malta, his preaching at Athens, his making a speech to the people from the stairs of the Castle when they had conspired to murder him, his converting the jailor, his curing the lame man and the people's going to sacrifice to him upon it, the story of Elymas, the sorcerer's being struck blind by Sergius Paulus, the story of the people at Ephesus bringing their books of curious arts and burning upon Paul's preaching and doing miracles there. The models have a pretty good spirit in them, but there does not seem to me to be that air of grandeur and majesty in describing the postures and faces which appears in the most masterly pictures. Paul is everywhere drawn exceeding grave and old.

Mr. Thornhill came to me again and talked with me about painting and told me he supposed I was a virtuoso. I told him I took a pleasure in seeing fine painting. He asked me if I did not paint myself. I told him no. He took me, I believe, for one that understood it pretty well, but I was afraid of talking to him lest I should discover my ignorance. He at length seemed mighty complaisant and glad that anybody that was a judge would come to take notice of his performance. He said there were but few that took a pleasure in viewing these things, and would give themselves the trouble to come and see him, and therefore he was not much troubled upon that account with many people. I went up to the top of the scaffolds where the very top of the Dome is painted chiefly with roses gilded within squares. It will be exceeding rich. There are two or three more persons who are under-workmen that are working at these figures but Mr. Thornhill himself comes and overlooks them and directs them. When I came away I gave his man a shilling that opened the door for me.

Went with Cousin Joseph to the tavern where we talked about Mrs. Marshall and marriage. I could not help telling my Cousin Billio of my great exploit in venturing to address Mr. Thornhill and going through with the difficulty of seeing his painting. I cannot but fancy cousin would take notice of the little vanity in me to tell that and the pride I took in doing it.

Wednesday, August 29. Found Mr. Henry and his mother at our house. He is going to Edinburgh next Monday. Father is going to build a house in the room of that summer-house that belonged to the school-house. He does it in expectation of a great profit, having a great deal of lead of the summerhouse and other things, that the rest won't cost him £200.[1]

Thursday, August 30. Rose at 6. Went to Islington to drink the waters. My arm pained me very much by that time I got there. I find that the pain increases very much by walking, though I walk never so slow. This seems to favour what my Cousin Marshall thinks, that it is a nervous case.

Met with Dr. Tilly there again. Talking about Ireland he told me that almost all the churches in the country there were destroyed in the rebellion of '41 and a great many are not yet rebuilt or repaired. He told me that there are no vipers nor snakes nor moles there, but he has seen a great many spiders. He says a friend of his brought over some frogs on purpose to try whether they could live in the air of Ireland and he says they do live and increase very much, that he don't doubt but in time the whole island will be peopled with them. He told me also that the coal which they burn there never flames nor smokes but burns exceeding clear and strong like a red-hot iron. Blowing it will put it out and so will stirring it. The coal is large and very hard and requires an hour at least to light it. There was a Welsh gentleman by that said they had the same kind of coal in Wales and a great deal of it was brought to town, which was bought up chiefly by those that dry malt, because it did not give it any ill smell or taste as our coal is apt to do.

Went to brother's. Met Cousin Joseph Billio. We went to the coffee-house together. He desired to know of me what he should write to Dr. Tilson in Chester, about the will of Mr. Walker concerning what he left to his children upon the account of my brother William's courting one of his daughters, my mother having desired him to write about it. I referred him to my father. We talked about matrimony and agreed in this that the sorrows and cares and burdens to which it exposes a man don't seem to be sufficiently balanced by the joys and pleasures one can expect from it. I wish I could reason myself into an easy state of mind under the thoughts of never being married, but I find a strong inclination towards it, not from

[1] 'In October [1716] Mr. Richard Ryder began to erect a dwelling-house near Church Field in the place where the summer-house stood in the garden adjoining' [Newcome].

any principle of lust or desire to enjoy a woman in bed but from a natural tendency, a prepossession in favour of the married state. It is charming and moving, it ravishes me to think of a pretty creature concerned in me, being my most intimate friend, constant companion and always ready to soothe me, take care of me and caress me. Cousin Billio said for a young man not in business that had 2 or £3,000 to marry a woman of perhaps 1 or £2,000 it would keep him low all his life. This I must confess gave a great turn to my thoughts with respect to Mrs. Marshall. Why should I think of having her when it would expose us both to want?

Went to Hamlin's Coffee-House to inquire about the Italian master for Mr. Porter as I promised him. I found out there that his name is Castilio, but not where he lived.

The Prince and Princess admit everybody of any fashion, the meanest persons whatsoever, to come and see them at dinner. One day they interested themselves with seeing the country folks come in their straw hats and because one came without her straw hat the Princess sent her back again to fetch it. Upon this several of the gentry came in with straw hats very fine with footmen attending. They gain very much upon the people by that means.

Friday, August 31. Mrs. Ironmonger's came to see my mother. We were pretty merry upon the subject of matrimony. Cousin Billio's wife was there and she told me I talk just like an old bachelor, and men that talked in that manner were never likely to marry. It really concerned me to have this believed of me.

Father came to Hackney. He talked with me about Mrs. Walker. He said he thought to write to her mother about it and tell her that he understands by her son that her daughter has a £1,000 fortune, and whatever she shall think to add to it he will equal in my brother's fortune. But I am at a loss to know how such affairs are to be managed. If she should add a £1,000 more to her fortune when she dies I can scarce believe my father can give my brother William so much without injuring me and my brother Ryder.

Saturday, September 1. Rose between 5 and 6. John rubbed my arm with a flesh brush in bed, but did not find it did my arm any good. Went to the Wells. My arm was not so bad in writing as it used to be in walking. Had the company of Dr. Lee at the Wells and Dr. Tilly.

At supper father and mother had some little dispute, as they generally have every time they meet at table. I have been thinking which is in fault, my father or mother, but indeed they are both very much in fault, my mother for saying everything in a cross way and taking everything ill, and my father for continuing the matter that gave offence and pushing it on. When he sees my mother peevish and fretful, instead of endeavouring to put an end to it he loves to say the thing over again that made her uneasy.

Sunday, September 2. Mr. Smith preached at our meeting both morning and afternoon.

I thought within myself what should be the reason of the little success that preaching meets with and the few persons that are bettered by it, and I can give no other account of it but this, that people don't, I believe, generally come to church with a design to grow better, to have their hearts bettered and more disposed to their duty. The general view of most people seems to be either because it would be disreputable not to go to church or else to hear a well-composed discourse or else to know something more of the matter than they did before so as to be able to give a better account of their religion and talk better of it. I judge this partly from reflection upon myself, who am too conscious that I seldom propose that end to myself in going to church, to have my mind and heart and whole self bettered, and partly from the little care I observe in mankind to govern their passions and watch over themselves, and partly from the disposition I observe in the generality of people to exercise upon and censure the sermon; either the delivery or style or words or thoughts or method does or does not please them. If people were sincerely concerned to find benefit from what they hear they would not be so ready to pass a judgement upon these things. I am indeed very much concerned to find in myself so much of this temper that I seem to hear a sermon only with a design to judge of the composition or the parts and qualifications of its preacher.

Mr. Smith and Mr. Burroughs came with me after sermon

and drank a glass of wine and tea. When they were gone father asked me why I did not go and see Mr. Blundell and told me that he had said he was mightily pleased with my company.

Monday, September 3. Breakfasted at Cousin Billio's. Mr. Christopher Fowler came there also. Our conversation turned very much upon the travels of Cousin Billio into Flanders and the army and Mr. Fowler told some very good stories upon that head.

Dined at home. Sent to Mr. Burroughs to come and see me in the afternoon and send his viol which he did and we played together a great while. At 6 came to London with father. We talked about the new house he is going to build.

Was a little tired by walking, but went to the Gill House. Mrs. Marshall came into my thoughts with a great deal of regret and sorrow but after I had eat some oysters I found a sudden cheerfulness diffuse itself quite through me.

Wednesday, September 5. Rose at 6. Went to Islington; drank the waters there. Talked with Dr. Lee about my pain in my arm. He thinks my blood is purified pretty much already by the waters by the alteration of my complexion. I asked him about the Bagnio. He thought it would do me good, but he said it would be better to stay till my blood is more purified before I used it.

Met with a gentleman that had been at the East Indies several times. He talked about ships and sailing and gave us pretty good accounts of the nature of it. It requires a great deal of judgement and penetration to be a good sailor and manage a ship well. There are such a variety of things and circumstances to be considered in it.

I talked with Captain Pierce and he told me that he drank the waters upon the account of a pain in his breast which he is now quite cleared of, but he said he gained an accidental benefit from them which he did not expect or think of when he first came. When he first came he was so deaf that he could not hear across a room a common voice and was going to have his ear syringed, but after he had drank the waters three or four days his head was cleared and he heard as well as ever he did in his life. He says since he has been informed that the waters are often drank upon that account.

Came home after dinner. Read some parts of Rushworth's *Collections*[1] as the argument of Justice Crook against the Ship Money.

Went to brother's. Brother and sister were just come from the Hay. I soon began to talk to sister about Mrs. Marshall but there is no beating her off a notion when she has once taken it into her head and therefore she says she would not have me come when Mrs. Marshall comes to her house, that my father and mother take notice of it.

Father was at brother's. He said he had writ to brother William's mistress's mother last night. He had been talking with Mr. West about partnership. Mr. West said he was dissatisfied with Mr. Bailey's management. He also mentioned to my father that he should like very well to have brother William partner in his room. This pleased my father and I am extremely glad of it. There is now a very fair prospect for brother of making his fortune in the world and living very happily in it. The encouragement he has met with in his affair of matrimony hitherto, and the thoughts of settling in the world and being a master has given a perfect new turn to his behaviour. He applies himself very well to business and thinks of coming into the world.

Came home at past 9. To bed at 11.

Thursday, September 6. Rose before half-hour after 5. Drank the waters at Islington. Spent most of my time there with Dr. Lee. He talked with me about whoring. The old man talks of it with a very sensible relish of it, but I talked with him very gravely about the danger of a clap or pox by using it and also the great villainy of debauching and seducing young virtuous girls as is so common a practice.

Went to Uncle Marshall's to dinner, but neither he nor my cousin was at home and they had just done dinner when I came in, and I was forced to make my dinner off the almost cold remains of a shoulder of mutton. Mrs. Allom was there to beg some charity as Uncle Marshall do give her now and then out of his own money or what he has from others to dispose

[1] *Historical Collections.* By John Rushworth (d. 1690).

of to charitable uses, for I cannot but take notice that my whole family is very much disposed to charity and very willing to do a kindness to any of their friends and ready to serve them, which I think is an admirable good quality and which I cannot but be sorry when I see so much wanted in my father. He has very little notion of generosity that way and thinks much to do a kindness to anybody.

Cousin Marshall told me that Mrs. Allom had told them a story of old Mr. Stevenson's [1] appearing to her and telling her he was in a place of misery and has wronged her. My Aunt Marshall seems to give some little credit to it so far as to think she may have some foundation for it in a dream, but my cousin looks upon it in another view and it makes her suspect the truth of her former story of the apparition of her husband's mother to her and discovering to her her son's right to the estate in East Smithfield and indeed this is enough to make one suspect both.

Went at 7 o'clock to Button's Coffee-House. There was Dr. Cairns, a man that pretends to have discovered the philosopher's stone and the occult qualities of matter, pretends to show gold vegetable-like trees and shrubs and plants, and talks in a most unintelligible style about materia prima, elementary fire, &c. He is treated as a kind of a madman there and ridiculed and bantered by all that talk with him, though he does not seem to be at all sensible of their ridicule but is himself perfectly serious.

My barber as he was shaving me this morning told me that he was last Sunday night in Dr. Sutton's [2] company where the doctor told them in a very grave and serious manner that he had a friend who had bought a precious stone that was found in Scotland, for £50. It had in it a picture of three crowns and under them writ 'James the Third'. His friend carried the stone to a goldsmith's upon Ludgate Hill and the goldsmith told him he was imposed upon. He would go and take out these figures presently and accordingly took it into an inward room and tried it with some liquor that he had proper for that purpose, but could not get it out. However,

[1] Grandmother's second husband.
[2] Possibly Thomas Sutton, who graduated M.D. at Oxford in 1692 and was admitted a member of the College of Physicians in 1693.

he told him he might depend upon it it was only marked upon it. However, says he, 'Let me see it once more. I am sure I can get it out now.' And takes it in with him and stayed for half an hour, when his friend was impatient and told him he was afraid he would spoil his stone, and told him if he spoilt the stone he should pay for it. But the goldsmith came out again and told him. 'Sir,' says he, 'all the art of man cannot get them out. This is natural, I am sure. I was before a Whig but now from this moment I am a Jacobite.' The doctor had the confidence to tell this with the greatest seriousness and positiveness in the world, and when my barber seemed to doubt of it the person at whose house he was says, 'What! Do you doubt the doctor's veracity?' But the doctor did not affirm he had seen the stone, only he had a friend that had it and could see it at any time. This story gives a very just and good idea of the manner in which the parsons and cunning politicians of the Tories and Jacobites promote their cause. This is something akin to the famous pear that has been talked of that had the Duke of Ormonde's name grown upon it.

Friday, September 7. When came to brother's, met Mrs. Marshall there. I found a strange beating at my heart and concern upon my spirits how to approach. However, I bore her presence pretty well and, as I conceived, methought she carried it to me better than the last time I saw her.

When sister and Mrs. Marshall were going in the coach alone and sister was to come again to-night, I thought it proper to offer my service, and when they were got into the coach I asked Mrs. Marshall whether there would be any room for me. She said she did not know certainly whether her brother Deison could go, but he would if he could. I was getting into the coach to go as far as her house to wait upon them if he could not go, but sister whispered me that it was very silly. So I stepped out again and told Mrs. Marshall what sister said. But then sister desired me to come again, but I refused it positively.

At 6 went to the Grecian Coffee-House. There were several gentlemen, some of those that had been at the Old Bailey to-day at the trial of the rioters in Salisbury Court. Five were indicted and all found guilty of felony by the late Statute of

Riots. There were four or five positive witnesses against every one of the prisoners, that they were in the house and active pulling down the sign, breaking the windows, &c.[1] Mr. Read, the mug-house man, was also tried for the death of one of the rioters and acquitted. By the evidence for him it was proved by several witnesses that the mob cried out, 'No King George! No Hanoverians! The Duke of Ormonde! The High Church! Down with the Mug-house!' and Vaughan the man that was killed was the foremost of them all and to encourage the rest of the mob told them that the Duke of Ormonde was landed in the West of England with 20,000 men.

It was affirmed by one witness, a writing master, that he happened to be at the shop by Fleet Bridge when a little mob gathered thereabouts and increased as they went along. He out of curiosity joined himself with them and as they went along one of them told them they should go to such houses for clubs and particularly they went to a soap boiler's, where they received about 26 clubs. From whence they went to Shoe Lane to a house where they had another good quantity given them and then they were distributed to them that would accept of them and they went in a body into Salisbury Court and talked of pulling down the mug-house when they came there, and began to attack the house. Some gentlemen in the house sallied out and drove them away into Fleet Street, but they soon rallied and came on again, but they were beat back again. But a third time they rallied and came up near the mug-house and then Mr. Read and a soldier who was there presented, one a blunderbuss and the other his musket, and told them they would shoot the first man that came upon them. However, this Vaughan, being a very brisk stout fellow, advanced before the rest of the mob ten yards and came throwing stones and insulting the soldier, still advancing and endeavouring to get upon them unawares, when he came so near that he was forced to fire upon him and shot him dead. Then Mr. Read was forced to retire into his house and defend that as well as he could. But they soon broke in upon him but they defended themselves above stairs by the narrowness of the stairs a good

---

[1] The mob was led by Tom Beau, a valet to two condemned Jacobites. He was among those hanged. Read escaped narrowly: the jury were divided on the verdict of justifiable homicide.

while. But the gentlemen in the house were forced to get away behind the house by climbing down a large church wall, where they met the clerk who set a great dog upon them that they drew their swords and told him if he did not call off his dog they would first kill the dog and then run him through too. So he called off the dog and they got away. At length the guards came and secured the remainder of the house.

The evidences that were brought against Mr. Read were all very bad. There was the fullest proof that could be desired for Mr. Read, that if he did kill the man he did it in his own defence and there was no full proof that he did kill him.

It was also swore in court that the constables and watchmen were by when the mob was there. But instead of doing their duty by suppressing them, they encouraged and abetted as much they could do without actually assisting them or speaking to them. They stood by, never offered to lay hold of any of them. The mob came and brought baskets of stones and set them between the constables and watchmen and when one of the constables who was an honest man and got into the house to defend it, called out to his brother constables to cease the mob, they told him there was no mob, all the mob was theirs.

The gentleman that was then president in the mug-house was asked whether he ever knew them drink any healths that were reflecting upon the Church, &c. He said never any but such as might be drunk in any company. He said they always began with the King's and Prince's and Princess's and Royal Family, then the immortal memory of King William and never without the Church as by law established. ' But did you never drink any healths by way of confusion to any set of men?' He said they never did. This is false to my own knowledge, for when I was there [1] they drank confusion to all the enemies of King George, &c.

Saturday, September 8. Rose before 6. Went to the waters. Got into company with Dr. Oldfield and his brother. They came to Dr. Lee to advise about making a record of the remarkable cures that have been wrought by these waters. There is one pretty remarkable one. A young man went upon Hampstead Heath the day of the great eclipse on purpose to see it and when it

[1] On 20 July.

came it struck him with a sudden dampness and chillness that as soon as he was got home took away the use of all his limbs and so he continued for a good while. Doctors and surgeons were applied to, but in vain; he only recovered so much as to be able to get to go with crutches. He was advised to drink these waters and he found benefit from them immediately and was cured perfectly before he left there.

Dr. Lee told me a story of his widow. He took a fancy to her by her conversation but when he made his addresses to her she told him she had resolved never to marry again and therefore desired if he would expect to be treated civilly never to mention that again. However, the Doctor resolved not to be put off, so every now and then in the midst of different discourse would put in a word of the matter, but she still pressed him not to mention it. But the Doctor was resolved to push it forward and he did it so much that he perfectly enraged her and after he had by almost violence kept her in the room for six or seven hours she went away in anger and vowed never to see him more. But the Doctor by his pleasant manner of treating her and persuading her and almost forcing her, partly in jest and partly in earnest, had so wrought upon her mind that, a half-year afterwards, the widow by a message gave intimation that she should be willing to admit of his addresses. But he was then engaged to another.

Went to Hackney on foot. Received a letter from Mr. Leeds, a very long one, wherein he vindicates love against philosophy and ridicules my philosopher [1] under the title of the Stoic. It is writ with a pretty tolerable good spirit, but methinks we are running the matter too far to fill so many letters with the same subject. I shall endeavour to give some other turn to it in my next if I can.

Went after dinner to Mr. Blundell's. Mr. Blundell talking of Mr. Freke who died last night and the strangeness of his marrying when he was so ill as to be put to bed by his nurse. That at that time there were two ladies of his congregation [2] that were both in love with him, his present widow as is and one Mrs. Chandler, a young lady of a good fortune and agreeable person. Their love was so great that they perfectly [despaired] which of them should have him. They used at last to go about (especially Mrs.

---
[1] A character-sketch sent in a letter to Leeds.
[2] At Bartholomew Close, Smithfield.

Chandler) to the people of the congregation and make it their business to speak ill of one another and complain of each other's forwardness with regard to Mr. Freke, that it came to almost an open breach and hatred. Mrs. Chandler said that she loved him so as she should hang herself if she had him not and endeavoured to recommend herself to him by showing the qualifications of a nurse, while he was in such a condition as not to be capable of helping himself. And this though he was so little, deformed a man as one shall seldom meet with one more so. At last, however, he marries his present widow as is and then the other young lady resented it so much as not only to go from the congregation but upon that account to leave the dissenters also and turn High Church, saying that she would never go among them again.

Sunday, September 9. Rose at past 7. Was half an hour putting on my shoes, being new yesterday. Mr. Mayo preached upon the necessity of Faith in Christ in order to salvation. He dined with us. After dinner he gave us an account of what was done about the choice of a minister for our place. They have several of the gentlemen met and talked about it and agreed to choose Mr. Smith. Father was concerned for Cousin Billio,[1] and told him his concern, but Mr. Mayo said the gentlemen had him proposed to them but they all agreed that though they had a great value and respect for him, yet they thought him not so proper and so acceptable to the congregation.

Went to London with Cousin Joseph Billio in the afternoon. I told him that I believed Mr. Smith would be chosen to-night. He was surprised at it and I also told him how much father was concerned that he could not press his brother, but he had tried it and all in vain. He said his great defect lay in his prayers, but it was entirely owing to his own will and pleasure, for he would not budge the least to make himself popular from what he thought just and reasonable and that he did not like the manner of praying among the dissenters in general, which is so acceptable to the people.

Went to sister's. She was in a very good pleasant humour, but when Joseph was gone I asked her whether I might not go with her and Mrs. Marshall to the Hay. She was very much vexed with that proposal and presently run out upon my folly

[1] i.e. Robert Billio.

in endeavouring always to see her, and besides it would be likely to make Mrs. Marshall herself never come to see her and would break off her acquaintance to have it reported as if I courted her, which was already done.

At last brother William came in and told us of a little quarrel he had with Mrs. Bailey. Cousin Ned Harding came up to him one morning and Mrs. Bailey asked why he brought up that boy into his chamber to dirty the room, that she would not suffer him to come into the house again. They keep a most wretched house, that the servants have scarce victuals enough to eat, and they don't treat my brother in a very civil manner.

Brother William begins to be less assured of success with his mistress than before. She talks to him in a pretty lofty style about fortunes and manner of living and genteel appearance and presents before marriage for such and such a fortune, and intimates as if she expected considerable things for herself. I believe she does this only to spur him on and raise his notion of her. But brother likes her extremely and thinks he shall never be so happy in any wife as her.

At dinner Mr. Mayo talked about the hardship of English juries, that they might not eat or drink till they brought in their verdict and agreed every man. By this means honest [men] are forced to bring in their verdict contrary to their conscience and oath.

Monday, September 10. Rose at 6. Went to Islington. Conversed chiefly with Dr. Lee. He gave me an account of some things that passed concerning the revolution, and as he was in his prime at that time I thought it proper to inquire a little about these affairs.

I asked the Doctor what popular noise there was before the revolution and how the people conceived of it. And he says that three or four months before, the people had got it into their heads and talked of it very much and healths were drank at all the taverns, with oranges in their hats.

He told me he was very intimately acquainted with Lord Delamere [1] and was present at his trial for Monmouth's rebellion.

---

[1] Henry Booth, 2nd Baron Delamere. He was imprisoned in 1683 on the charge of being concerned in the Rye House Plot but was released on bail. In 1685 he was charged with attempting to raise the North in support of Monmouth's rebellion; the evidence was inadequate and he was acquitted.

THE DEATH OF KING CHARLES II

After he was acquitted he went to the King to kiss his hand. The King told him he believed he was sensible he had a very fair and free trial. He answered 'Yes' and said he hoped His Majesty thought him very innocent and a good subject. The King replied, 'Lord Delamere was innocent but Brown was guilty.' For he had taken upon him the name of Brown during the time of his acting for the Duke of Monmouth.

I asked the Doctor also about the death of King Charles. He says he was a papist all his life as well as at his death but he does not the least doubt but he was poisoned. After the murder of the Earl of Essex [1] Mr. Braddon [2] writ a pamphlet to prove that he did not murder himself but was murdered, and indeed the circumstances were so plain and evident as not to be doubted but he was murdered. And that book was laid in the King's chamber by an unknown person. The King finds it and reads it and immediately sends for my Lord Arlington and advises with him. And the Duke of York was immediately sent for and the King told him he would have him to go into Scotland now and commanded him to do so, but the Duke replied, 'By God, I will not.' This passed and in two or three days the King and Lord Arlington were invited by the Duchess of Portsmouth [3] to supper and they drank chocolate and ate turkey eggs. The next morning the King found a swooning and dizziness in his head and while he was under concern upon that account news was brought him that Lord Arlington was dead. This startled him and he said then, 'I am gone.' He was soon taken with a fit but recovered out of it and died about four or five days after. This, the doctor says, is a sufficient proof that he did not die of an apoplexy, for he was quite out of the fit before he died and that, if it kills, does it very soon. Sir John King, the King's physician or surgeon, let him blood which spread the poison all over the veins and effectively killed him, for which King James gave him £500, and when his

---

[1] In 1683 he was found dead, his throat cut, in the Tower, to which he had been committed for his share in Monmouth's rebellion.

[2] Laurence Braddon (d. 1724): imprisoned 1683-9. Among his many pamphlets on this subject was *Murder Will Out*, 1692.

[3] Louise de Kéroualle (d. 1734), mistress of Charles II. The suddenness of the King's death led to popular suspicions against the Catholics at Court, including the Duke of York and herself. She herself seems to have believed that the King was poisoned by his brother.

body was opened one of the physicians said he was poisoned and in a little time he was heard of no more.[1]

Dined with Mr. Bowes, Mr. Franklin and another gentleman. Mr. Bowes told us of a remarkable case that happened in the King's Bench as it is particularly set down by Serjeant Maynard in the 4th year of Charles I's reign. A woman was found murdered in bed at some town in Hertfordshire and her sister and brother and husband only being in the house. And the Coroner's Inquest that sits upon her brought it in self-murder. However, the neighbours not being satisfied with this had these persons taken up for it and the body of the woman [was] taken up again a good while after it was buried. The first evidence that was sworn was a clergyman who swore that when the body was taken up, the woman's sister, being by and also being one of them that were accused of the crime, fell down upon her knees and prayed to God Almighty that He would be pleased to show some mark as a testimony to her innocence. The people that were about were immediately for making the usual trial in this case and desired her to touch the dead body and she did upon the forehead, upon which the skin immediately changed from a black colour of a dead body into something of a more vivid colour and a kind of a dew arose upon it, which distilled in drops that run down her face to her eyes, one of which opened and she stretched out her left arm. The mark of her wedding ring appeared upon her finger, from which several drops of blood gushed out. This was sworn also by another clergyman who was present. Upon this and one or two more circumstances the sister and husband of the deceased were condemned and executed.

Went to Mr. Bowes's chambers to drink tea with him. Happening to mention Dr. Williams [2] he immediately fell foul upon him and called him villain. I don't find he has any very particular reason for this but he has conceived a prejudice against him and is ready to receive anything that may contribute to create any ill opinion of him. He told me that when his father and mother had a mind he should go to Scotland Dr. Williams came to their house and talked to him in so insolent and proud a

---

[1] Sir Edmund King (d. 1709) bled the King when he was struck with apoplexy on 2 February 1684. His promptitude was rewarded by the Privy Council with a grant of £1,000, which, however, was never paid.

[2] Dr. Daniel Williams, the minister.

manner and so haughty that his blood perfectly set against him and he could not treat him civilly. When we had talked together for above an hour he asked me to play at picquet. I consented and played till it grew dark and in the whole won 2s. of him.

Tuesday, September 11. Dined at the Marlborough Head with Mr. Bowes. He told us a remarkable story of a strange adventure. He had the story from Mr. Jeremiah Burroughs who also told it me himself this afternoon from a gentlewoman at Dr. Williams's to whom one of the persons concerned told it. A German officer was a little while ago in town and told her this story. He had been in Spain and upon some account during the late war there was sent into France by the King of Spain and put into the Bastille at Paris, where he contracted a particular intimacy with a young gentleman who was also in the Bastille.

The young gentleman told him his story; that he was a son of Muley Mulock, the late emperor of Morocco about 15 years ago.[1] His elder brother and he raised a rebellion against their father but were taken. His elder [brother] was punished with the loss of an arm and leg of which he soon died. He himself got an opportunity to escape and came into Portugal where he continued some time till he found he was discovered by his father's ambassador there. From whence he made his escape to Madrid, where he continued a good while, getting his subsistence in what manner he could. Till at length he was taken notice of as a foreigner and stranger and appearing to have no business was taken up as a spy and sent to France into the Bastille there, where he got this acquaintance where he was kept for several years. But at length the King, not finding anything against him, gave him his liberty and the German officer gained also his soon after.

The officer now bethought himself he might have an opportunity of making his fortune if he could any way assist this young prince to regain his father's favour and pardon and made terms with the young prince what he should do for him if he could bring this about.

[1] The Emperor of Morocco at that time was Moulay Ismā'īl the Bloodthirsty, who reigned from 1672 until 1727 and, by slaughter on the grand scale, united the Empire. His children, begotten in a harem rivalling Solomon's, were numbered by the hundred. His concubines may have included Europeans; he once sought Mlle. de Conti, a natural daughter of Louis XIV, as an inmate.

And now they resolved to come into England and as soon as they came hither the German officer, who was a polite genteel man, went to the Morocco ambassador here and inquired about his master's family. When he found the young man had told him true, he told him that he could produce the young prince if he could promise the pardon of his father, and being received into favour. The ambassador desired to see him, but he refused that but told him several marks by which he might be assured that he was the real young prince. The ambassador then told him he could assure him of a very kind welcome from his father, who had been extremely concerned at his cruelty to his brother and had a great desire to have him, his only son and heir, to succeed him. This message the officer brought back to the young prince, but he said he could not trust to any promise or words of the ambassador but only desired that his father might have notice of it and wrote a letter to him himself, telling him he was afraid to trust any other person but himself, but could entirely rely upon his word and promise if he would think fit to give it him in writing, and this letter was sent. And King George had notice of it, who, if his father owned him, intended to have sent him over in the quality of a prince. But in this interval of time the Morocco ambassador died, which put a stop to the affair and also Muley Molock himself died soon after. And how ends the narration, was it further proceeded in, it is not known.

There is this further remarkable in it, that the young prince had often said that his mother was an Englishwoman who was [brought] into the seraglio about 30 years ago, but did not know her name. Mr. Bennett happened to be by when this story was told and he said he knew a lady and her daughter about that time was sent for by her husband into the West Indies, who were taken by a Salleyman as they were sailing into the West Indies. The young lady being very handsome was sent as a present to court and the emperor took a fancy to her and married her after she had been forced to turn Mahometan. The emperor was so well pleased with her that he sent for her mother and treated her with all the imaginable respect and gave her the liberty of her religion, though he could not to her daughter because he could marry none but a Mahometan. Her mother lived with her four or five years and then had liberty given her to come to England to see her friends, and Mr. Bennett saw her when she returned, and thinks she went back again to her daughter, where she died. This story appeared to be the same with the other and she to be the mother of this young prince and his brother.

Went to brother's, where talked with sister about Mrs. Marshall. We happened to talk about agreeable men. Sister is become very much of late given to criticizing upon others and talks mightily of agreeableness since Mrs. Marshall's acquaintance. She says she does not know ten agreeable persons of both sexes together in the world. My sister plainly said my brother, her husband, he was not one of them.

Mr. Hunt whom I met in the street told me that the Princess is certainly with child, for my Lord Townshend at a feast lately, when the King and Prince and Princesses and Family were drank, proposed *Hans en Kelder*, which he said they might depend upon. My Lady Cobham, they say, is very bad of the venereal disease given her by her husband and also Ned Harley's lady.

Wednesday, September 12. Rose before 6. Went to the waters. Dr. Lee gave us an account of the difference that is between Dr. Read and his curate Mr. Henley. Dr. Read being taken ill of the palsy so as not to be capable of preaching constantly was obliged to take a curate. This Mr. Henley was recommended to him as an honest man and he accepted of him and entered into an obligation to give him £30 per annum till he should have better preferment. Soon after this settlement Mr. Henley shows himself to be a very high churchman, a great Tory and associates only with such, frequently goes to the Jacobite coffee-house and has endeavoured as much as possible to set the parish against Dr. Read. He has also railed at Justice Fuller [1] in the pulpit so as that the whole congregation knew who he meant. This made both the Doctor and the Justice resolve if possible to get him out and to that end complained to the bishop who sent for him last Saturday. When he came back he went to the tavern with some of his friends, where he stayed till past 11 o'clock and did not go home that night, but came at the clerk's about 10 o'clock. The clerk sends Dr. Read word that Mr. Henley was sick abed and had vomited half a pail full of blood (claret I suppose) and desired him to provide. Accordingly the Doctor was forced to go into

---

[1] Apparently a Hackney J.P., cf. 'Cash, p^d expences going to Justice Fuller 00·03·06'. Hackney Churchwardens' accounts.

the pulpit unprovided. As soon as he entered the pulpit several of the congregation went away saying that Mr. Henley was turned out and crying out extremely against the Doctor, and it was soon reported that Dr. Read pulled Mr. Henley's surplice off his back and Justice Fuller led him out of the church by the nose. Though there was not a word of truth in it.

There was a gentleman said upon occasion of talking concerning Mr. Young's drinking much, that he was like the New River pipes hard by that had water run through them so long that they would grow rotten if the current was stopped.

Came home. Dressed and went to dinner. In the way met father who told me he would meet me at the Marlborough's Head where I was to dine. Accordingly he came and talked with me very seriously about his affairs and circumstances. He told me he was now very much at a loss for money and could not tell what to do upon that account. He owed as much as the stock in his shop came to, particularly £500 to grandmother, £450 to Aunt Billio for which two of his houses in Leadenhall Street were mortgaged, and £200 to Mr. Stratford. That he had £400 per annum coming in entire and clear besides all taxes and encumbrances, that he had made me sole executor, given brother William only £1,400 by his will and settled about £150 a year upon brother Ryder besides what he has already given him, and that he had left all the rest to me excepting mother's jointure that was above £100 per annum. He said in general what I should have after mother's death would be above £3,000.

He then told me he would ask me one question and desired me to answer him ingenuously and plainly. I said I would. It was whether I had not a kindness for Mrs. Marshall (which my mother guessed I had). The colour came in my face and only answered, how could my mother guess at such a thing. My countenance so betrayed me that I could not help owning it and the tears flowed out of my eyes. My father was then very sensible of my passion and told me the inconvenience of marrying so soon out of business, and besides said her fortune could not be anything considerable, a £1,000 or £1,500 would be the most could be expected. Besides her family was nothing, could bring me no acquaintance nor friends that could serve me in my business. That her father was nothing but a common ordinary tailor at first, but by great industry arrived at something considerable.

He might perhaps be worth 5 or £6,000 but hardly more. As for Mrs. Marshall, she was agreeable but nothing extraordinary. But he said if I was so deeply engaged in love as to interrupt me in my study or that I could not be easy without her, he could freely consent to my marrying of her, and would go himself to Mr. Marshall and make up the match. Nothing can be more obliging and endearing than such a tender regard to me shown by my father. I desired my father not to mention anything of this to anybody, that I intended to stifle it as soon as possible within my own breast. He promised that he would not tell it to brother or sister or anybody but mother who he said was very private and secret in anything entrusted to her. But desired he would not mention it to her because Aunt Billio is apt to inquire. He said he would not.

I think I find my mind much more easy now than it was and I am in hopes to be able to overcome my passion. When I told my father I was afraid that she herself would be against marrying me, he said then I should scorn to be in love with her. This has had some effect upon me. I wish I had that self-sufficiency as to be able to despise those that despise me.

Thursday, September 13. Rose at before 6. Went to the waters. Dr. Lee upon my asking him told me that when it was reported that James II's queen was with child of the present Pretender not one in ten believed it, but lampoons were made upon it and papers stuck in her train with these words, 'Madam, your cushion does not sit right to-day.' Such as these were laid also upon her toilet and a general disbelief of it went through the Kingdom. Indeed Dr. Lee said that a physician of the King's told him his blood was corrupted and his seed so bad by the pox that it was impossible for him to get a child that could live.[1] When the Queen was thus pretended to be with child it was given out that she would be brought to bed sometimes in one place and sometimes in another, till at last all of a sudden she came to town and was brought to bed at St. James's. There were indeed a great many lords and noblemen in the room at the time of the pretended birth and heard her cry out but they saw nothing, the

---

[1] Of James's fifteen legitimate children, only the Pretender and Louise Maria Theresa (d. 1712) survived him. His many illegitimate children were longer lived.

bed being all round shut with vallance and open only of one side, just by which was a private door. When the child was taken out of the bed it looked all black and was thought to be have been almost stifled.

Came back to the Bell Inn at 8 o'clock in order to see sister and Mrs. Marshall take coach for the Hay. Sister charged me to come on Monday and bring Joseph Billio with me.

Went to Hackney to dinner. Cousin Joseph Billio came in the afternoon. Our first discourse was about Mrs. Marshall. He is extremely smitten with her.

I told him I was under a great perplexity what to do, whether to go to the Hay while she is there or no. He wondered at that and said surely I was very serious. I would not go to the Hay while she is there upon father's account, who is privy to my passion. Only my sister will take it ill and I don't know how to think of Joseph Billio's enjoying her company and having an opportunity of engrossing her affections while I am absent.

Friday, September 14. Rose between 6 and 7. The wind was extremely high all night, that put me under some consternation remembering the former great wind in which the stack of chimney was blown down into our room. In the morning went to the waters on horseback.

Went to North's Coffee-House. A story was told of Dr. Garth [1] who is now at Paris, that being in company with several English gentlemen the King's health was proposed and drank round, till it came to one gentleman who said the word 'King' was so general that he thought it proper to be explained, and supposed they meant James III. Upon that Dr. Garth asked him what he meant, that he knew no other king than King George, and that was the sense in which the company and he drank it. Upon which the other gentleman said there was no other but King James and said he should drink it too. Upon that Dr. Garth without any more words gave him a blow over the face with his fist and immediately rose up and drew his sword and so did the other. But they were soon parted. This made a mighty noise at Paris and the Regent has put the gentleman who proposed King James's health into the Bastille.

[1] Dr. Samuel Garth (1661-1719), author of *The Dispensary*. He was knighted in 1714.

Came home part of the way with father and told him I intended to go to the Hay next Tuesday. He said he thought I would not have gone and I should do well not to encourage that foolish passion. It was only for novices to fall in love with a girl by being in her company and hearing her talk.

Saturday, September 15. Came home. Read some account of Venice in the *Voyage du Levant*, particularly the manner of performing the Quarantain for ships come from the Levant.

Went to father. He has seen a horse which he likes if he can agree about the price. Went to Mr. Deison [1] to acquaint him with my design to go to the Hay Tuesday next and that I shall be glad of his company since I hear he goes to meet sister and Mrs. Marshall at Watford. I was under some concern and uneasiness at the thought and prospect of going into Mrs. Marshall's house and behaving before any of her relations. However, I went and come off very well. I saw her father and brother and sister and spoke with them all. They received me very kindly and pleasantly and I have appointed to call him at between 6 and 7 at his house.

When I came home, read some of Pitt's account of the religion of the Mohametan religion and manners and customs, &c. The book seems to be writ with a very good air of truth and sincerity but a very indifferent style and without any kind of method or order. There appears in it the marks of a very honest, well-meaning, rude man that has not polished his mother tongue at all by study or reflection or learning. Upon reflection now, I find but little that I can remember of what I read that is particular or that is fit to tell again. Only in general with regard to matrimony there is no such thing as courting or wooing. A match is made up without so much as the young man's seeing his wife as is to be, by the father of the woman. When all things are agreed upon the man goes to the officer of the city and promises them to give her a certain sum of money if they part and that is all the ceremony there is.

Sunday, September 16. Rose at 7. Read a sermon of Tillotson's. Mr. Tonge preached at the meeting both parts of the day. At the time of praying it came into my thoughts that the

[1] Mrs. Marshall's brother-in-law.

manner of praying might be much improved and bettered to what it is if persons would but keep in their minds a view of the design and end of prayer and retain upon them the impression of the Deity and the sense of the goodness of the God they approach.

Came to London at 6 o'clock with brother William. He tells me his mistress begins to treat him a more distant forbidding manner than usual and seems as if she expected better terms of matrimony than she has an account of from her mother, to whom my father wrote. She talks to him also of former addresses to her by others and seems to expect great things, that brother almost despairs. I am apt to think she does this only to enhance her price and try him.

Went to Tom's Coffee-House. No company that I knew. I heard there that the five rioters are to be hanged next Wednesday in Salisbury Court.

Monday, September 17. Rose at 6. Went to the waters. Conversed chiefly with Dr. Lee. He told us a story of the mischief that happened lately at Manchester. It seems the Tories there instead of crying 'Down with the Rump' as was usual before when they would insult a Whig, they hem. Two officers were going through the streets and some ladies looking out of the windows cried hem and did so a second time. One of the officers looks back at them and says, 'We don't want a whore,' and went on their way. A third hem followed them and the officer cries 'Cuckoo'. Upon that a tradesman going by said, 'I know of no cuckold but King George.' The officers pursued him to his house where they surrounded the house with some soldiers they had and he fired a pistol out of the window and shot one of them upon the eye. This created some disturbance. The man was taken and is bound over to the assizes.

After dinner went to Paul's to hear the Anthem. Went to brother's to meet Cousin Joseph. He was in a great perplexity what to do about going to-morrow with me to meet sister and Mrs. Marshall. He had no mind at all to go. I believe his chief difficulty lies in this, that he did not care to be obliged to any of the company for his club.[1]

We went with Mr. Burgess to the tavern together. Our

---
[1] i.e. his share of the cost.

conversation turned chiefly upon the manner of preaching among the dissenters. I said I thought the chief difference between the preaching of the dissenters and the churchmen lay in this, that the dissenters were for making men good at once, whereas the churchmen were for rooting out evil habits by degrees and implanting virtues one by one. The dissenters preach as if they thought that regeneration or confession was but one single act to be done at once and all the virtues and graces of the Christian life would follow upon it. Whereas the churchmen preach as if they thought that it was to be brought about by degrees and through various stages.

Went to John's. Met Mr. Porter and Mr. Witnoom. We went together to Tom's to drink hot punch. We were pretty merry and I was more free than usual. We talked pretty much about the manner of preaching, whether Tillotson's style was better than the more copious, fluent, enlarged style and I made this note of my sentiments, that the more enlarged style was more proper for preaching, because the bulk of the audience are vulgar ordinary persons who cannot receive things without it is impressed upon them with some warmth and vehemence.

I had a great mind to a whore and wandered about the streets till I found one to my mind, and gave her 6s., but she picked my pocket of a handkerchief.

Tuesday, September 18. Rose at between 5 and 6. Was shaved. Went to father's. From thence to Mr. Howard's [1] in order to have his horse to go into the country. It put me under some concern that I was to go as far as Watford and could not let him know I was to go above four or five miles. Went to Mr. Marshall's. It was now 7 o'clock and I should have been there half after 6. Drank some chocolate there, talked with Mr. Deison about public affairs. Cousin Joseph Billio soon came in and we set out a little before 8. We were pretty merry upon the road. We went to Watford. Soon after we came my brother and sister and Mrs. Marshall came in. Mrs. Marshall was very much disappointed that Dr. Avery did not come along with us. At Watford at first I observed that Mrs. Marshall favoured

---

[1] The Hackney church records often mention Matthew Howard. John Howard, the father of the philanthropist, also lived at Hackney, where he died in 1727.

Cousin Billio much more than me. Mr. Deison was chiefly applied to to divert her. His discourse run chiefly upon what had a tendency to bawdy and it a little surprised [me] to hear a married man give such a loose to himself upon that head.

We went together through my Lord Essex's park.[1] When we came to the house we were to part, my brother and Mr. Deison for London and we to the Hay. Cousin Joseph and I had desired my sister and Mrs. Marshall to let us ride with them in their coach, there being none but themselves, but she showed an unwillingness to gratify us, particularly Mrs. Marshall, that we should dirty their petticoats. So we kept our horse, but we were both vexed at it and were once going to resolve not to speak to them all the way and indeed cousin did not for a good while. In a little when I came again to the coach I perceived a want of conversation between them, as I thought, a little distance and difference, and sister asked me to come into the coach, but I told them there was not room and we should dirty their petticoats.

We passed away the evening in comical conversation enough. It chiefly turned upon bawdy and *double entendres*, than which I perceived nothing is more touching to Mrs. Marshall. I don't know that I ever talked so much to any woman in that way as I did at that time. But it made me very uneasy every now and then to observe Mrs. Marshall show more respect and familiarity to Cousin Billio than to me. Only once I ventured to attack her for a kiss by open force upon some proper occasion, but I could not conquer it at first and left off. But then sister upbraided me with cowardice, that I could not do it and then I resolved to go through with it and they both assisted one another against me and made a prodigious hideous noise, but still I did get a kiss of her.

At night in bed I talked a good while with Cousin Joseph about this and Mrs. Marshall. He is extremely enamoured with her.

Wednesday, September 19. Rose at 8. Before we rose we talked a good while together and very, very merry, Cousin Joseph and I. It pleased to think that we laughed so loud as to make the ladies in bed hear us and Mrs. Marshall might think me more merry than when I am in her company. In the morning

[1] Cassiobury Park. Part of it had been laid out by Le Notre.

when they were up and got dressed I went into their room, upon which sister immediately fell into a vehement exclamation against me in earnest for coming before they were dressed, though they were dressed more than I have seen them both.

After breakfast we went out together to gather mushrooms. In this time Mrs. Marshall was very touchy and would not bear to be meddled with by me and but a little by cousin. Out of pure malice to them and envy to Joseph Billio I had a mind to gain him to go along with me and separate from them and therefore endeavoured to persuade him to go the next morning to Hatfield House,[1] about 12 miles off, and could have been contented to have lost their company so I could but prevent them having his. Sister took an opportunity to tell Joseph Billio very seriously that he was very rude, that we teased Mrs. Marshall so that she said she was weary of her life with us. We went together to Dame Butler's where I found the same temper in her; that made me exceeding heavy and melancholy that I could scarce speak a word, and told Cousin Joseph that I would go to-morrow. At 10 they went to bed and I was glad of it.

Thursday, September 20. Rose between 6 and 7. Went to Hemstead with Cousin Joseph to be shaved. At 4 we went to meet the ladies and found them at Mr. Johnson's. He has an agreeable, sensible wife but he is so vile a fellow that he treats her in the most barbarous manner imaginable, coming home drunk, swearing he will murder her, forcing her to run away to avoid him, &c.

When we came home I grew very uneasy because of the freedom and familiarity which Cousin Joseph was permitted to use with her and I could not. However he was not allowed to be very free neither. But he resolved to endeavour to kiss her by main force and he did it after some striving. She seemed a little ruffled, but I think not much displeased. But sister took it into her head to be angry at this and called Joseph rude and said he knew nothing at all of the world for conversation and knowledge, only lay at Hamlin's and among the parsons and did not know how to behave in company of genteel, well-bred persons. This nettled him a little and he could not help saying some harsh things of her and talking to her a little warmly by telling her she knew

[1] The residence of the Earl of Salisbury.

nothing of good breeding or the world, one that had been pent up all her life in the country [1] and removed from thence into Cheapside.

Friday, September 21. Rose at 8. Mr. Birch came with some greyhounds to hunt with us. We were very unwilling to leave the ladies for such dull sport. However, we went out and stayed two hours beating the ground to find a hare, without any success. I think this is the dullest sport that can be. We were both tired and longing to get loose and we were I believe both jealous of one another lest either of us should give the other the slip and go to Mrs. Marshall.

I was extremely faint and out of order that I could scarce move my limbs without shaking. I attribute it to my want of appetite to victuals and the very little that I have eat since I came from London, for indeed I have not eat one hearty meal since. It is all owing to Mrs. Marshall's neglect of me.

Saturday, September 22. The time now draws nigh when I had resolved to go from the Hay and leave Mrs. Marshall, chiefly because I find myself disagreeable to her and could [not] bear to live continually under the sense of it. However, sister now pressed me stay very much. My sister put it to the vote of the company whether I should go or stay and they all said stay, excepting Mrs. Marshall who would say nothing at all. I took this as a plain indication that she did not like my company, especially when she afterwards said why could not we both stay. Cousin Joseph was himself very unwilling to go but could not help it, so at 2 o'clock, after I had shown as I thought sufficiently to Mrs. Marshall that she was the cause of my going but especially the chief reason that inclined me to stay, we went away in the midst of a great shower of rain.

Came to Hackney mighty dull and melancholy. I heard my brother Richard has been very bad of the colic and continues something ill. It grieves me to find that upon the mention of his illness my mind immediately flew to the thought of his death and the advantageous circumstances it would put me into. I hope this is no crime in me, for it is entirely involuntary and I endeavoured to check myself in it.

[1] At Childwick, Herts.

Monday, September 24. At 4 Smith and I went to London and took Cousin Joseph Billio by the way. I was pretty merry upon the road and talked a little wittily to them. The thoughts of Mrs. Marshall which had possessed my mind in the night and great part of the day now began to wear off. Cousin told me he had been doing nothing but thinking of her. It had cast a perfect gloom over his countenance and made him taken notice of by the family as strangely dull and grave.

We went together to Tom's Coffee-House, where I found myself so very heavy that I thought some hot punch might be of service and we drank 1*s*. 6*d*. of it. We talked of little else but her. He extolled her as the finest woman and the best that ever he saw. He was perfectly ravished with the thoughts of her. The talking in this manner encouraged very much my passion and uneasiness and I told cousin that I had suffered a great deal upon her account and could not bear the mention of her without the greatest emotion. He told me he longed to see me, it was a mighty ease to his mind and alleviated his sorrow to talk her over and give a vent to the dullness of his mind. That he could do this to nobody but me and therefore was mighty glad to meet with me that he might be able to say whatever his heart dictated. At last we talked of this love of ours as a very foolish vain thing that proceeded from an impotency of mind and ought not to be encouraged. By talking in this manner with him my passion subsided by degrees, my thoughts grew more free and disengaged and a cheerfulness run through me. If I could often talk with Cousin Joseph in this manner concerning Mrs. Marshall it would be a mighty ease to me.

Went to brother's. Father being there told me that one Mr. Short had been at his shop to inquire for me and that lodged at the Saracen's Head in Friday Street. I went there and he soon came in. We talked over the concerns of our former friends. Upon the subject of matrimony I told him a dream of mine which I had a good while ago, and I don't know that I have writ it down. It is that one night I dreamt I was married to a young lady, bedded her, and the next morning found myself in the greatest hurry and confusion of mind in the world, longing to be unmarried, in which trouble I awaked. I fell asleep again and dreamt I was married to another young lady and enjoyed her and then repented again with the same or greater trouble and concern of mind and regretted exceedingly to find it was only a dream. The impressions that these marriages made upon me were so strong and great that they still leave behind them a strong sense of them. I think I never felt greater trouble and perplexity, greater uneasiness and remorse when awake than I did upon these occasions. Came home at 10.

Tuesday, September 25. Rose past 6. Went to Islington. Drank the waters there. Five robbers were hanged last Friday and this morning the speech of Bean, one of them, was in the *Flying Post* with remarks upon it. Dr. Lee told me that he was assured that the day before his execution there came an old woman to him in Newgate. When she was going away Bean bid her be sure to send him clean linen, for he was resolved to die in clean linen and also bid her take care to send him his speech time enough. And this speech of his was given him in the cart upon Fleet Bridge as is supposed because a man stepped up to the cart and gave him a paper. The speech is plainly calculated for nothing else but to incense the people against the Government and is filled with the most evident falsehood in the world. It shows plainly that the present set of Jacobites have no manner of regard to the salvation or lives of others that can thus make a fool of a dying man.[1] A rogue cannot be hanged but he must become a saint upon the gibbet.

In the afternoon went to father's for some money to buy cloth for a winter coat. Stayed there a long time before I could have an opportunity of speaking to him, there was such a crowd of customers. Among the rest there were three young ladies. I had a mind to speak to them and talk a little merrily with them, but I had not courage enough. At length father gave me 5 guineas.

Went to the Fountain with Cousin Joseph Billio. There were Mr. Short, Mr. Burroughs and several others. The conversation was taken up chiefly between themselves. It ran upon astrologers, the conjurers that pretend to tell fortunes, of which Mr. Burroughs gave us an account of an old woman to whom he and

---

[1] In a letter to his father on 28 September, Ryder said, 'Howell the parson in Newgate is thought to be the common speech maker to the party'. This was Laurence Howell, who died in Newgate in 1720. He had written the speech which Paul the clergyman read at his execution; cf. p. 277.

another went on purpose to entertain themselves with her humour. He carried on the jest admirably well with her and made her give him the whole history of his life by seeming to believe all she said, though she did not tell one word of truth or any one circumstance that had the least affinity to his life, for she told him he had been at sea and a merchant, met with losses there, &c., but he observed the method she took to amuse her customers. At first she, as soon as he entered the room, put herself into a most majestic woman and looked like one exalted in raptures and in a kind of a prophetic voice that puts the poor people into a consternation and makes them sooner ready to make discoveries of themselves. But she had not only this trade of prophesying but she told him she had a great many ladies and quality that came constantly to her and upon occasion she could make him as happy as ever a duke or nobleman in the kingdom.

Brother William told me he was yesterday to see his mistress after a week's absence. She was surprised at his long absence but received him more favourably than before and gave him some intimation that she expected him to write to her, for she had a mind to see a man in all lights and how he can do everything. He therefore desired me to write for him, which I promised.

Wednesday, September 26. Signior Castilio came to see me to thank me for a scholar. I recommended to him Mr. Porter. I took it into my head to have him talk Italian to me. At first I could not speak scarce a word but before he went away I was so much improved that I hemmed out almost anything and I was in hopes by his conversation I might in time be able to talk it pretty well.

Read some little law. After dinner went to father's to see brother William who wanted to speak to me about his mistress and writing to her as I believe. When I came there father told me grandmother was extremely ill and he was in doubt whether she could live so long as the end of the week, and he would have me go to Hackney and be with her. He was mightily concerned about her will and afraid lest she should have altered it.

Thursday, September 27. After dinner read some of the *History of Queen Zarah*.[1] It is designed as a satire upon the Duchess of

[1] *The Secret History of Queen Zarah and the Zarazians,* 1705, &c. It is attributed to Mrs. De la Rivière Manley.

Marlborough chiefly, whose character is painted as a vast politician, very ambitious, lustful and revengeful.

At night found myself very indolent and inactive. I fell into a kind of a dozing between sleeping and waking that put me when I awaked into a very heavy sickish state. However, after some time I recovered myself and read some of *Telemachus* in Italian.

Friday, September 28. Rose at 6. Went to the waters. Dr. Lee told me that King George was now upon a treaty with France.[1] There indeed seems some difficulty if the King enters into an alliance with France how to reconcile the several jarring interests of Germany and Spain, with whom he has already alliances, but it will show a great deal of dexterity and authority in Europe if he is able to accomplish that. The Prince was last Monday at Tunbridge Wells where he dispensed a great deal of money among the several persons and places that belong to it, as the parson, the poor, the coffee-houses, the water-dippers, the music, &c.

Dined at brother's. Brother William came there to go with brother to the Hay. He desired me to write a letter for him to send out of the country to his mistress. I was pretty much at a loss what to say, not knowing the several circumstances of their courtship and her manner of treating him. However, he pressed me so to it that I sat down to write and after some time wrote a short letter for him. It was pretty much in the hyperbolic strains of lovers to their mistresses, but not so much as some are. There were some good thoughts in it.

Saturday, September 29. Read *Telemachus* in Italian. While I was reading it Mr. Mayo came in. I was not ill-pleased that he found me reading Italian. Was pretty merry with him and pleasant.

Cousin Joseph Billio came to see me. When he was going we soon fell upon Mrs. Marshall as that which was the most present to our thoughts of any subject whatsoever, but we took a fancy to talk in Latin together. We were both pretty much

---

[1] Since July the King had been in Hanover with Bernstorff and Stanhope. The visit was largely concerned with the negotiations which were consummated in the triple alliance between Great Britain, France and the United Provinces, concluded on 4 January 1717.

at a loss to express our thoughts. However, we continued the conversation a good while in that language.

Sunday, September 30. After dinner we were surprised with a call upstairs. My grandmother was just seized by death. We came up and found her gasping for breath in her chair. We could do nothing but look on and in about seven or eight minutes' time she died. I never saw any one die before. It did not shock me near so much as I should have expected. Indeed she died as one on whom Nature had entirely finished her work, the fabric of the body seemed to fall by its own natural weight, and life to depart as a lamp goes out for want of oil. I was a little at a loss how to behave upon this occasion, but I did not make any great show of sorrow, but rather bore it with a kind of manly strength and firmness. I said but little, not knowing what to say that was proper.

My mother fell into a strange kind of fit of crying and taking on that put us more into concern and confusion than the death of my grandmother. I cannot say I thought it was all feigned in my mother, but, I don't know how, I believe the death of my grandmother entered into her thoughts and mind as a thing of great moment and importance and what required a great deal of concern. Indeed she seemed all the afternoon to put on a sighing, sobbing air, as a thing becoming and proper, much as I guess in the same manner as when she groans and looks dismal at the reading a good book or hearing an affectionate prayer.

My father immediately sent to Uncle Marshall's to let them know she was dead and my mother desired Mr. Mayo would come to see her after sermon.

Monday, October 1. Rose at past 7. Did very little. Mr. Reynolds [1] came to inquire about the funeral. My father was very much at a loss how to manage with him. He determined upon nothing concerning the funeral, but put it off till the afternoon.

At noon Uncle Marshall came and we then opened the will and read it. It was the same which I wrote for my grandmother almost three years ago. Mother is left sole executrix and £400

[1] Possibly Samuel Reynolds of St. Dunstan's in the West, who married Ann Parker at Hackney in 1709.

is given to uncle's family and £450 to ours. My uncle expressed a surprise that he was not left joint executor with mother and seemed to think it hard that her estate was not equally divided. However, it passed off very well, but my father very imprudently, as he is apt to do, began to show the reasonableness of it by saying that the overplus would be very little more than she in reality owed him upon the account of coals which she had used of his without paying for them.

Uncle Marshall stayed with us till past 4 and then Mr. Mayo and Mr. Smith came in and stayed about an hour, and after that father sent for Mr. Reynolds again to talk about the funeral expenses and so he began to calculate the expense and object against little trifling articles and he went away again without any determination except just of the coffin and shroud.

Tuesday, October 2. Went to father's. He gave me £5 to buy mourning. After dinner came into the City; bought some black cloth, 5¼ yards at 18s. per yard.

Went to North's; found father there and Mr. West who it seems were met in order to talk about their partnership, and father asked me to go along with them. Mr. West seemed not to like Mr. Bailey as a man not so fit nor so diligent and careful in business as he should be, but then the question was how brother should come in partner. Mr. West proposed that he should come in for only fifth part and he and father for two-fifths apiece. When they had talked some time I told Mr. West I thought it would be hard that my brother should come in upon such disadvantageous terms. However, the matter ended here in order to be thought over again. If brother should marry it would be but a little matter to maintain a family with a fifth part of the business, supposing my father and Mr. West to take every week each £4 out and him only £2.

Wednesday, October 3. Went to Mr. Fernley and paid him 2 guineas, all that I owed him upon the account of dancing. Father committed to me the charge of writing to Gresley of grandmother's death and some other business.

Thursday, October 4. Rose at 7. Brother William came to me for me to go to father's. He told me he had been with his mistress last night. She talked very freely with him and told him that she wondered his father would not give him more than a £1,000. It gave me a great deal of concern to think of their marriage, for I don't know how my father will be able to give him down a £1,000, for he is very much at a loss for money. I perceive brother himself is not so very warm upon the matter himself, and if they are married it will be but, as I believe, entered into on both sides with more indifference than I think the affair of matrimony ought to be. She herself seems to have nothing else in view but a bettering her circumstances and gaining a husband of a good fortune.

Cousin Joseph Billio came to see me. I talked with him a little about her till I was very sensibly touched with the thoughts of her, but mother coming in we talked about death and the difficulty of conceiving ourselves in another world.

At past 7 Aunt Billio and Aunt Lomax came from the Hay. Mentioning Mrs. Marshall, Aunt Billio said she was very much disappointed in her; she thought her face too large for a beauty and that she was extremely high and in a manner proud, talking very big about dress and furniture.

Friday, October 5. Rose at 7. Read in Quintilian concerning the education of children in private or public schools. This chapter, viz. the 3rd *De Institutione Oratoria*, is writ with an admirable spirit and true solid judgement.

Father came at 12. Went with him to Mr. Reynolds and by my solicitation he settled the whole matter of the funeral in a genteel manner.

Went to brother's at 8 o'clock. Found Dr. Cox [1] with him and he in a very weak condition in a great chair. My father was very much concerned. His fever was much worse than in the morning and I asked Cousin Watkins what he thought of him and he said he thought him very ill. I was concerned with myself to find that upon this I felt a little kind of pleasure rising in my breast at the thought of my gaining his estate by his death. But it is entirely involuntary and I am angry with myself I should have such risings in my mind.

Mr. Rusheer in the coffee-house told me that a friend of his was lately come from Hanover. He says the young Prince

[1] Daniel Cox, M.D.; died in 1730, aged 90.

Frederick[1] talks very much with the English gentlemen there and will ask them questions about the state of affairs in England and the Tories, which are looked upon in that country by the ordinary sort of people as a strange kind of fretful creatures as bad as wild beasts and by the best quality as a very vile set of people that are irreconcilably set against the King and the royal family.

Saturday, October 6. Brother is something better than he was, but yet not out of danger. My father would have him have another doctor, but it is a difficult matter to mention it to him, he is so apt to fancy himself very bad. However I mentioned it, but he was extremely averse to it.

I sat with sister all the evening till 11 o'clock and talked about Mrs. Marshall. She owned that she has not a very free genteel behaviour, is a little stiff in her manner, and seldom says anything in mixed company. She is more dull than I am. She has conceived strange notions of me, that I hate all mirth, never take any of the diversions of the playhouses, public places or assemblies. Sister told me that she has had several matches offered her since she came from Bath and after, since she came from the Hay, but has rejected them all, though very considerable fortunes, most of them tradesmen that have great business and good estates. Sister showed me a copy of verses that were made upon her. They are a complaint of her cruelty. I read them and thought there was nothing at all extraordinary in them but yet Mrs. Marshall seems mightily pleased with them, for she has got them by heart and can repeat them word for word. This made me fancy I might raise my character with her if I could furnish out a copy of verses, which I thought I could at least equal to those. And I told sister I did not know but I might attempt to make one if she would give them her, which she promised she would.

Came home. In the way I thought of making some verses and made several and when I came home increased the number to about twenty. To bed at 1.

Sunday, October 7. Rose at 8. Set about making more verses in order to show them Mrs. Marshall. I find I have no

[1] The Prince of Wales's son who had remained in Hanover to be educated. He was created Prince of Wales in 1729.

genius for poetry. Thoughts don't flow in easily and I am very long in making the rhyme. But I have so much of the poetic genius as to know what poetic fire and rapture is. I find sometimes myself carried a little away by a little poetic fit in which I find harmonious numbers jingle in my head and my thoughts almost naturally run into something like verses. But these fits hold but a very little while. A little thought or study or endeavour to form and polish my lines quite puts an end to it and then it is extremely difficult to recall it.

Went to brother's. Father and mother and Aunt Lomax were come from Hackney this morning to see him. They thought him better than last night but Cousin Watkins afterwards said he did not think him a whit better, that the fever was pretty much upon his spirits and he thought it proper to have another physician.

Father took an opportunity when Mrs. Marshall was mentioned to say that he had observed her very narrowly last night and he thought her a very clumsy woman, her face broad and flat, her hands thick and big and her voice very rough and masculine and he was sure she had not much wit. This did not make much impression upon me and I did not answer a word.

Monday, October 8. Awaked in the night, was restless and my head ached. I found myself extremely uneasy, tumbling from one side of the bed to the other.

In the morning awaked and found myself much better. Did nothing all the morning but make verses in order to show them to Mrs. Marshall.

After dinner went to brother's. He had Dr. West [1] come to him. His case is yet doubtful, not past danger nor the fears very great. Found my father at brother's. He was extremely concerned and troubled. It grieves to see him so troubled. I wish it does not break his heart if my brother should die.

My father and I came to Hackney alone in the coach, and upon the road he talked to me very gravely about my brother and his affairs. But my father chiefly talked to me about his own affairs, said he had entangled his affairs very much. He repented he had ever laid out his money in houses,[2] which has not only

[1] Possibly Thomas West, M.D. (1668-1738), of Red Lion Square.
[2] In Leadenhall Street and Hackney.

cost him a great deal of time and pains and anxiety but also been a great loss to him. He took an opportunity to advise me about my management of myself in the world, said he observed a very generous temper in me that might lead me into many inconveniences and therefore warned me not to be too good-humoured. My father told me he had done his estate prejudice by too hasty counsels and management; he had been apt to do things without due consideration, which he thought was my temper pretty much and advised against it.

Tuesday, October 9. My grandmother being to be buried at night[1] we were in some little hurry and confusion about it. However, it was managed pretty well and at 3 o'clock we set out in the coaches. I went in the coach with Cousin Marshall. We had some discourse about the Bill that was brought into the House of Commons the last session and carried in that House for the regulating vestries. He says that that Bill was designed chiefly against the charity schools which it would very much have discouraged if not totally stopped. My grandmother was buried at Marylebone in the vault there.

Wednesday, October 10. Made verses all the morning till Mr. Castilio came to visit me at before 10 o'clock. I conversed with him all the while in Italian, though I made but sad work of that language.

Went to sister's, when I showed her my verses. She seemed to like them very well and desired a copy of them. Sat up till past 3 a-mending of them but could not finish them.

Yesterday after the funeral of grandmother, Cousin Marshall in the coach speaking of Aunt Lomax said she looked very ill and was but of a short life, could not live above a year and half at most. She had a complication of illnesses, the scurvy and dropsy.

Thursday, October 11. Continued mending and polishing my verses all the morning. Went to sister's, gave them her. After dinner Cousin Joseph Billio came. We talked about Mrs. Marshall.

When Cousin Joseph talked of conquering his passion, which

---

[1] Cf. *Hackney Burial Register* for 1716: 'Mrs. Frances Stevenson, widow, 9 October'.

he hoped he should do in a month's time if he did not see her, it gave me a very sensible pleasure because he would not then be my rival. I thought of showing him the verses I had made concerning her, but I thought it would only make him the more envious and jealous if they were good and, if not, it would be the better for my own reputation not to show them.

Thought when I was alone about death, finding myself a little oppressed about my lungs. I fancied I might be in a consumption. I was almost pleased with the prospect of it. At least nothing shocking appeared in it and I thought if I was plainly in a dying condition I could with a great deal of calmness and serenity resign up my life. The greatest sorrow to me would be the grief that it would give my father who I know is extremely fond of me, but as for myself I did not then observe anything in the present world very desirable.

Friday, October 12. Came to London in the coach with Mrs. Whittaker, a granddaughter of Mrs. Wallis. She is mighty pretty and something very sweet in her countenance. There was an old woman in the coach who talked very much, gave advice about matrimony, how to behave in that state and the necessity of mutual forbearance between man and wife. She talked really very well upon that subject. She made us pretty merry and gave me an opportunity of talking much more than I should have done else.

Went to brother's. From thence to father's about some rings for Mr. Smith and Mr. Mayo and he ordered to bespeak them and one for myself of Major Pitts,[1] which I did. I was ashamed that my father should so many times order rings, as he has now no less than four several times, but my father has a very unhappy method of managing business.

After dinner went to father again about the receiving his rents in Leadenhall Street. Went to my father's tenants. They all put me off till next week.

Went to brother's. Mrs. Lee and Mr. Utber[2] came in there. He is a pretty sort of a man, talks very well and pleasantly. She now makes no scruple of owning she is to be married to him and

---

[1] Captain Pitts, goldsmith, next door to the Cross Keys Tavern, Holborn.
[2] Jeffery Utber (or Uther), goldsmith, at sign of the Golden Ring, Fenchurch Street, bankrupt 1719.

they treat one another upon these terms. She was so complaisant to me as to tell me she thought me a very pretty gentleman and very genteel. This is some consolation to me under the contempt Mrs. Marshall has of me, that other women like me.

Came home at 9. Read *Telemachus*. I am perfectly charmed with that author. There is so much of nature and judgement shown in it that I think I cannot read it over too often.

Saturday, October 13. Read law till 10, when Major Pitts came to bring me the rings I bespoke yesterday. He breakfasted with me and told me of his having been formerly a juryman in a great many very considerable trials and resisting the insinuations of bribery.

Sent a ring to Mr. Smith by Mr. Page the undertaker. Sent by John to Mr. Mayo and Mr. Dolins a ring, gloves and hatband.

Read some *Spectators* at night. Have resolved to read them over with very great care and attention in order to observe the peculiar thoughts upon gallant subjects such as are proper to entertain the ladies with.

Sunday, October 14. Rose at past 7. Read a sermon of Tillotson's about the difficulty of religion. It made me reflect upon the difference that there is between young and old persons upon that account. I observe in myself, and it seems to be so in other young persons, that I have more delicate and tender sentiments of virtue, gratitude, generosity than appears in elder persons. A long practicedness in the world seems very much to have wore off that nice sense of virtue that makes young persons startle at the appearance of dishonesty, dishonour, or ingratitude. From this observation I think it very naturally follows that religion ought to be then set about while the impulses of nature are strong towards virtue and goodness.

After sermon in the afternoon went into the vestry where my father happened to be talking about the manner of assessing estates for the land tax and the very unequal assessments that are made, some persons' estates not being taxed near so high as others, and this without the least foundation in reason, but mere favour, there being no justice to be had in these cases. I could not help making this reflection, that virtue and justice is regarded only according to the custom and is little else in most people's esteem, but as it is received; so that some kinds of doing justice, if not received by custom, is not regarded. For in this case of assessments by what they talked there was no manner of equality regarded in that. The authority of a considerable man shall be sufficient to fix or alter any assessment or lower his taxes and raise those of other people. That the commissioners in these cases seem to have very little regard to equality of the distribution as the law expects and designs them for.

Monday, October 15. Rose at 7. Took some cream of tartar, having found myself sickish yesterday and the night before.

Went to London in the coach. Aunt Billio had spoke to me about making interest for Cousin Billio's being chose at Mr. Freke's. She desired me to mention it either to Dr. Avery or Mr. Marshall's family. I promised her I would and indeed it pleased to think that I might be able to do my cousin any service.

Received a letter from Mr. Powell with a copy of verses in them about the ladies at Bath from an officer there. When I had read them over they seemed to me so indifferent that I thought I might venture to let him see the verses I had made in regard to Mrs. Marshall.

Tuesday, October 16. Rose at 8. Read law all the morning. My mind would every now and then make a sally to Mrs. Marshall and interrupt my reading.

I went to father's tenants in Leadenhall Street. I was put off by two of them and was paid by the third. I don't like it to be thus put off from time to time.

Dined at the tavern with Cousin Joseph Billio. Our conversation turned very much upon Mrs. Marshall. He told me that she had a notion of me as one that did not at all value women. I wonder very much she should have so wrong a notion of me and has not yet been able to discover my extreme love for her. At last, talking pretty vehemently about Mrs. Marshall I was perfectly melted with the thoughts of her. She quite overcame my soul and introduced a softness and tenderness in it that made me ready to dissolve almost in love and passion for her. It almost drew tears into my eyes. My cousin I believe perceived it and endeavoured to divert by mentioning what might appear disagreeable in Mrs. Marshall. Among other things I told him I have had very serious thoughts of death upon occasions relating to her. I am capable of conceiving in perfection that state of mind which persons are in when they make away with themselves. A very small degree more of the same temper in which I have been in at Bath would have made me imitate their examples.

Went to brother's with Cousin Joseph. Mrs. Deison came in. I was extremely merry and pleasant with her and sister. Our conversation turned chiefly upon matrimony and children. I rallied sister upon her big belly and talked in a very humorous strain.

Went to John's Coffee-House. There was one Mr. Doliff lately come over from France. He says the Regent is extremely hated among the generality of people and spoke ill of. They have all a notion that he has a design upon the life of the young King, whom they are prodigiously fond of. He says the Regent gives himself up very much to debauchery, wine and women, and that the court of France is at present in a very debauched condition. There are scarce any ladies at court but what have openly their gallants and it is looked upon as very unfashionable and ungenteel for their husbands to take notice of it or to think much that they can be contented with them alone. It is confidently reported there that the Regent himself ravished Madame Rochefoucauld,[1] the wife of the captain of the Duchess of Berry's guard and that the Duchess of Berry[2] herself assisted him in it by inviting her to take a game at cards with her and then throwing her upon the bed and holding her for the Regent to lie with her.

Went to the playhouse. Stayed almost an Act in the side-box. I believe it would have a very good effect upon me to learn me a good manner of speaking to go there often.

Wednesday, October 17. Rose at 8. Read law all the morning. After dinner went to brother's. From thence to Leadenhall Street for rents of the houses there, but found none of them at

---

[1] Wife of François, duc de la Rochefoucauld (1663–1728), Master of the Wardrobe.

[2] Marie-Louise-Elizabeth, duchesse de Berry, eldest daughter of the Regent. The debauchery of her father and herself was notorious.

home. Gave sister the verses Mr. Powell sent me and desired her to send mine with them to Mrs. Marshall to-morrow.

Thursday, October 18. I had but a restless night, but just before it was light I thought I heard somebody come into my room and open the curtains and put their hand on my bolster to feel for my breeches. I did not in the least doubt but that it was a rogue come to rob, and I lay extremely still, pretty much frightened. He still kept feeling for my breeches. I thought he felt several times but my breeches being over my head he could not find. In this condition I lay very still for a good while hoping that he would go away and then I would get up and pursue them. While I was thinking this, methought the person went away and I immediately heard my watch beat. This made me wonder that he should not find it and I began to think that it was only a dream, and I opened the curtains and looked about. Could see nor hear anything, nor observe anything out of order. This was the strangest dream or rather vision I ever had. I attribute it to my eating pretty heartily last night of a turkey and drinking.

As soon as I was thoroughly awake I thought of writing some more verses upon Mrs. Marshall and indeed made some upon her curling locks. Intended to set about law, but my mind so run upon the verses I was making that I found it a difficult matter to divert these thoughts.

Went to Hackney in the coach with Mr. Moreland. He entertained with some of his notions, particularly about the folly and unreasonableness of practising the Roman virtue, Caesar and Augustus, Cato, &c., who were only so many great highwaymen.

Friday, October 19. Rose at 7. Took some cream of tartar before I rose. Read some *Spectators* now and then and thought about making verses upon Mrs. Marshall's curling locks. Did not make any more. Played upon my viol; pleased myself very much.

Went to Cousin Joseph. We talked a good while about Mrs. Marshall. He thinks of her night and day. She possesses all his thoughts and enters into his very study. I said Mrs. Marshall had nothing at all of that genteel becoming air, nothing of a good address and manner of appearing in company. This gave me a great deal of ease with respect to her and I could bear to think of her with indifference. I thought, why should I be so fond of a woman who is so much excelled by others and who wants what is so necessary an accomplishment in a fine lady, a genteel behaviour and admirable address. I mentioned Mrs. Oileman as one much preferable to her in these respects. What she has that is charming consists only in her beauty and good humour.

Went to brother's. Sister told me all of sudden Mrs. Marshall was going to be married. This struck me with a strange surprise and astonishment, though I had but just before been thinking I could bear the loss of her with indifference. But this gave me such a surprising turn to my spirits, filled me with anxiety and threw me into a perfect trembling and amazement, that I was all in a flutter and my spirits in a hurry. But it was only a jest of my sister's.

Mr. Boyd came in and I took an opportunity of talking to him a little in a jesting manner by asking him whether he had solved a case of conscience that he put to me the other day about going to dine with Mr. Behmen because he was a debauched kind of a man. But he took it very ill of me and told me he would have me to do [know?] that he knew more of these things than I and was a man of more consideration and figure than I thought him to be.[1]

Brother William came in and told us he had been with his mistress last night and they fell out and are now entirely parted and all his courtship at an end. She told him that he has appeared of late too indifferent to become a husband. That she believes his friends were against it and therefore desired to have no more to do with him upon these terms. This produced some discourse and it at last grew to such a height that they reflected upon one another's conduct and management in pretty hot terms. This dispute ran so high that he was afraid they could not be reconciled again. He said he believed there never was such a courtship in the world before as his has been. She told him the first time she rejected him, with a kind of disdain, she did it only to try him. And also told him that if she appointed a gentleman that came to court her any particular day for him to come to see her, she would tell him the day wherein she was absent to try him and show her superiority. I think this is a very happy accident for brother, that

[1] He was a parson.

he has by this an opportunity of getting off from a match which seems to promise so little peace and happiness to him.

Saturday, October 20. Went to Hackney at 5, nothing extraordinary. Read some *Spectators*, endeavoured to observe the connexion and see how the several thoughts naturally and easily arise in the mind, one after another. I observed that there is not that scrupulous exactness in the manner of connexion and methodizing thought in these papers as I am apt to desire and expect in what I write myself. It is sufficient if it have a remote agreement to it and be upon the same subject. Took some cream of tartar.

Sunday, October 21. Mr. Smith preached both morning and afternoon upon repentance and made two very good discourses. When he came to answer the excuses and objections that sinners are apt to make against repentance, I could [not] help looking into my own mind. My great difficulty as to repentance lies here, that I cannot bring myself to that strong aversion to sin, detestation of it which is necessary in order to repent from good principle. It does not seem to be in my power to make me thus affected. I can conceive how I may indeed be able to resist temptation, but how to do this from such a love to holiness and strong hatred of sin I cannot tell. The best method I can conceive of in order to bring myself to this temper with regard to sin is to possess my mind as fully as possible with the view of God.

Monday, October 22. Rode out with Cousin Joseph Billio. My heart was full of the thought of passing by Mrs. Marshall's house at Highgate. Our conversation turned chiefly upon her. We stayed at an inn there.
Would have gone to London but not finding a coach went to Aunt Bickley's. Mr. Papillon[1] furnished us with some discourse. His strange humorous manner of living was the subject of discourse for us. It is thought his wife's death is very much owing

---

[1] Mr. Samuel Papillon, vestryman of Hackney in 1716; his wife Fidacia died on 10 October 1716. His eccentricity seems to have been hereditary. Thomas Papillon's will (proved 1702) contains the item: 'I do give and bequeath . . . a Black person, commonly called Brown, whom I take to be in the nature of my goods and Chattles'.

to that confined stifling kind of life which she was obliged to live with him. He would scarce admit of any visitants lest by opening the doors often they should let in too much air and endanger his catching cold. This made him always keep fire in the parlour, stop up every little hole and not suffer the least breath of fresh air to enter the room. He lay in bed with about seven blankets over him. If he took her out in the coach for an airing a little he would not suffer her to speak a word to him all the way till he came to such a place, lest by her speaking she should excite him to speak too and so let in bad air into his lungs. He would never sit down in anybody's house but his own lest it should not be so well aired as it should be. He himself always narrowly observed the holland of which his shirts was made, and would pick out those parts of the same piece that were thicker than the rest to make them of and would weigh his new shirts when they were made to take care that they be exactly of the same weight with the old ones, otherwise he would not wear them. And in this strange manner does he bring up his children, not suffering them to do anything or be anywhere where the least cold might come to them.

Tuesday, October 23. Rode out as far as Edmonton by myself. I did it upon the account of my health and very much because I thought it might have a good effect upon my breath to prevent it stinking as I am almost sure it does now. As I was alone I had a mind to set myself to think upon some particular subject, but could not set my mind to it because of the motion of the horse and the almost necessary diversions that one meets with upon the road from the variety of objects that present themselves.

Came home at 12. Went to London after dinner in the coach with a servant-maid of Mr. Brookbanks.[1] She soon began to complain of her mistress and her manner of living, that they had no company at all, lived in a kind of nunnery. She said she did not know whether she might venture to go into any place in the house but where she was expressly sent. I began to think that it was not proper for me to give attention to or encourage servants talking of their masters and therefore would not encourage it.

[1] Joseph Brooksbank, an eminent merchant of Hackney. Died in 1726. Cf. note, p. 259.

Came to London at 5. Found Mrs. Marshall and her sister Deison at brother's and Joseph Billio. It was a mighty consolation to me to find Joseph as dull and heavy as I used to be myself and scarce speak a word. I was myself in a pretty good humour for conversation and I believe one cause of it was the finding Joseph in the contrary extreme.

Brother William came in. We talked about his affair with Mrs. Walker. She appears to me to be very much of a coquette, to have a good knack at talking, but wants prudence, but also she seems to have nothing at heart but a man with a good fortune and determined to make the best of her market. I proposed Mrs. Gifford to brother as a very agreeable, good-humoured woman: he seemed to be pleased. I promised to go to-morrow and see her father's will.

Wednesday, October 24. Rose at 7. Read a little law. Went to Mr. Leeds. Went to Westminster with Mr. Samson and Horseman. Came home with Mr. Wollaston with whom dined and another gentleman. I made a pretty tolerable figure among them in conversation. It pleased me very much and flattered my vanity that Mr. Wollaston after dinner invited me to his chambers and, when I could not go then, told me he should be glad if I would at any time come and see him, which I promised.

Went to Doctors' Commons to see Mr. Gifford's and Mr. Anthony's [1] wills but it cannot be known by his will because they gave their cyphers in their personal estate without any sum in certain, only Mr. Gifford has disposed of some annuities of £10 per annum among his children.

Thursday, October 25. Went to Mr. Horseman's chambers in Lincoln's Inn till 1. After dinner went home and dressed myself and went to sister's. Found Mrs. Marshall there, much to my surprise. I, when I opened the parlour door, made a little pass as I usually do to look about me and Mrs. Marshall told me she believed I took her for a ghost. I answered, 'No, Madam, I never saw better flesh and blood in all my life.' I was pretty tolerably merry with her and she seemed better pleased with me

[1] Edward Anthony of Hackney and freeman of London; will proved 31 March 1716. His daughter Apphia married Mr. Opie; he left a great estate, Newcome says.

than usual and I got a kiss when she went away because she was going to Highgate.

Met with a book in Moorfields concerning the art of pleasing in conversation in French [1] and found it wrote well with a good many very just and polite reflections with regard to conversation.

Came to Hackney on foot. Overtook Cousin Joseph Billio in Hackney. We soon talked about Mrs. Marshall. He was very much cast down about her and tells me has not had scarce a quiet thought since last Tuesday when he saw her. I wanted mightily an opportunity of introducing the verses I sent to Mrs. Marshall but could not prevail upon myself to tell him of them.

Friday, October 26. Rose at 7. Rid out on horseback as far as Enfield and back again by little past 12. I thought of the verses I made upon her curling locks and her neck and a new thought came into my head upon that subject. It was to charge the lappets, tippets and hoods that should have the honour to cover her neck and become the guardians of those locks to take care to secure them against all rough winds and everything that might discompose or ruffle them.

Cousin and Aunt Billio dined with us. I was pretty merry and pleasant with Aunt Lomax in a little of the luscious strain which she loves dearly. Anything that has some remote hint towards bawdy is what she delights in. At length the discourse happened to turn upon Mrs. Marshall, which my Aunt Lomax brought in. All the company, Cousin Robert Billio himself, said there was nothing at all extraordinary in her, she was rather clumsy than gentle and wanted address and politeness. I only vindicated her and I did it in a style of raillery. Aunt Lomax talks against her with a peculiar kind of dislike, but I perceive the great matter that offends her is her being the daughter of a tailor as was and another thing is that she has a daughter herself which she thinks extremely handsome.

Cousin Billio took into his hand Mr. Henry's Life,[2] which was the occasion of a little conversation that he and I had upon the folly of writing lives in such a manner as that is, by exposing all

---

[1] P. d'Ortique de Vaumorière : *L'Art de plaire dans la Conversation*, 1690, &c. This work is mentioned by Swift in the introduction to his *Polite Conversations*.

[2] W. Tonge, *An Account of the Life and Death of the late Reverend Mr. Matthew Henry*, 1716.

the little trifling transactions and private affairs of a man's life. It did a great deal of injury to his character.

Saturday, October 27. Aunt Lomax told me that my sister's maid, Mrs. Jane, was discovered this week to be with child and was examined by brother and sister about [it]. She was very unwilling at first to make any confession about it, but at last by threatenings was brought to give them satisfaction about it. We suppose that she is married to Mr. William his prentice.

Sunday, October 28. Went with Cousin Joseph Billio to hear Mr. Biscoe [1] at Newington Green. He is but a very dull preacher and looks exceeding silly in the pulpit.

Joseph says he is now in a fair way of getting over the uneasiness he has been under upon Mrs. Marshall's account. He has affected himself with the views of another world and touched his mind so sensibly with those things that it is but turning his thoughts at any time towards God and death and eternity and this is enough to conquer every irregular desire and cool and abate his affections to and anxieties about any temporal felicity. As we came home I brought myself to tell him of the verses I sent to Mrs. Marshall, but I did it in a very hesitating and trembling manner, especially when I repeated some of them to him. He seemed pretty well pleased with those which I repeated to him and wanted to hear the rest.

Monday, October 29. Rode out this morning from 9 o'clock with Cousin Joseph till past 1. Our conversation turned chiefly upon Mrs. Marshall. We could not help going through Highgate to see her house, but we did not see herself or any of the family. We had a pleasant ride as far as Edmonton and so across the country to Highgate.

Came to town in the afternoon at 5 o'clock. It was my Lord Mayor's Day. Found Mrs. Lee as was and her husband at brother's. She is married to one Utber, a goldsmith, a pretty agreeable man. She has as sister tells me £2,000 fortune, £700 of which her two uncles gave her. We had a good deal of raillery upon the subject of matrimony and her new marriage.

---

[1] Richard Biscoe (d. 1748), minister at the meeting in Old Jewry. He conformed and became rector of St. Mary Outwich and minor canon of St. Paul's.

However, she bore it as one satisfied with what she had done. She is a woman that has as I really believe a very great value for me and esteems me very much. I wish she could communicate her good opinion of me to the rest of her sex.

When they were gone went with brother William to Ironmongers' Hall, where I sent to Mr. Jackson who let me in. I danced there for some little time with a relation of Mr. Glover's, the master of the Company. He had a niece there that I was extremely taken with, that was mighty pretty and agreeable, and though I had not her for my partner yet I was always next to her in dancing and took all opportunities of talking to her and did it in a merry agreeable manner I believe. I handed my partner into the coach where both of them went together with two other ladies. The rest of the company was chiefly but indifferent. Came home. To bed at 11.

Tuesday, October 30. At 7 went to Court with a design to get into the ball there, having dressed myself out of mourning. When I came to St. James's I attempted to get upstairs but was repulsed. Upon that I went to the coffee-house and stayed half-hour and came back again and resolved to try again. And I attempted and was repulsed, but I immediately put one shilling into his hand and he let me go. Now I was got among a vast crowd of nobility and gentry waiting for the opening of the door into the dancing room. And about half-hour after the door was opened, we all rushed in as fast as we could and got in among the rest and got into a pretty good place. After some time the Princess and then the Prince came in and the dancing was begun by the Princess and the Duchess of Bolton. The method of dancing at court is to take out one another and I observed that it was usual for them to dance twice with the same persons out of civility, to take out those who took out you before. The Princesses Anne and Amelia[1] both danced several times and mighty finely. There were several pretty agreeable women there but I thought not a sufficient number in proportion to the multitude of women that were there. Met Mr. Emmett and Swain and Skinner and Gould there. Came home with Gould at 1 o'clock. To bed at half-hour past 1.

[1] The eldest daughters of the Prince of Wales: Anne (1709–59), Amelia (1711–86).

Thursday, November 1. Rose at 8. Rode out alone to Enfield Chase. Endeavoured to think but could not apply my mind with any attention to any subject.

Cousin Joseph Billio came hither, stayed but a little while but told me he had seen Dr. Avery and he intends to go to hear him next Sunday. It gave me some uneasiness and anxiety to think that this would be an opportunity of his being introduced into Mrs. Marshall's house, for he intends to go into the vestry to the doctor, with whom I don't doubt but he will go and drink a dish of tea with Mrs. Marshall.

Read some of the *Art of Pleasing in Conversation.* There is a chapter about the method of flattery and the manner of introducing and using it among the ladies.

Friday, November 2. Went to father, received of him £8 12s. Dined in commons. Paid for my two last terms in commons £2 2s. 6d.

Went to Cousin Watkins's to supper. Played at cards. Was very merry and laughed. She is mighty fond of her husband and there appears a peculiar kind of delight when she looks upon him and so does he upon her with a great deal of pleasure. Came home at past 10.

Saturday, November 3. Took some rhubarb in the morning because it is a great sweetener of the blood. Intend to do so every morning for some time. I only chew it.

Came to Hackney to Aunt Billio's. She told me she had been with Mrs. Anthony and took an opportunity of asking her whether her daughter was engaged. She told her she could not well tell. There was a gentleman had made some overtures, so that she could say nothing about it yet, but her daughter herself was averse to marrying yet. Her fortune will be considerable, above a £1,000.

At supper mother told a very moving love story about the hard disappointments of two ardent lovers and their strange and surprising marriage afterwards. The circumstances of their case moved me extremely and I was almost ready to cry. I am very sensible of any affecting circumstances of this nature and can easily feel the sorrows of lovers.

Sunday, November 4. Mr. Smith preached both morning and afternoon upon these words: 'The repenter is more excellent than his neighbour.' He made two very good sermons, only I think he is apt to be rather too long. He seems to have a good invention and thought and a good way of spreading out the subject and pressing it. He gave us an account of the nature of repentance and the character of a repentant man. And indeed when I hear or read discourses upon this subject methought I felt something within me that answered to them and I was a little touched and charmed with the beauty of holiness and repentance.

Mr. Smith in the afternoon after sermon came and drank a dish of tea together. No extraordinary conversation. Though he preaches well he has not a talent for conversation.

Monday, November 5. Heard Mr. Smith upon the day. He dined at our house and so did Aunt Billio and Cousin Billio. I was very merry with sister: her being with child gave a handle for our mirth and I think I have not laughed more nor been so much the cause of it this great while. Aunt Billio is a little invidious and could not help saying she wondered what they could see in Mr. Smith to choose him before others. Cousin Billio, though she did not say so, I perceive was full of a like envy. Her husband being not chosen here makes her very ready to take every opportunity of reflecting upon those that seemed his rivals and those that neglected him. I was a little vexed at Aunt Billio for her giving Mr. Smith hints of what people say of his being to have Mr. Denn's daughter, but my aunt is apt now and then to let out some improper things and it is no wonder, she is a pretty great tattler. Her acquaintances will tell her anything that they hear or fancy of her relations and nothing is more common than for our family to be subjects of their conversation with her. By this means she learns all the ill things that are said of us; and she told me that she heard something said of me that would mortify me, which she told me afterwards to myself alone, upon my asking her. It was that I was not very sharp. I must confess this moved me a little. There is nothing touches a man so sensibly as what reflects upon his sense or understanding, especially because I thought I had maintained a very considerable character in Hackney in that respect. However, I am persuaded yet that I have in the general in Hackney the character of a man of good sense at least and, by some, that of an ingenious man. I believe indeed there are few persons who have so very different a character among different people as I have. Those that are thoroughly acquainted with me and see me upon all occasions, have been alone with me and are themselves of a pretty free temper and ready to raise subjects of conversation, conceive, I believe, a pretty good opinion of me, but others who see me only in a large company or assembly take me to be very stupid and dull.

A letter came to my father from Mr. Boyd accepting a little matter of business. The rest was entirely writ upon the account of the little quarrel that he had with me when he was last in town.[1] He desires my father to use his paternal authority to rebuke me for my ill treatment of him. He says in it I magnify my office and cannot suffer any contempt or reproach to be thrown upon me without resentment. I could not have thought a man would have been so foolish as to have taken any notice of a quarrel that lies entirely at his door and was so much to his disadvantage.

We had a report that the Princess was in labour to-day and we expected to hear of her being brought to bed.

Tuesday, November 6. Went to see the tragedy of *Tamerlane*[2] which was acted with a new prologue in honour of King William and in memory of what he did for us. The play itself is good, but I find myself too much moved and affected with tragedies to take much pleasure in them. And besides they fill in and justify too much my natural humour, that I think comedy much more proper for me. I am apt to interest myself so much in the concerns of the principal person in the drama that I am always in pain for his senses or honour, that I could not help feeling a great deal of uneasiness lest Tamerlane after all his glorious actions should be murdered by a felon's hand. Mills who acted the part of Bajazet did it mighty well and expressed that furiousness and rage and malice and ambition admirably well in his gesture at the end, but, which is his distinguishing character, very well kept up

[1] Cf. p. 350.
[2] Nicholas Rowe's play (published 1702) which was having a week's run at Drury Lane. It was the chief Whig play of the period, revived annually in November on the anniversary of William's landing. Rowe intended Tamerlane to represent William and Bajazet, Louis XIV.

throughout. I observed in the general that the manner of speaking in our theatres in tragedy is not natural. There is something that would be very shocking and disagreeable and very unnatural in real life. Persons would call it theatrical, meaning by that something stiff and affected.

Supped at the tavern with Mr. Samson. Nothing extraordinary, only he told me something I never knew nor suspected before, viz. that Mr. Warren had maintained such a familiarity and intimacy with Mrs. Newbury [1] that he expected her for a wife and she herself seemed to design it. It was what was in a manner agreed upon before his father fell into misfortune. And he says Mr. Warren in a great measure owed his death to his disappointment in that affair, which threw him into melancholy and impaired his constitution.

At the play there were the ladies that I danced with at Ironmongers' Hall in the first row of the front box and one of them extremely fine. She is married as I believe.

Wednesday, November 7. Signior Castilio came to see me, that I could not go to Westminster Hall. He told me upon my inquiring about it, that in Naples his country the priests there are not under any secular authority, but the Nuncio, or Inquisition in his absence, had the cognizance of all criminal cases of ecclesiastical persons and though they seldom condemned any priest to death yet they often did to the galleys. And as soon as they are condemned to the galleys the skin is taken off the palm of their hands because the consecrated oil with which they used to anoint the sick was handled and put into their hands, and also the tops of their thumbs and forefingers with which they have taken the Host, and have the skin taken off, that nothing that has been concerned in consecration of them may be left.

He told me also concerning the theatres at Naples that they are much finer and more magnificent than ours here, and he admires their manner of acting much beyond ours. He thinks we have not enough of action and gesture, our players say their parts as if they were reading a book and have nothing of that expressive force of looks and voice and gesture which gives life and spirit and nature to their action. He told me their tragedies were

[1] Probably a daughter of Samuel Newbery, of Stepney, and Katherine Watson, who were married at Hackney on 1 February 1686/7.

formed only upon sacred stories from the Scriptures and that it is a common thing for Christ to be introduced upon the stage and His passion to be acted.

Thursday, November 8. Went to Westminster Hall. Nothing extraordinary there. After dinner at commons, came home and Mr. Samson, Leeds and Horseman came to see me. Our conversation turned very much upon the reasons of dissension from the Church of England and I said I thought the differences between us were very small and trifling. For my own part I could communicate with either of them. I looked upon the several churches according to the English establishment in the same light with those of the dissenters, only as congregations of Christians met together to worship God without any regard at all to their being established.

Went to our club at the Mitre. There is Mr. Foster, Samson and Abney that are very discontented Whigs and so set against the present ministry that they would be glad to be revenged upon them, at any rate for their ingratitude to the dissenters, and say they cannot be worse used by the Tories themselves. Lord Chief Justice Parker and the Lord Chancellor they look upon as no friends at all to the dissenters but that [show] love to the court and make their addresses to the Church, by that means to become popular. They say they know that it will be moved the next session of Parliament to take away the Schism and Occasional Conformity Act, and they don't doubt but it will either break the present ministry or else remove these Acts. If the court be against it and the Whigs in House of Commons refuse to vote for their repeal, it will give the dissenters a full view and insight into the ministry and Whigs, and they will do their utmost to prevent the dissenters voting for their men again. And without their assistance they can never be chosen.

It was said that Lord Chief Justice Parker [1] had this vacation given him a pension of £2,200 per annum from the Crown. This was looked upon as a very unjust thing for a judge to take a pension from the Crown, by which he must be a little biased

---

[1] Thomas Parker, 1st Earl of Macclesfield, was a favourite of George I who, when Parker became Chancellor in 1718, presented him with £14,000 and a pension of £1,200 per annum for his son. On being created a baron in 1716 he had been granted a pension of £1,200 per annum.

towards the Crown and upon that account Judge Eyres [1] was complained of by the Recorder in the Parliament for accepting the place of Chancellor to the Prince which brings him in £800 per annum while he is Judge at the same time of the King's Bench.

Our club is set up with a design to encourage the dissenters and doing what we can for them. Upon that account it was proposed by Mr. Foster to write a weekly paper in defence of them and whatever tended to encourage those true Protestant principles of private judgement and liberty of conscience. It was pretty much approved of by the whole company that were there, viz. Mr. Blenman, Samson, Leeds, Horseman, Abney and myself. It was at first proposed to call it *The Protestant* but afterwards I proposed the name of *Freethinker*. For myself I like the proposal well enough but, as we are a variety of geniuses, I am afraid lest the spirit and life of the paper should not be kept up.

Sunday, November 11. At meeting hearing Mr. Mayo upon the subject of trusting and relying upon God I found my affections more raised and I found myself pleased with the thought of religion and ravished with the prospect of living a life of dependence and sincere confidence in God. But it grieves to find that these impressions that are often made upon me by hearing or reading so soon wear off and I cannot tell how to bring my mind into such a frame again.

Brother William has Mrs. Burton of Hackney recommended to him by Aunt Billio who has mentioned the matter to her mother who seems to favour it.[2] Brother William is under some concern how he shall do to prosecute on his part with the young lady. I told him he must write to her often. He said he expected assistance from me in that respect, which I promised him.

Monday, November 12. At 6 went to the playhouse. Saw a comedy called *The Double Gallant or Sick Lady's Cure*.[3] It is full

---

[1] Sir Robert Eyre, a Queen's Bench judge, was appointed Chancellor to the Prince of Wales upon the accession of George I. In 1729 he was charged with corruption, but was acquitted.

[2] William married Mrs. Burton of Hackney on 14 November 1717, the ceremony being performed by Uncle Marshall.

[3] By Colley Cibber, 1707.

of little sneers and rubs upon matrimony and now and then some *doubles entendres*.

Tuesday, November 13. The Duke of Marlborough is very ill and has lost much of his senses that he often falls into fits of crying.[1] Methinks the frailty and mortality of the human nature never appeared in a more moving and affecting light than in him. To see a man that was but just now the glory and pride of a nation, the hero of the world, of such vast abilities and knowledge and consequence sink almost below a rational creature, all his fine qualities disappear and fall away!

The Princess who was brought to bed last Friday morning of a dead son and has been exceeding bad is better and in a fair way of recovery. It is said by Dr. Hollier and most people that she might have been delivered the Tuesday before of a live child if she would have made use of Sir David Hamilton [2] and suffered herself to be laid then, but she refused both.

Went to sister's with some distinct hopes of seeing Mrs. Marshall there but she was not there. Cousin Joseph Billio came there. We talked with sister about Mrs. Marshall. She told Joseph she would take him with her at any time to see her but she would not me. And when I desired her to take me she said I should be as welcome as snow in harvest. This moved me extremely and made me almost mad.

Went with Cousin Joseph to the Fountain Tavern to see Dr. Whinnell. Dr. Hollier was there also and many others. I talked a good deal about painting and poetry and some plays and Addison and trade. Such subjects as these suit my capacity and give me an opportunity of conversation.

Supped at sister's. While we were at supper there passed by through the street a mob with the effigy of the Pretender holding a taper in one hand and a gallows in the other, with a pair of wooden shoes hanging upon them. It seems this is the day that the rebels were beat last year at Dunblane.[3] Came home at 11.

Thursday, November 15. Mr. Bowes according to his promise to-day came to see me. He gave me an account of a law club

[1] He had had a paralytic stroke on 10 November.
[2] Sir David Hamilton (1663-1721), physician to Queen Anne.
[3] The battle of Sheriffmuir was fought about two miles from Dunblane.

that he is a member of. There are about nine of them. They have each of them a title or head of the law assigned to them which they are in their turns to discuss and go through all its branches. They do it in the method of a commonplace by bringing in all the cases that are found in the law books on that head and proposing them to the company, who each of them in his turn gives his opinion of it till it comes back again to the person who first proposed it, who then gives a resolution and judgement upon it as it is in the books and the arguments for it. In this manner they go on till they have gone through their several titles. But beside this every week they have an argument made upon a case between two. The two persons who are to argue the next week bring each of them a case wherein there is some moot point not yet determined in the books. When the company have determined which of the cases to pitch upon, these two persons make arguments upon it to be spoke the next week. I could be very glad to be admitted of this society, but I am afraid I am not likely to gain that. Mr. Bowes did not himself in the least hint at any such thing, though I made such questions to him as might very naturally lead him to mention it if he thought fit.

When Mr. Bowes was gone, I sat down in order to study the title of Errors but before I did much I heard somebody knock at the door. As I am very apt to be alarmed with the thoughts of Mrs. Marshall, it came into my head that my sister had upon some account relating to her sent to me, and it proved so, that she sent to desire me to go with her and brother and Mrs. Marshall to the playhouse, which I did. But it vexed me that I was to have so little of her company and yet be at the charge of 9s. as I was by sitting in the front box and paying 4s. besides myself towards the rest. I sat at the playhouse but could scarce mind what was transacting upon the stage, my thoughts were so fixed upon Mrs. Marshall. There was one thought which seemed to me to be mighty good and just in the play. The play was *Tamerlane*. Bajazet in the fury of his wild passion, when his wife Arpathia fell down dead upon the death of her former lover Monetis, cries out in the utmost rage, ' Where is royalty and majesty, the power of kings and emperors, if vile slaves can thus mock my anger and free themselves from my service,' or to that effect.

When the play was done I told Mrs. Marshall I did not intend they should leave me to walk alone, as I came there on foot, but was resolved some of them should accompany me in the coach, and I bespoke her. She refused it and I did not expect she would. However, when we came as far as Mrs. Thomas's where we left her. I got into the coach with Mrs. Marshall and ravished almost I was to come so near her. When we parted I gave her a kiss after my sister and brother had introduced it. Came home. To bed at 12.

November 16. Supped by myself. After supper Mr. Foster met me. Sat with me and went to Tom's where met with some of his friends, particularly one Mr. Martin, who entertained the company with stories about himself at Oxford, how he treated the Master and Fellows and how insolent he was to them. Though I did not much admire his conversation yet I cannot but envy his memory which I saw was very considerable. But the subject turned upon witches and Mr. Martin bantered very well our laws for punishing it and said that since Judge Hales no one had been punished for witchcraft. There was not long ago in the Devonshire assizes before Baron Price two women accused of witchcraft and a man and his wife were sworn who said they were pinched and beat most sadly, but who did it was Jane such a one. 'Why then,' says the Judge, ' you should bring your action of assault and battery against her.' 'No,' but say they, 'we did not see her.' 'Why then, how do you know it?' The Baron would have discharged her, but the parsons made a body and got in a quantity of affidavits that he was forced to satisfy the Church by continuing them in prison, and one of them died in prison.

Saturday, November 17. Rose at past 7. Read law. To Westminster at past 10. After dinner made haste to go to sister's in expectation of seeing Mrs. Marshall. Found her there but my stock of conversation was soon out and I was mightily at a loss what to say. I longed for Cousin Joseph Billio to tell the state of my mind to and had a design to have told him it was too much for me to bear and beg his assistance to ease.

Read some *Spectators*, among others the 447th concerning the force of custom to render anything pleasant. This is an observation that I might make every day upon what happens to myself. I am now extremely concerned and troubled about Mrs. Marshall. If I could but use myself to bear her absence and for a few times resist the inclinations I have to see her, by refusing to take any opportunity that offers of coming into her company, I should soon become easy and indifferent with respect to her.

Sunday, November 18. Rose at 8. Heard Mr. Smith both parts of the day. One very good observation which he made was that in order to be prepared for all conditions and circumstances of life a man must behave himself well and suitably, be easy and contented under his present circumstances.

When Mr. Smith was at prayers the thought of the glorious and vast perfection of God struck me with such an idea of greatness and grandeur that I could not help thinking it must be the noblest and most exalted employment of the soul to address itself to its Maker and a prayer suited to the condition of an innocent rational creature who is possessed with the full sense of his obligation to his God must be the most sublime lofty composition in the world. David has furnished us with some of the noblest and most sublime addresses to the Divine Being of any that ever were composed. There is something of rapture and exalted style in his psalms that suits the divine subject of them. To bed at 10.

Monday, November 19. Rose at 7. Went to London early. Stayed at sister's all the morning, though I intended to go to Westminster, but she being in a good humour I could not help staying with her. Came home at 12. Spent the afternoon very idly.

In the morning Major Pitts was at brother's and he, happening to mention Serjeant Whittaker,[1] I told him he had a pretty daughter, that the old gentleman thought I had a fancy for her and told me if I had a mind that way he believed he could introduce me into her company. I humoured him in his good design for me and thanked him for his kind offer. He thought me in earnest and told me he would do nothing without my father's knowledge and consent. It pleased me, though in fancy and imagination only, to have the prospect of such a pretty girl for a wife, and I could not help almost hoping that it might be so.

---

[1] Edward Whittaker of the Middle Temple was appointed Sergeant-at-law in 1714.

Tuesday, November 20. Went to the Grecian Coffee-House. Nothing extraordinary. Met with Mr. Abney and Mr. Leeds. Supped with them. We were a little merry. Mr. Abney is a man of good sense and memory and good entertaining company. He gave us an account of the assemblies they have at Derby whereabouts he lives in the summer. They have them every fortnight and very good company. The scarcity of men in proportion to women creates a little emulation and envy among the ladies, who are very solicitous about getting partners. The old mothers and aunts enter into this rivalship and by their civilities to the gentlemen and sometimes sly hints or plain requests gain partners for their daughters or relations. Came home at 10.

Wednesday, November 21. Rose at between 7 and 8. Read civil law. To Westminster Hall. After dinner went to brother's. Saw sister. She was out of humour because she heard that Mrs. Marshall was going to Highgate to-day without coming to see her as she promised she would yesterday. She said she believed she did it upon my account. She finds I am constantly there when she is there.

I inquired about what my father had done concerning brother William's marriage with Mrs. Burton, for he had been to meet her yesterday at her son-in-law's, Mr. Atwell. When he came there she would say nothing at all about the matter till her son came in. When he came they sat silent for a little while before anybody opened and then my father began. He put it upon this foot, that whatever fortune she had he would give his son equal, and desired to know what she had. They refused to tell that, but asked him what he had heard. He said £1,000 or £1,500. He said she had that, but this finished the conversation, only that Mr. Atwell said the man ought to have double the woman's fortune, while my father answered by his trade. But nothing at all was done and my father parted telling her that whenever she should think fit he should be glad to wait upon her.

Went to our club at Change at 8. I found Mr. Heathcote, Jackson, Crisp and Porter at the tavern. It seems Mr. Isles is not pleased with the coffee-house and the gentlemen have a mind to change it to the tavern. Mr. Crisp was rather for continuing, though not absolutely. He thinks that Mr. Isles is rather weary of the company than the place and makes that only as an excuse, but I don't find the rest think so. However, it is determined to try the tavern and to change the night from Wednesday to Thursday, at the Castle Tavern in Lombard Street. Our conversation went on very briskly and merrily and Mr. Porter and Heathcote attributed it to the spirit of the wine and took this occasion to recommend the tavern before the coffee-house. Upon that our conversation turned partly upon women and wives.

Mr. Witnoom gave us an account of Sir Richard Steele's manner of treating his duns. He has now a bill upon him for about £50 for which he has been dunned almost fifty times. The man that duns him goes to his house early in the morning, inquires for Sir Richard and is admitted. He finds there altogether in one hall twenty or thirty men come upon the same errand. They presently inquire of one another what sum of money they each have come for and sometimes quarrel who shall first speak to Sir Richard when he comes downstairs. One demands the preference upon the account of the long standing of his debt, another the greatness of the sum, another that it is for goods sold in the shop at the common rate of ready-money customers. Till at last perhaps they inquire for Sir Richard and they are told he has been gone out these three hours. Or if he is caught coming downstairs they find him to be sure engaged in some very deep and earnest discourse with a friend that comes down with him, by which means he passes through the clamours of the multitude of duns without hearing a word they say.

Mr. Witnoom told us a pun that was made by a Dutchman, a very good one. The word 'stemm' in Dutch signifies both the root of a tree and also the lineage of ancestors. When a man was boasting of the antiquity of his family and the many great names that belonged to it, he said, 'I don't know what this gentleman may be, but it is a common saying that an old stemm seldom bears good fruit.' Upon the subject of punning Mr. Porter told us another which he admired. When some company were diverting themselves with the play of asking of each person what an unknown thing is like which they are afterwards when known to find out some likeness to, one of the company said a thing was like a watch. The thing proved to be an Oxford scholar, upon which he answered immediately that it was like him because it went continually tick-a-tick as he did (viz. in debt). I don't much admire this pun.

As I came home at 1 o'clock I had a mind to feel a whore and went about the streets on purpose to find one which I did, but she would not let me before I gave her money, which I would not do and so came away. To bed at past 1.

Saturday, November 24. After dinner went to brother's. Met Mr. Ramsey there. I inquired of him, when he was like to be drowned and was so long under water, how he felt himself, what thoughts he had. He says when he had been in for some time he felt a prodigious weight upon his breast, as if all St. Paul's lay upon him, that he could scarce breathe, but he could give me very little account of himself. When he was taken up he was senseless to outward appearance, and he could not tell me whether he was sensible himself, but that I believe he could not be because he did not know when they took him up.

I told my sister I would not for a great while see Mrs. Marshall and she might be assured that if I knew at any time of her being at her house I would purposely avoid coming there. My sister seemed to be pretty well contented with that.

Sunday, November 25. Rose at 8. Read some of Hoadly's sermons upon the terms of acceptance. He has not a very good style, but he has a pretty strong way of expressing himself and a very clear way of arguing. The sacrament was administered to-day and Mr. Mayo pressed it very much as a necessary duty upon those that neglected it. But I am very much concerned to find in myself such a strong disinclination to these external duties of religion, as prayer, meditation, receiving the sacrament of the Lord's Supper. It proceeds I believe chiefly from the want of due and lively sense of spiritual things and the vast importance of them. They don't affect me as they ought to do.

Tuesday, November 27. To father's in order to see an account of his whole estate as he promised to show it me, and he did so. He appears to have £500 per annum chiefly in houses, and, all his debts paid, about £1,000 personal estate. He advised with me about brother William's affair and seemed to be in great perplexity what to do. However, at last he was very pleased with the proposal that if she had £1,500 he would settle £100 per annum in houses upon him and her instead of an estate in money equivalent, since her £1,500 would be sufficient to employ in trade. This matter has given me a good deal of trouble, for though I perceive my father seems to have my interest at heart, yet he does not seem much to understand it, for he does not propose to give me anything at all till after his death and after mother's death about £220 per annum. But this is what I cannot be pleased with at all, since it will quite destroy my prospect of marrying and keep me low as long as he and mother live.

Wednesday, November 28. Read law. At 9 o'clock Cousin Benjamin Ryder came to me. Cousin and I breakfasted alone. He is a lad of a very shallow head and little sense that makes me wonder what should be the reason that several of my uncle's friends, as Mr. Stratford and others, are so mighty civil to him as to invite him to come and see them and receive him into their company, especially when he goes so meanly dressed as to be a disgrace to them that keep him company.

At 11 o'clock Mr. Castilio came to see me, with whom I spent all the morning. He is a man of good sense and informs me of affairs and things which I did not know, in relation to the condition of the ecclesiastics of the Church of Rome. He himself was an abbé, that is, a secular ecclesiastical order of which there are two sorts, such as are given and confirmed by the Pope and such as belong to a certain family and may be disposed of by will and descent as temporal inheritances. Of this sort his abbacy was ; his father was a Marquess, his eldest brother had a marquisate descend to him, his second brother was a baron by descent ; he himself as the third son had no title or honour, but he had an uncle who was an abbé, a very rich man, who left his abbacy to him for life. An abbacy is a spiritual jurisdiction or lordship, contains lands and villages and houses, and stocks of sheep and herds of kine commonly go along. The abbés wear a peculiar distinguishing habit like a bishop, with a crosier on the left breast. Those kind of abbacies that come by inheritance and go in families are not under the jurisdiction of any bishop nor of the Pope himself, nor can be taken away by him.

Went to brother's where were Mrs. Henry and Mr. Bunkley and his wife and his sister. They supped there that evening and played cards. I played at cards with them and was very merry with them, but, I don't know how, Mrs. Bunkley puts on a strange kind of frowning, dissatisfied countenance that she does not appear pleased at all. I observed that the women at cards are generally very much out of humour if they lose. Sister would now and then check me in what I said which made me very angry with her, though I did not in the least express but carried it off with a jest. But she vexed me very much once when, upon my talking very merrily and in jest, she grew grave all of a sudden and told the company in a very serious and angry humour that she would never tell me anything but what she would have all the world know, for I told everything in the next coffee-house or company I came into.

Thursday, November 29. After dinner went to see Mr. Mills but not at home, then to the coffee-house, from whence to father's. He told me what he had done at Mr. Atwood's.[1] He told them that he would settle an equivalent in land upon him and her for her fortune and they told him her fortune was £1,500, but they expected to have £150 per annum settled upon him, but that my father refused and they parted in great civility but not absolutely. I desired some money of him for books, but he could give me then only £6, which he did.

Friday, November 30. Went to Mr. Abney's chambers according to appointment. He is to go to Hyde Park to see the review of the regiment of horse, Churchill colonel,[2] which the Prince has made his own regiment. I never saw a review before. There was a pretty great crowd of people, coaches and horses. Coming home in the coach we talked about the mottoes of the nobility and great men. It was said that the greatest part of them were taken up within the last seven years, it having been mightily in vogue since that time.

After dinner went to Mr. Bowes's. After some little time spent in conversation he asked me to play at picquet which I did and won about 4s. of him, when he seemed uneasy and resolved, as I

---

[1] *Sic*, although previously *Atwell*. There was an Atwood family at Hackney related to Sir Josiah Child.

[2] Charles Churchill, a natural son of Marlborough's brother, M.P. for Castle Rising.

guess by what followed, to recover it though by cheating, for having suspected him one time I took particular notice another time and saw him lay down a card which belonged to his hand and take up another which he had before laid out and by that means won the game. I did not think fit to take any notice of it, but I shall take care how I play again with him, for I am pretty careless in my playing and it is the easiest thing in the world to cheat me if he pleases.

Sunday, December 2. Heard Mr. Biscoe in the morning and Mr. Smith in the afternoon. Mr. Biscoe does not become the pulpit well at all. He has a very dull manner of delivery and has a very simple air in it. I could not help observing what a vast advantage it is to appear lively and brisk in what a man does. I find this fault in myself at home. I can sit hours together without speaking or regarding what is done. But I am persuaded I ought to endeavour to rouse myself out of that indolence and use myself more to activity and not indulge that humour.

Monday, December 3. Rose at 7. Read some of Quintilian's *Institutio.*

Quintilian is an admirable writer. He has a peculiar strong, masculine style that is very sublime and concise. He has a very just sense of nature, and the various turns, properties, inlets, accesses, and passions of the human soul. He often makes use of very lively and strong images that set his subject in a new and surprising light, so that I think to read him often.

Played upon the viol. Read some *Spectators.* I think I can very plainly distinguish Steele's style and manner of writing from Addison's, which is indeed much the best.

Tuesday, December 4. Went to Mr. Samson's where met Mr. Foster. We talked about politics. He said that Grey Neville conceives mighty hopes that the Parliament will take off the Occasional Conformity and Schism Acts, but Mr. Barrington who converses very much with the Court thinks otherwise.

Mr. Leeds told us that he heard for certain that the Duke of Argyll is forming a party to attempt the doing something in favour of the Kirk of Scotland and he has applied to the dissenters to desire them to join in with him that their case also may be taken care of. But the dissenting ministers who assembled upon this occasion were mostly agreed to have nothing to do with it. It seems Lechmere is in with the Duke of Argyll and is to be the head of his party in the House of Commons as he is to be in the House of Lords.

Duke of Argyll is a strange, restless, troublesome man and so as he may but govern, be at the head of affairs, does not care how he disturbs and perplexes the King and Parliament. It was the Duke of Argyll when the King was going to his own dominions that persuaded the Prince that the patent by which he was made Regent during his absence was not so ample and so honourable as it used to be formerly in the like cases, and Lechmere was the counsel who advised about it and brought precedents of former patents to confirm that notion, so that the Prince seemed discontented to the King and told him the reason of it and also the persons who put it into his head. But the King told him if he would not accept of it as he had given it him he must prepare his equipage and go along with him. Upon which the Prince complied and all was well again, and when the King went the Prince went with him as far as Greenwich, where he landed and in the open air upon the shore took his leave of the King and the King kissed [him] and a great deal of reverence appeared on the side of the Prince and as much love and tenderness from his father. This Mr. Foster said was thought to be done so on purpose that there might not appear the least difference, but that they parted in entire friendship and good understand[ing].

Mr. Foster gave a very different character of the King than I had all along conceived of him or ever heard before. He says he is a man not of an active temper but loves his ease very much and cannot bear fatigue. He is mighty good-natured, but does not love much application to business. Methinks this is very disagreeable to the common character that he bears both here and abroad of a wise prudent man of great penetration into business and much influence in foreign affairs. It is very inconsistent with that steadiness and constancy and resoluteness of temper which he is noted for. A king that loves his ease and cannot bear application to business, is shocked and disturbed by every solicitation of courtiers, does not know how to resist them and is glad to shake off the weight and burden of public affairs at any rate upon his ministry. All of which seems directly contrary to the King's management.

Went to brother's at past 7. There was Mr. Utber and his wife. We played at cards and were very merry. Home at 12.

Wednesday, December 5. Went to John's. Met Mr. Porter. I find a strange alteration in myself in the company met with at John's from what I am in the company at Sue's. I don't know how it is but I am much more free and talk with much more ease and indifference in that than in the other and by that means I am more merry and facetious and sometimes say things that are very tolerable and good. But at John's I have a kind of awe upon me that keeps me at a distance, my thoughts are not so much at large but more confined, that I am very much at a loss for conversation. Came home at past 10.

Thursday, December 6. Read law. At 11 Signior Castilio came to see me and talked about his family. I asked him whether he had heard any news from Italy, which brought in an account of the treatment that his relations gave him. His eldest brother is a Marquis and his second brother is Archbishop of Rossano.

Friday, December 7. Dined with Mr. Leeds. He came with me home after dinner and Mr. Bowes also came in. He told me he heard there was a club set up upon a religious account of which I was a member and that the design of it was in opposition to atheism, deism and conformity. I told him that religion was no further the business or subject of our society than as most of its members were dissenters, but any subjects, the most promiscuous, were equally allowed and favoured in our conversation. I was concerned that there should [be] such a report go about and indeed I believe I shall not so commonly frequent the club upon that account. He told us that he was last night at the play when the Prince was there. This . . .

INDEX

So detailed is the diary, that a complete index would exceed the diary itself in length. Many items of minor importance, therefore, have not been indexed, e.g. his visits to Hackney and to his father and brother in London, unimportant references to friends and acquaintances and minor repetitions.

An asterisk following a page number means that there is a relevant note on the page.

The indexing of the names of nobles follows the form in the diary.

Abney, Mr., friend : 154*; begins dissenters' club, 226, 233 ; his talents, 234, 265, 361 ; character, 367 ; account of Derby, 367, 371

Act for Preventing Tumults : passed in House of Lords, 59*, 66 ; discussed, 94

Actors : their bad morals, 101 ; style in tragedy, 359

Addison, Joseph : on translations of Homer, 33* ; Mr. Whatley sends him essays, 69 ; his genius, 94 ; compared with Steele, 121, 372 ; *The Freeholder*, 169, 183 ; *The Drummer*, 195* ; *Cato*, 202*, 263*, 268 ; compared with the French *Cato*, 268*, 270

Address, manner of : 32, 66

Alchemy : Dr. Cairns's experiments, 314

Aldersgate Street : a coffee-house in, 164

Aldgate Ward, 156

Allen, Aunt, of Gresley : her suit with Lord Huntingdon, 44* ; oranges and lemons bought for, 166 ; her affected gentility, 252*

Allen, Mary, cousin : about to be married, 120 ; to 'Don Cholerick', 122 ; diarist's fondness for her, 151, 262 ; not married, 252

Alliances : between France and England, 74 ; rumoured league between France, Italy, and Sicily, 157 ; treaty with France, 338*

Allom, aunt : 313 ; her vision, 314

Allowance : father gives diarist money, 44, 117, 276, 336, 357, 371

Alworthy, Mr., of Clapton : bonfire before his house, 287*

Alworthy, Mrs., her strange behaviour in church, 191*

Amelia, Princess : cf. Royal Family

Amsterdam Coffee House, 124*

Anatomy : Mr. Porter recommends the study of, 292

Anecdotes, 42, 124, 152, 167, 202, 321, 330, 368

Anglesey, Earl of : opposes repeal of Triennial Act, 220

Anne, Princess : cf. Royal Family

Anne, Queen : her bed, 72 ; interview with Pretender, 193

Anstis, John, M.P. : order for arrest, 103

Anthony, Mr., of Hackney : his will examined, 353*

Anthony, Mrs., daughter of the above : her position in relation to marriage, 357

Apothecaries : arrangements with doctors, 227

Argyll, John Campbell, Duke of : goes to meet rebels, 103* ; reported battle at Sheriffmuir, 139, 140 ; his character, 139 ; pursues Mar, 178 ; at the playhouse, 195 ; deprived of office, 267, 271 ; his character, 267, 373 ; movement to assist Kirk of Scotland, 372 ; promotes difference between King and Prince of Wales, 373

375

Aristotle, 206
Arlington, Earl of : Charles II advises with him, 321
Army : discussion of a standing army, 60
Army camp in Hyde Park : description of, 60*, 64 ; visit with ladies, 72-3 ; exercising a regiment, 80
Artificial Memory : used to remember law cases, 93, 115
Arts and Manufactures : indebtedness to immigrants, 181
Ashridge Park, Herts, 99*
Astor, Rev. Mr. : preaches a loyal sermon at Hackney, 173
Astrologers : discussed, 336 ; visit to an astrologer-bawd, 337 (cf. also Dr. Cairns)
Atkins, Mr., friend : 42*
Atwell, Mr., brother-in-law of Mrs. Burton : opinion on marriage settlement, 367 ; expectations for Mrs. Burton, 371
Atwood : cf. Atwell
Aurora Borealis : described, 192* ; discussed, 192 ; Tory interpretation of, 213
Avery, Dr. Benjamin : story of Convocation, 129* ; gives 'inside information' about execution of Derwentwater and Kenmure, 193 ; love for Mrs. Marshall, 242, 277, 282 ; visits Ryders, 286, 297, 331, 347, 357
Aylesbury, Vale of : 112
Aylesford, Heneage Finch, Viscount : anti-Whig activities, 176* ; turned out of office, 190 ; opposes repeal of Triennial Act, 220

Bagnio : therapeutic value of, 237, 312
Bailey, Mr., partner to Richard Ryder, senr. : dinner with, 152* ; brother William's treatment at his house, 178 ; problem of his partnership, 212, 227, 255, 313, 340
Bailey, Mrs., wife of above : lies in, 279 ; rebukes brother William, 320
Baire, Dr., physician at Bath : advises diarist on his regime, 243

Baker, Rev. Mr. : familiarity with Mrs. Marshall, 261*, 263
Bale, University of : account of, 89
Balls and dances : at Cousin Watkins's, 68 ; at a tavern in Cornhill, 92 ; Lord Mayor's Day, 127, 356 ; at Mr. Fernley's, 147, 151, 152, 192 ; at Mrs. Wallis's, 151, 154, 157, 203, 235 ; at Clothiers' Hall, 152 ; at Mr. Bunkley's, 163 ; 204 ; Sir John Fryer's feast, 213 ; at Bath, 245 ; at Court, 340
Banqueting House : Rubens's paintings there, 59
Barker, Rev. John, of Hackney : style in preaching, 43*, 71, 115 ; controversy about, 117, 155, 216, 219, &c.
Barker, Mrs., 68*
Barker, Mrs., whore : 138*
Barrington, Shute, M.P. : asked reasons for repealing Schism and Occasional Conformity Acts, 154* ; pessimistic about repeal, 372
Bartholomew Close, 260
Bartholomew Fair, 86
Bashfulness : a method of curing it, 104
Basinghall Street, 55
Bastille, The, 323, 328
Bates, Rev. Dr. William : minister at Hackney, 3 ; his sermons read, 170, 263
Bath : Mrs. Richard Ryder, junr., goes there, 211 ; diarist thinks of going, 230 ; prepares for, 237 ; journey to, 238-9 ; stay there, 239-50 ; baths, 240 ; plays, 241 ; church and meeting, 244 ; Mr. Blathwayt's estate, 248. Cf. also Court Bath, 240 ; Harrison's Walks, 239, 246, 248 ; King's Bath, 240 ; Leper's Bath, 240 ; Beau Nash, 240, 245 ; Poem on ladies there, 347 ; Pump Room, 240 ; Pump Woman, 250, 296
Bathing, effects of : cf. Cold bath, Baire
Battle of the Books : cf. Boileau, Dacier, De la Motte, Wotton
Baxter, cousin : character, 261*
Bayes, Rev. Joshua : 161*
Bean, robber : hanged, 336 ; his last speech, 336

INDEX

Beheading : reflections on, 204 ; experiment with a viper, 205
Behmen, Mr. : 350
Bell Inn, London : 328
Bennett, Mr., acquaintance : his story of an Englishwoman in a seraglio, 324
Bentley, Dr. Richard : 31*, described, 214
Berkeley, George, philosopher : *Principles of Human Knowledge*, discussed, 56*, 59, 65, 93 ; borrowed, 94 ; read, 95 ; objections to the theory of abstract ideas, 93, 94, 95, 102, 117 ; Joseph Billio reads, 263 ; *Of Passive Obedience*, 114*, Mr. Porter puzzled by it, 300 ; his opinion of Pope's *Homer*, 102 ; reputed author of *Advice to the Tories*, 117*
Berkhamstead : visit to, 98
Bernoulli, Jean, mathematician : professor at Bale, 89*
Berry, Marie-L.-E., duchesse du : her debauchery, 348*
Bethnal Green, 56
Beverages : arrack punch, 145 ; ale, 98, 171 ; birch wine, 81 ; cardus tea, 257 ; cherry brandy, 112 ; chocolate, 97, 109, 331 ; coffee, 89 ; green tea, 96 ; milk, 276 ; punch, 35, 194, 331, 335 ; rack, 115 ; tea, 50, 89, 109, 120, 133, 182, 199, 299, 311, 358 ; wine, 76, 115, 187, 192, 205, 206, 216, 247, 268, 311
Bible : sublime passages in 33, 94, 366, reading of, 39, 56, 61, 94, 228 ; authority of New Testament, 104
Bickley, Aunt, of Hackney : 71* ; her house robbed, 87 ; met in Mare Street, 94 ; visits to, 118, &c. ; dinner with, 122 ; tactlessness, 208 ; Mrs. Loyd takes leave of her, 268 ; wish to match brother William and cousin Abigail, 269 ; her son, 288 ; discusses Mr. Papillon, 351. (Cf. also Abigail Ryder and Mrs. Loyd)
Billio, Rev. Robert : husband of following, 3, 30*
Billio, Sarah, aunt : treatment of her daughter-in-law, 30* ; quarrel with her son, 43 ; pleasantness in company, 54 ; suspects brother William of highway robbery, 84 ; her gossip, 108 ; advice about William, 173 ; rallies diarist, 268 ; discusses William, 285 ; Mr. Ryder's debt to her, 326 ; her curiosity, 327 ; opinion of Mrs. Marshall, 341 ; seeks a place for her son Robert, 347 ; inquires about Mrs. Anthony, 357 ; is invidious and tattles, 358 ; recommends Mrs. Burton for William, 362
Billio, Joseph, cousin : 30* ; opinions on preaching, 33 ; quarrel with his mother, 43 ; agreeable conversationalist, 50 ; talent for entertaining ladies, 51 ; discusses bashfulness, 104 ; garrulousness, 135 ; skates, 165 ; walks with diarist, 185 ; his defects, 200 ; discusses Mrs. Marshall, 261 ; admires her, 268 ; discusses story-telling, 270 ; bawdy discourse, 271 ; discusses Mr. Powell, 272 ; discusses conversation, 281 ; failure in conversation, 286 ; sister Ryder displeased, 299 ; discusses Mrs. Marshall, 301 ; asked to write about Mrs. Walker, 309 ; opinion on dowries, 310 ; discusses his brother's defects, 319 ; smitten by Mrs. Marshall, 328 ; perplexity about her, 330 ; goes to Westbrook Hay, 332 ; enamoured, 332 ; mushroom-gathering, 333 ; rebuked for rudeness, 333 (twice) ; retaliates, 333 ; returns from Westbrook, 334 ; melancholy with love, 335 ; recovers on punch and misogyny, 335 ; discusses Mrs. Marshall, 338 (in Latin), 341, 344, 347, 349, 354 ; dullness, 353 ; recovering from love, 355 ; likes diarist's poem, 355 ; rides to Edmonton, 355, 363, 365
Billio, Rev. Robert, cousin : 30*, 35* ; bad preaching and praying, 46 ; journey to Westbrook, 96 ; skates, 164 ; preaches, 195 ; reports debate on Triennial Act, 219 ; a sermon, 254 ; defects, 265 ; attempt to get place at Hackney, 305 ; not acceptable, 305, 319 ; defects, 319 ; seeks Mr. Freke's ministry, 347 ; his opinion of Mrs. Marshall, 354

Billio, Mrs. Robert, wife of above: 30*; pregnant, 35; birth of son, 47; a cleanly child, 64; timorousness, 97
Billio, Rev. Joseph, of Maldon: 48*
Birch, Mr., of Hemel Hemstead: 97*; courses with diarist, 99, 334; wrestles, 99; at Hackney, 105; frightened, 105; buys straw hat, 107, 109
Births: 47, 166, 363
Biscoe, Rev. Richard, of Newington Green: preaches, 355*, 372
Black and White House, Hackney: 14
Blackbourn, Mr., acquaintance: high steward for Essex, his character, 53
Blackmore, Sir Richard: his *Essays* discussed, 194*
Blathwayt, William, M.P.: a visit to his estate at Durham Park, near Bath, 249*
Blencowe, Sir John, judge: rebukes University of Oxford, 207*
Blenman, Mr., member of Nonconformist Club, 362
Blount: *Characters* read, 285*
Blue flannel: remedy for rheumatism, 278, 286
Blundell, Mr., friend: discusses persecution of French Protestants, 300, 303; esteem for diarist, 312; tells story about Mr. Freke, 318
Boileau; Reflections on Longinus, 30*, 31*; Satires, 60; epistles, 97, 108; opinion of Fontenelle, 122; diarist's admiration of 62, 110
Bois, Mr., reader at Middle Temple: 225*; discusses exercises, 230, 258
Bolingbroke, Henry St. John, Viscount: impeachment, 32
Bolton, Henrietta, 2nd Duchess of: at Bartholomew Fair, 86*; at Court, 356
Bonfires: 66, 121, 138; at Hackney, 287
Booth, Barton, actor: his debauchery, 101*; style, 157
Borrett, Mr. and Mrs.: best example of married bliss, 76*, 123, 135
Bossu, René le: *Traité du poème épique*, 140*

Bothmer, Hans Caspar von, Hanoverian minister: alleged relations with dissenters, 47*
Bovingdon, Herts, 213
Bow Church, London: great bonfire at, 121
Bowes, John, friend: 93*; sees diarist's prints, 103; suspected of freethinking, 104; diarist's respect for, 104: plays picquet, 113; walks with diarist on Thames, 167; character, 172; discusses Pope and women, 178, 183; hatred of Scotchmen, 226; story of supernatural, 322; hatred of Dr. Williams, 322; story about son of Muley Mulock, 323; account of his law club, 364; cheats at cards, 371, 374
Bowls: cf. Sports
Boyd, Rev. Mr.: at Hemel Hemstead, 98; stinking breath and singularity, 98; affronted by diarist, 350; complains to Mr. Ryder, 359
Bradbury, Dr. Thomas, congregational divine: style, 50*, 71
Braddon, Laurence, agitator: pamphlet on death of Earl of Essex in 1683, 321*
Bragg, Mr., of Hackney: a suspicious letter, 82, 83; character, 83; charged with sending letter, 85
Brainthwaite, William, serjeant-at-law: his practice, 106*
Breath, bad: 97, 195, 205, 221, 276
Brerewood Family: met at Court, 77
Brian, Mr., poet; met at Button's, 78; his poems, 78
Bridgewater, Scroop Egerton, 4th Earl of: his estate at Ashridge, 99, 111
Bristol: 241; visited, 241; Hot Wells, 242; customs there, 243; Mrs. Loyd leaves for, 268
British Coffee House: 62, 89*
Brookbanks, Mr., of Hackney: visits Ryders, 259*: his maid abuses his household, 352*
Brown, Mrs., parson's wife: 295
Brown, Tom: *Lindamira*, discussed, 209*; read, 210

INDEX 379

Bruet, Mr., Mr. Horseman's uncle : 187
Brydges, James, 1st Duke of Chandos : his estate at Edgware, 100*
Buchanan, George : *Franciscanus et Fratres* read, 237*
Buckingham, George Villiers, 2nd Duke of : *Essay on Poetry*, 102 ; *The Chances*, 114* ; performed in Inner Temple Hall, 177
Budget, Mr. : his course of physic, 227
Bulkeley, Mr. : visits Ryders, 285*
Bullock, Christopher : *Cobbler of Preston* seen, 241*, 101
Bunbury, Mr., fellow-lodger : 164, 187
Bunbury, Mrs., fellow-lodger : frightened by strange appearances in the air, 192
Bunkley, Mr. : dance at his house, 163 ; reasons for not inviting diarist, 177 ; plays cards, 370 ; his wife dines with Ryders, 135, 370
Burgess, Dr. Daniel, Nonconformist minister : his meeting pulled down by Sacheverell mob, 41*
Burgess, Mr., friend : discusses education, 65 ; discusses preaching, 331
Burmann, Pieter, Dutch scholar : his oration at Leyden, 195*
Burnet, Gilbert : his *History of the Reformation* read, 111*
Burnet, Sir Thomas, cf. *The Grumbler*
Burroughs, Rev. Jeremiah, friend : discusses preaching and plays music, 59* ; anecdote about choice of Archbishop of Canterbury, 167 ; discussed, 285 ; plays viol duets, 299 ; entertained, 311, 312 ; story about son of Muley Mulock, 323 ; goes to an astrologer, 336
Burton, Mrs., of Hackney : proposed for brother William, 362*, 367, 369, 371
Butler, Goody : entertains family on visit to Westbrook, 98 ; her husband's loyalty to King, 98, 333
Butler, Samuel : *Hudibras*, 261, 271
Button's Coffee House : visits to 37*, 49, 78, 314
Byam, Mrs. : partner at a ball, 213
Byfield, Adoniram : 3

Cairns, Dr., alchemist : 314
Calamy, Dr. Edmund, Nonconformist divine : preaches at Hackney, 224*
Calderwood, William, rebel, 197*
Cambridge, University of : 115 ; its Toryism, 189, (twice) ; and Dr. Bentley, 214
Campbell, Mr., acquaintance : 88
Canons Edgware : described, 100*, 111
Card games : backgammon, 285 ; picquet, 113, 200, 323, 371 ; ombre, 217 ; whisk, 99, 158 ; unspecified, 126, 131, 161, 178, 357, 371, 374
Carnwath, Robert, 6th Earl of : impeachment, 168 ; sentenced, 179
Carpenter, Major-General George : report of victory over rebels, 132* ; pursues rebels, 133 ; assembles troops at Warrington, 135* ; witness in trial of Lord Wintoun, 198
Cassiobury Park : visited, 332*
Castilio, Signor, teacher of Italian : 310, 337, 344 ; account of Italian priesthood and Neapolitan drama, 360 ; his family, 370 ; Italian abbacies, 370 ; his family again, 374
Castle Tavern, Lombard Street : new home of diarist's club, 368
Celebrations, public : King George's accession, 66, 287 ; King's passage through City, 100 ; King Charles's martyrdom, 173 ; King George's birthday, 245 ; Charles II's Restoration, 247 ; failure of rebellion, 253 ; Pretender's birthday, 254
Chandler, Mrs. : her infatuation for Mr. Freke, 318
Chapman, Rev. Mr. : heard at Bethnal Green, 56
Character, the diarist's : cf. Dudley Ryder, character
Charades, 99
Charing Cross, 81, 180
Charity Schools : evils of, 165, 344
Charles I : portrait at Kensington, 72 ; martyrdom, 173
Charles II : Waller's flattery, 196 ; Triennial Parliaments, 221 ; celebration of Restoration, 247 ; Popish Plot, 302 ; witticism about Lord Delamere, 321 ; an account of his death, 321
Charles VI, Emperor, 259, 296*

380   THE DIARY OF DUDLEY RYDER

Cheapside, 333
Chelsea, 49
Chester, 309
Child, Mr., of Hackney : his gaiety, 261 ; his daughter suggested as wife for diarist, 271
Childwick, Herts : 107*, 334*
Chillingsworth, Dr. William, antipapist writer : 155* ; read, 172, 219, 264
China, Emperor of : cf. Orrery
Churchill, Colonel Charles : witness in trial of Lord Wintoun, 198 ; review of his regiment, 371*
Cibber, Colley : acts as Lord Foppington, 148 ; *The Double Gallant*, 362* ; *Love Makes a Man*, 241*
Cicero : character 128, 133 ; as stylistic model, 140, 143 ; discussed at club, 200, 206 ; *Orations* : Anthony, 128, Archia, 140 ; Catiline, 132, 136 ; Milo, 142, 143 ; *De Finibus*, 170 ; *Paradoxes*, 204, 206 ; *De Legibus*, 219 ; *De Officiis*, 41
Civil Law Club : cf. Law Club ; John's Coffee House
Clark's Bookshop : 77*
Clark, Sir Samuel, acquaintance : at Skinner's ball, 40*
Clarke, Dr. Samuel : *Scripture Doctrine of the Trinity*, 114*, 115
Claudian, 116
Clergymen, Church of England : a disloyal prayer, 66, 152 ; story of one, 152 ; their mischief-making, 161 ; objects of their preaching, 331
Clerk, Richard, of Westbrook : 109*
Clothes, &c. : breeches from silk stockings, 51 ; greatcoat, 115 ; material, 30 ; mending, 35, 61 ; mourning, 91, 340, 345, 346 ; new clothes, 37 ; nightgown, 131 ; ruffles, 66 ; suit, 217, 218, 219, 279 ; sword, cost, 118 ; remorse at its fineness, 119, fear of its being stolen, 132 ; wigs, 30, 45, 77, 258, 281 ; winter coat, 336
Clothiers' Hall : a ball there, 152
Club for discussion of useful subjects : proposed by Mr. Whatley, 200 ; agreed to meet at Hamlin's, 200 : projected members, 200 ; discussion, 206 ; diarist draws up rules, 214 ; 221.

Clubs : cf. Bowes, Club for discussion of useful subjects, Freethinkers' Club, Dissenters' Club, Hamlin's, John's, Law Club, Sue's
Coach : accident, 230 ; hire of, 240 ; purchase of a new coach, 300
Coachmen : truculence of, 109, 243
Coal : Irish and Welsh smokeless, 309
Cobham, Anne, Viscountess : has venereal disease, 325
Coffee Houses : cf. list under Dudley Ryder
Coke's Reports : cf. Law Reading
Cold bath : its benefits, 58 ; visit with Whatley and cost, 79, 89, 190, 194 ; expected benefits, 196, 200, 204, 233 ; discussed, 243, 276, 288, 295, 296
Colebrook, 238
Colebuck, Mr., wigmaker : 30, 258
Committee of Secrecy : its report, 32*, 39 ; attitude of Tories, 41, 48
Common Council : 153, 154
Commons : cf. Inner Temple
Conformity, Act of : 153* ; expected repeal, 154 ; 163 ; 176 ; 361 ; 372
Conversation, chief subjects of : actors, 101 ; art, 88, 96, 363 ; bawdry, 85, 88, 179, 271, 283, 332 ; casuistry, 101 ; criticism, 57, 163 ; economics, 52, 363 ; education, 92, 133 ; etiquette, 156 ; law, (cf. Law Club) ; love, 40, 85, 123, 126, 178, 209, 244, 299, 335, 368 ; mathematics, 150 ; matrimony, 47, 113, 161, 173, 224, 262, 284, 295, 309, 310, 326, 348, 367 ; medicine, 276, 278 ; nonconformity, 153, 361 ; philosophy, 56, 59, 65, 69, 92, 93, 102, 161, 190, 206, 224, — ; poetry, 94, 102, 124, 178, 195, 363 ; politics, 39, 40, 41, 59, 60, 93, 112, 124, 154, 162, 163, 165, 182, 184, 202, 208, 274, 302, 309, — ; preaching, 33, 59, 215, 331 ; prose style, 183, 363 ; religion, 52, 103, 161, 172, 176, 228, 271 ; secrets, 83 ; ventriloquism, 149. (Since so much of the diary consists of reports of conversations, this list is merely a selection of the chief general discussions : conversations about people and events are indexed under the particular subjects)

INDEX

Conversation : diarist's love of general subjects, 36 ; female, 45, 73, 90 ; repetition, 74 ; necessary qualities for, 94, 282 ; bashfulness in, 104 ; satisfactions of, 141 ; dullness in Ryder family, 143 ; benefits of, 143 ; of the aristocracy, 217 ; trifling, 218 ; double entendre, 247, 332 ; stories, 270 ; notes and thoughts about, 286, 287
Conversation, L'art de plaire dans : bought, 354* ; read, 354, 357
Convocation : account of its dispute about a form of prayer, 130
Conway, Francis Seymour, 1st Lord : at Bath, 245*
Cornhill : dance at a tavern there, 92
Cotton, Colonel : witness in trial of Lord Wintoun, 198
Country Customs : assisting new farmers in Herts, 99
Country Fairs : statute, 112*
Country sports : cudgelling in West country, 35 ; in Herts, 98 ; on Whit-Monday, 238
Coursing : cf. Sports
Court, visits to : cf. Drawing Room
Court bath : cf. Bath
Courtship : cf. cousin Watkins, Mr. Whatley, William Ryder, Mr. Hampshire, Samuel Humphries, &c.
Covent Garden Church : loyal sermon there, 253
Cowley, Mrs. : a lovely young widow at Westbrook, 97
Cowper, William, Lord Chancellor : stylistic debt to Locke and Chillingsworth, 155* ; part in impeachment of rebel lords, 169*, 179 ; passes sentence, 180 ; trial of Lord Wintoun, 197 ; supports repeal of Triennial Act, 220
Cox, Dr., physician : attends brother Richard, 341*
Cradock, Mr., of Leicester : story about him, 152
Crisp, Robert : 48 ; defends dissenters, 65 ; at club, 100, &c. : affectation of gentility, 114 ; 154 ; 367
Crisp, Thomas : rumoured grant from King, 237

Crisp, William : account of Liverpool during rebellion, 174 ; captain of Government troops, 175 ; helps to smoke out rebels, 175 ; dying of consumption, 210*, 234 ; prepares for death, 263
Crisp, Mrs. : diarist dines with her, 106 ; dines with diarist, 113 ; her manner, 113 ; new lodgings, 121 ; compliments diarist, 210 ; attitude to her son's illness, 234 ; 237 ; 263
Criticism, literary : discussed, 57, 163
Cromwell, Oliver : Waller's flattery, 196
Cross-bows, the Pretender's, 176*
Crown Tavern, Ironmonger Lane : 65*, &c.
Cucantellus's balsam, 170
Cudgelling : cf. Sports, Country sports
Cummin, Captain, friend : 6 ; Edinburgh law examinations, 30* ; discusses Berkeley, 92 ; discusses translations of Homer, 102
Cupping, 233 (twice)
Cynelum, music master : visits to, 58, &c. ; gives lessons, 120, 223

Dacier, Madame : attack on de la Motte, 30, 31*, 37
Daily Courant, 277*
Dancing : at Hampstead, 30 ; his defect in, 31 ; etiquette, 156 ; desire to dance well, 195, 204 ; at Bath, 245 ; 340 ; minuet, 37, 194 ; rigadoon, 137, 138 ; country dances, 37, 68, 127, 152, 194 ; the Briton, 127 (cf. also Balls and Dances)
Dawson, Mr., of Hackney : puts diarist at ease, 105*
Day, Colonel : his son, 36
Deafness : a cure at Islington, 312
Dear, John, tenant of brother Richard : character, 165
Death, thoughts on : 188, 210, 263, 291, 294, 339, 345, 348
Defoe Daniel, 5, 17, 39*
Defoe, Mr., son of Daniel Defoe : met, 39* ; at Westminster Hall, 125 ; character, 129 ; at Hackney meeting, 140
Deism : inclination of young physicians to, 161

Deison, Mr., brother-in-law of Mrs. Marshall: his wife's gentility, 295, 315; goes to meet Mrs. Marshall, 329*; talks bawdy, 332; his wife discusses matrimony, 348
De la Fond, musician: concert, 171
Delamere, Henry Booth, 2nd Baron: Charles II's witticism about him, 320*
De la Motte, Antoine, author: 31*, 37
Demodore, Mr., music-master: with Mr. Smith, 69, 89, 114, 138
Denn, Mr., of Hackney: agreeable character, 70*; negotiations for new meeting house, 86; at Ryders', 299; his family, 299; gossip about his daughter, 358
Dent, Mr.: method of curing bashfulness, 104
Deptford, 138
Derby: its assemblies, 367
Derby, James, 10th Earl of: Whig activities, 176*
Derham, William: *Astro-Theology* read, 275*
Derham Yard, Strand: cf. Tiltyard Coffee House
Derwentwater, James, 3rd Earl of: imprisoned, 147; in Tower, 147; impeachment, 168; Mr. Owen's story of his defeat at Preston, 173; sentence passed and his speech, 179; wife seeks reprieve, 183; her petition, 185; read, 186; King's attitude, 187; execution described, 187; rumours about his conduct during execution, 193
Deschamps, François: *Caton d'Utique*, read and compared with Addison's *Cato*, 268*, 270
Devonshire, William 2nd, Duke of: moves repeal of Triennial Act, 217; his cascade, 249
Diary: his own, 29, 37 (twice), 177, 223; one kept by Mr. Henry's grandfather, 87
D'Iberville, Monsieur, French ambassador: 172
Dissenters' Club at the Temple: formation and members, 226; proposal of general correspondence, 233; meets at Mitre to discuss politics, 361; its reputation, 374; diarist resolves to neglect it, 374

Dissenters: their political interests, 65, 153, 163, 176 (cf. also Conformity Act and Schism Act); style of preaching, 265, 331; in Ireland, 182; Court attitude to them, 233
Dixon, Mr.: fights a duel, 123*
Doctors' Commons: wills examined there, 353
Doliff, Mr., acquaintance: account of Court of France, 348
Dolins, Daniel, of Hackney: discusses public affairs, 184*: sent mourning, 346
Don Cholerick: to marry Mary Allen, 122
Dormer, Mr.: gives breakfast at Bath, 243
Dorrell, Captain, Jacobite: trial for high treason, 136, 137, 141*
Dowries: Mrs. Anthony, 357; Mrs. Burton, 367, 371; Mrs. Gery, 177; Mrs. Lee, 355; Mrs. Marshall, 252, 255, 273, 326; Mrs. Partridge, 110; Mrs. Walker, 291, 296, 309, 310, 341; a widow, 265
Drapers' Gardens: Mr. Whatley flirts there, 191
Drawing Room: visits to, 62, 66, 77, 221, 253, 356
Dreams: of Pretender, 46*; of marriage, 335; of burglary, 349
Drowning: sensations of, 369
Drury Lane: Theatre, 195; whores, 273
Dry, Mr., acquaintance: a rake, 57*; at Islington Wells, 297
Dryden, John: *Spanish Friar* seen, 181*
Duckett, George, 37*
Dumont, Duke of: interview with Pretender and Queen Anne, 193
Du Mont, Jean: *Nouveau Voyage du Levant*, read, 286*, 287, 294, 329
Duels: Tyssen and Henley, 157; Mr. Humphries challenges Captain Hilliard, 236; diarist settles the affair, 237; Mr. Musgrave, 255; Mr. Dixon, 123
Dunblane, battle at: cf. Sheriffmuir
Duplin, George, Viscount: arrested, 102
Durham Park, near Bath: cf. Blathwayt
Dutch Troops: arrive at Deptford, 137*; leave for Scotland, 137, 141
Dyer's Reports: cf. Law Reading

INDEX

Earle, John : *Microcosmographie*, 285*
Eclipse, the great : 317
Edgware : 100 ; talk with taverner, 112
Edinburgh : 103 ; University, 30, 279, 308
Edmonton, 42* ; 187, 352, 355
Education : cf. Cambridge, Leyden, Oxford, Edinburgh ; charity schools, Quintilian, religion, Dudley Ryder
Election, doctrine of : dispute with father, 170*
Elizabeth, Queen : Birthday riot, 138, 139* ; orders stopping up of Islington Wells, 298
Elliot, Rev. Mr., chaplain to Lord Wintoun, 169
Emmett, John, friend : good company, 81* ; plays flute, 83 ; admires diarist's prints, 88 ; preferences, 96, 252 ; at Court Ball, 356
Enfield, 354
Enfield Chase, 357
Englishman, The, journal : 58* (cf. Steele)
Epistolary Style : Farquhar's, 47 ; Mr. Leeds's, 77 ; Voiture's, 125, 164, 168 ; Locke's, 295 ; the diarist's, 48, 49* ; his excessive care, 75 ; vanity in, 254 ; consideration of, 260 ; merry, 265 ; in love letter, 338 ; compared with the *Spectator*, 351
Epitaph, 148
Epsom, visit to, 32, 33, 283, 288
Epsom Wells : diversions at, 33, 249
Essex, Arthur Capel, 1st Earl of : Braddon's pamphlet on his death in 1683 and its sequel, 321*
Essington, Mr. : his estate near Berkhamstead, 98
Established Church : arguments about, 172, 271, 361
Etiquette : walking with ladies, 31 ; salutes, 97 ; dancing, 156
Eugene, Prince of Savoy : victory over Turks, 295, 296*
Evans, Mrs., of Watford : her Toryism, 213
Examiner, The, journal : its impudence, 62*

Executions : cf. Derwentwater, Kenmure, hangings
Exeter, 150
Eyre, Sir Robert, judge : complaint about his accepting Chancellorship to Prince of Wales, 362*

Farmers : their complaints, 112 ; a good one, 165
Farming, 52
Farquhar, George, author : his letters, 44*, 47
Fashions : gentility, 74, straw hats, 310 ; mottoes, 371
Fénelon, François : *Dialogues des Morts*, 104*, 113
Fernley, Mr., dancing master, 31 ; his politics, 40 ; character, 133 ; fees, 137, 138, 340 ; teaches diarist, 138, 142, 147, 190, 192, 261
Filmer, Sir Robert, philosopher : Locke's arguments against him, 45, 47*
Finall, Mr. : taverner near Berkhamstead, 98
Flamsteed, John, astronomer : opinion of an invention, 67
Flanders : stories about, 312
Flavel, Rev. John, Presbyterian divine : *Of the Immortality of the Soul* read, 266*
Fleet Bridge, 316
Fleet Street, 284, 316
Flemming, Rev. Mr. : tells stories about public affairs, 124*
Flirting and Romping : 76, 126, 127, 164, 191, 238, 239, 248, 251, 269, 270, 272, 300, 332
Flying Post, journal : a letter in, 176
Fontenelle, Bernard le-B. de : his pastorals, 122*, 123, 289 (twice)
Foreigners : a projected essay on the advantage of admitting them, 181
Forester, Lord : witness in trial of Lord Wintoun, 198
Formosa, customs of : according to Psalmanazar, 132, 133
Forster, Thomas, M.P. : order for arrest, 103 ; imprisoned, 147 ; in Newgate, 147*, 198 ; escapes, 218*

Foster, Mr., friend : starts dissenters' club, 226*; character, 234 ; discusses politics, 361 : proposes to establish a weekly journal, 362 ; at Tom's, 365, 372 ; opinion of George I, 373
Fountain Pen : diarist makes one, 87
Fountain Tavern, 153*, 231, 263, 336
Fowler, Christopher, acquaintance : stories about Flanders, 312
Fowles, quack doctor : diarist consults him and takes his medicine, 276, 277, 278, 282, 283, 284, 285, 287, 288
France : diarist's visit to, 166, 297 ; persecution of Protestants, 300 ; debauchery of Court, 348 ; new treaty with England, 338*
Franklin, Mr., acquaintance, 322
Frederick, Prince : cf. Royal Family
Freeholder, The, journal : answer to Pretender's declaration, 169*, 183, 194*; diarist examines its style, 232
Freethinkers' Club : at Grecian Coffee House, 79
Freke, Rev. Thomas : offers to introduce diarist to L. C. J. King, 164*; diarist dines with him, 203, 294 ; dies, 318* ; loved by two ladies, 319 ; cousin Robert seeks the vacancy, 347
French : conversations in, 31, 203 ; ousting Latin, 195 ; benefits of translating, 258 ; books bought, 37, 40, 102, 354 (for his French Reading, cf. Dudley Ryder, Reading)
Friends and acquaintances : cf. under Dudley Ryder
Frogs : cf. Ireland
Fryer, Sir John, Sheriff of London : at execution of Derwentwater and Kenmure, 188 ; his feast, 213*
Fuller, Samuel, M.P., 186*
Fuller, Justice : abused by Rev. Mr. Henley from pulpit, 325*
Funerals : Richard Ryder, 91 ; grandmother, 344

Gags, the Pretender's : Mr. Owen's letter, 176
Gambling : temptations, 34, 158 ; losses, 161
Games : on Twelfth Day, 163 (cf. also Card games, Charades)

Garrick, David, 37*
Garth, Dr. Samuel, poet : quarrel about the Pretender, 328*
Gascoigne, tailor : measures diarist, 218
Gay, John : *The What D'Ye Call It* read and discussed, 146*
George I : cf. Royal Family
Gery, Mrs., of Hackney : partner at dance, 163 ; rumours of diarist's intentions, 177
Gifford, Mrs. : proposed for brother William, 353 ; her father's will, 353
Gill House : visits to, 37, 39, 183, 279, 312
Glaziers : rumoured encouragement of window-smashing, 41
Glover, Mr., master of Ironmongers' Company, 356
God, attributes of : cf. Religion
Goodall, Mr., friend : 42 ; a sceptic, 79
Gore, Mr., acquaintance : at Button's, 78*
Gorthan, Mrs., of Hackney, 284*
Gossip, 108, 135, 202, &c.
Gould, Ichabod, of Hackney : visits diarist, 120
Gould, Mr., of Hackney : his impudence, 75*; affects the rake, 86, 90 ; passionate in Hackney controversy, 155 ; at Court Ball, 356
Gower, John Leveson-Gower, 1st Earl : goes bail for Wyndham, 259
Gray's Inn Walks : 201
Grecian Coffee House : visited, 79*; Freethinkers' Club, 79 ; company there, 185, 189, 315, 367
Greek : a method of learning, 44 ; its strength, 163 (cf. also Homer)
Greenor, Rev. Mr. : his style in preaching, 95
Greenwich : 64, 373
Greenwood, Mr., a meal at his (inn ?), 112
Gregg, Mr., friend : races with diarist, 31 ; love for Tristram, 35 ; fondness for diarist, 48, 91 ; discusses stewards of manors and legal practice, 106 ; visit to him at Putney, 216

INDEX

Gresley, Derbyshire: home of Aunt Stevenson and Aunt Allen, 151, 340
Grotius: *De veritate religionis Christi* read, 105
Grumbler, The, journal, 37*
Guardian, The, journal, 39, 214

Habeas Corpus Act: suspension of, 59, 60, 171
Hackney, Middlesex: diarist visits his home there, 30, *et passim*; ladies there, 75; character of people there, 203; schoolgirls, 81*, 84, 102, 151
Hackney, new meeting house: controversy about successor of Matthew Henry, 43*, 116, 155, 216; zeal of women in the quarrel, 219; site for new meeting house, 86*; opening, 215; Mr. Mayo preaches, 215; choice of new minister, 305; Mr. Smith chosen, 319. Cf. also names of preachers: Calamy, Billio, Mayo, Smith, Tong, &c.
Hackney coaches: encounters in, 37, 46; a lift in, 77; petition of coachmen, 183
Hackney Marsh: skating there, 164, 165; walks there, 208, 210
Haddon, Mr., acquaintance: seen at Court, 62
Hales, Judge, 365
Hall, John, of Otterbury: hanged, 274*; his last speech, 277
Hamilton, Sir David, physician, 363*
Hamilton, James, Douglas, Duke of: duel with Lord Mohun, 257*
Hamlin's Coffee House: 192; discussion club meets there, 206, 221, 227, 231, 263, 283, 310, 333
Hammond, Mrs., Hackney Schoolmistress: at church, 81
Hampden, Mr., M.P.: opens trial of Lord Wintoun, 197
Hampshire, Mr.: inclination to Mrs. Loyd, 201
Hampstead: 90; slough near, 90; man struck lame, 317; Hampstead Wells described, 30, 292, 294; Hampstead Walks, 76

Hampton Court: Prince and Princess of Wales there, 298, 310
Hand Court: 77
Hangings: Oxburgh, 234; Hall and Paul, 274; Bean and other robbers, 336
Harcourt, Simon, 1st Viscount, 169
Harding, Aunt: 71*; treated, 199
Harding, Ned, cousin: given old clothes, 49; fears that brother William is corrupting him, 285*; Mrs. Bailey abuses him, 320
Harley, Sir Roland: he and his son sought as rebels, 175
Harris, John, journalist: main author of *The Patriots*, 156
Harris, Mr., Steele's secretary, 183
Harrison, Lady: visited at Epsom, 34; attempts fine manners, 34; her daughters and son, 34
Harrison's Walks: cf. Bath
Harvey, Edward, of Combe, M.P.: order for arrest, 103
Hatfield House: 333*
Haversham, Maurice Thompson, Baron, 156*
Hawksbee, Mrs., landlady: politics, 164; frightened by strange appearance in the air, 192
Hay, The: cf. Westbrook Hay
Hayward, Mr., friend and druggist: at Cousin Watkins's dance, 68*; astonishing ability to entertain ladies, 92
Heathcote, Mr., friend: 52*; character, 79, 154, 165; fondness for bawdy, 179; opinions on Triennial Act, 208; at bonfire, 287, 367
Hemel Hemstead, Herts: visited, 97, 107, 108, 333
Henley, Mr.: fights with John Tyssen, 157, 158
Henley, Rev. Mr.: quarrel with Dr. Read, 325
Henry, Rev. Matthew, Nonconformist divine: his sermons, 43*, 50; Expositions on New Testament, 50; his *Life*, 354*
Henry, Mrs., widow of the above: her excessive dejection at husband's death, 63; dines with Ryders, 135, 308; plays cards, 371

Henry, Philip, son of above : 63*; jumps with diarist, 85; his relations, 88*; good scholar, 92; at Twelfth Day party, 163; going to Edinburgh, 279, 308; visits, 285

Hide, Mr., acquaintance : 73

Highgate : visits to Mrs. Marshall, 272, 351, 354, 355, 367

Hilliard, Captain : at Hackney dance, 236*; quarrel with Samuel Humphries, 236

Hiot, Mrs., of Hackney : 87; her gravity, 131

History of Queen Zarah : cf. Pamphlets

Hoadly, Dr. Benjamin : 183; his sermons read, 245, 369

Holidays : arguments against, 52

Hollier, Dr., acquaintance : discusses Whigs and Dissenters, 153; liveliness, 231; opinion on Princess of Wales's accouchement, 363

Homer : 30, 31, 33*; Tickell's translation, 32, 102; Pope's, 32, 102

Honour, thoughts on : 147

Horace : Satires, 208, —; translation bought, 77, its defects, 81; Odes, 78, 87, 264, 91, 134; discussion at Club, 207, 221

Horse : purchase of, 231, 234, 273, 289, 292, 329; hire of, 237; race with Gregg, 31; journeys on horseback, to and from Epsom, 33-4; to Canons, 111; Edmonton, 187: Slough and Westbrook, 212; to Bath, 238-9; from Bath, 250-2; Islington, 303; to and from Westbrook, 331, 334; Highgate, 351; Edmonton, 352, 355; Enfield, 354; Enfield Chase, 357 (This list of journeys includes only the chief ones)

Horseman, Mr., friend : understanding of law, 171*; discusses Mr. Humphries, 183; rides to Edmonton, 187; member of dissenters' club, 226; visited, 353, 361

Hot Wells : cf. Bristol

Housekeeping : cost of, 96, 287, 295, 340

House Property : Mr. Ryder's, 326, 369; the worries of, 343

Howard, Mr., of Hackney : ability as raconteur, 200; entertains diarist, 218; diarist borrows his horse, 331*

Howard, coachmaker : makes a coach for Aunt Lomax, 300

Howell, Rev. Laurence : 336*

Hoxton : cannon foundry near, 205

Hudson, Mr., friend : meeting with Hackney schoolgirls, 81*, 82; opinion of Bragg, 83; discusses schoolgirls, 102; character, 102, 115; education, 115; entertained, 120; becomes clerk to Mr. Marsh, 166; breakfasts with the Ryders, 297

Hudson, Mrs., Hackney : supper with diarist, 273; goes to bonfire, 287; comparison of two sisters, 287; breakfasts with Ryders, 297

Hughes, John, author : 195; vanity, 202*; connection with Addison's *Cato*, 202

Hughes, musician : sings at St. Paul's, 35

Hulse, Dr. Edward, physician : freethinker, 161*; discusses patient with cousin Watkins, 227

Hulst, Mr., friend and druggist : at Cousin Watkins's dance, 68*; sells tea and coffee, 89; at dance in Cornhill, 92

Humphreys, Samuel, friend and author : Letter to Mrs. Loyd, 95; part author of *The Patriots*, 156*; sweet on Mrs. Loyd, 157; reputation, 171; part author of *The Instructor*, 183; esteemed by Mrs. Loyd, 210; challenges an admirer of Mrs. Loyd, 236, 254; willing to marry her, 260; assignation with her, 269

Hungary Water : embrocation, 86

Hunt, Mr., acquaintance : 139, 325

Hunt, Dr. Jeremiah, Nonconformist divine : his style, 50*, 148; his congregation, 148

Huntingdon, Earl of : suit with aunt Allen, 44

Huntly, George Gordon, 4th Marquis of : about to submit to Government, 172*

Hutchinson, Captain : intended visit to his tent, 73*

Hutton, Mrs., Hackney schoolmistress, 82

INDEX 387

Hyde Park : entertaining ladies there, 55, 62, 260 ; review there, 371 ; camp there (cf. Army camp)

Illness, the diarist's : vomiting, 33 ; fever, 37 ; cold, 39 ; tumour in hand, 44, 45 ; toothache, 119 ; cough, 134 ; curing a cold, 134 (twice), 135 ; results of tooth extraction, 142 (thrice) ; shoulder pain, 170 (twice), 171 ; scurvy, 190 ; rheumatic pains, 190 ; summary of complaints, 196 ; fever, 209 ; pain in his arm, 231, 233, 257, 258, 288, 301, 309, 312 ; consultation with Dr. Baire at Bath, 243 ; drastic cures, 257, 258 ; itch, 259 ; consultations with Dr. Wadsworth, 257, 268 ; cures for rheumatism, 268 ; vomiting, 269 ; consumption feared, 269 ; visits to Fowles the quack, 276, 277, 278 ; his medicine, 278, 282, 283, 284, 285, 287, 288 ; wasp sting, 285 ; improved appearance, 305 ; giddiness, 306 ; discussed with Dr. Lee, 312 ; faintness, 334. (Cf. also visits to Bath and Islington Spa)

Immigrants : cf. Foreigners

Impeachment of Rebel Lords : 164 ; described, 168

Indemnity : Lechmere proposes Act of, 178 ; opposed, 178

India House : orrery at, 138, 139

Inner Temple : diarist enters into commons, 227 ; exercises, 258 ; dines there, 230, 258, 357, 361 ; pays dues, 357

Inner Temple Hall : play performed there, 177

Inquisition, Spanish : an account of an interview, 145

Instructor, The, journal : partly written by Samuel Humphries, 183 ; its style, 183

Ireland : feared invasion, 182 ; frogs and coal in, 309 ; Protestantism and courage of Irish Parliament, 144

Ironmonger, Mrs., of Hackney : 51*, 310

Ironmongers' Hall : Lord Mayor's Day Ball, 127*, 356 ; a lady met there, 356, 360

Isaac, Mrs., of Hackney : censorious behaviour, 108

Islay, Lord : supports repeal of Triennial Act, 220

Isles, Mr., friend : sprightly conversion, 39, 120, 155, 201, 217 ; desires club to move to a tavern, 367

Islington : New River Head, 79 ; skating there, 164

Islington Spa : 295* ; described, 296 ; Mr. Suly there, 279 ; Mr. Dry there, 297 ; Dr. Lee's account of its history, 298 ; its merits, 298* ; Dr. Tilly there, 301 ; effect on diarist, 306 ; Cures, 312, 318 ; other visits, 306 (twice), 309, 311, 312, 327, 330, 336, 338, &c.

Italian : books bought, 40 ; Italian songs, 95 ; diarist reads, 165 ; speaks, 337, 344 ; *Telemachus* read, 338 (twice), 346. (Cf. also Castilio and Porter)

Italian abbacies : described, 370.

Italian priesthood : punishment of crime among, 360

Jackson, Mr., friend : his humour, 32 ; character, 42 ; reads *Tale of a Tub*, 114 ; discusses public affairs, 274 ; at a Ball, 356, 367, &c.

James II : calls in Irish, 70* ; death of Charles II, 321 ; birth of the Pretender, 327*

Jane, Mrs., servant to Mrs. Ryder, junr., 250* ; with child, 355

Jeffries, Mrs., Robert Billio's mother-in-law : 96*

Jekyll, Sir Joseph, M.P. : to present petition for reprieve of rebel lords, 185* ; speaks in trial of Wintoun, 197

Jermyn, Mrs. : met at Westbrook, 97

Jersey, William, 2nd Earl of : arrested, 102

Jewel, a political, 314

Jobson, Mr., acquaintance : met in Hyde Park, 55 ; his lady cousins, 55

John, servant to Mr. Ryder, 171*, 237, 310, 346

John's Coffee House : visits to club there, 32*, &c. : estimate of the club, 120 ; diarist's cheerfulness there, 146 ; his awe there, 374

Johnson, Mr., of Hemel Hemstead: his barbarity, 333
Jones, Mr., ex-proprietor of Islington Spa, 298
Journals: cf. *Daily Courant, Englishman, Flying Post, Freeholder, Grumbler, Guardian, Instructor, Nonconformist Journal, Occasional Paper, Patriot, Spectator, Tatler*
Journeys: cf. Horse-Riding, Thames, Dudley Ryder and Place-Names
Judgment, good: prejudice in favour of, 145
Jumont, Lord: goes bail for Wyndham, 259
Juries: their hardships, 320; Major Pitt's service, 346
Justice, Mr., of Hackney: plays bowls and discusses Barker, 216
Juvenal: diarist's translation, 134

Kelly, Mr., acquaintance: account of his interview by the Spanish inquisition, 145
Keniston, Mrs.: brother William's intrigue with, 255
Kenmure, William Gordon, 6th Viscount: impeachment, 168; executed, 187
Kennedy, Mr., friend, 88
Kensington Gardens, 253
Kensington Palace: described, 72
Kentish Town: visits to Uncle Marshall, 40*, &c.
Kielmansegg, Charlotte von, mistress to George I: sells places, 299*
King, Sir Edmund, physician: attends Charles II on deathbed, 322*
King, Sir Peter, Chief Justice: Mr. Whatley's acquaintance with him, 34*, 69*, 150; proposed introduction of diarist, 164, 203, 177
King's Bath: cf. Bath
King's Chapel: service there, 253
King's Evil: and venereal disease, 206
Kingsford, Mr.: his wealth and avarice, 161, 259; his account of the Court, 299
Kingston-on-Thames: Mr. Mayo minister there, 306
Kirk of Scotland: Argyll's movement to help it, 372
Kissing: cf. Flirting

Knot, Mrs., servant: fondness for diarist, 199, 252*
Kynaston, Cuthbert, M.P.: order for arrest, 103*

Lacy, Mr., of Hackney: feelings about new meeting, 100*, 199; his wife's covetousness, 115*
Lambeth Wells: visited and described, 57*
Lancaster: rebels at, 135; Mayor proclaims Pretender, 136
Land Tax: unjust assessments, 346
Lancaster, county of: Whig activity there, 174
Lansdowne, George Granville, Baron: arrested, 102*; to be charged with conspiracy, 156*; *Jew of Venice*, 114*
Latin: its strength, 163; Burmann on its neglect, 195; Mrs. Marshall discussed in, 338 (cf. also names of writers)
Law Club: Mr. Bowes's, 364; the diarist's, 165, 190, 207, 223, 226, 256, 264, &c.
Law Practice: 31; judges who encourage litigation, 106, 166; diarist's familiarity with, 180
Law, Study of: misgivings about, 30, 64, 91, 93, 115, 184, 192, 219; Inn exercises, 258, 283, 291, 347, 353, 364, 365, 367; Reading: Coke, 49, 91, 147, 184; Dyer, 281; Perkins, 87, 113, 116. (These entries are not exhaustive. Cf. also *Trials*)
Lea, River, 216
Leadenhall Street: Mr. Ryder's property there, 345, 347, 348
Lechmere, Nicholas, M.P.: proposes indemnity for rebels, 178*; blocks Bill for speedier trial, 184; alliance with Argyll, 373
Lee, Dr., physician, 306*; his account of Islington Spa, 297; advises diarist, 312; relish of whoring, 313; courtship of a widow, 318; account of 1688 Revolution and death of Charles II, 320; describes quarrel between Dr. Read and Mr. Henley, 325; describes Pretender's birth, 327; account of political disturbance at Manchester, 330; account

INDEX 389

of Bean's hanging, 336 ; discusses new treaty with France, 338

Lee, Mrs., friend : 30 ; vindicates diarist's gallantry, 32 ; opinion on courtship, 67 ; kindness for diarist, 76, 90 ; rumours of engagement to him, 96*, 128, 177, 286 ; marriage to Mr. Utber, 345*, 355 ; her fortune, 355 ; visited, 374

Lee, Mr., father of above : 30

Lee, Sir William, L.C.J. : dies, 25

Leeds, Edward, friend : letter makes diarist envious, 77*, 302 ; Mr. Defoe's opinion of, 129 ; character, 130, 154, 205, 207 ; intellect, 223 ; member of dissenters' club, 226 ; letter to, 265 ; letter from, 318 ; visited, 353, 361 ; account of Duke of Argyll, 372, 374

Legal oratory : Roman and English, 136

Leicester : manifestations of loyalty, 152

Le Sage, A. R. : *Le Diable Boiteux*, 46*

Letter of application for a job : Mr. Whatley's, 221

Lewis, Aunt : 122, 185* ; her tact, 208

Lewis, Jack, cousin : present for, 208

Leyden, University of, 65, 195

Lies : lawfulness of official lies discussed, 100

Lincoln's Inn, 353

Lincoln's Inn Fields Theatre, 128*

Lindamira : cf. Tom Brown

Literary style : his own, 232 (cf. also Epistolary Style)

Little, Mrs., of Hackney : funeral sermon, 258

Liverpool : during the rebellion, 174

Locke, John, 29 ; *Two Treatises of Government*, 45, 47* ; *Reasonableness of Christianity*, 75 ; *Letters on Toleration*, 89, 155, 156, 164, 295 ; *On raising the value of coin*, 231* ; *Letters*, 295* ; style, 75

Lomax, Caleb, 107, 109

Lomax, Joshua, father of above : 89* ; met and described, 107*-8 ; litigation with Mr. Ryder, 107, 108 : account of his villainy, 148

Lomax, Thomas, decd., brother of above : his will, 56*, 107* ; villainously treated by his brother, 148

Lomax, Aunt, widow of above and brother Richard's mother-in-law, 41 ; her odd sayings, 97, 98 ; provides handsome dinner, 110 ; recounts old Joshua's villainy, 148 ; valetudinarianism, 213 ; buys a coach, 300 ; visits brother Richard, 343 ; opinion of Mrs. Marshall, 354, 355

London Coffee House, 162

London Fields, Hackney, 56

Longinus, 30

Lonsdale, Henry Lowther, 3rd Viscount : flees from rebels at Penrith, 135*, 136

Lord Mayor's Show, 127 ; Day, 355

Louis XIV : expected death, 74 ; reported death, 81 ; attitude to Turkish War, 296

Lovat, Simon, Lord : diarist conducts his trial, 24

Love affairs : cf. under Dudley Ryder, Borrett, Freke, Humphries, Powell, William Ryder, Utber, Watkins, Whatley

Love-story, an affecting, 357

Loveits, Mr., swordmaker : sword bought from, 118

Lovel, Mr., dancing master : his great ability, 204

Loyd, Mrs., friend living with Aunt Bickley, 71 ; visit to Hyde Park with diarist, 72 ; liveliness, 73 ; critical humour, 85 ; projected letters to her, 94 ; fondness for brother William, 94 ; diarist's fondness for her, 115 ; excuse for seeing her, 119 ; likes diarist, 119 ; visited, 122, &c. ; kicks over traces, 124 ; petting with diarist, 126, 127, 131 ; lent books, 127 ; Sam Humphries's love for her, 157 ; at Twelfth Day party, 163 ; good breeding, 163 ; never seems obliged, 176 ; letter to, 171 ; suitability as a mistress, 177 ; courted by Mr. Woolridge, 185 ; amorous disposition, 194 ; Mr. Hampshire enamoured, 201 ; pleased with diarist's company, 205 ; discusses romances and love, 209 ; esteem for Mr. Humphries, 210 ; blooded, 211 ; obstinacy, 211, 228 ; at Mrs. Wallis's ball, 235 ; Hum-

phries quarrels about her, 236; preens herself on this, 237, 238; reputation, 254; attitude to Mr. Humphries, 259; diarist's cheerfulness with her, 262; leaves for Bristol, 268; assignation with Mr. Humphries, 269
Lucan, 116
Lucas Square, 93
Lully, J. B.: *Songs from Psyche*, 207★

Macartney, General George: outlawry reversed, 235, 257★
Machine 'for performing an equal at sea', 67★
McIntosh, General William, of Borlum: imprisoned, 147; in Newgate, 147; story of how he lost battle of Preston, 173–4★; escapes, 232★
Madrid, 323
Mahometan Customs: Pitt's account of, 329
Manchester: a political disturbance, 330 (cf. also Mrs. Walker)
Manley, Mrs. de la Rivière, 337★
Mar, John Erskine, Earl of: raises Highlanders, 103★, 135★; defeated, 139, 140; pursued, 178; flees to France, 179★, 181
Mare Street, Hackney: 16, 94, &c.
Marlborough, Wilts: meeting with a dairymaid, 238; the downs and wells, 239: an adventure near there, 239
Marlborough, John Churchill, 1st Duke of: character in Steele's *Englishman*, 85; falls out with Walpole, 299; seriously ill, 363★
Marlborough, Sarah, Duchess of: satirised, 337★
Marlborough Head Tavern: dinner there, 114, 166, 323, 326
Marriage: hopes of an agreeable wife, 45, 47; necessary to restrain peevishness, 49; danger of ill-tempered wife, 54; an ideal couple, 77; rumoured engagement to Mrs. Lee, 96; thoughts about Mrs. Partridge, 110; improbability of perfection, 123; thoughts about Mrs. Lee and Mrs. Loyd, 177; about Mrs. Marshall, 251, 254, 256, 273; qualifications of a wife, 274; copulation,

284; Mr. Powell's views, 288; necessary dowries, 310; a pleasing fancy, 366; financial prospects, 370
Marsh, Mr., attorney of Hackney: engaged in family litigation, 109★, 166
Marshall, John, uncle: his Toryism, 41; character, 144; plays cards, 200; political prejudice, 255; visits Mr. Rollison, 301; charitableness, 313, 339; legacy from grandmother, 340
Marshall, Aunt, wife of above: 41; hurt in coach accident, 230; Toryism, 255; advises diarist to use blue flannel, 286
Marshall, Nathaniel, son of above: 40★, 42; edition of St Cyprian's Works, 40★, 190; describes Dr. Bentley, 214; preaches, 262; discusses diarist's illness, 276; goes to quack, 278, 301, 314
Marshall, cousin, of Wisbech, 53★
Marshall, Sally, of Highgate: diarist falls in love at first sight, 211★; her beauty, 211; desire to see her, 230; met at Bath, 239; admired, 240; her gaiety, 242; attitude to a lover, 244; fondness for Mr. Powell, 244; refuses to dance with diarist, 245–6; her character, 246; unkindness to diarist at Bath, 247, 249, 250, 251; diarist's love for her, 249, 251, 253, 256; familiarity with Sam Powell, 248; love of secrecy, 248; diarist thinks of marriage, 251; her fortune, 252, 255; letter from, 256; returning from Bath, 257; walk in Hyde Park with diarist, 260; discussed with cousin Joseph Billio, 261; missed by diarist, 262, 263 (twice); character, 264, 267; admired by cousin Joseph, 268; her admiration for officers, 270, 271; diarist visits her family, 272; visits Mrs. Richard Ryder, 273, &c.; diarist's consuming love, 275; Dr. Avery's fondness for her, 242, 277, 278, 279; breakfast with her, 280, 281, 282, 285; views on housekeeping charges, 287; love of gentility, 287, 295; attitude to diarist, 287, 288; amorousness and

father's fortune, 288, 290 ; diarist imagines a proposal, 290 ; visit to Westbrook Hay, 292 ; courted by wealthy men, 294 ; views on love, 295 ; shown Mr. Powell's verses, 297 ; diarist's talk of her causes trouble, 299 ; discussed with Joseph, 301 ; displeased, 302, 306, 312, 313 ; diarist offers his services, 315, 319 ; inspires sister Ryder to criticism, 325 ; Mr. Ryder discusses her, 326 ; her father the tailor, 326 ; goes to Westbrook, 328 ; diarist visits her family, 329 ; unkindness, 332 ; mushroom-gathering, 333 ; rivalry of diarist and cousin Joseph, 332, 333, 334 ; further unkindness, 334 ; discussed by diarist and cousin Joseph, 335, 341, 344, 347, 349 ; discussed in Latin, 338 ; Aunt Billio's opinion of her, 341 ; diarist's poem to her, 342, 343, 344, 349 (twice), 354, 355 ; her opinion of diarist, 347, 353 ; diarist pleases her, 353 ; his family's opinion of her, 354, 355, 357, 363 ; diarist accompanies her to the play, 364, 365, 367, 369
Marshall, Mrs., mother of above : at Bath, 245
Marshalsea : rebels imprisoned there, 147 ; jury there, 235
Marten, Mr., acquaintance : character, 73
Martin, Mr., acquaintance : account of a ventriloquist, 149 ; stories of Oxford, 365
Marylebone : grandmother buried there, 344
Massery, Rev. Mr. : impudent style, 262
Mathematics, study of : recommended by Mr. Whatley, 150
Maynard, serjeant-at-law : story of the supernatural, 322
Mayo, Rev. Richard : 155* ; preaches first sermon in new meeting at Hackney, 215 ; character, 215 ; administers sacrament, 228 ; at Mr. Crisp's, 234, 254 ; funeral sermon, 258 ; visits Ryders, 259, 275, 293 ; favours Smith as new minister at Hackney, 305 ; account of choosing new minister, 319, 338, 339, 345, 346, 362, 369

Mead, Dr. Richard, physician : a deist, 161*
Meals : meat pie, 33 ; boiled beef, 39 ; toast and milk, 49 ; fish, 64 ; mutton chops, 65 ; eggs, bacon and boiled beef, 66 ; plum cake, 80 ; bread, butter and birch wine, 81 ; fowls, tarts and fruit, 92 ; cold pork and ale, 98 ; trouts, 99 ; roast beef, 112 ; oysters and cold fowl, 194 ; cold dishes, 246 ; oysters, 312 ; turkey, 349
Mears, Mr., of Hackney : 48, 106*
Medicines, Empiric : their value, 276
Memory : memorising sermons, 144 (cf. also Artificial Memory)
Mermaid Tavern, Hackney, 16, 38*
Merreal Family, friends : 67*
Merryweather, Mr., acquaintance, 156*
Mesees, Mrs., acquaintance, 213
Miller, Mrs., musician : concert at London Bridge, 140
Millex, Mr., friend : lives in Wine Office Court, 53 ; character, 53, 79
Mills, John, actor : virtuousness, 101* ; acts in Rowe's *Tamerlane*, 359
Mills, Mr., friend : his polite Latin, 57*, 64, 371
Milton, John : 124 ; *Il Penseroso*, 214*
Mimicry : usefulness in conversation, 121
Miracles of New Testament : authority for, 104 ; Grotius on, 105
Mitre Tavern : Club there, 361
Molesworth, Colonel Richard : at Bath, 246* ; gallantry, 248
Molière : *Les Précieuses Ridicules*, 114 ; *Cocu Imaginaire*, 114 ; *L'Escole des Maris*, 125 ; *L'Escole des Femmes*, 128, 166 ; *Le Misanthrope*, 141, 142
Molyneux, William, Viscount Maryborough : house searched for rebels, 175*
Molyneux, William : Locke's letters to him, 295
Montagu, Mr. Wortley : ambassador to Constantinople, 221 ; Mr. Whatley's letter to him, 221
Montague, John, Duke of : at Southwark Fair, 101*
Montaigne, Michel de, 70
Montrose, 179

Moor, Mrs. : at Bath, 247
Moorfields : books bought there, 44, 104, 122, 211, 354
Moreland, Samuel : 75★ ; reflected on, 158 ; political views, 163
Moreland, Samuel, son of above : plays whisk, 158 ; views on Roman virtue and Romans, 349
Morocco : cf. Muley Mulock
Mottoes of the nobility : 371
Mountebanks : at Hemel Hemstead, 97
Mourning : cf. Clothes
Mug-houses : proceedings at, 279 ; value to Whigs, 280 ; songs, 279 ; toasts, 317 ; riots, 280, 283, 315
Muley Mulock, 'Emperor of Morocco' : an account of 'his son's' adventures, 323★-4
Mundy, General : witness in trial of Lord Wintoun, 198
Mungor, Mr., brewer : chosen common councilman, 155 ; how chosen, 156
Musgrave, Mr., officer : wounded in political fight, 255
Mushroom-gathering : 333
Music : diarist plays viol or flute, 29, et passim : at Epsom, 33 ; church anthems, 34 ; plays with Mr. Burroughs, 59 ; with John Emmett, 83 ; sings and plays with cousin Billio, 87 ; sings Italian songs, 95 ; viol and flute duets, 95 ; Mr. Spering plays harpsichord, 118 ; flute and viol sonatas, 120 ; viol lesson, 120 ; concerts, 140, 171 ; sonatas with Mr. Whatley, 177 ; practice, 192 ; music-master sings 'Genius of England', 203 ; a musical evening, 207 ; hopes of improvement in playing, 223 ; a book on the bass viol, 226 ; at King's Chapel, 253 ; Mrs. Oileman sings, 271 ; its consolation, 295 ; Mr. Suly sings, 297 ; viol duets, 299

Nag's Head, Hackney : 17
Nairne, William, 2nd Baron : impeachment, 168 ; sentence, 180 ; reprieved 187★ ; makes discoveries to the King, 194

Naples : theatres and drama there, 360
Nash, Richard 'Beau' : account of, 240★ ; at a ball, 245
Neve, Mr., of Hackney : at the Ryders', 299
Neville, Grey, M.P. ; in communication with Shute Barrington about Schism and Occasional Conformity Acts, 154★ ; a letter from, 265 ; hopes of repeal, 372
Newbury, Berks : 238 ; famous for crayfish and trout, 238
Newbury, Mrs., Mr. Warren's love for her, 360★
New Exchange : collection of glass there, 130★
New Inn, 258
Newcastle, Sir Thomas Pelham-Holles, Duke of : promotes Whig riots, 255★
Newcome, Henry, of Hackney, 15, 66★ ; preaches at Hackney, 180★
Newcome, Rev. Peter, vicar of Hackney and father of above : 15, 43★, 66 ; preaches a Whiggish sermon, 132 ; politics 173 ; quoted, 253★, 309★
Newdigate, Sir Richard : his character, 260★ ; his father's cunning, 266
Newgate, 147 (twice) ; attempted escapes, 178 ; escapes, 218, 232
Newington Green, 38, 40★ ; cf. also Biscoe
Newnham, Anne, of Streatham : meets diarist, 20 ; marries him, 21★
Nithsdale, William Maxwell, 5th Earl of : impeached, 168 ; sentenced, 179 ; escapes, 189★
Noble : French author : his dialogues, 102
Nonconformist Weekly : a proposed journal, 362
Norris, Henry, actor : farce at Bartholomew Fair, 86★ ; at Southwark Fair, 101
Northey, Sir Edward : Attorney-General : profits, 106★ ; trial of Lord Wintoun, 196
Northey, Edward, barrister : character as a lawyer, 183★

INDEX   393

North's Coffee House : visits to, 182, 297, 328
Northumberland : risings in, 265
Nottingham, Daniel Finch, 2nd Earl of : 176 ; turned out of office, 190 ; opposes repeal of Triennial Act, 220, 267
Nye, Philip, 3

Oates, Titus : part in Popish Plot, 302
Oaths : administered to City of London and Westminster, 155 ; possible effect of, 155
Occasional Conformity Act : cf. Conformity, Act of
Occasional Paper : a projected essay, 181 ; proposed letter, 300
Oileman, Mrs., of Hackney : her charm, 271, 350 ; her pictures, 289
Old Bailey, 315
Oldfield, Rev. Joshua : strange style in preaching, 238*
Oldfield, Dr. : 232* ; at Islington Spa, 317 (possibly same person as above)
Oldsworth, Rev. Dr. : preaches, 71 ; met at Hackney, 116
Oldsworth, Mr. : his history, 217
Operas : 166 ; in France, 207
Opie, Mr., acquaintance : comes to breakfast, 118*, 353*
Oratory : differences between Roman and English, 136
Orleans, Duke of, Regent of France : expected to succeed Louis XIV, 74, 81* ; connexion with Pretender, 103 ; rumoured help for Pretender, 157 ; rebuked by George I, 172, 191; attitude to Turkish War, 296, 328 ; his debauchery, 348
Ormonde, James Butler, Duke of : proposed impeachment, 40 ; escape, 60* ; poem on his running away, 78 ; reported off Torbay, 131 ; his pear, 315 ; rumours, 316
Ormonde Street, 93
Orrery : Emperor of China's, 138 ; described, 139*, 140
Overall, Mrs., of Hackney : 83*
Ovid, 116
Owen, Rev. Charles, of Warrington : at brother Ryder's, 136* ; hated by Tories, 136 ; account of battle of Preston, 173 ; letter in *Flying Post*,
176 ; defects in arguing, 177 ; recounts political rumours, 181
Owens, William : diarist prosecutes him, 24
Oxburgh, Colonel Henry : hanged, 234*
Oxford, Robert Harley, 1st Earl of : impeached, 32 ; discussion about his trial, 154 ; incriminating letters, 182*
Oxford : trial of rebels, 136, 137, 141 ; rebellion subdued, 141
Oxford, Mr., friend : at Mr. Bowes's, 178, 183
Oxford, University of : infested with Toryism, 74 ; poverty of its education, 133 ; debauchery there, 143 ; rebuked for rebelliousness, 207, 365

Page, Mr., undertaker, 346
Page, Mr., acquaintance : strange manner of speaking, 144-5
Painting and prints : discussed, 88, 363 ; diarist's collection, 88, 96, 103 ; Mrs. Oileman's, 289
Pakington, Sir John, M.P. : order for arrest, 103
Pamphlets : *Advice to the Tories*, 117 ; *An Answer to the Bishop of Canterbury's . . . Declaration against the Rebellion*, 153 ; *Pretender's Declaration*, 169 ; *On the Nature of Study*, 201 ; *Proposals for easing the nation's debts*, 230, 231 ; *History of Queen Zarah*, 337*
Papillon, Mr. : his eccentricity, 351*
Parents : necessity of gratitude to, 215 ; children's reliance on their judgment, 229 ; evils of faultfinding, 293
Paris : memoirs of a visit, 59, 166, 297 ; Dr. Garth there, 328
Parish duties : increase in, 96
Parker, Thomas, L.C.J. : Nonconformist opinion of him, 361 ; his pension, 361*
Parry, Mr., suitor to Abigail Ryder, 185
Parsimony : cf. Venner, Richard Ryder, senr.
Partnerships : Mr. Ryder discusses partnerships in his firm, 212, 256, 291, 340

Partridge, Mr., of Hemel Hemstead, 109*; dines with Aunt Lomax, 110; his wife, 110; his daughter proposed for diarist, 110
Passive Obedience, doctrine of: disputed at Bath, 247; cf. also Berkeley
Patriot, The, journal: written by Harris and Humphries, 156*
Patten, Rev. Robert, renegade rebel: witness in trial of Lord Wintoun, 197*
Paul, Rev. William: hanged, 274*; last speech, 277
Paulet, Charles, 62*
Penkethman, actor: his farce at Southwark Fair, 101
Penrith, 135*
Pepys, Samuel, vii, 6, 13, 15, 82*
Percival, John, Baron: met near Bristol, 242*
Perizonius: his *Universal History* read, 171
Perrault, Charles, 30, 31*, 264
Persian Tales, read in Westminster Hall, 130
Perth, 103*, 178
Peterborough, Charles Mordaunt, Earl of: at Skinners' Company Ball, 36*, 40: opposes repeal of Triennial Act, 220
Phelps, Mrs.: visits Mrs. Richard Ryder, 273
Phipps, Sir Constantine: defends Lord Wintoun, 198
Pierce, Captain, acquaintance: benefits from Islington Spa, 312
Pilkington, Lady: 84*; visit to her at Putney, 217
Pillories: Fleet Street, 284
Pinner's Hall: 50; cf. Hunt
Pitt: Account of Mahometan Religion, 329
Pitts, Major, goldsmith, 345*, 346; mentions Serjeant Whittaker's fondness for diarist, 366
Play-going, 58, 115, 128, 137, 148, 177, 181, 348, 359, 362, 364
Ploughing: easiness of, 99
Plumbers' Hall: visited, 127*
Plumtre, Dr. Henry, physician: deist, 161*

Poetry-writing: projected Epithalamium for Mary Allen, 122; translation of Juvenal, 134; projected versification of Psalms, 178; poem to Cousin Abigail, 203; translation of Virgil, 264; poem to Mrs. Marshall, 342, 343, 344, 349, 354, &c.
Political colours, 245, 253, 255, 320
Pope: rumoured help for Pretender, 182
Pope, Alexander: translation of Homer, 32, 33*, 102; *Essay on Criticism*, 117; *Rape of the Lock*, 300; thought to be author of *The What d'Ye Call It*, 146, 194*
Popery: opposition of Irish Parliament, 144
Popish Plot: described by Dr. Tilly, 302
Popper, General: subdues rebellion at Oxford, 141, 207*
Porteus Riots, 23
Porter, Mr., apothecary: 58; arguments against Berkeley's ideas, 65, 102, 178, &c.; sings, 71; character, 79; opinions on venery and polygamy, 85; goes to Southwark Fair, 101; lends book, 114; stories of his sister's death, 117; opinions on clergymen, 165; goes to trial of rebel lords, 179; describes experiment with a viper, 205; discusses King's Evil, 206, 237; on marriage, 284; recommends study of anatomy, 292; puzzled by Berkeley, 300; discusses Tillotson, 331; Italian teacher, 310, 337, 367; quotes a bad pun, 368; at John's, 374
Portsmouth, Louise de Keroualle, Duchess of: death of Charles II, 321*
Potter, Mr., acquaintance, 40
Pottery-making: by Ryder women, 58
Poussin, Nicholas: diarist owns prints, 96
Powell, Samuel, friend: discusses Oxford politics, 74*; affects gentility, 74; gallantry, 123; discusses Oxford education, 133; vices at Oxford, 143; effect of Oxford on him, 143, 157 (twice); at Bath,

INDEX

239, 241, &c.; character among ladies, 241; quarrel with coachman, 243, 244; success with Mrs. Marshall, 244; double entendres, 247; looseness, 247; romps with Mrs. Marshall, 248; offers to assist diarist in love affairs, 249; diarist writes to him, 253, 257, 260; writes about diarist's love, 270; reforming and his character, 272; to study at Temple, 283; diarist jealous of him, 285; views on marriage, 288; attitude to parents and Mrs. Marshall, 288; captures conversation, 290; verses on Pump Woman, 296; shown to Mrs. Marshall, 297; sends verses about ladies at Bath, 347, 349
Powys, Sir Lyttleton, judge: his sharp practice, 107*
Prayer: private, 45, 275; in family, 33, 38, 166; public, 129; diarist's defect in, 113
Preaching: its lack of effect, 311; difference in style between Churchmen and Nonconformists, 331; style of, 33, 46, &c. (For criticism of individual preachers, cf. under their names)
Predestination: diarist argues about it with Mr. Owen, 177
Preston, battle of, 135*; report, 137* (twice), 152; 'General' Wood's part, 234
Pretender, The: feared invasion by him, 59, 81; Highlanders rise, 103; his declaration, 169; in Scotland, 172; tries to escape from Montrose, 179*; flees to France, 181; rumours of foreign help, 181, 191; interview with Queen Anne, 193; birthday, 254; another declaration, 297; a marvellous jewel, 314; his birth described, 327; a quarrel about him, 328; carried in effigy, 363 (cf. also Rebellion)
Price, Robert, Baron: conducts trial for witchcraft, 365
Price, Mr., friend, 42*, &c.
Prince of Wales: cf. Royal Family
Prince's Street, 121
Prints: cf. Painting and Prints.

Processions, political: a loyalist demonstration, 121; anniversary of Sheriffmuir; 363 (cf. also Celebrations, Pretender, Riots)
Proposal of Marriage: a fancied, 290
Proposals for easing the Nation's Debts: cf. Pamphlets
Protestants, French: persecution, 300
Psalmanazar, George: *Historical and Geographical Description of Formosa*, 132*, 133
Pufendorf, Samuel von: his account of England read, 298*
Pump Woman at Bath, 250; a poem on, 296, 297
Puns: good and bad, 368
Purcell, Henry: *Dioclesian* seen, 166*
Purging, 44, 45, 50, 190, 195, 205, 235, 269, 278, 295, 257 (cf. Illness)
Putney: visit to Mr. Gregg and Lady Pilkington, 216

Quakers: their general correspondence, 233
Quarantine in the Levant, 329
Quintilian: *Institutio Oratoria* borrowed, 267; read, 272, 287, 341; appreciation of, 372

Racine, Jean: Boileau's epistle to, 108
Rackley Church: described, 243
Rakes: why young men become rakes, 270
Ramsey, Mr., acquaintance: his sensations of drowning, 369
Rapin, René, critic, 57*
Ratcliffe, Dr., physician: character, 232*
Read, Mr., acquaintance, 38*, 231
Read, Rev. Dr.: quarrel with Mr. Henley, 325
Read, landlord of Salisbury Court Mug-house, 279*; kills a man in a riot, 283; trial for murder, 316
Reading, Hugh, organist at Hackney, 15
Reading, Berks: George Inn, 238; election day, 252
Reading, the diarist's: cf. under Dudley Ryder
Reading: aims in, 37; a plan of, 219; poetry-reading to improve style, 199 (For books, &c., read, cf. under *Dudley Ryder*)

Rebellion of 1641: burning of churches in Ireland, 309
Rebellion of 1715: pretended hunting match, 89; association in favour of Pretender, 102; Mar raises Highlanders, 103; attempt on Edinburgh, 103; failure, 131; reported Government victory, 132; arrival of rebels in Lancashire, 133; rebels arrive at Lancaster, 135*; Government troops assemble at Warrington, 135; surrender of Lancaster to rebels and flight of Lord Lonsdale's militia, 136; report of Government victory at Preston, 137; lack of confirmation, 137; Wills forces rebels to surrender, 138; reported Government victory at Sheriffmuir, 139*, 140; chief rebel prisoners arrive in London, 147*; end of rebellion in Scotland, 185; rumours of new rebellion, 259 (cf. also Pretender)
Rebel Lords: impeachment, 164; described, 168; Wintoun pleads Not Guilty, 172; sentence passed, 179; their speeches, 180; diarist's friends advocate mercy, 182; warrant for execution, 184; Lady Derwentwater petitions for reprieve, 185; petition read, 186; King's attitude, 187; rumoured reprieve, 187; reprieves, 187; executions, 187; rumoured behaviour of executed lords, 193, 213 (cf. also under their names)
Rebels: Bill for speedier trial, 184; surprising proceedings of Government, 261; proposed indemnity, 178, 261; escapes, 179, 189, 218, 232, 289; smoking out rebels at Liverpool, 175
Red House, Westbrook Hay, 110
Reed, Mr., of Hackney, 38*
Regnard, Jean F., dramatist: *Attendez-moi sous l'orme*, 51*; *Le Légataire*, 59; *Le Distrait*, 66; character of his plays, 59
Religion, diarist's thoughts about: cf. under Dudley Ryder
Rent: diarist pays, 164, 208, 265; collects, 345, 347, 348
Reputation, 32

Revolution of 1688: Dr. Lee's account of, 320
Reynolds, Mr., undertaker: makes arrangements for grandmother's funeral, 339*, 341
Rhubarb: as a purifier, 278, 357
Ribble Bridge, Lancs, 231
Richmond, Charles, 1st Duke of: to present petition for reprieve of rebel lords, 185*
Richmond Beauties: a poem on them by Mr. Brian, 78
Rioters' Act: cf. Act for Preventing Tumults
Riots: by High Church mobs, 41*, 134; at Roebuck, 138; Tory and Whig, 255; at Salisbury Court Mug-house, 280, 283 (twice), 315
Robberies: at Aunt Bickley's, 87; at Mr. Ryder's, 95
Robert, Sir Thomas, of Stepney: his character, 120
Robinson, General: visit to his tent in Hyde Park, 64
Rochefoucauld, Madame: raped by Duke of Orleans, 348*
Rochester, Henry, 2nd Earl of: goes bail for Wyndham, 259
Roebuck Tavern: headquarters of Williamite Club, 121*; project of anti-Jacobite procession, 121; riots, 138, 280
Rollison, Mr., apothecary of Hackney: diarist consults him, 235*; entertains diarist, 268; entertains the family, 301; his garden and his wife, 301
Romance reading: cousin Abigail, 164; Mr. Humphries, 171, 209
Romping: cf. Flirting
Roper, Moses: his strange conversation, 110*
Roscommon, Wentworth Dillon, 4th Earl of: translation of Horace's *Ars Poetica*, 94*, 134
Rowe, Nicholas: *Tragedy of Jane Shore* read, 143*; *Tamerlane* seen, 359*, 364
Rowley, J., inventor: his orrery for Emperor of China, 139*, 140
Royal Exchange: visited, 58
Royal Family: George I: good humour, 62; his statesmanship, 162;

INDEX

speeches to Parliament, 172 ; refusal to reprieve Derwentwater, 183, 186, 187 ; diarist's praise, 188 ; rumours of promised reprieve, 193 ; familiarity, 221 ; leaves for Hanover, 271 ; Mughouse toasts, 279, 299, 323 ; new treaty with France, 338★ ; difference with Prince of Wales, 267★, 373 ; character, 373

    Prince of Wales : at playhouse, 195 ; refuses office, 267★ ; difference with King, 271 ; popularity, 298 ; sets fashion, 310 ; toasts, 317 ; at Tunbridge Wells, 338 ; at Court Ball, 356 ; Judge Eyre's office, 362 ; reconciliation to King, 373

    Princess of Wales, 62 ; sympathy with Lady Derwentwater, 183 ; familiarity, 221 ; at Thanksgiving service, 253 ; at Hampton Court, 298 ; toasts, 317 ; enceinte, 325 ; at Court Ball, 356 ; in labour, 359 ; birth of dead son, 363

    Frederick, Prince, 342★

    Amelia, Princess : at Ball, 356★

    Anne, Princess : at Ball, 356★

Royal George : great ship described, 63, 91

Rubens, P. P. ; paintings in Banqueting House, 59

Rusheer, Mr., acquaintance, 341

Rushworth, John : *Historical Collections* read, 313★

Ryder, Rev. Dudley, grandfather of diarist, 3

Ryder, Richard, father of the diarist : quarrels with his wife, 38 ; his rashness and bad memory, 41 ; generosity to diarist, 44, 49, 117, &c. ; hastiness, 96 ; legal dispute with Joshua Lomax, 107, 108 ; vast trade in riding-hoods, 115 ; purblindness to William's extravagance, 151, 212 ; shocked by diarist's views, 170 ; boasts of diarist's cleverness, 199 ; indifferent financial circumstances, 206 ; partnership difficulties, 212 ; lack of prudence, 225 ; his trade, 226 ; negotiations for a horse for diarist, 231, 234, 273, 289, 292, 329 ; wedding anniversary, 232 ; concerned about diarist, 249 ; disturbed about William, 255 ; discusses partnership, 256 ; attitude to diarist's love affairs, 262 ; solicitous about diarist's health, 264, 269 ; complains of poverty, 265 ; thinks marriage a cure for diarist, 271 ; hastiness, 272 ; concern about William, 273, 274 ; rallies diarist, 275 ; settles diarist's allowance, 276 ; negligence, 277 ; fickleness, 289 ; fault-finding, 293 ; discusses William's proposed marriage, 293, 296, 310 ; tries to get Robert Billio chosen at Hackney, 305, 319 ; builds a new house, 308, 309★, 312 ; love of provoking his wife, 311 ; discusses partnership, 313 ; financial position and will, 326 ; discusses Mrs. Marshall, 326, 329 ; fears about grandmother's will, 337 ; inefficient management of grandmother's funeral, 339, 341, 345 ; legacy from grandmother, 340 ; partnership, 340 ; worried by Richard's illness, 342, 343 ; opinion of Mrs. Marshall, 343 ; losses on house property, 344 ; negotiations for marriage of William and Mrs. Burton, 357, 371 ; his estate, 369

Ryder, Mrs., diarist's mother : her peevishness, 38, 49 ; wedding anniversary, 232 ; confusion at her entertainments, 232, 265 ; her temper, 271 ; wears a scandalous gown, 298 ; fretfulness, 311 ; her jointure, 326 ; guesses diarist's love, 326 ; dismal behaviour at grandmother's death, 339 ; legacy from grandmother, 340 ; tells a moving love-story, 357

Ryder, Richard, diarist's elder brother : visited, 36 *et passim* ; kindness to his wife, 54 ; good judgment, 145 ; estate cumbered by debt, 180 ; birthday, 194 ; discusses William's conduct, 212 ; discusses father's defects, 224 ; thinks of becoming King's Draper, 230 ; freedom with ladies, 230 ; returns from Westbrook Hay, 313 ; legacy in father's will, 326 ; at Watford, 331 ; ill of colic, 334, 341, 343 ; obstinacy, 342

Ryder, Mrs., wife of above: exhibition of ill temper, 53; her jointure, 56*; lack of education, 81; acts charades well, 99; obstinacy, 100; ill of smallpox, 145; has good symptoms, 146; recovers, 161; miscarriage, 166; sets out for Bath, 211; at Bath, 239, 250; leaves Bath, 250; diarist grows familiar with her, 254; a letter from Mrs. Marshall, 256; diarist wishes to make a present, 264; romps with diarist, 269, 270; her liveliness, 272; perversity, 277; Mrs. Marshall breakfasts with her, 280; comforts diarist, 282; attitude to Mrs. Lee, 286; mentions Mrs. Marshall's courtships, 294; repeats Mrs. Marshall's views on love, 295; anger at diarist's mentioning Mrs. Marshall, 299; romps with diarist, 300, 301; leaves for Westbrook Hay, 306; returns, 313, 315; angry with diarist, 319; becomes critical, 325; reproves diarist for cowardice, 332; and for boldness, 333; rebukes cousin Joseph Billio, 333 (twice); Joseph retorts, 333; wishes diarist to stay at Westbrook, 334; opinion of his poem to Mrs. Marshall, 344; enceinte, 348; frightens diarist about Mrs. Marshall, 350, 363; at the playhouse, 364, 367, 369; rebukes diarist for tattling, 371

Ryder, Dudley, the diarist: his diary vii, shorthand vii, nature viii, present edition viii-ix, 1

His life: introduction 1-25; reputation 2, family and relations 3-5, education 5-6, legal studies 6-9, accomplishments and reading 9-10, tastes 9-10, his friends 10-11, discussions 11-12, amusements and sightseeing 12-13, life at Hackney 13-17, diversions 17-18, love affairs 19-21, marriage 21, legal advancement 21-2, Attorney-General 22, his abilities 22-3, his chief cases 23-5, Lord Chief Justice 25, death 25

Character: peevishness 38, lack of decision 40, 48, ill nature 43, good husbandry 44, lack of application 45, love of esteem 45, bashfulness 51, gallantry 58, unfilial conduct 61, lack of ease in speaking 62, speaks best among strangers 65, fond of objecting 37, 69, restlessness 70, snobbery 73, religious resolves 75, flirting 76, envy 78, anxiety about brother William 82, 83, hankering for female applause 87, humanity 90, ashamed of fast companions 90, uneasiness with women 91, unaffected by cousin's death 91, envy of brother William 95, 105, fear of bad breath 97, finds country boring 99, desire of esteem 113, made dull by wine 115, lack of concentration 118, vanity 119, fretfulness in illness 119, affectation 121, envy 124, desire for gallantry 123, enervated by argument 125, suspiciousness 127, influenced by others' opinions 129, ill-humour and solicitousness 132, peevishness 134, courage under pain 142, dread of illness 142, excessive gaiety in dancing 151, temptations to gamble 158, perturbed by losing 162, jealousy of father 166, hopes of success as lawyer 180, misgivings 184, cheerfulness at arrival of Spring 185, snobbery 190, negligence at Church 191, desire to dance well 195, gatecrashes trial of Wintoun 196, annoyed by father 199, contrariness 201, jealousy 202, offended by Mr. Whatley 203, temptation to sloth and resistance to it 204, desire to be a dancing master 204, further worries about William 205, failure in romantic fancies 209, fears consumption 209, jealousy 210, falls in love at first sight 211, posing 215, poor memory 217, makes reading plan 219, summary of his strength and weakness 223, melancholy 224 desire for children 224, uneasiness at behaviour to Mrs. Loyd 225, revulsion from gallantry 228, reflects on life and death 228, shyness 230, melancholy over his defects 241, love for Mrs. Marshall and despair 242, bashfulness 243, jealous of Mr. Powell 245, love sickness 249, 250, thoughts of suicide 250, epistolary

INDEX

vanity 253, melancholy over Mrs. Marshall 254, 256, 263, 273, 281, 282, 288, 289, 294, 295, 296, 334, 341, 348, 363, &c., consoled by melancholy of others 261, weeps at *Cato* 263, difficulty in expressing appreciation 264, inordinate affection to the world 266, reputation for gravity 267, perplexed about his love 270, fears on visiting Mrs. Marshall 272, lack of boldness 274, fears of impotency 279, anger 281, makes pose of fortitude 285, envious pleasure 286, thinks about peace of mind 289, imagines proposing to Mrs. Marshall 290, fears for legal future 291, envies his brother's happiness 294, harshness to his mother 298, envy of Mr. Leeds' writing 302, made uneasy by cousin Joseph's love for Mrs. Marshall 306, vanity 308, ravished by thought of marriage 310, 366, reputation for misogyny 310, comforted by oysters 312, hopes of overcoming his passion 327, disturbed at deceiving Mr. Howard 331, talks bawdy 332, tries to impress by merriment 332, jealous of cousin Joseph 333, 357, &c. shocked by thinking of his advantage from his brother's death 334, 341, new cheerfulness 335, disturbed by dream of matrimony 335, bashfulness 336, writes brother William's love letter 338, exhibitionism 338, pleased by thought of dying 345, consoled by Mrs. Lee's good opinion 346, frightened by story of Mrs. Marshall's marriage 350, pleases her 353, moved to tears by a lovestory 357, reputation in Hackney 359, religious vacillation 362, reflections on mutability 363, plans to neglect Mrs. Marshall 365, 369, lack of spirituality 369, rebuked for tattling 371, carelessness at cards 372, indolence 372, different behaviour at different clubs 374, resolve to neglect Dissenters' club because of its reputation 374

Whoring : his ventures in 67, 71, 85, 138, 218, 274, 292, 331, 369, remorse 72

Religion : thoughts on 45, resolution to follow God's laws 75, evil of idolatry 235, consolation 258, sin 266, works of God 275, deplores his lack of concern for eternity 281, effects of education 293, nature of God 303–5, object of prayer 330, youth and age 346, aversion to sin 351, living with God 362, perfection of God 366, thoughts on sacrament 228, intention to receive it 275, private prayers 45, 275, family prayers 33, 38, 166, 281, his defect in prayer 113, thoughts on death 188, 210, 263, 291, 294, 339, 345, 348

Attendance at church and meeting, &c. For description and criticism of sermons and preachers, cf. Astor, Barker, Robert Billio Biscoe, Bradbury, Calamy, Chapman, Greenor, Hunt, Nathaniel Marshall Newcome, Oldfield, Oldsworth, Sherlock, Smith, Tong, Trapp, Wiggett. For his reading and criticism of sermons and other religious works, cf. Bates, Chillingsworth, Clarke, Flavel, Matthew Henry, Hoadly, Sharrock, Tillotson, Tong

Love affairs : for his love affairs, cf. Mary Allen, Mrs. Gery, Mrs. Lee, Mrs. Loyd, Mrs. Marshall, Mrs. Partridge, Mrs. Whittaker, Flirting, Marriage

Education : cf. under Cambridge, Edinburgh, Leyden, Oxford, Inner Temple, Law, Trials, Castilio, French, Greek, Italian, Latin

Health : cf. under Bagnio, breath, cold bath, Fowles, Epsom, illness, Islington Spa, Purging, Tunbridge

Reading : For his reading, cf. under the names of theologians given above and also : Addison, Berkeley, Bible, Blackmore, Blount, Boileau, Bossu, Tom Brown, Buchanan, Buckingham, Burmann, Burnet, Butler, Cicero, *L'Art de plaire dans la Conversation*, Dacier, Du Mont, De la Motte, Derham, Deschamps, Farquhar, Fénelon, Gay, Grotius, Homer, Horace, Juvenal, Le Sage, Lansdowne, Perizonius, Persian Tales, Pitt, Pope, Psalmanazar, Pufendorf, Quintilian, Regnard, Roscommon, Rushworth, Sallust, Seneca, Shakespeare, Spenser, Steele, Strada, Swift, Tickell, *Turkish Spy*, Vanbrugh, Virgil, Voiture, Waller, Wotton, Young ; cf. also Pamphlets and the following journals : *Daily Courant, Englishman, Examiner, Freeholder, Grumbler, Guardian, Occasional Paper, Patriot, Spectator, Tatler* ; cf. also *Flying Post Instructor.* For his law reading, cf. under Law Reading.

Writing : for his own writing, cf. under diary, epistolary style, poetry-writing

Amusements : cf. under Balls and dances, dancing, Fernley, Bartholomew Fair, Spring Gardens, Southwark Fair, Card games, charades, gambling, games, Conversation, Drawing Room, Music, Mushroom-gathering, Painting and Prints, Poussin, Rubens, Thornhill, Van Blope, Playgoing (cf. also under names of playwrights, Sports)

Journeys and visits to towns, &c. Cf. under Horse-riding ; Aylesbury, Bath, Bristol, Edgware, Edmonton, Enfield, Epsom, Greenwich, Hackney, Hampstead, Hemel Hemstead, Highgate, Hoxton, Hyde Park, India House, Islington Spa, Kensington, Kentish Town, Lambeth Wells, Reading, Slough, Southwark Fair, Spring Gardens, Stepney, Watford, Westbrook Hay, Woolwich ; and names of London Streets, &c.

Clubs. For his clubs, see under : Club for discussion of useful subjects, Dissenters' Club, John's, Sue's.

Coffee houses and taverns. For his visits to London coffee houses and taverns, see under : Amsterdam Coffee House, British Coffee House, Button's Coffee House, Castle Tavern, Crown Tavern, Fountain Tavern, Gill House, Grecian Coffee House, Hamlin's Coffee House, John's Coffee House, London Coffee House, Marlborough Head Tavern, Mitre Tavern, North's Coffee House St. James's Coffee House, Salisbury Court Mughouse, Saracen's Head, Sue's Tavern, Sugar Loaf Tavern, Temple Chop House, Temple Tavern, Tiltyard Coffee House, Tom's Coffee House, Waghorn's Coffee House. Cf. also references to : Roebuck Tavern, Tavistock Mughouse

Family : For his relations with and his opinions on the family and its connections, see under : Allen, Allom, Baxter, Bickley, Billio, Harding, Lewis, Lomax, Marshall, Ryder, Stevenson, Watkins, Wilkinson

Friends and acquaintances : For references to his friends and acquaintances, see under : Abney, Atkins, Avery, Bailey, Barker, Birch, Blackbourn, Blenman, Blundell, Borrett, Bowes, Boyd, Brerewood, Brian, Brookbanks, Brown, Bulkeley, Bunbury, Bunkley, Burgess, Burroughs, Byam, Campbell, Child, Cowley, Crisp, Cummin, Dawson, Defoe, Deison, Denn, Dolins, Dry, Evans, Foster, Fowler, Franklin, Freke, Gery, Gore, Gorthan, Gould, Gregg, Haddon, Harrison, Hawksbee, Hayward, Heathcote, Henry Hide, Hilliard, Hiot, Hollier, Horseman, Howard, Hudson, Hughes, Hulse, Hulst, Humphries, Hunt, Hutton, Ironmonger, Isles, Jackson, Jermyn, Jobson, Justice, Kelly, Kennedy, Dr. Lee, Mrs. Lee, Leeds, Marsh, Marshall, Marten, Martin, Mears, Merreal, Merryweather, Mesees, Milley, Mills, Molesworth, Moore, Moreland, Neve, Newdigate, Oileman, Oldsworth, Overall, Oxford, Owen, Page, Papillon, Partridge, Perceval, Pilkington, Pitts, Potter, Powell, Price, Ramsey, Read, Reynolds, Robert, Rollison, Rusheer, Samson, Serjeant, Lady Shaw, Short, Sikes, Skinner, Smith, Spering, Spragg, Stancliff, Stratford, Street, Suly, Sutton, Swain, Thompson, Thornhill, Tilly, Tillyard, Tindall, Tomson, Tyssen, Utber, Venner, Wadsworth, Walker, Wallis, Ward, Warren, West, Whatley, Whinnell, Whittaker, Witnoom, Wollaston, Wood

INDEX

Miscellaneous. The chief other headings relating to the diarist himself are: artificial memory, memory; allowance; beverages, meals; clothes; dreams; highwaymen

Ryder, Nathaniel, son of diarist, 6

Ryder, William, diarist's younger brother: fears evoked by a letter, 82, 83, 84*; suspected of highway robbery, &c., 84; dispels suspicion, 84; success with the ladies, 93; with Mrs. Loyd, 94, 105; lack of sense, 95; carries letter to Mrs. Loyd, 95; association with her, 115; extravagance raises fears, 151; foolish conduct with women, 164; finishes apprenticeship, 173; gives a treat, 178; further extravagance, 184; another treat, 194; at a ball, 204; extravagant finery, 205; discussed, 212; proposed partnership in father's business, 213; Aunt Billio complains of him, 225; further misdeeds, 254, 255, 259; arranges assignation for Mrs. Loyd, 269; Aunt Bickley's plan to marry him to cousin Abigail, 269; father's misgivings, 273, 274, 277; thought to lead cousin Harding astray, 285; courts Mrs. Walker, 291; concern about marriage, 292 (twice); discussed by family, 293; diarist envies his happiness, 294; hot upon marriage, 296; Mrs. Walker's dowry, 309; partnership, 313; his reform, 313; quarrel with Mrs. Bailey, 320; doubts about Mrs. Walker, 320; legacy in father's will, 326; his mistress grows cool, 330; gets diarist to write to her, 337 (twice), 338; partnership, 340; breaks with Mrs. Walker, 350; her coquetry, 353; Mrs. Gifford proposed for him, 353; at a ball, 356; Mrs. Burton proposed for him, 362; negotiations, 367, 371; difficulty of a settlement, 367

Ryder, Dudley, uncle, of Nuneaton: 48*; uncommunicativeness, 48; strong aversion to his daughter's love affair, 56; at church, 180; disagreeableness, 190, 260; observations on persuasion and Sir Richard Newdigate, 266

Ryder, Benjamin, cousin: character, 370

Ryder, Dudley, cousin: 128; views on honour, 147; leaves for East Indies, 167

Ryder, John, cousin: account of Toryism at Cambridge, 189*; discusses philosophy, 189; discusses strange appearance in the sky, 192; plays bowls, 195, 205, 206; walks to Hackney Marsh, 208; reads a sermon with diarist, 209; rudeness, 215; goes to Putney, 216; goes to Court, 221

Ryder, Richard, cousin: dies, 90; buried, 91

Ryder, Robert: 181

Ryder, Robin, cousin: 189. (Same as Robert Ryder?)

Ryder, Abigail ('Bibby'), cousin, living with Aunt Bickley: 71*; visits Hyde Park camp, 72; attitude to men, 73; offended by diarist's attentions to Mrs. Loyd, 131; jealousy, 163; ignorance, 164; never obliged, 170; letter to her, 171; courted by Mr. Parry, 185; diarist's poem to her, 203; discusses love and romances, 209; affected ignorance of love, 211, 228; at Mrs. Wallis's ball, 235; envies Mrs. Loyd, 237, 262; attitude to Mrs. Loyd, 268; Aunt Bickley's wish to match her with brother William, 269

Ryder, Katherine, cousin: ill with love, 56; love for cousin Baxter, 261*

Sabine, General Joseph: pursues Pretender, 179*

Sacheverell, Dr. Henry: riots, 41; used as threat, 152*

Sacrament: diarist's thoughts on: cf. Dudley Ryder

St. Cyprian's works: cf. Nathaniel Marshall

St. James's, 66, 76, 327; cf. also Drawing Room

St. James's Church: cousin Richard Ryder buried there, 91

26

St. James's Coffee House, 76
St. Paul's : singing there, 34 ; paintings in dome, 306–8 ; anthem there, 330
St. Thomas's Hospital : Governors grant land for new meeting at Hackney, 86
Salisbury, Bishop of : preaches Whig sermon, 253
Salisbury Court, 315
Salisbury Court Mughouse : described, 279* ; riot there, 280, 283 ; reprisal, 283 ; trial, 315 ; verdict, 316* ; hanging of rioters, 330
Sallust : *Catiline Conspiracy*, 67 ; compared with England, 70, 75 ; *Jugurthan War*, 92
Salter's Hall : 50, 71 ; cf. Bradbury
Samson, Mr., friend : his regard for diarist, 31, 266 ; recounts West Country custom, 35, 125, 172, 190 ; does Inn exercise for diarist, 258 ; dines with diarist, 266 ; lends book, 267, 353 ; discusses Mr. Warren's death, 360, 361, 372
Sal volatile, excuse for visiting ladies, 119
Sandylane, 238, 251
Saracen's Head, Friday Street, 335
Scandal : female, 45
Schism Act, 153* ; expected repeal, 154, 163, 176, 233, 361, 372 ; cf. also Conformity, Act of
Schoolgirls at Hackney : cf. Hackney and Hudson
Scoley, Dr. : his daughter marries Mr. Witnoom, 257
Scotch people : their cunning, 88 ; character of, 227
Seaforth, William Mackenzie, 5th Earl of : submits, 172*
Seneca : opinion of his letters, 69
Septennial Parliaments, Bill for : cf. Triennial Acts
Serjeant, Mr., friend, 40, 93, &c. ; affectation, 202
Sermons, reading of : cf. Dudley Ryder
Shakespeare, William : *Timon of Athens*, 144 ; *Merry Wives of Windsor*, 104
Sharrock, Dr. Robert : *De Officiis*, read, 71, 215*

Shaw, Lady : diarist dances with her daughter at Bath, 246
Sherbourn, Mr. : writes suspicious letter to brother William, 85
Sheriffmuir : battle of, 139*, 140 ; anniversary celebrated, 363*
Sheriff's Feast : cf. Sir John Fryer
Sheriffs, pricking of, 130
Sherlock, Dr. Thomas : 61* ; preaches at Temple, 148 ; his style, 148 ; Toryism at Cambridge, 189
Shipbuilding at Woolwich, 64 ; cf. also *Royal George*
Ship Navigation : discussed, 312
Shoe Lane, 316
Shoe-Patterns : made for Aunt Billio, 111
Shore House, Hackney : 48*, 50, 116 ; account of a lady who lodged there, 265
Short, Mr., friend : visited at Saracen's Head, 335 ; at Fountain Tavern, 336
Shorter, Mrs., Walpole's sister-in-law : at Bath, 246*
Shorthand : letter in, 94, diarist's, vii
Shortsightedness, diarist's : discussed with Mr. Street, 58
Shrewsbury, Charles Talbot, Duke of : influences choice of Archbishop of Canterbury, 167*
Shute, Barrington : cf. Barrington Shute
Sikes, Mrs. Betty, of Hackney, 51* ; has vapours, 131
Sikes, Mr., of Hackney, 51
Six Clerks' Office : visit to, 44 ; value of a seat there, 44
Skating : cf. Sports
Skinner, Mr., friend, 29* ; character, 30 ; his gravity, 86, 200 ; with his music master, 203, 218 ; at Court Ball, 356
Skinners' Hall : ceremony of choosing Master, 36 ; dances 37, 127*
Slough, 212, 252
Smallpox : cf. Mrs. Richard Ryder, junr.
Smith, George, friend : ill manners, 32* ; difficulty of talking with him, 36 ; talks about Berkeley, 56, 65 ; plays music, 69 ; his cousin, 70 ; offends Mr. Street, 78 ; prepares a sermon, 86 ; lends Berkeley, 94 ;

INDEX 403

quotes an epitaph, 148 ; preaches, 157 ; attitude to Mr. Whatley, 200 ; defects, 200 ; music, 207, 214, 227 ; plays backgammon, 285 ; preaches at Hackney, 299, 311 ; liked at Hackney, 299 ; rallies diarist on his love, 299 ; favoured as new minister at Hackney, 305 ; chosen, 319, 340, 345, 346 ; two sermons, 351, 358 ; Aunt Billio is invidious, 358, 366

Smith, Mr., Mr. Moreland's usher : gets a living, 75

Smithfield : buying horses there, 274, 292

Smoking, 77, 116, 217

Snuff : bought for sister-in-law, 211

Somerset, Charles Seymour, 6th Duke of : goes bail for Wyndham, 259

Somerset House Walks, 61

Sorbonne : doctors' letter to Archbishop of Canterbury, 297

Southwark, 217

Southwark Fair : a visit to, 101*

Spectator : characters of, 46 ; opinion of Seneca, 69 ; indebtedness to Boileau, 111 ; diarist resolves to model his style on, 117 ; Club, 117 ; method of writing, 120 ; Addison and Steele compared, 121, 372 ; its style, 183, 223, 287, 300 ; used for conversation with ladies, 346 ; style criticised, 351 ; on the force of custom, 365

Speeches : last speeches of Paul, 274, 277 ; Bean, 336

Spenser : *Faerie Queen* read, 172

Spering, Mr., acquaintance : plays harpsichord, 118 ; sings, 119

Sports : bowls, 33, 195, 216 ; its absurdities, 200 ; coursing, 99 ; dullness of, 99, 334 ; cudgelling, 35 ; jumping, 85, 208 ; skating, 164, 165 ; wrestling, 99 ; cf. also Horse-Riding

Spragg, Mr., silkman, 252

Spring Gardens : a visit to, 217*

Stair, John Dalrymple, 2nd earl of : ambassador at Paris, 172 ; purchases evidence of Lord Oxford's guilt, 182*, 191

Stancliff, Mrs., of Hackney : censorious behaviour, 108* ; talk with her, 260

Stanhope, James, Secretary of State : reported attitude to dissenters, 153* ; seeks reasons for removing Acts, 154 ; encourages Harris, 156 ; opposes Act of Indemnity, 178, 184, 186, 267

Stanley, Sir Roland : his rebel son caught, 175

Statianus, 116

Steele, Richard : *Account of State of Roman Catholic Religion*, 31 ; *The Englishman*, 58*, 85 ; politics, 186 ; compared with Addison, 121, 372 ; answer to Pretender's declaration, 169* ; manner of treating duns, 368; style, 372 (cf. also *Tatler, Spectator*)

Stepney : visit to Mr. Warren there, 120

Stevenson, old Mr., 44* ; his ghost, 314

Stevenson, Mrs., grandmother, 44* ; visits to, 37, 55*, 144 ; her temper, 54 ; pleasant to diarist, 60 ; Mr. Ryder's debt, 326 ; seriously ill, 337 ; dies, 339 ; her will, 339 ; buried, 344*

Stevenson, Aunt, of Gresley : letters from, 55, 131, 151 ; letters to, 62, 64, 75, 164, 168, 252, 288, 340

Stewards of Manors : their profits, 106*

Stillingfleet, Dr. Edward, 167

Stirling : loyalist camp there, 103

Stocks Market : visit to, 49*

Stoke Newington : cf. Newington Green

Story-telling : the art of, 53, 73, 270, 282 ; cf. Isles

Strada, Famianus : Account of poetic contest in his *Prolusiones*, 116*

Strafford, Thomas Wentworth, Earl of : impeachment, 89*

Stratford, Mr., acquaintance, 326, 370

Streets, Mr., friend : habits, 10 ; character, 42 ; shortsightedness, 58 ; drunken anger, 78

Strype, Rev. William, 15 ; preaches at Hackney, 181*

Sue's Tavern : visits to, 67, 182, &c. ; his cheerfulness there, 374

Sugar Loaf Tavern : dinner there, 141*

Suly, Mr., acquaintance : sings, 93*, 297 ; his history, 104 ; met at Islington Wells, 297

Sunday Mornings : idleness on, 50, 66
Supernatural : Mr. Porter's stories of his sister, 117 ; Mrs. Allom's story of old Mr. Stevenson, 314 ; Mr. Bowes repeats an old story, 322 ; trial for witchcraft, 365
Surgeons' Hall : lectures there, 292
Sutton, Dr. : story of a marvellous jewel, 314*
Swain,Mr., friend : 29* ; goes to Hackney, 75, 151 ; at Court Ball, 356
Swearing, habit of, 74
Swift, Jonathan : *Tale of a Tub*, 114 ; cf. *The Examiner*
Sword, the diarist's : cf. Clothes

Tatler, The, journal : appreciation and intention to model style on, 38, 45 ; characters, 46 ; indebtedness to Boileau, 111 ; style, 183 ; application to diarist, 210
Tatton, General William : seen exercising troops in Hyde Park, 80*
Taverns visited by diarist : cf. list under Dudley Ryder
Tavistock Mughouse, 280
Telemachus in Italian : read, 338 (twice), 346
Temple : piazzas, 93, 115, 283, 294
Temple, Sir William, 31*, 264
Temple Chop House : political argument there, 124
Temple Church : Dr. Sherlock preaches, 148
Temple Stairs, 167
Temple Tavern : music there, 118
Tenison, Dr. Thomas : account of his being made Archbishop of Canterbury, 167*
Thames : frozen, 162, 165 ; diarist walks on, 165, 167 ; booths on, 167 ; journeys to the park, 62 ; to Woolwich, 63 ; to Whitehall, 80 ; to Putney, 216
Thompson, Mrs. : at Mrs. Wallis's ball, 235
Thomson, old Mr., of Hackney : his youthful sports, 38*
Thornhill, James, painter : diarist talks with him about his paintings in St. Paul's Dome, 306*, 307
Tickell, Thomas, poet : translation of the *Iliad*, 32, 33*, 102 ; read and compared with original, 103 ; lent, 114
Tillotson, Dr. John : reason for not being made Archbishop of Canterbury, 167 ; his style, 199, 219, 265, 331 ; his sermons read, 199, 209, 219, 265, 271, 275*, 293, 329, 346
Tilly, Rev. Dr. : met at Islington Spa, 301 ; describes Popish Plot, 301 ; discusses frogs, coals and rebellion in Ireland, 309, 311
Tillyard, Mr., friend, 182
Tilson, Dr., of Chester, 309
Tiltyard Coffee House, 276, 278
Tindal, Dr. Matthew : talk with, 89*
Tips, 55, 64, 72, 248, 250
Tom's Coffee House : visits to, 37*, 49, &c.
Tonge, Rev. William : preaches funeral sermon, 38* ; preaches at Hackney, 329 ; Life of Matthew Henry, 354*
Tooth Extraction, 142
Torbay, 131
Tories : their prejudices, 41, 42, 255 ; insolence, 253 ; cunning, 315 ; Princess's opinion of, 62 ; Hanoverian view, 342 ; cf. also Conversation : politics
Tower Hill : execution of Derwentwater and Kenmure, 187
Tower of London, 63, 147 ; escape from, 189, 289
Towneley, Richard, of Towneley : his trial, 234, 235*
Townshend, Charles, 2nd Viscount : rumoured attitude to dissenters, 153, 176, 267, 277
Townshend, Dorothy, Viscountess : her beauty, 77*, 325
Tracey, Robert, judge : his malpractice, 107
Tracey, Mrs., daughter of above : a coquette, 61*
Trade : its advantages over a profession, 291, 293 ; difficulty of calculating balance of trade, 52
Trapp, Joseph, poet : uncouth preacher, 33*
Trials : at Westminster, 134 ; of three Oxford rebels, 136, 137 ; of Captain Dorrel, 141 ; of rebel lords, 164, 168, 172, 179, 182 ; Lord

Wintoun, 196 ; Richard Towneley, 234 ; McCartney, 257 ; Sir William Wyndham, 259 ; Salisbury Court rioters, 315 ; diarist conducts trials, 24

Triennial Act : proposed repeal of triennial Parliaments and substitution of septennial Parliaments discussed, 202*, 208 ; repeal moved, 217 ; report of debate, 219 ; arguments for and against, 220 ; its passage through Parliament, 223*, 226, 227 ; diarist fails to get into debate, 225

Tristram, Mrs. : loved by Mr. Gregg, 35

Tunbridge Wells : 249, 257, 288, 298 ; Prince of Wales there, 338

Turkish Spy : read, 290*

Turkish War : its purpose, 296

Twelfth Day : party on, 163

Tyburn, 277

Tyssen, John, of Hackney : fights Mr. Henley, 157* ; reflects on Mr. Moreland and King George, 158

University education : poverty in England, 65 ; cf. also Cambridge, Edinburgh, Leyden, Oxford, Bale

Utber, Geoffrey : marries Mrs. Lee, 345*, 355, 374

Van Blope, painter : paints sister's portrait, 302

Vanburgh, Sir John : *The Relapse, or, Virtue in Danger* seen, 148*

Vapours and spleen : cf. Betty Sikes and Whatley

Vaughan : murdered in riot at Salisbury Court mughouse, 316

Vaumorière, P. d'O., 354*

Vauxhall Gardens : cf. Spring Gardens

Venereal Disease : cousin Watkins makes medicine for, 45 ; and the King's Evil, 206, 313 ; society victims, 325 ; James II, 327

Venetian Ambassador : his coach, 77*

Venner, Mr. : son-in-law of Mr. Kingsford, 161

Ventriloquism : account of, 149

Vernon, Mr., M.P., 184

Vestries : Bill for regulating them, 344

Viner, Sir George, 14, 15

Viper : an experiment with one, 205

Virgil : 30, 116 ; read, 165, 171 ; attempt to versify, 264

Voiture, Vincent : excellence of his letters, 125, 164*, 168

Wadsworth, Mr., acquaintance : complaints against dissenters, 65 ; describes visit to Bartholomew Fair, 86

Wadsworth, Dr. Thomas, physician, 256* ; a consultation with him, 257, 268

Waghorn's Coffee House, 58

Wake, Dr. William : consecrated Archbishop of Canterbury, 167

Wales, Prince of : cf. Royal Family

Walker, Mrs., of Manchester : her fortune, 291*, 296, 309, 310, 341 ; brother William's attitude to her, 291, 292, 296 ; her expectations, 320, 330, 341 ; letter to her, 337-8 ; breaks with brother William, 350 ; a coquette, 353

Walker, Mr., brother of above : visits Ryder's, 293

Waller, Edmund : his poems read, 181, 196 ; life and character, 196*

Wallis, Mrs., Hackney schoolmistress : 81* ; dances at her house, 151*, 154, 157, 203 ; her granddaughter, 345

Wallis, Martha, niece of above : her suicide, 194*

Walpole, Horace : on diarist, 22, 23, 24

Walpole, Mrs. Catherine : at Bath, 241, 246

Walpole, Robert : opposes Lechmere's motion of indemnity, 178*, 184 ; moves adjournment of House, 186 ; falls out with Marlborough, 21, 22, 299

Warburton family : Philip Henry's account of, 88* ; his grandfather's diary and poems, 88

Ward, Edward, writer, 7

Ward, Mr., of Hackney : discusses criticism, 163 ; retails rumours about execution of rebel lords, 193* ; discusses escape of Wintoun, 289

Warren, Mr., friend : 34, 36 ; seriously ill, 120* ; death and love for Mrs. Newbury, 360*

Warrington: Government troops assemble to oppose rebels, 135; cf. Rev. Charles Owen
Warrington, George Booth, Lord: reported death at Preston, 137*
Watermen, 62; repartee, 64
Watford, 90, 100, 213, 329, 331
Watkins, Mr., cousin: setting up apothecary's shop, 30; matrimonial hopes, 46; dancing at his house, 67-8; recounts his courtships, 84; dancing in Cornhill, 92; entertains ladies, 102; discusses his many courtships, 113, 117; his wife, 178, 227; love of merriment, 216; bantered at Spring Gardens, 217; his salesmanship, 227; gives diarist a vomit and blister, 257, 258; advises diarist, 259; diarist rallies him, 262, 268, 288; opinion of brother Richard's illness, 341, 343; happy marriage, 357
Watkins, Mrs., wife of above, 178, 227, 262, 288, 357
Weather: notes on, 38, 48, 50, 77, 98, 185, 190, 213, 262, 264, 328, 334, &c.
Wells: cost of, 110; on Marlborough Downs, 239
Welton, Rev. Dr. Richard: political influence, 156*
Wesley, John, vii, 205*
West, Mr., friend, 31*, 35, 291
West, Mr., partner of Mr. Ryder senior, 212, 256, 313, 340
West, Dr., physician: attends brother Richard, 343*
Westbrook Hay, Herts, visits to brother Richard's estate, 36, 89*, 96, 213, 306, 332-4
Westminster Hall: trials there: cf. Trials: bookshop in, 130
Whatley, Mr., friend: influences Ryder to keep a diary, 29; visited, 34*; conversational powers, 36; affects singularity, 39; philosophy, 48, 69; sends essays to Addison, 69; unsettledness, 48; acquaintance with L.C.J. King, 69*; law reading, 80; his parson friend, 81; melancholy, 91; account of unsuccessful courtship, 125-6; seeks diarist's company, 141; grows troublesome, 146; describes his acquaintance with L.C.J. King, 150; recommends study of mathematics, 150; plays sonatas, 177; flirtation, 191; paper on the vapours, 200; proposes a discussion club, 200; pedantic ostentation and contrariness, 201; offends diarist, 203; paper on *totus aptus*, 206; *Pensées detachées*, 206; his melancholy, 214; letter of application, 221; discusses philosophy and matrimony, 224; melancholy, 227; reasons for unsteadiness, 229; failure of his application, 233; egotism, 233; at Bath, 250; a merry letter from him, 265
Whigs: attitude to Dissenters: 176, 361; cf. also Conformity and Schism Acts
Whinnel, Dr.: met at Fountain Tavern, 363
Whittaker, Edward, Serjeant-at-law: his fancy for diarist, 366*; his daughter, 366
Whittaker, Mrs.: granddaughter of Mrs. Wallis, 345
Whores: near theatre, 49; at Lambeth Wells, 57; Dr. Lee's relish for, 313; cf. also under Dudley Ryder
Widdrington, William, 4th Baron, 147; impeachment, 168; sentenced, 179
Wiggett, Rev. Mr.: says prayers when cousin Richard buried, 91
Wilkinson, cousin, 53*, 58
William III: choice of Archbishop of Canterbury, 167; prologue in his honour, 359
William, Mr.: prentice to Richard Ryder junr., 355
Williams, Peer, barrister: defends Lord Wintoun, 198
Williams, Dr. Daniel: opinions about him, 155*; his meeting, 157; Mr. Bowes's hatred, 322, 323
Willis, Dr. Richard, Bishop of Gloucester: dispute with Convocation, 129*
Wills, Major-General Sir Charles: commends Government troops, 135*; reported victory at Preston, 137; forces rebels to surrender, 138; Mr. Owen's account of his victory, 173; witness in trial of Lord Wintoun, 198

INDEX

Winter, Rev. Mr., acquaintance, 234

Wintoun, George Seton, 5th Earl of: impeachment, 168; pleads Not Guilty, 172; trial described, 196*; gibe at Cowper, 198*; makes no defence and found guilty, 199; escapes from Tower, 289

Witchcraft : cf. Supernatural

Witnoom, Mr., friend, 32*; opinions on politics, 59, 61, 162; character, 79; goes to Southwark Fair, 101; reflects on others, 202; marries Mrs. Scoley, 257; congratulated, 267; grows thin on matrimony, 284, 331; recounts Steele's treatment of duns, 368; quotes a pun, 368

Wollaston, Mr., acquaintance : invites diarist, 353

Woman at Cards, 371; cf. also Cards

Women's attitude to men : 51; necessity of preserving distance before marriage, 225; cf. also under names of women

Wood, Rev. James, 'General': account of his raising dissenters against the rebels, 231*, 234

Woolridge, Mr.: suitor to Mrs. Loyd, 185

Woolwich : visit to *Royal George*, 63, 91; visit of George I, 100

Wotton, William : *Reflections upon Ancient and Modern Learning*, read, 31*, 263*, 276

Wrestling : cf. Sports

Writing-masters, 122, 316

Wyndham, Sir William, M.P.: thought to be raising rebellion, 60; order for arrest, 103*; reward for capture, 105*; examined, 259

Yarmouth : meeting with ladies from, 46

York, Duke of : cf. James II

Young, Edward, poet : *The Last Day* criticized, 137*

Young, Mr.: his drinking, 326

Zarah, History of Queen : cf. Pamphlets

Printed in Great Britain
by Butler & Tanner Ltd.,
Frome and London

For Product Safety Concerns and Information please contact our EU representative GPSR@taylorandfrancis.com
Taylor & Francis Verlag GmbH, Kaufingerstraße 24, 80331 München, Germany